INTRODUCTION TO THE CANONICAL BOOKS OF THE OLD TESTAMENT

BY

CARL CORNILL
PROFESSOR OF OLD TESTAMENT THEOLOGY AT THE
UNIVERSITY OF BRESLAU

TRANSLATED BY

G. H. BOX, M.A.
FORMERLY SCHOLAR OF ST. JOHN'S COLLEGE, OXFORD
VICAR OF LINTON, ROSS, HEREFORDSHIRE
SOMETIME HEBREW MASTER AT MERCHANT TAYLORS' SCHOOL, LONDON

Wipf & Stock
PUBLISHERS
Eugene, Oregon

Wipf and Stock Publishers
199 W 8th Ave, Suite 3
Eugene, OR 97401

Introduction to the Canonical Books of the Old Testament
By Cornill, Carl
ISBN: 1-59752-456-5
Publication date 2/16/2006
Previously published by G. P. Putnam's Sons, 1907

PREFACE

THE volume which now appears for the first time in an English dress under the title "Introduction to the Canonical Books of the Old Testament" is translated from the fifth thoroughly revised edition of my "Einleitung in das Alte Testament" ("Introduction to the Old Testament"), which was first published fifteen years ago (in 1891). It is a source of unqualified satisfaction to me that in its new form the "Introduction" is confined to the Canonical Books of the Old Testament. The sections on the Apocrypha and Pseudepigrapha, which were included in the last edition, have, at my earnest desire, been omitted from the present work. These will form the subject of a separate volume, for the preparation of which the publisher has been fortunate enough to secure the services of Professor Gunkel.

In a work which is intended to serve primarily as a Handbook for students, it would obviously be impossible, nor indeed would it be fitting, that every view which has been propounded regarding the various problems raised by the science of Biblical Introduction in this department should be discussed. It has been my endeavour, however, to lay due emphasis on all the important factors that have co-operated in the development of Old Testament

Introductory Method, and especially to assign credit, where credit is due, to pioneers whose work is in danger of being forgotten. I have also tried to take account of all important contributions to Criticism in its recent phases, and to estimate the weight of critical opinion in relation to problems which are still being discussed. Since 1891, when the first edition of this work appeared, the movement of Criticism has been continuous, and of this fact due account is here, I hope, taken.

In this way, the student will, I trust, find in the volume here presented a faithful picture of the present state of Old Testament critical science, both as regards the problems that still call for final solution, and as to assured results.

In sending it forth in its English dress, I venture to express the hope that the volume may find, at the hands of English students and readers, as warm a welcome as it has been fortunate enough to secure in Germany, and that it will be found to serve a useful end, especially as a Handbook for the purposes of study.

In conclusion, I wish to express my thanks to the English publishers for the worthy manner in which they are placing my volume before English readers.

C. CORNILL.

January 1907.

CONTENTS

CHAPTER I.—PROLEGOMENA PAGE
§ 1. Name and Idea 1
§ 2. History of the Method 3
§ 3. Order of Treatment of the Material . . . 12
§ 4. Age of the Practice of Writing among the Hebrews 13
§ 4A. Hebrew Metre 15

Division I.—Special Introduction

BOOK I.—A. HISTORICAL BOOKS

CHAPTER II.—THE PENTATEUCH
§ 5. Of the Pentateuch in General 27
§ 6. History of the Analysis of the Pentateuch . . 37
§ 7. Analysis of the First Four Books of the Pentateuch 42

CHAPTER III.—DEUTERONOMY
§ 8. Analysis of Deuteronomy 46
§ 9. Time of Arrangement and Composition of Deuteronomy 50
§ 10. The Literary Implications of Deuteronomy . 69

CHAPTER IV.—THE JAHVISTIC-ELOHISTIC HISTORY
§ 11. The Jahvistic-Elohistic History 76
   The Work of the Elohist . . . 79
   The Work of the Jahvist . . . 84

CHAPTER V.—THE PRIESTLY WRITING
§ 12. The Priestly Writing 92

CONTENTS

Chapter VI.—THE PENTATEUCH
§ 13. Special Passages of the Pentateuch . . . 117
    1. The Blessing of Jacob, Gen. xlix. 1b–27 . 117
    2. The Red-Sea Song, Ex. xv. 1–18 . . 118
    3. The Little Songs in Numb. xxi. . . 120
    4. The Oracles of Balaam, Numb. xxiii. and xxiv. 121
    5. The Song of Moses, Deut. xxxii. . . 122
    6. The Blessing of Moses, Deut. xxxiii. . 125
    7. Genesis xiv. 126
    8. The Book of the Covenant, Ex. xxi.–xxiii. 128
    9. Leviticus xvii.–xxvi. . . . 132
§ 14. The Pentateuch as a Whole and its Formation . 136.

Chapter VII.—JOSHUA AND JUDGES
§ 15. The Book of Joshua 149
§ 16. The Book of Judges 156

Chapter VIII.—SAMUEL AND KINGS
§ 17. The Books of Samuel. 180
    Contents of 1 and 2 Samuel . . . 181
    1 Samuel i.–xv. 183
    1 Samuel xvi.–2 Samuel viii. . . 191
    2 Samuel ix.–xxiv. 198
    Poetical Pieces in the Books of Samuel . 202
§ 18. The Books of Kings 205

Chapter IX.—EXILIC BOOKS AND CHRONICLES
§ 19. The Exilic Book of the History of the People of Israel 222
§ 20. The Book of Chronicles 225
    Contents of 1 and 2 Chronicles . . 226

Chapter X.—EZRA AND NEHEMIAH; RUTH AND ESTHER
§ 21. Ezra and Nehemiah 240
    Contents of Ezra-Nehemiah . . . 241
§ 22. The Book of Ruth 254
§ 23. The Book of Esther 256

CONTENTS ix

BOOK II.—B. PROPHETIC BOOKS

CHAPTER XI.—ISAIAH   PAGE
§ 24. Isaiah 262
    The Genuine Parts of the Book of Isaiah . 266
    Special Passages of the Book of Isaiah . . 269
    Isaiah xl.-lxvi 284
    The Composition of the Book of Isaiah . . . 292

CHAPTER XII.—JEREMIAH AND EZEKIEL
§ 25. Jeremiah 295
    Oracles against Foreign Nations . . . 304
§ 26. Ezekiel 313

CHAPTER XIII.—MINOR PROPHETS
§ 27. Hosea 320
§ 28. Joel 325
§ 29. Amos 329

CHAPTER XIV.—MINOR PROPHETS—*continued*
§ 30. Obadiah 334
§ 31. Jonah 336
§ 32. Micah 339
§ 33. Nahum 348
§ 34. Habakkuk 351
§ 35. Zephaniah 355
§ 36. Haggai 358

CHAPTER XV.—MINOR PROPHETS—*continued*. DANIEL
§ 37. Zechariah 361
    Zechariah ix.-xiv. 363
§ 38. Malachi 372
§ 39. The Book of the Twelve Prophets . . . 378
§ 40. The Book of Daniel 382

BOOK III.—C. POETICAL AND DIDACTIC BOOKS

CHAPTER XVI.—THE PSALTER, LAMENTATIONS
§ 41. The Psalter 392
§ 42. Lamentations 411

CHAPTER XVII.—THE BOOK OF JOB
§ 43. The Book of Job 419

CONTENTS

CHAPTER XVIII.—PROVERBS, KOHELETH, SONG OF SOLOMON

PAGE
- § 44. The Book of Proverbs 437
- § 45. The Book of Koheleth (Ecclesiastes) . . . 447
- § 46. The Song of Songs (Canticles) 456

Division II.—General Introduction

CHAPTER XIX.—HISTORY OF THE CANON
- § 47. The Idea and Division of the Canon among the Jews. The Number, Titles, and Order of the Canonical Scriptures 463
- § 48. Formation and Close of the Canon . . . 470
- § 48A. The Alexandrian Canon 483

CHAPTER XX.—HISTORY OF THE TEXT
- § 49. Materials for Writing, and the Written Signs . 487
- § 50. Perfecting of the Writing 493
- § 51. The Massoretic Text 496
- § 52. The Relation of the Massoretic to the Original Text 505
- § 53. Aids towards Reaching an Approximation to the Original Text 509
  - The Samaritan Pentateuch 511
  - The Alexandrian Translation . . . 512
  - The Later Greek Translations . . . 515
  - The Activity of Origen and its Consequences 519
  - The Citations in the Fathers . . . 523
  - The Secondary Versions of the LXX. . . 524
  - The Targums 527
  - The Old Syriac Version 531
  - Hiéronymus (Jerome) 533

APPENDIX.—SURVEY OF THE PROCESS OF DEVELOPMENT THROUGH WHICH THE OLD TESTAMENT LITERATURE PASSED, IN ACCORDANCE WITH THE RESULTS REACHED IN THE SPECIAL INTRODUCTION 537

INDEX I.—SUBJECTS 543
„ II.—PASSAGES OF THE OLD TESTAMENT REFERRED TO IN THE INTRODUCTION 553

PRINCIPAL ABBREVIATIONS EMPLOYED

A G.G.W. = "Abhandlungen der Göttinger Gesellschaft der Wissenschaften."
B.C.A.T. = "Biblischer Kommentar über das A.T."
B.Z.A.W. (or B.Z.A.T.W.) = "Beihefte zur Zeitschrift für die alttestamentliche Wissenschaft."
E = Elohist (see Index I.)
G.G.A. = "Göttinger gelehrte Anzeigen."
G.G.N. = "Nachrichten von der Göttinger Gesellschaft der Wissenschaften."
G.V.I. = "Geschichte des Volkes Israel."
H.B.A. = "Handwörterbuch des biblischen Altertums."
H.J.P. = "History of the Jewish People."
H.K.A.T. = "Handkommentar zum A.T."
J = Jahvist (see Index I.)
Jb. W. = Ewald's "Jahrbücher der biblischen Wissenschaft."
J. d. Th. = "Jahrbücher für deutsche Theologie."
J. pr. Th. = "Jahrbücher für protestantische Theologie."
K.E.H. = "Kurzgefasstes exegetisches Handbuch zum A.T."
M.B.A.W. = "Monatsberichte der Berliner Akademie der Wissenschaften."
M.T. = Massoretic Text.
N. J. d. Th. = "Neue Jahrbücher für deutsche Theologie."
P = Priestly Writing, Priestly Code, Foundation-Writing ("Grundschrift") (see Index I., *s.v.* P).
P. Jb. = "Preussische Jahrbücher."
R.E. = Herzog's "Real-Encylopädie."
S.B.A.W. = "Sitzungsberichte der Berliner Akademie der Wissenschaften."
S.B.O.T. = "The Sacred Books of the Old Testament."
St. Kr. = "Theologische Studien und Kritiken."
S.W.A.W. = "Sitzungsberichte der Wiener Akademie der Wissenschaften."

xii   PRINCIPAL ABBREVIATIONS EMPLOYED

S.Z. = Strack-Zoeckler, " Kurzgefasster Kommentar zu den heiligen Schriften Alten und Neuen Testaments."
Th. T. = " Theologisch Tijdschrift."
W.Z.K.M. = " Wiener Zeitschrift für Kunde des Morgenlandes."
Z.A.T.W. = " Zeitschrift für die alttestamentliche Wissenschaft."
Z.D.M.G. = " Zeitschrift der Deutschen Morgenländischen Gesellschaft."
Z.K.Th. = " Zeitschrift für katholische Theologie."
Z.L.Th. = " Zeitschrift für die lutherische Theologie und Kirche."
Z.T.K. = " Zeitschrift für Theologie und Kirche."
Z.W.L. = " Zeitschrift für kirkliche Wissenschaft und kirkliches Leben."
Z.W.Th. = " Zeitschrift für wissenschaftliche Theologie."

ERRATA[1]

Page 14, line 25, *for* " Meša " *read* " Mesha."
,, 21, ,, 14, *for* " Qînā " *read* " Kînā."
,, 22, ,, 20, *for* " Qînā " *read* " Kînā."
,, 35, ,, 8, *between* " by " and " Hobbes," *insert* " Aben Ezra."
,, 81, ,, 8, *for* " Ex. xix.-xxiv." *read* " Ex. xix.-xxxiv."
,, 99, ,, 1, *for* " xxv. 6-19 " *read* " xxv. 6-9."
,, 138, ,, 27, *for* " xx. 17-19 " *read* " xxiii. 17-19 "
,, 141, ,, 26, *for* " xxi. 23-35 " *read* " xxi. 32-35."
,, 143, ,, 26, *for* " ch. i." *read* " ch. i. 1."
,, 144, ,, 18, *for* " xxxv. 1-5 " *read* " xxxvi. 1-5."
,, 178, ,, 19, *for* " xi. 1-xxii. 7 " *read* " xi. 1-xii. 7."
,, 184, ,, 9, *for* " xiii. 23 " *read* " xiii. 22."
,, 237, ,, 17, *after* the three Hebrew words *insert* (" Midrash of the Book of Kings)."
,, 273, ,, 28, *for* " Jona " *read* " Jonah."
,, 287, ,, 1, *for* " Esra " *read* " Ezra."

[1] The attention of readers is particularly requested to this list. It would be well if the corrections could be embodied before using the book.

Introduction to the Canonical Books of the Old Testament

CHAPTER I

PROLEGOMENA

§ 1. NAME AND IDEA

AUTHORITIES: H. Hupfeld, *Ueber Begriff und Methode der sogenannten biblischen Einleitung*, etc., 1844; and *St. Kr.*, xxxiv. 3 ff., 1861, against H. J. Holtzmann, *St. Kr.*, xxxiii. 410 ff., 1860.

1. The name "Introduction" owes its origin to the Ancient Church: εἰσαγωγή first certainly occurs in Adrianus († *circa* 440), while *introductio* can be traced back indirectly to Cassiodorus Senator († *circa* 570). The German term "Einleitung" was employed for the first time by J. D. Michaelis († 1791) in his "Einleitung in die göttlichen Schriften des neuen Bundes" (1750). While the name has remained unchanged, the thing denoted by it has in the course of the centuries undergone essential modifications of meaning. What is now understood under the term "Introduction" can best be defined as *that branch of theological discipline which is concerned with Holy Scripture on its literary side.* Its function is to ascertain how and when the individual writings

originated which, in their collected shape, form Holy Scripture (= the so-called "Special" Introduction); and, further, to ask how and when these individual writings became united into the common whole of the existing collection, and how this collection has come down to us (= the so-called "General" Introduction). These questions can only be resolved scientifically along the lines of historical-critical investigation, and so it has been customary, since the time of G. L. Bauer († 1806), to designate such Introduction as "historical-critical."

2. More particularly the *Introduction to the Old Testament* has to deal with, as the subject-matter of its investigation, *those products of Israelitish and Jewish literature which are recognised, or have been recognised, by the Christian Church as sacred.* To this fact is due its theological character as well as its organic position in the whole vital structure of Christian theological science.

3. Since the inquiry, both in its character and process, partakes of the nature of an investigation of the history of a literature, the title "History of Biblical Literature" or "History of Hebrew Literature" has been proposed. But, apart from the fact that in a History of Hebrew Literature much would call for treatment which in an Introduction to the Old Testament would have no organic place, in the present position of scientific investigation—and perhaps for all time—a real history of Biblical literature is impossible. In a word, so long as such points can be debated in this connexion as "Moses or Ezra?" "Solomon or Alexander Jannaeus?" a history of Hebrew literature is out of the question. If the

name "Introduction" be rejected altogether as unscientific, and as insufficiently indicating what is intended to be described, no objection can be taken on this ground to "Critical History of the Old Testament" (R. Simon), or "History of the Sacred Writings of the Old Testament" (Spinoza, Hupfeld, Reuss).

§ 2. HISTORY OF THE METHOD

LITERATURE: L. Diestel, *Geschichte des A.T. in der christlichen Kirche*, 1869.

1. The material collected by the Ancient Church in the form of "Introductions" or "Guides" to Holy Scripture is throughout stamped with a purely hermeneutical character; its aim is to offer guidance to the right understanding of Holy Scripture, and to lead onward to that end. Compare the following characteristic words of Adrianus: οἱ σπουδαῖοι οὖν τὰς ἀφορμὰς ἐντεῦθεν δανεισάμενοι ὁδόν τινα καὶ πύλην τῇ φιλομαθίᾳ εὑρήσουσι πρός τὴν τῆς ἱερᾶς γραφῆς ὁδηγηθῆναι διάνοιαν.[1] The εἰσαγωγὴ εἰς τὰς θείας γραφάς [Guide to the Holy Scriptures][2] of Adrianus, which has given its specific name to our branch of theological method [Introduction], is simply an explanation of the Hebraisms in Biblical Greek. Tyconius († *circa* 390) and Eucherius of Lyons († 452) belong exclusively to the hermeneutical school. The "Doctrina Christiana" of Augustine († 430) only deals with a few questions of Introduction in II. 8-15; and even Junilius Africanus († 552), who most clearly grasped the problem of Introduction on the side of the history of literature, in his "Instituta regularia divinae legis" [ed. H. Kihn, 1880] only devotes nine chapters to it, under the characteristic title of *Quae pertinent ad superficiem scripturarum*, while the remaining forty-one, *Quae scriptura nos edocet*, may be described as Biblical theology.

---

[1] "Thus those who have sufficient diligence in utilising the means here provided, will by zealous study find a way and an entrance through which to be led to the understanding of Holy Scripture."

[2] Ed. F. Goessling, 1887.

4   INTRODUCTION TO OLD TESTAMENT

2. The mediaeval period did nothing independently to advance the study of Introductory method; the latter received its first impulse to new life from *Humanism* and the *Reformation*. Here the Roman Church leads the van. The " Isagoge " [Introduction] of St Pagninus († 1541), dating from the year 1536, is still quite mediaeval in character; while, on the other hand, the " Bibliotheca Sancta " of Sixtus Senensis († 1599), which first appeared in 1566, and was repeatedly reprinted and reissued down to the eighteenth century, can be described as an attempt in the direction of a history of Biblical literature, even though the larger part of its pages is still occupied with hermeneutical matter and the history of the interpretation. On the Protestant side the long line of the Reformers is inaugurated by A. Rivetus († 1651) with his " Isagoge " (appeared 1627), in which, in consequence of its author's strict reforming ideas of inspiration, all discussion of the questions of Special Introduction is, by the premisses, excluded as meaningless; and by the Lutheran M. Walther († 1662), whose " Officina biblica noviter adaperta " (appeared 1636), which is dependent upon Sixtus Senensis, though it is marked by a strong dogmatic bias, yet, in a manner entirely consonant with a history of the literature, sets forth the whole Introductory method with a clearer distinction of General from Special Introduction, and must therefore be recognised as the first " Introduction " in the modern sense.

3. A new direction was given to investigation by the appearance of *Criticism* on the scene, which first came in contact with the Bible in the guise of the so-called " lower criticism." Its gifted pioneer was the French reforming theologian L. Cappellus († 1658), who was the first to achieve, with anything like exactness and clearness, and on a consistently high level, a purely scientific philological treatment of the O.T. In his " Arcanum punctationis revelatum " (1624) he strikingly demonstrated the unoriginal character of the punctuation of the Hebrew text, and also showed in the " Critica Sacra " (1650) that the consonantal text of the O.T. had been handed down in a form that was by no means free from uncertainty and error. Side by side with Cappellus stands J. Morinus († 1659), with his two volumes of " Exercitationes biblicae " (appeared 1633 and 1660). Tendencies in the direction of the so-called " higher criticism "

first meet us in the work of the philosopher Th. Hobbes († 1679), whose " Leviathan " (iii. 33) treats " Of the Number, Antiquity, Scope, Authority, and Interpreters of the Books of Holy Scripture."

A searching literary investigation of the Pentateuch was produced by I. Peyrerius († 1676) in Book IV. cap. i. and ii. of his extraordinary work, published anonymously in 1655, "Systema theologicum ex Praeadamitarum hypothesi"—he, however, extended the results there attained expressly to the other Biblical books also; while B. Spinoza († 1677), in the "Tractatus theologico-politicus" (1670), cap. vi.-x., requires already *ad Scripturam interpretandum . . . ejus sinceram historiam adornare* [for the interpretation of Scripture . . . that its true history be provided]; here, in a manner truly classical, the problems and aims of the Introductory method were defined, and, with the intuition of genius, many of its most important results anticipated. This section of the "Tractatus theologico-politicus" must be reckoned among the most significant of the contributions that had hitherto been made to the literature on the O.T. For the science of Introduction the "Histoire critique du Vieux Testament" (appeared 1678) of R. Simon († 1712) can only be described as epoch-making; it is a very learned and thorough literary-critical investigation of the O.T., which might be regarded as an "Introduction" in the modern sense, if Simon had not exclusively limited himself to General Introduction. For Simon's life and the history of his "Histoire critique," *cf.* especially A. Bernus, " R. Simon et son Hist. crit. d. V.T." (1869).

4. From this Criticism contemporaries and the generation that followed held themselves stiffly aloof: in the century which falls between the years 1670 and 1770 the only noteworthy work is the "Introductio ad libros canonicos bibliorum V.T. omnes" (1714–1721) and the "Critica Sacra" (1728) of the extreme Lutheran controversialist J. G. Carpzov († 1767); the sole object of these books is the polemical one of refuting the *Pseudo-critica.* Before a truly scientific treatment and investigation of the O.T. could be made possible it was essential that a firm and immovable foundation of principle should be laid. To have achieved this is the abiding merit of the "Father of

the Neo-Theology," J. G. Semler (†1791). This scholar, by the publication of his "Abhandlung von freier Untersuchung des Kanons" (4 vols., 1771–1775), prepared the way for *a strictly historical treatment of the Canon, and for determining the sense of the individual books of the Bible in the light of the historical circumstances surrounding their origin,* and thereby dealt the orthodox Protestant doctrine of inspiration its death-blow. It is true that his own effort in the "Apparatus ad liberalem V.T. interpretationem" (1773) can only be described as singularly unfortunate; but still the right way had been pointed out, and the right principles clearly recognised. It was not so much a scholar of the regular type, but a poet—J. G. Herder († 1803) —who to an astonished world made known in a certain measure a new aspect of the O.T., and revealed its splendour and its beauty. Herder taught the world to appreciate the O.T. as an artistic self-presentation of the Israelitish national consciousness, and as a document of religion. To the O.T. he devoted a whole series of works: "Aelteste Urkunde des Menschengeschlechts" (1774-1776), "Salomons Lieder der Liebe" (1778), "Briefe das Studium der Theologie betreffend" (1780); and, above all, "Vom Geist der Ebräischen Poesie" (1782). Though Herder's point of view is essentially the aesthetic one, yet in every part of his work the profound and independent thinker is manifest who was destined to exercise a lasting influence over scientific investigation. Building on the basis of Herder's results, and keeping his work always in view throughout, J. G. Eichorn († 1827) produced the first "Introduction to the O.T." (1780–1782), in fact as well as in name. In this treatise all the materials which are now comprehended under the term "Introduction" are dealt with and marshalled with a wealth of learning, a literary grace, and a completeness that are remarkable. Eichorn's work won a great and well-deserved reputation, and determined the lines of Introductory method for a generation. The works of Jahn († 1816), "Einleitung in die göttlichen Bücher des Alten Bundes" (1793), of G. L. Bauer († 1806), "Entwurf einer Einleitung in das A.T." (1794),[1] of

---

[1] Second edition, "Ent. einer historisch-kritischen Einleitung in das A.T." (1801).

J. C. W. Augusti († 1841), "Grundriss einer historisch-kritischen Einleitung in das A.T." (1806), are essentially dependent upon Eichorn; the six-volume treatise also of L. Bertholdt († 1822), "Historisch-kritische Einleitung in sämtliche kanonische und apokryphische Schriften des A. und N.T." (1812–1819), marks no real advance on Eichorn.

5. A new factor was introduced into the science of Introduction by the appearance of *religious-historical Criticism*, as the pioneer of which the name of W. M. L. de Wette († 1849) calls for recognition. The first-fruits of his work, the three volumes: "Dissertatio critica qua Deuteronomium a prioribus Pentateuchi libris diversum, alius cujusdam recentioris auctoris opus esse monstratur" (1805), and "Beiträge zur Einleitung in das A.T."— first small volume, "Kritischer Versuch über die Glaubwürdigkeit der Bücher der Chronik mit Hinsicht auf die Geschichte der mosaischen Bücher und Gesetzgebung" (1806), and the second volume, "Kritik der mosaischen Geschichte" (1807),[1]— are brilliant examples of this method of treatment, and secured for O.T. science several permanent results of far-reaching significance. The "Lehrbuch der historisch-kritischen Einleitung in die kanonischen und apokryphischen Bücher des A.T.," which first appeared in 1817, is the first really independent and noteworthy work of Introduction since Eichorn; it marks, however, no advance on the brilliant "Beiträge," but has rather a suspicion of wavering in the direction of the mediatising type of theology. It was reserved for W. Vatke († 1882) to be the first to bring to full maturity, in his "Biblische Theologie wissenschaftlich dargestellt" (1835), the bud which had burst into blossom in the work of the youthful De Wette. Here, on the basis of a history of the religion which is as boldly conceived as it is firmly constructed, Vatke gives a pragmatic recital of the evolution of the O.T. literature which for the first time clearly conceives, and to a large extent lays hold of the facts of, the actual process of development. For the most part, indeed, this pioneering work was doomed to be neglected and without influence; for neither in the domain of criticism

---

[1] Described [under the general title] as "Kritik der israelitischen Geschichte, Erster Teil." It was not, however, continued any further.

nor apologetic was it taken into account. It was rather the mighty figure of the Göttingen scholar H. Ewald († 1875) who entered into the inheritance of Eichorn and De Wette, and who for a whole half-century remained the standard authority in the domain of O.T. science. We do not, indeed, possess a formal treatise of Introduction from Ewald's pen; but in " Die Dichter des Alten Bundes" (1835-1839), "Die Propheten des Alten Bundes" (1840-1841), and the first volume of his " Geschichte des Volkes Israel" (1843) he has given us an isagogic treatment of all the books of the O.T.

6. The critical treatment of O.T. Introductory method seemed firmly set on a course of unchallenged and irresistible triumph. But there came a set-back. Once more the strict ecclesiastical view gathered its forces in an effort to overthrow Criticism by means of an apologetic which borrowed its weapons from the armoury of the opponent whom it proscribed, and to re-establish the old Protestant point of view in regard to inspiration. In his " Beiträge zur Einleitung ins A.T. " (3 vols., 1831-1839) E. W. Hengstenberg († 1869) attempted to revise and reverse the verdicts of Criticism with regard to three questions which were to a special degree the subjects of discussion, and to "demonstrate" the "authenticity of Daniel," "the integrity of Zechariah," and "the authenticity of the Pentateuch." The most thorough-going and complete presentation of Introductory method in this sense is the " Handbuch der historisch-kritisch Einleitung in das A.T." (5 vols., 1836-1849)[1] of H. A. C. Hävernick († 1845), and the shorter but thoroughly practical and useful " Lehrbuch der historisch-kritischen Einleitung in die kanonischen und apokryphischen Schriften des A.T." (1853) of C. F. Keil († 1888). In opposition to this school, the cause of Criticism, from Ewald's standpoint, was represented by F. Bleek († 1859) in the " Einleitung in das A.T. " (edited by J. Bleek and A. Kamphausen, 1860), by J. J. Stähelin († 1875) in his "Spezielle Einleitung in die kanonischen Bücher des A.T." (1862), by Th. Nöldeke in his " Die A.Testamentliche Literatur" (in a series of essays published 1868), and by E. Schrader, who in 1869 published what was

---

[1] Completed after Hävernick's death by Keil.

nominally the eighth edition of De Wette's "Einleitung," but was in reality an entirely new and altogether independent work.

7. Occupying essentially and fundamentally the same critical position as Ewald, but yet in important details already pointing the way beyond, the Dutch scholar A. Kuenen († 1891), in his "Historisch-kritisch Onderzoek naar het ontstaan en de verzameling van de Boeken des Ouden Verbonds" (3 vols., 1861-1865), gave the world the work of a specialist who did not merely sum up and register previous results, but tested and investigated every problem independently. The so-called "Modern School of Criticism," which recognises and reverences in him its leader and master, dates from K. H. Graf († 1869). In this scholar's "Die geschichtlichen Bücher des A.T." (1866), in close dependence on the precedent set by the youthful De Wette and Vatke, a larger amount of space is accorded to the criticism of the history of the religion, and to it the decisive word is given. An elaborate exposition of the history of the religion of Israel from this point of view was put forth by Kuenen in his monumental "Religion of Israel to the Fall of the Jewish State" (3 vols., 1869 and 1870), while Germany for the most part held itself aloof from the "Grafian hypothesis"—in fact, it was only A. Kayser († 1885) who in his "Das vorexilische Buch der Urgeschichte Israels und seine Erweiterungen" (1874) developed it any further in public. The turning-point was reached with the publication of J. Wellhausen's brilliant "Geschichte Israels" (first part, 1878 ; the later editions [fifth, 1899] under the altered title "Prolegomena zur Geschichte Israels"). Since the appearance of this epoch-making work the whole science of O.T. Introduction has ranged itself round the question, "for or against Wellhausen." To the modern critical school belong the following :—Wellhausen's revision of Bleek's "Einleitung" (1878). E. Reuss († 1891), "Die Geschichte der heiligen Schriften A.T.'s" (1881 ; 2nd ed., 1890); B. Stade, "Geschichte des Volkes Israels" (1881-1888), which includes an extremely thorough treatment of the history of the literature. W. R. Smith († 1894), "The Old Testament in the Jewish Church" (1881 ; 2nd ed., 1892), which first secured an assured position in Germany through the translation of W. Rothstein under the title "Das A.T.: Seine Entstehung und Ueberlieferung"

(1894). A. Kuenen, second thoroughly revised edition of the "Onderzoek," the first two volumes 1885-1889; after Kuenen's death, in 1893 the first part of the third volume, edited by J. C. Matthes, completed the translation into German of all that had hitherto appeared; yet the work necessarily has the appearance of remaining a torso; and so A. Kuenen's "Gesammelte Abhandlungen zur biblischen Wissenschaft," translated by K. Budde (1894), is doubly welcome as a supplement. The author's "Grundriss," first published 1891. G. Wildeboer, "Die letterkunde des Ouden Verbonds" (1893; 2nd ed., 1903); German translation by F. Risch (1895). Here also belongs the "Abriss der Geschichte des A.Testamentlichen Schrifttums," by E. Kautzsch (1894),[1] an outline of the subject sketched by a master-hand for the wide circle of the educated laity generally; as also S. R. Driver's "Introduction to the Literature of the Old Testament" (first appeared 1891; German translation by W. Rothstein, 1896). The latter work occupies in the main the position of the modern critical school, even though in many details it maintains a thoroughly conservative attitude.

In conscious opposition to the newer criticism are ranged the following:—the posthumous Introductory work of W. Vatke ("Historisch-kritische Einleitung in das A.T.," edited from lecture-notes by H. G. S. Preiss, 1886); E. Riehm († 1888), "Einleitung in das A.T.," edited by A. Brandt (1889, 1890), and the exposition of Introductory method given in the volume of the series edited by Zoeckler, from the pen of H. L. Strack ("Einleitung in das A.T.," including the Apocrypha and Pseudepigrapha; fifth much enlarged and improved edition, 1898). A peculiar combination of free criticism and bold apologetic, but with varying emphasis on the two elements, is manifest in the work of F. E. Koenig ("Einleitung in das A.T.," including the Apocrypha and Pseudepigrapha of the O.T., 1893): in Deuteronomy, *e.g.*, he affirms the existence of elements derived from the time of the Judges, while, on the

---

[1] In the supplement to "Die heilige Schrift des A.T. übersetzt und herausgegeben von E. Kautzsch" (1890-1894; 2nd ed., 1896; published separately in 1897, and in this form translated into English and published 1899).

other hand, on the subject of the "Grundschrift" the accepted view according to the hypothesis of Wellhausen is advocated. Still, for all this, on account of the extraordinary wealth of material that is brought together, as well as the independent and penetrating thoroughness with which the whole method of Introduction is handled throughout, this piece of Introductory work must be recognised as the most noteworthy that has appeared in recent years. Finally, an altogether conservative character marks the comprehensive "Einleitung in die Bücher des A.T." of W. W. Baudissin, which appeared in 1901. As the title already indicates, the author pursues a way characteristically all his own. In opposition to the essentially analytic method of procedure, as it has been usually practised since the time of Eichorn, Baudissin aims at describing the individual books "exactly as they present themselves to the mind of the observant and judicious reader, as a concrete whole compounded, for the most part, out of parts of very different character." This quite laudable and justifiable object is attained by the author in superlative fashion. In an exposition of the individual books of the Bible, on the side of their positive and particular characteristics, and of an estimate of their finer and aesthetic features, it is possible for those to rejoice who do not share the author's scientific standpoint.

8. Of modern *Catholic scholars* the following call for mention:
—J. G. Herbst († 1836), "Historisch-kritische Einleitung in die heiligen Schriften A.T.'s" (4 vols., 1840–1844, edited by B. Welte); A. Scholz († 1852), "Einleitung in die heiligen Schriften A.T.'s" (3 vols., 1845–1848); F. H. Reusch, "Lehrbuch der Einleitung ins A.T." (1859; 4th ed., 1870); F. Kaulen, "Einleitung in die heilige Schrift A. und N.T.'s" (1876–1881; 4th ed. of the "A.T.," 1899); W. Schenz, "Einleitung in die kanonischen Bücher des A.T." (1887); R. Cornely, "Historicae et criticae introductionis in V.T. libros sacros compendium" (1889). Of *Jewish scholars*:—J. Fürst († 1873), "Geschichte der biblischen Literatur und des jüdisch-hellenischen Schrifttums" (1867, 1870); D. Cassel († 1893), "Geschichte der jüdischen Literatur" (1871); A. Geiger († 1874), "Einleitung in die biblischen Schriften" (1877).

§ 3. ORDER OF TREATMENT OF THE MATERIAL

1. In accordance with § 1, our Introductory method is divisible into Special and General Introduction. The question arises: in what order should these two divisions be treated? M. Walther, Eichorn, Bauer, Jahn, Augusti, Bertholdt, De Wette, Hävernick, and Vatke begin with General; Keil, Bleek, Kuenen, Nöldeke, Strack, and Riehm with Special Introduction. What is demanded both by the actual facts to be dealt with and by right method can only be satisfied by the latter order of treatment: the particular writings must first be brought clearly to view before they can be combined into the collection of Holy Scripture. We shall, therefore, begin with Special Introduction, which exhibits the history of the particular Biblical books, and conclude with General Introduction, which treats of the history of the Bible as a whole; and in the latter case we shall again commence with the history of the Canon, and then set forth the history of the Text. The order of treatment followed by König—History of the Text, Special Introduction, History of the Canon—I find it impossible to adhere to.

2. But in the case of Special Introduction also the question as to the right order of treatment of the material arises. Should this be a purely historical one, or determined by the character of the subject-matter? As we expressly exclude the designation of our Introductory method as a history of Biblical literature, the historical order of treatment is, by that fact, ruled out. In addition, it has the dis-

PROLEGOMENA 13

advantage of violently disintegrating many books of the Bible and relegating their different parts to the most various periods of Hebrew literature. For the purposes of a text-book practical considerations must be given the first place. In the interests of precision and clearness it therefore seems to be demanded that the individual books should be treated by themselves, and arranged, according to the categories of their subject-matter, into historical, prophetic, and poetical-didactic writings.

§ 4. AGE OF THE PRACTICE OF WRITING AMONG THE HEBREWS

As, according to the tradition, the Pentateuch is the oldest book of Biblical literature, the question as to the age of the practice of writing among the Hebrews must be investigated; a work like the Pentateuch could not have been transmitted merely by word of mouth. While many peoples possess a definite tradition regarding the time when, and the source whence, writing was introduced among them, this was not the case with the Hebrews; they have no recollection of a time when writing was not practised. For Moses and his age it is simply presupposed: *cf.* Ex. xvii. 14, xxiv. 4, xxxiv. 27 ; Numb. xxxiii. 2 ; Deut. xxxi. 9 ; *cf.* also Ex. xxviii. 9, 21, 36 ; Numb. v. 23. In the Papyrus Anastasi, iii., we possess documentary proof that at the time of the Pharaoh Merenptah there was in existence a vigorous and regular official correspondence from Egypt with Palestine and Phoenicia—and according to what is still the most probable view Merenptah is the Pharaoh of the Exodus, and therefore Moses' contemporary. Then again the find of clay tablets at Tell-el-Amarna in 1887 opened up unsuspected prospects and possibilities. In view of such facts as these, it would be altogether unwarrantable to assert dogmatically that Moses could not have been possessed of a knowledge of writing. It is true the name קִרְיַת סֵפֶר ("Book Town"?), Judges i. 11, proves absolutely nothing; and whether any conclusions can be drawn from the fact that סוֹפֵר occurs in the extremely ancient Song of Deborah with the meaning "leader" ("instructor") is at least by no means certain. On the other hand, the use of writing for the time of David is firmly guaranteed by the existence at the royal court of the office of סוֹפֵר ("scribe," "secretary"), 2 Sam. viii. 17, xx. 25, as well as by the indubitably authentic Uriah-letter preserved in 2 Sam. xi. 14, 15. That the art of reading and writing was tolerably widely diffused among the Hebrews at a relatively early period is suggested by the instructive passage Judges viii. 14—a passage which, of course, is evidence not for the age of Gideon, but for that of the narrator; and it must be remembered that Judges viii. belongs to the oldest historical part of the O.T. The monumental stone, also, of the Moabite King Meša, which was erected some 125 years after David's death, exhibits in the form of its letters such a finished type of cursive script as only long usage and a well-advanced development of the art of writing could produce. *Cf.* further Is. viii. 1, x. 19, xxix. 11, 12.

§ 4A. Hebrew Metre

As poetical pieces appear in all branches of Hebrew literature, the historical books not excepted, it follows that the Prolegomena is the appropriate place for dealing with the metrical question: at the present time, indeed, it has the distinction of being the burning question of Old Testament science, so that even an Outline of Introduction cannot afford to pass it by. A full discussion and exhaustive treatment of details can be attempted here even less than elsewhere: our task must be limited to a brief introduction to those metrical systems which at the present time are of importance, and to a characterisation of their essential governing tendencies.

1. It would be natural to suppose that a poetry which has produced works of such imperishable beauty as Job and the Psalms should have possessed an artistic form; for the essence of all art lies not in the material but the form. In the poetic art, form consists in the regularity with which syllable is arranged with syllable, word with word, verse with verse, strophe with strophe—in other words, it consists in a *system of metre*. More especially where the poetic art has not yet been divested of its twin relationship to music, where the poem is at the same time a song, the presence of metre is necessarily assured; for singing, above all singing in chorus, is simply inconceivable without fixed form and definite rhythm. The only positive information on the subject of a Hebrew metre that we possess on the Jewish side is found in Josephus, who (Ant. II. xvi. 4)

considers the Song of the Exodus (Ex. xv. 1-19) to have been written ἐν ἑξαμέτρῳ τόνῳ ["in hexameter verse"]; in Ant. IV. xviii. 44 he also describes the so-called "Song of Moses" (Deut. xxxii. 1-43) as ποιήσις ἑξάμετρος [a hexameter poem], and in Ant. VII. xii. 3 he speaks of the Psalms of David as being composed "of several sorts of metre" (μέτρου ποικίλου), "some trimeters and some pentameters" (τοὺς μὲν τριμέτρους τοὺς δὲ πενταμέτρους). But Josephus writes with the deliberate intention of making his people presentable and intelligible to a Graeco-Roman public, to whom a poetry without metre would naturally have seemed an absurdity. The most that can be said is that in these accounts we are dealing with a casual expression of Josephus, not with any real tradition; and the same remark may be applied to the assertions of Hieronymus [Jerome] on the subject of Hebrew metre, the best known of which occur in the Prologue of his translation of Job. In any case, the metrical tradition—if any such existed—has disappeared without leaving a trace: the Jews themselves have no knowledge of any system of Hebrew metre.

Jewish tradition obviously regarded the characteristic difference between poetry and prose as embodied in the *stichometrical structure of the poetical pieces*: it distinguishes the longer poetical texts which occur in the body of the prose-literature—such as the Song of the Exodus (Ex. xv. 1-19), the Song of Moses (Deut. xxxii. 1-43), the Song of Deborah (Judges v.), and the double-text of Ps. xviii. which occurs in 2 Sam. xxii.—by a stichic arrangement of the writing, the individual lines being separated from each other by a space. And these lines are no mere arbitrary groupings or mechanical divisions of the text, but organic formations, since they everywhere coincide with the logical breaks demanded by the sense. They never appear as isolated and unrelated units, but sometimes as verses of three lines (tristichs) — as Ps. xxiv. 7–10, lxxvii. 18–20, xciii. 3–5—or (which is the case in the vast majority of instances) as distichs (verses of two lines), so constructed that it is not so much the external symmetry but the inner connexion that forms the predominating factor — both lines giving expression to one and the same thought, whether it be in the direction of the second line amplifying the first, or merely varying the expression of the thought contained in it. This fundamental law of Hebrew poetry had, of course, long been understood; but it was R. Lowth who, in his " De sacra poesi Hebraeorum " (1753), was the first to coin the extraordinarily happy designation of it as *parallelismus membrorum*. Thus Hebrew poetry appears throughout as divisible into distichs or tristichs (two-lined or three-lined verse), and unmistakable traces indicate further that from these verse-combinations alone has it compacted *regular strophes*. In such passages as Pss. ii., iii., or cxiv. the strophic arrangement is obvious, and is demonstrated by the occurrence of the verse-refrain in Pss. xlii.–xliii., Is. ix. 1–x. 4, and such cases. In this connexion the alphabetic poems of the O.T. are specially significant, for here the author, by means of the alphabetic acrostic-letters, has placed the articulation beyond dispute: in Pss. cxi. and cxii. these appear in each line; in Pss. xxv., xxxiv., cxlv., and Prov. xxxi. 10-31 in each verse; in Pss. ix.-x. and xxxvii., and in Lam. iv., after every second, in Lam. i., ii., and iii. after every third, and in Ps. cxix. after every eighth verse. The whole result, regarded as *data*, is the product of one tradition: the two problems which would have to be solved by a Hebrew system of metre would be, first of all, to resolve the question whether the individual lines possessed a regular metrical structure, and then, whether Hebrew poetry was constructed strophically.

2. Metre is always conditioned by *the character of the language* : what results if one literature, without regard to the character of a language, mechanically imitates the metres of another is shown clearly enough from a comparison of the products of German and French Alexandrine verse.[1] Since the Hebrew language—which, as is well known, does not tolerate short vowels in open unaccented syllables at all, and in open accented syllables only in certain isolated instances—is not a quantitative one, it follows that a quantitative metrical system of the kind exemplified in Graeco-Roman or Arabic poetry cannot be predicated of it. On the other hand, Hebrew is emphatically an accentuating form of speech; consequently an *accentuating system of metre* would correspond to its essential character. This was the line taken by J. Ley. In 1866, in his " Die metrische Form der hebräischen Poesie," he attempted to show that alliteration and rhyme, in their different varieties, formed an essential element in the Hebrew system of metre; this was followed in 1875 by the " Grundzüge des

---

[1] "Alexandrine," a verse of twelve syllables first used in a French poem on Alexander the Great.—TR.

Rhythmus, des Vers- und Strophenbaus in der hebräischen Poesie," accompanied by a selection of strophic poems; and this again in 1887 by a "Leitfaden der Metrik der hebräischen Poesie," accompanied by a metrical analysis of the First Book of Psalms. According to Ley, Hebrew is an accentuating form of speech, with an ascending rhythm, anapaestic-paeonic in character: it is only at the end of the verse that a falling tone is required, so that the final rise is succeeded by a toneless fall. The constituent element of the Hebrew system of metre is to be found in the accents or rhythmical risings (*ictus*): the number of syllables or tone-falls is a matter of indifference so long as the lines or verses have an equal number— or a number varying according to fixed rules—of accentual rises. In this way Ley secures hexameter, octameter, and decameter verse in which the place of the caesura may vary, as well as the elegiac pentameter, which always has its caesura after the third accentual rise. In 1875 Ley still employed in various ways the method of substitution, according to which one metre might be replaced by another with an equal number of accentual beats; and of compensation, which allowed an equal number of accentual rises to be taken from one verse and added to another; but in 1887 he overcame these defects and produced a consistent and self-contained system.

3. The weak side of Ley's method lay in the fact that such a system of metre as he postulates can only be made plausible on German premisses, whereas in the case of a Semitic language it is Semitic analogies that should be sought for. It is at this point that G. Bickell intervenes. There existed a Semitic

language whose phonetic system exhibits a similar formation to that of Hebrew, viz. the Syriac, which at the same time possesses a rich and varied poetical literature with a developed metrical system. A principal factor in this is the counting of the syllables: its lines consist of a certain well-defined and regulated number of syllables, *i.e.* full vowels. Taking up a hint that had been thrown out by A. Merx in his "Das Gedicht von Hiob" (published 1871), p. lxxxvi., Bickell—one of the most competent judges of Syriac poetry and metrical system—attempted to prove the existence in Hebrew, after the Syriac model, of *a metrical system determined by the counting of the syllables,* such as we find exemplified in the old-Indian poetry, where the *çlôka* consists simply of 16 syllables, without regard to their quantity or accent. In his "Metrices biblicae regulae exemplis illustratae" (1879) and "Carmina V.T. metrice" (1882), with which should also be compared the "Dichtungen der Hebräer zum ersten Male nach den Versmassen des Urtextes übersetzt" (3 parts, 1882, 1883), he distinguishes 6-, 8-, 10-, and 12-syllable trochaics, and 5- and 7-syllable iambic metres, which go to make up regular strophes. But this system was confronted by two serious difficulties. First of all, it was precarious in the extreme to make the counting of syllables the fundamental factor in the metrical system of a language whose pronunciation is quite unknown. And then the system lacked consistency. While Syriac quite consistently only counts the full vowels—giving them, however, at the same time their full value, Bickell, as need dictates, does or does not count in the half-vowels, and even goes to the extent of altering the value of the full-vowel system by means of drastic elisions and suffixions. The copula ן is read in the following ways—*v'*, *ve*, *vé*, *u*, and *ú*; דֶּרֶךְ becomes *dérech*, *dark*, or *darki*; יִקְטֹל, *j'kattél*, *j'káttel*, or *jékattél*; אָמַרְתִּי, *amárti*, *ámarti*, *ámart-*, *amárt-*, or *-mart-*. By this procedure Bickell obtains a "language of his own" which "can no longer claim the name of Hebrew." Thus his system has practically been rejected on all sides, while at the same time, in the domain of textual criticism, he can point to brilliant results achieved, and has assured to himself a great and abiding reputation.

4. The year 1882 was rendered epoch-making by K. Budde's elucidation of the *Qīnā-verse*, the existence of which Ley, indeed, had already clearly recognised in his elegiac pentameter. The importance of Budde's work, "Das hebräische Klagelied" ("Z.A.T.W.," ii. 1 ff., 1882), lies in its application of strict scientific method. Budde does not profess to offer here "an infallible master-key for opening all the closed doors" of the Hebrew metrical system, but will "confine himself strictly to the solution of a single clearly defined problem," and "stake the success of the experiment on its execution alone." He had observed that wherever the Hebrew text yields a song of lamentation a well-defined and characteristically constructed form, clearly distinguishable from its context, shows itself, and that this consists of two members of unequal length so arranged that the second is the shorter. This second shorter member is everywhere sharply marked off, and therefore as a rule follows on the first longer clause ἀσυνδέτως: normally a first clause was composed of three, a second of two, words.

This "elegiac scheme," Budde noticed, occurred not infrequently in other kinds of composition, but with unfailing regularity in the lamentation-song. Since there is no denying plain facts, Budde's theory on the subject was at once universally accepted, and firm ground and an assured starting-point were thus secured for the whole subject, from which it was possible to form a trustworthy estimate of the theories that had hitherto been proposed on the question of the Hebrew metrical system. If in the elegiac scheme such formations as *baḥḥûrîm mêrᵉḥôbôth* and *wᵉên mᵉassēf*, or *wᵉnāmēr ḥᵃbarbûrôthâw* and *wᵉên pôtēᵃḥ*, are metrically equivalent, it is obvious that the principle of syllable-counting cannot belong to the Hebrew metrical system; by this fact Bickell's system was shown to be untenable, while Ley on the whole and in the main was proved to be on the right path, in view of the fact that he had already proposed an "elegiac pentameter" which exactly coincides with Budde's Qînā-verse. It was in this direction, therefore, that the further development of the problem was bound to proceed.

5. The one principal ground of objection and hesitation regarding Ley's system was in the main removed when in 1893 H. Zimmern and H. Gunkel jointly discovered that *Old Babylonian*—an undoubtedly Semitic language—possessed an *accentuating metrical system* based upon the equal value of the rhythmical rises.[1] And thus Gunkel ("Schopfüng und Chaos," 1895, pp. 30 and 45) was able to affirm the existence in Hebrew poetry of "verses of 4, 5, and

[1] See Zimmern's essays in the "Zeitschrift für Assyriologie," viii. 121 ff., 1893; x. 1 ff., 1895; xi. 86 ff., 1896; and xii. 382 ff., 1897.

6 rises, divided by a caesura into half-verses, and frequently constructed so as to form distichs, tristichs, and tetrastichs"; and he distinguishes from these "an intermediate class, which, in common with poetry, possesses the logical relation that marks the connexion between its half-verses, as well as its lofty diction, but ignores the counting of the accentual rises," and which may be termed "rhythmical prose." It was, however, instinctively felt that the matter could not be allowed to rest here, but that an attempt must still be made to determine the relation of the accentual rises to each other according to fixed laws. To meet this need H. Grimme, in his "Abriss der biblisch-hebräischen Metrik" (published in the "Z.D.M.G.," l. 529 ff., 1896, and li. 683 ff., 1897) proposed " *a rhythmical law of 'morae,'* "[1] according to which the position of the tone-syllable "depends upon the sum of the '*morae*' which go to make up both it and the syllable behind the preceding and in front of the following principal-tone of the 'sprechtakt.'" Grimme attributes to every kind of syllable in the Hebrew language a definite '*mora*'-value: in this way he distinguishes syllables of 4, 3, and 2 "*morae*," and on the basis of his law of "*morae*" arrives at verses (*i.e.* lines) of 2, 3, 4, and 5 rises: that any of wider extent than these existed we have no right to assume. But this system is much too artificial, and at its very foundation—the determining of the value of the "*morae*" of the particular syllables—much too uncertain to have allowed of its winning acceptance.

6. The latest phase of the metrical question, and the most astonishing construction reared on the

[1] Lat. *mora* = lapse of time, stop.

foundation laid by Ley, are to be found in E. Sievers' "Studien zur hebräischen Metrik."[1] On the basis of the observation already made by Ley, that the rhythm of the Hebrew language is essentially anapaestic, Sievers proceeds to demonstrate the presence everywhere in Hebrew poetry of equal "sprechtakte" or verse-feet, whose groundwork is the *abnormal anapaestic measure* × × ∸, with its rhythmical displacements and varieties. Sievers comes to the subject having the advantage over all previous workers in this department of being a "trained versifier" and student of phonetics, which advantage, however, is counterbalanced by the fact that he is not a trained Hebraist and Semitist. Fully recognising, as I do, the compactness of his system, and admiring the acumen displayed in vindicating his thesis, yet I cannot allow that Sievers has solved the problem of the Hebrew metrical system. In particular, it appears to me a fatal defect that he has not taken, as his starting-point the one *datum* that up to the present time is assured and really proved, viz. the Qînā-verse: how such a complex of sounds as *wᵉnāmēr hᵃbarbúrótháw* and *wᵉên pótēᵃh*, which as a matter of fact are metrically equivalent, can possibly be brought to verse-feet of equal length I cannot conceive. Moreover, Sievers, in spite of his assertion that "the strange form of speech, peculiarly his own, and invented" by Bickell, separates him from the latter, himself constructs on an *a priori* basis of phonetic postulates an entirely new pronunciation of Hebrew, which is devised in the interest of metrical

[1] In the "Abhandlungen der phil.-hist. Klasse" of the Saxon "Gesellsch. der Wissenschaften," vol. xxi., 1901.

principles to eliminate the law of the falling tone at the end of the verse—a law which was deduced by Ley from the tradition of the Text, and which is stamped upon it as clearly as it possibly can be. But even if all this be conceded, the result gained at such cost is unsatisfactory. What avails the equivalence of particular verses if their arrangement is involved in confusion and disorder—and such metrical schemes as, *e.g.*, 3 : 4, 4 : 4, 4, 3 : 3, 4 : 3 for Judg. v. 2–4; or 4 : 4, 4 : 4, 3 : 3, 4 : 4, 3 : 3, 4 for Judg. v. 28–30; or 5, 6, 3 : 3, 4 : 4, 6, 6, 3 : 3, 3 : 3, 6, 6, 5 for Is. i. 21–27 can only be characterised as confused and disorderly? Sievers regards it as "a not unimportant defect in Ley's system" that the position of the beats is not so orderly and regularly articulated as "we should have a right to expect in a 'verse'"; I regard it as a much more important deficiency in his own system that the number and relationship of the verse-feet remain unregulated. The consequence is that in this metrical system the difference between poetry and prose disappears. A metrical system which can be applied indifferently to such passages as Gen. ii. and xli., Job i. and ii., Ruth i., Jonah i., and even to the Moabite Stone, is no metrical system at all—at least for the "untrained" metrical consciousness. I feel myself bound, therefore, to maintain my stand by Ley, although his system does yield "only conglomerations of numbered syllabic-masses of rhythmically indifferent form and constancy," because the facts prevent me from recognising anything more. The most successful and important follower of Ley is Duhm, whose commentary on Isaiah, published in 1892, was epoch-making for the study of the Hebrew metrical system.

7. The question of *strophes* still remains to be noticed. If these are to be regarded as satisfactory, and as according with the poet's invention, they must coincide with the internal articulation of the poem, and correspond with the logical divisions and transitions of the thought; in addition, an essential element belonging to them must be regularity of structure, or, at any rate, regularity of alternation. Where these essential conditions are lacking, there can be no question of strophes, if terminological accuracy is to be respected. Both Ley and Bickell have from the beginning worked on the assumption of such strophic arrangements in their systems, while Budde and Sievers stand in fundamental opposition to such. Here also I am compelled to decide in favour of Ley against Sievers. That poetry exists without strophe-formations is obvious; nobody would dream of looking for strophes in the Homeric songs, the Satires and Epistles of Horace, the Fables of Phaedrus, or Hans Sachsens' funny pieces. But that a purely lyrical poetry could exist totally destitute of strophe-formations is to me absolutely inconceivable: while at the same time such clear and unmistakable indications of strophic formation do occur in the Hebrew poems that have been handed down to us (see above, § 1), that I cannot but accept the presence of such as a fact, and pursue the investigation of them attentively, in all those parts of the literature where their appearance is not precluded by its special character.

Division I.—Special Introduction

CHAPTER II

BOOK I.—A. HISTORICAL BOOKS

§ 5. Of the Pentateuch in General.

LITERATURE: *Commentaries on the Pentateuch and Joshua*: K.E.H., A. Knobel, 1852–1861, rewritten by A. Dillmann, *Gen.* (6th edition), 1892; *Ex.–Lev.*, 1880; *Numb.–Josh.*, 1886. A 3rd edition of *Ex.–Lev.*, by V. Ryssel, 1897. H.K.A.T.: *Gen.*, H. Gunkel, 2nd edition, 1902; *Ex.–Numb.*, B. Baentsch, 1903; *Deut.–Josh.*, C. Steuernagel, 1900 (in this volume pp. 248–286 give a General Introduction to the Hexateuch). K.H.C.A.T.: *Gen.*, 1898, *Ex.*, 1900, *Numb.*, 1903, *Josh.*, 1901, by H. Holzinger; *Lev.*, 1901, *Deut.*, 1899, by A. Bertholet. S. R. Driver, *Genesis*, 1903; *Deut.*, 1895; G. B. Gray, *Numbers*, 1903. R. Kittel, *History of the Hebrews*, i., 1895, §§ 5–10. H. Holzinger, *Einleitung in den Hexateuch: mit Tabellen über die Quellenscheidung*, 1893. J. E. Carpenter and G. H. Battersby, *The Hexateuch*, 2 vols., 1900. J. E. Carpenter, *The Composition of the Hex.*, 1902. In S.B.O.T.: *Gen.*, C. J. Ball, 1896; *Lev.*, S. R. Driver and H. A. White, 1894 (English translation, with notes, 1898); *Numb.*, J. A. Paterson, 1900; *Josh.*, W. H. Bennett, 1895 (English translation, 1899).

1. The canonical Scriptures of the O.T. are opened by a comprehensive work, half narrative, half legislative in character, which narrates the history of Israel from the Creation to the death of Moses, and which contains an account of the giving of the Law by the Founder of the Israelitish religion, interwoven

with the story of his life and deeds. After its principal contents, it is called simply הַתּוֹרָה ("The Law"), Josh. viii. 34; Ezra x. 3; Neh. viii. 2, 14, x. 35, 37; 2 Chron. xxiii. 18, xxx. 16: more distinctly סֵפֶר הַתּוֹרָה ("Book of the Law"), Josh. i. 8, viii. 34; Neh. viii. 3: or סֵפֶר תּוֹרַת מֹשֶׁה ("Book of the Law of Moses"), Josh. viii. 31, xxiii. 6; 2 Kings xiv. 6; Neh. viii. 1: and more briefly סֵפֶר מֹשֶׁה ("Book of Moses"), Ezra vi. 18; Neh. xiii. 1; 2 Chron. xxv. 4, xxxv. 12: also תּוֹרַת יהוה ("Law of Jahve"), Ezra vii. 10; 1 Chron. xvi. 40; 2 Chron. xxxi. 3, xxxv. 26; תורת האלהים ("The Law of God"), Neh. viii. 18, x. 29, 30: ספר תורת יהוה ("Book of the Law of Jahve"), 2 Chron. xvii. 9, xxxiv. 14: ספר תורת האלהים ("Book of the Law of God"), Josh. xxiv. 26; Neh. viii. 18: and ספר תורת יהוה אלהים ("Book of the Law of Jahve Elōhîm"), Neh. ix. 3. It is divided into five books, and is therefore called correctly חֲמָשֵׁי חוּמְשֵׁי תורה ("Five-fifths of the Law"), in Greek ἡ πεντάτευχος, sc. βίβλος. This fivefold division, which has a good foundation in actual facts, is older than the LXX.; it is first positively attested by Philo de Abr., i.

2. THE FIRST OF THESE FIVE BOOKS gives a narrative of events from the creation of the world to the death of Joseph, in accordance with a uniform, clearly marked plan. Its arrangement may be compared with a series of ever-narrowing concentric circles. It sketches the prehistoric period which preceded the revelation of Jahve made to Israel through Moses, and describes how Israel became the recipient and bearer of this revelation through an ἐκλογή ("election") of the divine grace. The scheme

underlying the whole is a genealogical one, with the ten-times recurring formula אֵלֶּה(וְ) תוֹלְדוֹת, "these are the generations"; those branches of the stem are always dealt with first which are not destined to become the bearers of the revelation, and are summarily dismissed in a few words, from which point the narrative is concerned expressly with the direct ancestors of Israel. Ch. i.–iii.: creation of the world and of men; iv. 1–ix. 17: history of mankind till the Flood and God's covenant of mercy with Noah after the Flood. The first genealogy is that of the Cainites, and then follows that of the Sethites up to Noah, the hero of the Flood. As sin grows apace with ever-increasing power among mankind, God determines to annihilate the latter, and only saves the pious Noah with his three sons. Ch. ix. 18–x. 32: the three sons of Noah, and the derivation of all mankind subsequent to the Flood from these, in the famous "table of the nations": first Japhet, then Ham, and lastly Shem. Ch. xi.: cause assigned for the separation of mankind into different languages and nations through the building of a tower, and the genealogy of Shem through his son Arpachsad up to Terah and his three sons, Abram, Nahor, and Haran. Ch. xii. 1–xxv. 11: history of Abraham as the special founder of the People of the Promise. His migration into the Land of Promise, and the history of his life simply presented under the aspect of a trial and proving of his faith, in order to vindicate and sanction his position as being the worthy inaugurator of a new epoch in the history of salvation, in whose person Jahve concludes His special and eternal covenant of mercy with Israel. Ch. xii. 4–5,

xiii. 5–12, and xix. 29–38 give a short account of the line of Haran; xxii. 20–24, of the line of Nahor; and xxv. 1–6, of Abraham's descendants from a second wife Keturah. After Abraham's death first is given, ch. xxv. 12–18, the genealogy of Ishmael: then, ch. xxv. 19–xxxv. 29, the history of Isaac, which, however, is exclusively concerned with the history of his twin sons, Esau and Jacob. Ch. xxxvi. gives the genealogy of Esau-Edom. Ch. xxxvii.–l.: history of Jacob and his sons, among whom Joseph occupies the centre of interest—only ch. xxxviii. is specially concerned with Judah. Through the agency of Joseph, there then ensues the migration of Jacob and his whole family, in all seventy souls, to Egypt.

THE SECOND BOOK.—Ch. i. gives a picture of the subsequent fortunes of the children of Israel in Egypt, how they were hardly oppressed and kept in grievous bondage. Ch. ii. describes the birth and early history of Moses, the divinely chosen redeemer of Israel. Ch. iii.: the revelation of God at Horeb, and the call of Moses, which he after some resistance (ch. iv.) accepts. Ch. v. 1–vi. 1: the first fruitless negotiations with the Pharaoh. Ch. vi. 2–vii. 7: a fresh revelation of God to Moses, and a command to go to the Pharaoh. The fragment of a register of the heads of the Israelitish families, which breaks off with the name of Aaron; Aaron to be the speaker before Pharaoh. Ch. vii. 8–xi. 10: the wonders wrought by Moses and Aaron. The Egyptian plagues. Ch. xii.: the institution of the Passover. The departure from Egypt. Ch. xiii. 1–16: the law concerning the first-born. Ch. xiii. 17–xv. 21: the journey to the Red Sea and the marvellous crossing of the same. Ch. xv. 22–xix. 2: from the Red Sea to Sinai. Ch. xix. 1–25: the preparation for the revelation on Sinai. Ch. xx.–xxiv: the first revelation on Sinai. The Decalogue and Book of the Covenant; on the basis of the latter a solemn covenant is concluded between Jahve and Israel. Ch. xxv.–xxxi: the second revelation on Sinai. Minute regulation of the cultus in respect of place, persons, and actions: the Tabernacle, the Aaronite priesthood and its functions. Moses receives the tables of stone with the Law. Ch. xxxii.–xxxiv: the episode of the golden calf. The people to leave Sinai. Moses is permitted to view the majesty of Jahve from behind, and renews the broken tables of the Law. Ch. xxxv.–xl.: the renewal of the sacred furniture by Bezaleel and Oholiab, and the erection of the sanctuary.

THE THIRD BOOK sets forth first, ch. i.–vii., a detailed law of sacrifice, dealing with fire-, food-, peace-, sin-, and trespass-offerings. Ch. viii.: the consecration of Aaron and his sons. Ch. ix.: entry on their office by inaugural sacrifices and the blessing of the people. Ch. x.: the sin of Nadab and Abihu from using strange fire, and fresh prescriptions for the priests. Ch. xi.–xv.: laws concerning clean and unclean: animals, pregnant women, bloody flux. Ch. xvi.: law concerning the Day of Atonement. Ch. xvii.–xxvi. (Law of Holiness): a self-contained and coherent legislative corpus: prohibition of blood; laws concerning chastity. Various ethical injunctions. Idolatry, and renewed laws as to chastity. Priests and the High Priest. Use of the sacrificial gifts by the priests, and constitution of the sacrifice. Festival calendar. Lamps and show-bread. Blasphemers. The taking of life in the case of man and beast. The sabbatical year and year of jubilee. The blessing or curse pronounced upon the observance or non-observance of this law, and concluding remark. Ch. xxvii.: injunctions concerning vows and tithes. The valuation and discharge of these.

THE FOURTH BOOK.—With a view to the departure from Sinai, all the men of Israel capable of bearing arms are enrolled (ch. i.), to the number of 603,550, the tribe of Levi excepted, which is set apart for the service of the Tabernacle; an exact disposition of the camp is (ch. ii.) ordained. Ch. iii.: the relief of the Levites from military service in lieu of the firstborn who belong to God; their duties defined. A ransom of five shekels for those of the first-born in excess of the number of the Levites. Ch. iv.: more detailed distribution of the duties of the service among the individual Levitical families, and enrolment of all Levites liable to service (total, 8580). Ch. v. 1-4: maintenance of the purity of the camp. Ch. v. 5-10: enactment about fraud and priestly dues. Ch. v. 11-31: law concerning jealousy-offering and ordeal in the case of a wife suspected of adultery. Ch. vi. 1-21: law of the Nazirite. Ch. vi. 22-27: the Aaronite blessing. Ch. vii.: the consecration-gifts and sacrificial offerings of the twelve princes of the tribes to the sanctuary. Ch. viii. 1-4: directions concerning the lamps. Ch. viii. 5-23: presentation and consecration of the Levites. Ch. ix. 1-14: supplementary Passover and Passover for strangers. Ch. ix. 15-23: the pillar of cloud as signal for marching and halting. Ch. x. 1-10: the two silver trumpets. Ch. x. 11–36: the departure from Sinai. Moses' father-in-law joins Israel. Ch. xi.: Taberah. The seventy elders. Kibroth-hattaavah. Ch. xii.: Aaron and Miriam murmur against Moses. Arrival at Paran. Ch. xiii.: mission of the twelve spies. Ch. xiv.: despondency of the people. The whole generation to die in the wilderness. Defeat at Hormah. Ch. xv.: injunctions concerning fire-offerings and first-dough offerings. Sins of oversight or with a high hand. Sabbath-breakers. Fringes on the garment. Ch. xvi.–xvii.: rebellion of Korah's company. Confirmation of the exclusive priesthood of the tribe of Levi by the budding of Aaron's rod. Ch. xviii.: duty of the priests and Levites, and their revenues and dues. Ch. xix.: the water of purification mixed with the ashes of the red heifer. Ch. xx.: sojourn in Kadesh. Death of Miriam. Waters of strife (Meribah). Edom refuses to permit march through their land. Aaron dies on Mount Hor; his son Eleazar becomes High Priest. Ch. xxi.: victory over the king of Arad at Hormah. The brazen serpent. March to the Arnon. King Sihon of Heshbon routed at Jahaz, and the conquest of the whole of the East-Jordan region. Ch. xxii.–xxiv.: the episode of Balaam. Ch. xxv.: the sin at Baal-Peor. The Midianitish woman and Phinehas son of Eleazar. Ch. xxvi.: fresh numbering of the people with a view to the division of the land 601,730 Israelites capable of bearing arms; 23,000 male Levites. Ch. xxvii.: law of the inheritance of daughters. Moses views from the range of Abarim the promised land, and institutes Joshua as his successor. Ch. xxviii.–xxix.: minute and detailed code of regulations as to sacrifices for all the days of the year. Ch. xxx. : vows, in particular those on the part of women, and their validity. Ch. xxxi. : campaign of vengeance against Midian, and decision on the subject of booty. Ch. xxxii. : allotment of the East-Jordan region among the tribes of Reuben, Gad, and (the half-tribe of) Manasseh. Ch. xxxiii. 1–49 : itinerary of the journeyings. Ch. xxxiii. 50–56 : extermination of all Canaanites and disposal of their land. Ch. xxxiv. : boundaries of the land to be disposed of, and directions about its disposal. Ch. xxxv. : cities of the Levites and cities of refuge. Ch. xxxvi. : ordinance that heiresses should only be permitted to marry within their own tribe.

For the analysis of the FIFTH BOOK, see § 8.

3. Both Jewish and Christian tradition are agreed in regarding *Moses* as *the author of this fivefold book*, and, with the exception of some isolated protest, this opinion remained unshaken till the seventeenth century. According to the Jewish tradition, only the last eight verses of Deuteronomy, which narrate the death and burial of Moses, were additions to the Mosaic work. That such a view could grow up it is easy to understand ; all the same, however, it is entirely without confirmation in the Pentateuch itself. Neither by way of superscription, nor of introduction, nor otherwise does the work itself claim to have been written by Moses ; the latter is referred to throughout in the third person, and the manner in which, in the case of certain sections of the Pentateuch—viz. the sentence of extermination on Amalek (Ex. xvii. 14), the Book of the Covenant (Ex. xxiv. 4), the so-called "Second Decalogue" (Ex. xxxiv. 27), the itinerary (Numb.

xxxiii. 2), and several times in Deut. xxxi. 9, 22, 24, —the fact of their having been written down by Moses himself is expressly emphasised, leads rather to the conclusion that it is deliberately intended thereby to withhold this distinction from the rest of the Pentateuch. Add to this that a whole series of particular passages, which had already been pointed out by Hobbes, Peyrerius, and Spinoza, exists that cannot possibly be placed in the mouth of Moses or a contemporary. To this category belong such passages as Gen. xii. 6, xiii. 7 : the remark that *the Canaanite was then in the land*; Gen. xiv. 14 : the name *Dan*, which, as meaning the town of that name, first became current at a later time (Judg. xviii. 29) ; Gen. xxii. 14 : the allusion to the Temple on *Mount Moriah*; Gen. xxxvi. 31 : *a king over . . . Israel*; Gen. xl. 15 : Canaan described as *the land of the Hebrews*; Ex. xvi. 35 : reference to an event which, according to Josh. v. 12, first took place after the death of Moses ; Lev. xviii. 24–27 and Deut. ii. 12 : allusion to the *extermination of the Canaanites by Israel*; Numb. xv. 32 : *the children of Israel were in the wilderness*; Deut. i. 1, and seven times again : the East-Jordan region designated as *beyond (on the other side of) Jordan*; Deut. iii. 14 : *unto this day*, and similarly vs. 11 of the same chapter. In Numb. xxi. 14 a ספר מלחמות יהוה (" Book of the Wars of J.") is cited as authority for matters which must have been perfectly familiar to every contemporary of Moses ; *cf.* also vs. 27 *ibid.* A critical treatment of the legislation leads to the same results, since the greater part of the " Mosaic " Law implies an agricultural population firmly settled in Canaan.

4. It is not sufficient, however, to rest in the conclusion that the Mosaic composition, in view of such passages, is untenable; but, as Peyrerius was the first to recognise and Spinoza developed more fully and distinctly, it is necessary to go a step further. The Pentateuch cannot be regarded as the *connected and coherent work of a single author* at all. There occur a good many parallel narratives, double and even threefold accounts of the same events which are not always congruous throughout, but often actually contradict each other; and in addition many contrary time-specifications, definite chronological statements in particular narratives which cannot in any way be harmonised with the circumstances and the whole representation in other accounts. Holzinger, § 5, gives full details. And above all there is, to use Goethe's words, the "dreadful, incomprehensible redaction" of the whole work, to which Peyrerius has applied descriptive terms sufficiently strong: *Tam multa in illis legi obscura, confusa, inordinata, trunca et mutila, saepius repetita, omissa plurima, extra locum et seriem posita . . . confusa et turbata passim pleraque, imo quaedam invicem repugnantia.*[1] More especially the middle books of the Pentateuch, with their complex of historical and legislative elements, which are to a large extent inextricably woven together, present a *tout ensemble* that makes it impossible, in any unbiassed treatment of the problem, to regard the

---

[1] "There is so much to be perused in these books that is obscure, confused, in disorder, mutilated and imperfect, frequent repetitions, numerous omissions and misplacements . . . everywhere much disorder and confusion: some things indeed that are incompatible and mutually exclusive."

ANALYSIS OF THE PENTATEUCH 37

outcome as the work of one author, writing with any definite purpose in view. As the Pentateuch, however, in the result appeared as a compound of heterogeneous elements, it became the task of science to ascertain exactly what these elements were, and to determine the manner by which they were united into a single whole.

§ 6. History of the Analysis of the Pentateuch

LITERATURE: A. Westphal, *Les sources du Pentateuque*, i., 1888.

The analysis of the Pentateuch has advanced by several principal stages, each of which has resulted in bringing to recognition an element of truth, until finally it has become possible to estimate these elements at their right value, and to weld them into a single complete and coherent survey which satisfies all the demands of the problem.

1. THE EARLIER DOCUMENTARY HYPOTHESIS was started in 1753 by the publication anonymously at Brussels of the work of the French physician, J. Astruc(†1766), "Conjectures sur les mémoires originaux dont il paroit que moyée s'est servi pour composer le livre de la Genèse." Having observed that the divine names Elohim and Jehovah are regularly interchanged in Genesis, Astruc, on the basis of this fact, distinguished an Elohim-document and a Jehovah-document. As, however, the whole book of Genesis cannot summarily be divided into these two principal documents, he affirmed the existence of ten smaller ones by the side of the former. According to him, Moses had himself divided these twelve documents in the form of a tetrapla of four columns, the existing confusion being the result of later carelessness or mistaken attempts at improvement. Eichorn in his "Einleitung" accepted Astruc's conclusions, and propounded the view that there was a document which used the name Elohim,

and another which used the name Jehovah, with four or possibly five inserted pieces. A real advance was made by K. D. Ilgen († 1834) in his brilliant book, "Die Urkunden des jerusalemischen Tempelarchivs in ihrer Urgestalt" (1798), where he showed that the single Elohim-document of Astruc and Eichorn must rather be apportioned between a first and second Elohist; this momentous discovery, however, did not receive any immediate consideration.

2. THE FRAGMENTARY HYPOTHESIS goes back to the English Roman Catholic theologian, A. Geddes († 1802). Astruc and Ilgen had already called attention to the manifold fragmentary character of their documents. Geddes[1] analysed the whole Pentateuch into a number of larger and smaller Fragments, and explained the difference of the names of God employed as due to two different circles from whom the Fragments in question emanated. The Fragmentary Hypothesis was most fully developed, in the direction started by Geddes, by J. S. Vater († 1826) in his commentary on the Pentateuch (3 vols., 1802-1805), which is brought to a close by the 387 pages devoted to the essay on Moses and the authors of the Pentateuch. According to Vater, the Pentateuch is not by Moses, nor does it belong to the age of the events narrated in it, but originated somewhere about the time of the Exile as a collection of fragments of old accounts made with the object of preserving the latter from the danger of being lost. De Witte also ("Beiträge," ii., and "Einleitung," 2nd ed.) shows signs of having been strongly influenced by the Fragmentary Hypothesis. Its last energetic and consistent representative was A. Th. Hartmann († 1838), whose views are set forth in his "Historisch-kritischen Forschungen über die Bildung, das Zeitalter und den Plan der fünf Bücher Moses" (1831).

3. THE SUPPLEMENTARY HYPOTHESIS was the result of a natural reaction against the one-sidedness and extravagances of the Fragmentary Hypothesis. The latter received its deathblow from the first work of the youthful H. Ewald—then only nineteen years of age—"Die Komposition der Genesis kritisch untersucht" (1823). In this work a uniform and governing

---

[1] For the exact title of his writings, see Holzinger, p. 43.

ANALYSIS OF THE PENTATEUCH 39

purpose in the composition of Genesis was so strikingly demonstrated (*cf.* also § 5, 2, above) that the ground for the hypothesis of a dissection of the book into thirty-nine fragments, as Vatke maintained, was completely cut away. Tendencies in the direction of the Supplementary Hypothesis already assert themselves in the work of De Witte; but it was first clearly enunciated in the work of P. von Bohlen († 1840), "Die Genesis historisch-kritisch erläutert" (1835). Here an original writing is presupposed which an Israelitish compiler adopted and wove into his own representation. The same theory was supported by J. J. Stähelin in "St. Kr.," viii. 461 ff. (1835). In 1843 it was also extended by the last-named scholar to the historical books of the O.T. F. Bleek in his "De libri Geneseos origine atque indole historica observationes" (1836) accepted it, and in the "Kommentar über die Genesis" (1838) of F. Tuch († 1867) we possess the classical production of the Supplementary Hypothesis. De Wette also definitely took up the same position from 1840 onward, and likewise also C. von Lengerke († 1857) in "Kenaan" (1844), and F. Delitzsch († 1890) in his "Kommentar über die Genesis" (1852).

4. THE LATER DOCUMENTARY HYPOTHESIS gives due weight to the element of truth that exists in the Supplementary Hypothesis, viz. the unity of the Pentateuch as it stands, without impairing the independence of the individual sources. Its pioneer was C. P. W. Gramberg († 1830) in his book, " Libri Geneseos secundum fontes rite dignoscendos adumbratio nova" (1828). Here an Elohist, Jehovist, and compiler are distinguished; and the same conclusions were accepted by J. J. Stähelin in his "Kritische Untersuchung über die Genesis" (1830), and by Ewald in "St. Kr.," iv. 595 ff. (1831). For the whole Pentateuch, Ewald in 1843, in the "Geschichte des Volkes Israel," vol. i., works out the following results: Book of the Covenant ; Book of Origins ; third writer ; fourth writer, who worked over anew the three older sources; Lev. xxvi. 3–45; the Deuteronomist, who is at the same time the final author of the existing Pentateuch and of Deut. xxxiii. In the second edition, published in 1851, the work of the fourth writer is recognised as an independent one, and the complete working over of these

four sources is ascribed to a fifth writer. In the third edition, published in 1864, for the union of the work of the Deuteronomist with that of the fifth writer a special final editor is assumed, who also inserted Deut. xxxiii. By the publication in 1853 of his classical work, " Die Quellen der Genesis und die Art ihrer Zusammensetzung von neuen untersucht," Hupfeld († 1866) is justly entitled to rank as the real founder of the later Documentary Hypothesis. Here three entirely independent documents are assumed: an original writing, a younger Elohist, and the Jahvist, which have been worked into one by a redactor. Dependent upon Hupfeld, and in details improving upon and developing his master's work, the name of Hupfeld's pupil, E. Böhmer, deserves mention in connexion with his works, " Liber Genesis Pentateuchius," (1860) and " Das erste Buch der Thora: Uebersetzung seiner drei Quellenschriften und der Redaktionszusätze mit kritischen, exegetischen, historischen Erläuterungen " (1862). The first to carry through the dissection, according to the sources, of the whole Pentateuch verse by verse and word by word, was A. Knobel († 1863) in his commentary, " K.E.H. " (1852–1861). Here the Pentateuch is resolved into the " Foundation-Writing " (" Grundschrift "), which was supplemented by the Jehovist—who in turn made use of and worked over the " law-book " and the " book of wars " as documents—and by the Deuteronomist. Kuenen, in the " Onderzoek," i. (1861), introduced an important modification into the theory by accepting only a single post-Deuteronomic redaction. E. Schrader, " Studien zur Kritik und Erklärung der biblischen Urgeschichte " (1863), was the first to assail the literary unity of the Jahvistic stratum with success; and Th. Nöldeke, " Untersuchungen zur Kritik des A.T.," 1869, pp. 1–144, first rightly defined and differentiated " the so-called Foundation-Writing of the Pentateuch," and set forth its characteristic features in masterly fashion. In the eighth edition of De Witte's " Einleitung," published in 1869, Schrader dealt with the whole Pentateuch, and went back to Ewald's original view of the matter; resolving it into the work of an annalistic writer, a theocratic writer, a prophetic writer—who was at the same time the redactor of the pre-Deuteronomic Pentateuch—and the Deuteronomist. The most important representatives of the later Documentary Hypothesis are J. Wellhausen, "Die Komposition des Pentateuchs,"[1] and Kuenen, "Onderzoek," i., second edition (which embodies earlier essays published separately in "Th. T."). With these, occupying a position of equal importance in his way, is to be ranked A. Dillmann († 1894), in the rewritten edition of Knobel's "Kommentar" in "K.E.H." Very noteworthy also are the works of the French scholar A. Westphal, "Les sources du Pentateuque" (1888 and 1892), and of the American scholar B. W. Bacon, "The Genesis of Genesis" (1893), "The Triple Tradition of the Exodus" (1894). A thorough examination and independent investigation of the whole vast mass of material is given in synoptical form in Holzinger's masterly "Einleitung in den Hexateuch" (1893), decidedly the most outstanding monograph on our important theme that exists. Finally, K. Budde's "Die biblische Urgeschichte untersucht" (1893) calls for mention as being a highly important contribution to the literature of Introduction.

5. From the sketch just given of the work of the last century and a half it will be seen that the literary problem has, on the whole, been solved and brought to an assured issue. That the Pentateuch has been worked up out of four independent written sources—viz. a Jahvistic work J, an Elohistic E (identical with the earlier so-called "second" or "younger Elohist"), a Deuteronomic D, and a priestly writing (formerly denominated the "Foundation-Writing" or "first Elohist"), which I, following the example set by Kuenen, designate with the symbol P—will generally be conceded; and this fact is not altered in the least by the apologetic compromises that are always making their appearance in various quarters, or even by such an attempt as A. Klostermann's able revival of the Supplementary

[1] First published in "J. d. Th.," 1876 and 1877; now embodied in "Skizzen und Vorarbeiten," 3rd ed., 1899.

Hypothesis.[1] As to the distribution of the Pentateuch among these four sources there is essential agreement. The relative age of the latter is a subject of controversy, and on the answer given to this question, of course, depends the view that is to be taken of the origin and compilation of the Pentateuch as it lies before us.

§ 7. ANALYSIS OF THE FIRST FOUR BOOKS OF THE PENTATEUCH

LITERATURE: Best synopsis in Holzinger's Tables. Examples can be seen in E. Kautzsch and A. Socin's *Die Genesis mit äusserer Unterscheidung der Quellenschriften* (2nd ed., 1891); in general, in E. Kautzsch's *Die heilige Schrift. des A.T. übersetzt und herausgegeben* (2nd ed., 1896), and in the texts so far published in *S.B.O.T.*

I now give the results of the analysis of the Pentateuch for the first four books. Complete agreement as to all details has, of course, not been attained, but the main outlines may be regarded as firmly fixed. In order to eliminate any preconceived notions on the question of their age, I give the sources in the actual order in which they appear in the Pentateuch. The signs *a* and *b* denote the verse preceding and following the athnaḥ respectively;[2] the sign * indicates revision; † that the passage in question is to be attributed substantially to the source named.

[1] "Der Pentateuch, Beiträge zu seinem Verständnis und seiner Entstehungsgeschichte" (1893), continued in articles of the "Neue kirchl. Zeitschr."

[2] *I.e.* the first and last half of the verse, which is divided into two parts by the accent athnaḥ.—TR.

FIRST FOUR BOOKS OF THE PENTATEUCH 43

To P belong:

Gen. i. 1–ii. 4a; v. 1–21, 22*, 23, 24*, 25–27, 28*, 30–32; vi. 9–22; vii. 6, 11, 13–16a, 17a*; 18–21, 23b?, 24; viii. 1–2a, 3b–5, 13a, 14–19; ix. 1–17, 28–29; x. 1a, 2–7, 20, 22–23, 31–32; xi. 10–27, 31–32; xii. 4b–5; xiii. 6, 11b–12ba; xvi. 1a, 3, 15–16; xvii.; xix. 29; xxi. 1b, 2b–5; xxiii.; xxv. 7–11a, 12–17, 19–20, 26b; xxvi. 34–35; xxviii. 1–9; xxix. 24, 28b–29; xxx. 4a, 9b, 22a; xxxi. 18*; xxxiii. 18a*; xxxv. 6a, 9–13a, 15, 22b–29; xxxvi. 1a, 2a, 5b–8, 40–43; xxxvii. 1–2; xli. 46a; xlvi. 6–7, 8–27?; xlvii. 5–6a LXX., 7–11, 27b–28; xlviii. 3–6; xlix. 1a, 28b–32, 33†; l. 12–13.

Ex. i. 1–5, 7*, 13, 14*; ii. 23*, 24–25; vi.†; vii. 1–13, 19, 20a*, 21b–22; viii. 1–3, 11aβ–15; ix. 8–12; xi. 9–10; xii. 1–20, 28, 37*, 40–41, 43–51; xiii. 1–2, 20; xiv. 1–2, 4, 8, 9, 10bβ, 15*, 16aβ–18, 21–23†, 26–27aa, 28a, 29; xvi.†; xvii. 1a; xix. 1*, 2a; xxiv. 15b–18aa; xxv. 1–xxxi. 18a; xxxiv. 29–35; xxxv.–xl.

Leviticus.—The whole.

Numb. i. 1–x. 28; xiii. 1–17a, 21, 25, 26a*, 32; xiv. 1aa, 2, 5–7, 10, 26–38†; xv.; xvi.†; xvii.–xix.; xx. 1–13†, 22–29; xxi. 10*, 11*; xxii. 1; xxv. 6–xxxi. 54; xxxii. 1aa, 2b, 4a, 18–19, 28–30; xxxiii.–xxxvi.

To J belong:

Gen. ii. 4b–iv. 26; v. 29; vi. 1–8; vii. 1–2, 3b, 4–5, 7*, 10, 12, 16b, 17b, 22*, 23*; viii. 2b–3a, 6–12, 13b, 20–22; ix. 18–27; x. 1b, 8–19, 21, 25–30; xi. 1–9, 28–30; xii.†; xiii.†; xv. 1*, 2a, 3b, 4, 6, 9–10, 17–18; xvi.†; xviii.; xix.†; xxi. 1a, 2a, 6b, 7, 25–26, 28–30, 32–34; xxii. 20–24; xxiv; xxv.–xxvii.†;

xxviii. 10, 13–16, 19a; xxix.–xxx. †; xxxi. 1, 3, 19a, 21–22, 23b, 25b, 27, 31b, 36a, 38–40, 44, 46*, 48*, 51–53a; xxxii.–xxxiii. †; xxxiv. 1–2a?, 2baγ, 3*, 5*, 7*, 11–12, 13*, 19, 25*, 26, 29b–31; xxxv. 21*, 22a; xxxvi. †?; xxxvii. 3–4, 12–13a, 14b, 18b, 20a, 21*, 23a, 25–27, 28aβ, 32, 33*, 34b, 35a; xxxviii; xxxix. †; xl. 1*, 3aβb, 5b, 15b; xli. 30b, 31, 34a, 35–36, 38, 42a, 45b, 48, 49aβ, 53–57; xlii. 2, 4b–5, 9bβ–11a, 12, 27*, 28a, 38; xliii. †; xliv.; xlv. 1, 4b, 5a*, 10*, 12b, 13–14, 19*, 21*, 27aβ, 28; xlvi. 1aα, 5b, 28–34; xlvii. 1–5a, 6b, 13–26, 27a*, 29–31; xlviii. 2b, 9b–10a, 13–14, 17–19; xlix. 33aβ; l. 1–11†, 14, 26ba.

Ex. i. 6, 7aβ, 8–10, 14aβ, 20b, 22?; ii. 11–23aα; iii. 2–4a, 5, 7, 8*, 16–18†; iv. 1–16†, 19, 20a, 24–26, 29*, 30*, 31; v. †; vi. 1; vii. 14–15a, 16, 17b*, 18, 21, 24–29; viii.–x.†; xi. 4–8; xii. 21–27†, 29–39†, 42a; xiii. 3–16†, 21–22; xiv. 5–6, 10–14†, 19b, 20b, 21aβ, 24, 25b, 27*, 28b, 30–31; xvi. 4*, 5, 13b–15, 21, LXX. 27–30†, 35a; xvii. 1bβ, 2γ; xix. 9, 11–13a, 15a, 18, 20–21, 22b, 25a; xxxiii. 1–4†?, 12–23†?; xxxiv. 2a*, 2–3, 4*, 5, 6a, 8, 10–28†.

Numb. x. 29–32; xi. 4–6, 10–13, 15, 31–35; xiii. 17ba, 18–19, 22a, 28*, 29*; xiv. 3–4, 8–9, 11; xvi. 1, 2*, 12–14, 15*, 25, 26*, 27b–33†, 34; xx. 1aβ, 3a, 5; xxi. 1–3; xxii. 3a, 4, 5aαba*, 6, 7*, 11, 17–18, 22–34, 37, 39; xxiv. †; xxv. 1b–2, 4a; xxxii. 1aβb, 2a, 4b–6, 20–23, 25–27, 33*, 39, 41–42.

To E belong:

Gen. xv. 1*, 2b–3a, 5, 11, 12aβ, 13–14, 16; xx.–xxii. †; xxvii. 1b, 4b, 11–13, 16, 18b–19, 21–23, 28, 29aβ, 30aβ, 31b, 33b–34, 39 and 45b certainly;

FIRST FOUR BOOKS OF THE PENTATEUCH 45

xxviii. 11–12, 17–22†; xxix. 1 and 15–18 certainly; xxx. 1aβ–3bα, 6, 8, 17–20$\ddot{a}$, 22ba, 23b, 26 and 28 certainly; xxxi.†; xxxii. 1–3, 14b–22, 23b, 24b; xxxiii. 5b, 10b, 11a, 18b–20; xxxiv. 1–2a?, 2bβ, 3bβ–4, 6, 8*, 9–10bβ, 13*, 14*, 15*, 16–18a, 20–21, 22*, 23*, 24*, 25*, 27a, 28–29a; xxxv. 1–5, 6b–8, 14*, 16–19†, 20; xxxvii. 5–11, 13b–14a, 15–18a, 19, 20b, 22, 24, 28*, 29–31, 34a, 35b, 36; xxxix. 2aβ, 4aβ; xl.–xlii.†; xliii. 14*, 23b; xlv.†; xlvi. 1b–5a; xlvii. 12; xlviii. 1–2a, 7*?, 8b–9a, 10b–12, 15–16, 20–22; l. 3b, 4aα, 7b, 10a*, 15–26.

Ex. i. 11–12, 15–22†; ii. 1–10; iii.†; iv. 17–18, 20b, 27–28.; v. 1*–2?, 4?; vii. 15b, 17b, 20b, 23; ix. 22–23a, 24a*, 25a, 31–32, 35; x. 12–13aα, 14aαb, 15b, 20–23, 27; xi. 1–3; xii. 35–36, 39b; xiii. 17–19; xiv. 3?, 7*, 9aβ, 15aβ, 16aα, 19a, 20a, 25a; xv. 20–27†; xvii.–xxiv.†; xxxi. 18b; xxxii.†; xxxiii. 1–11†; xxxiv. 1*, 4*, 28b*?

Numb. x. 33*, 35–36?; xi. 1–3, 14, 16–17, 24b–30; xii.†; xiii. 17bβ, 20, 23–24, 26bβ–27, 30–31, 33; xiv. 22–24, 25b, 39–45†; xvi. 32a, 33b, 34; xx. 1b, 14–21; xxi.–xxiii.†; xxv. 1a, 3, 4b–5; xxxii. 3, 16–17, 24, 34–38.

Special Introduction

CHAPTER III

BOOK I.—HISTORICAL BOOKS—*continued*

§§ 8, 9, 10. *Deuteronomy*

§ 8. Analysis of Deuteronomy

1. In passing from the first four Books of the Pentateuch to Deuteronomy we feel that we have entered into another world. The three sources which so far, though they have not always preserved their original and unmixed integrity, we have yet been able to trace clearly and unmistakably enough all through each of the four Books, now disappear with startling suddenness: only in the account of Moses' death—an event of which all must naturally have given some account—do traces of the other sources reappear, Deut. xxxii. 48–52 and xxxiv. 1*a*, 8–9 being deducible with certainty from P, while in xxxiv. 1*b*–7 some features unmistakably point to the influence of J, and xxxi. 14–15, 23 appears to go back at least to an Elohistic basis. For the rest, Deut., both in language, mode of expression, and ideas, is something essentially and absolutely new, which is as clearly distinct from all that precedes as it is in itself a homogeneous whole throughout, and in spite of much variety in the nature of its subject-

matter presents, in contrast with the earlier sources, a well-defined unity.

2. When we come to consider Deut. more closely, it obviously falls into separate and distinct divisions. First of all, ch. i. 1–iv. 40: after a short notice of time and place (i. 1–5), a speech of Moses, which the latter delivers to Israel in view of his approaching death, is given. With many digressions of a historical and archæological character interposed, Moses here surveys the events of the Desert-march from Horeb up to the arrival on the other side of the Jordan in the land of the Moabites, and his discourse resolves itself into an emphatic commendation of statutes and laws which he will "to-day," by Jahve's command, lay before them. Ch. iv. 41-43 is a short passage, of purely historical content, on the subject of the establishment of three cities of refuge on the other side of the Jordan by Moses; the passage obviously stands in no close connexion with what precedes. Ch. iv. 44 gives the impression that now at last the promised Law is to make its appearance; but in ch. iv. 45–49 we have a fresh announcement—exactly parallel and in every respect corresponding to ch. i. 1–5—of *testimonies, statutes and judgments, which Moses spake unto the children of Israel beyond Jordan in the valley over against Beth-peor*; and in ch. v.–xi. another long speech of Moses, of a parenetic character throughout, marked by the express admonition to keep scrupulously *the law which I command thee this day*. This speech also contains more than one historical retrospect; in its whole tenor, however, it is essentially different from the first in ch. i. 6–iv. 40. From this second speech, ch. x. 6–9, which

contains a historical notice of the death of Aaron and of the setting apart of the Levites for the service of the Ark of the Covenant, is easily separable, from its marked incongruity with its context; the whole section x. 1–9 is clearly an interpolation. The actual *statutes and judgments* now follow in ch. xii.–xxvi. They form a collection of laws of very various content, but wholly framed in a theocratic spirit. In ch. xxvii. several injunctions are given, which follow no very clear line of ramification from each other, but have this in common, that they are brought into connexion with Mount Ebal and Gerizim: on Ebal an altar is to be erected and sacrifices offered thereon; in addition great whitewashed stones are to be set up, so that *this law* may be inscribed clearly and legibly upon them, and then curse and blessing are to be pronounced upon the non-observance or observance of the law—in the one case the blessing by six of the tribes on Gerizim, in the other the curse by the six remaining tribes on Ebal. Specially worth notice are vss. 9 and 10, which come in very abruptly, and stand in no immediate connexion either with what precedes or follows. Ch. xxviii. 1–68 introduces again an express blessing and curse on the observance and non-observance of the law, and vs. 69 is clearly a subscription which, in the words בְּאֶרֶץ מוֹאָב ("in the land of Moab"), appears to revert in connexion to ch. i. 5. The contents of Deut. are also described as a *Covenant* (דִּבְרֵי הַבְּרִית) in ch. iv. 23 and xxix. 8, 11, 13, 20. Ch. xxix. and xxx. form a single and connected speech of Moses, with a repeatedly emphasised admonition to observe *the words of this covenant*. As the blessing and curse with which these chapters are concerned are obviously those pronounced in ch. xxviii., it is clear that the former constitute the immediate continuation of the latter. In ch. xxxi. two divisions are clearly distinguishable: vss. 1–13, transference of the chief command to Joshua, and commission to the Levites publicly to read this law-book at the Feast of Tabernacles every year of release; and vss. 16–30, the promulgation of a song which predicts to the people its later sinfulness and the consequent punishments, and which is, therefore, to be learnt by them by heart as a stimulus to reflection and a standing warning. In this passage, which otherwise is a closely-knit and coherent whole, vs. 23 is out of harmony with and disturbs the continuity, forming an exact verbal doublet as it does of vss. 7–8; the verse stands as much out of connexion as itself breaks the connexion of its own immediate context. On the other hand, it seems to connect closely with vss. 14–15, which in their present context are equally isolated; they in fact belong before vs. 1, and are clearly the first announcement of the impending death of Moses. The terms *tent* and *pillar of cloud* point to E. The song announced in vss. 16–30 is given in xxxii. 1–43; here in vs. 44 is inserted a final historical remark. Vss. 45–47 do not produce the impression of having been written with the Song in view, but rather as the close to the whole Book of Deut. as it then existed; they cannot in any case be regarded as the immediate continuation of vs. 44. Finally, ch. xxxiii., *the Blessing of Moses the man of God with which he blessed the children of Israel before his death,* is an altogether independent and isolated passage, without any sort of connexion either with what precedes or follows. Ch. xxxii. 48-52 and ch. xxxiv. have already been referred to in this section (par. 1 above).

§ 9. Time of Arrangement and Composition of Deuteronomy

LITERATURE: De Witte, *Dissertatio critica*, 1805 (§ 2A); E. Riehm, *Die Gesetzgebung Mosis im Lande Moab*, 1854; P. Kleinert, *Das Dtn. und der Deuteronomiker*, 1872; J. Hollenberg, *Das Dt. und sein Rahmen*, St. Kr., xlvii. 467-472, 1874; J. J. P. Valeton, *Studien*, 1879, pp. 157-174, 294-320; A. Westphal, *Le Deuteronome*, 1891; W. Staerk, *Das Dt., sein Inhalt und seine literarische Form*, 1894; C. Steuernagel, *Der Rahmen des Dtn.*, Dissertation, 1894, and *Die Entstehung des deut. Gesetzes*, 1896; J. Cullen, *The Book of the Covenant in Moab*, 1903.

1. Having completed the analysis of the Pentateuch, we address ourselves to the question of the *origin* and *time of composition* of the individual sources. The investigation of this question must begin—in what appears to be an unsystematic way— with the end, viz. with Deuteronomy, because only here do we possess a fixed point of departure which can be dated even to the very year. At an early period, in the work of some of the Patristic writers,[1] and later in Hobbes—who of the whole Pentateuch only admitted Deut. ch. xi.-xxvii. to have been written by Moses—a knowledge is already shown of what has since the time of De Witte (1805) become a commonplace of O.T. science, the fact, namely, that the סֵפֶר הַבְּרִית ("Book of the Covenant") mentioned in 2 Kings xxiii. 2, 3, 21 is to be dis-

[1] See E. Nestle, "Z.A.T.W.," xxii. 170 f., 212 f., 1902.

covered in our Deut. One of the most important events, and fraught with momentous consequences for the religious history of Israel, is narrated in 2 Kings xxii. 8–xxiii. 24—the so-called "Reformation" of Josiah of the year 621. It is true the account "of this turning-point in Israelitish history" has only reached us in a revised form, and one that must be used with caution,[1] but in its essential features it is thoroughly historical and trustworthy. On the basis of a book which was discovered in the Temple, and which is described as a "Book of the Covenant" and is recognised in a solemn assembly of the people as embodying the law binding on the whole nation, King Josiah in 621 carried through a far-reaching and drastic change of all matters connected with public worship. That a book of such importance and significance could have disappeared without leaving a trace—at a time, too, of the most prolific literary activity in Israel—is inconceivable; but if extant it could only be looked for within the Pentateuch, which alone contains all the ordinances and prescriptions of public worship. From the character of the Reformation, however, it may be inferred with considerable precision what the contents of the book that evoked it were. If, in accordance with the requirements of this book, all the high places throughout the whole land were overthrown and defiled, and all the affairs of public worship were concentrated in a single place, the Temple at Jerusalem; if the cultus was purged from all heathen and syncretistic elements, particularly if all the *maççebôth* were broken in pieces and the *ashērîm* were hewn down

[1] See Stade, "G.V.I.," i. 649–655.

and burnt—it can only be the Deuteronomic legislation that is in question, because it alone requires just these points precisely, and that too as something specifically new, ch. xii. 8. The celebration of the Passover, also, that follows the promulgation of this "Book of the Covenant" accords best with Deut., which alone gives special prescriptions about the solemnisation of the Passover, in ch. xvi. 2-8. The one disagreement that exists, that between 2 Kings xxiii. 9 and Deut. xviii. 6-8, is easily explained on circumstantial grounds; in this case the demand of the Lawgiver could not be insisted upon without any thought being at the same time given to the ill-will of the Jerusalem Temple-priesthood. These empirical critical considerations are reinforced by literary criticism also. In Jer. xxxiv. 13, 14, the law about the emancipation of the Hebrew slave after six years' service is cited in a form closely dependent on Deut. xv. 12, and not on the parallel passage in Ex. xxi. 2, while in 2 Kings xiv. 6 a verbal quotation from Deut. xxiv. 16 is adduced.

2. Our next task must be to redintegrate this *Book of the Covenant* of the year 621. That it was not identical with Deut. in the form in which it lies before us will be sufficiently evident from the analysis already given in § 8, which implies anything but a uniform work preserved intact. An important clue is furnished in 2 Kings xxii. 8 and 10, according to which the book in question was read through twice in quick succession in the course of a single day, first before the scribe Shaphan in the Temple, and then by the latter before the king. It cannot, accordingly, have been unduly voluminous. As,

ARRANGEMENT OF DEUTERONOMY

moreover, the priest Hilkiah hands it over to the scribe as סֵפֶר הַתּוֹרָה ("Roll" or "Book of the Law"), and as it has the effect of a law-book, we shall naturally look for the "original Deuteronomy" of 621 more particularly in the legal portions of the existing Deuteronomy, consequently in ch. xii.–xxvi.; and now the question arises, can Deut. xii.–xxvi. be this *original Deuteronomy* (D)? Against this identification ch. xii. at the outset offers protest. This chapter contains two quite palpable doublets, which were long ago recognised as such by J. S. Vater, viz. vss. 5–7 compared with 11–12, and—even more strikingly evident—vss. 15–19 compared with 20–28. Thus at least three different hands must have worked on ch. xii. in its existing form. If in the very first chapter with legislative subject-matter suspicion is aroused, other indications very soon appear which suggest that in ch. xii.–xxvi. we do not possess a document which has preserved its original unity and integrity intact. Ch. xiv. 1–21 equally gives ground for grave doubts. Such expressions as עַם קָדוֹשׁ לִיהוה ("A people holy to J."), xiv. 2–21, and בָּנִים אַתֶּם לִיהוה אֱלֹהֵיכֶם ("Ye are children of J. your God"), xiv. 1 —the former occurring again in vii. 6, xxvi. 19, and xxviii. 8, the latter never recurring at all—are without parallel in the rest of the legislative part of Deut., while the prescription in xiv. 1 is involved in a material difficulty by Jer. xvi. 6, where the practice which is here expressly and strongly forbidden is assumed to be an obvious and natural one; the doubts excited by vss. 3–20 are less of a circumstantial and positive, and more of a formal character. For the existence of enactments of this kind respecting prohibited food

Ezek. iv. 14 is sufficient evidence; but the manner in which the subject is here treated throughout is not that otherwise characteristic of Deut., which gives its enactments a broader historical setting, and does not introduce directions of so detailed and pronouncedly casuistic and formulated a character. Further, the relation of this passage to Lev. xi. has to be taken into account. An additional difficulty of a formal character, which militates against the whole section, also exists. While elsewhere in the legislation proper the people are invariably addressed in the second person singular, here we are suddenly confronted with the address in the second person plural, which is only again found in isolated cases in xii. 1–xiii. 1—a passage that, as we have already seen, bears marks of drastic revision—and besides this only in xvii. 16, xviii. 15 (18), xix. 19, xx. 3, 4, 18, xxii. 24, xxiii. 5, and xxiv. 8, 9. On the other hand, xiv. 2 has the usual formula, and vs. 21aα, with its distinction of Israelite and stranger, is genuinely Deuteronomic. These two verses are therefore to be regarded as original. Of vs. 21b, which is a verbal citation from Ex. xxiii. 19, xxxiv. 26, it is possible to hold a different opinion. In ch. xv., vss. 4–6 (vs. 6 cannot possibly be separated from vs. 5) clearly form a correction of vs. 11, and by that circumstance reveal themselves as a later insertion. In ch. xvi. 1–8, vss. 3–4 obviously break the connexion between vss. 2 and 5, and vs. 7b stands in irreconcilable contradiction to vs. 8, so that here also an alteration of the original text must be admitted. The passage ch. xvi. 21–xvii. 7 has at the least suffered dislocation, as xvii. 8 is palpably the immediate con-

ARRANGEMENT OF DEUTERONOMY

tinuation of xvi. 20. In themselves, indeed, the particular precepts of this section bear the characteristic marks of Deut., and there is no material difficulty in deriving the passage from the latter work. Ch. xvii. 8–13 in its traditional form is of a mixed and conflicting character. If the more serious cases are as a matter of course reserved for the priestly tribunal to determine (and in favour of a priestly tribunal being intended the repeated use of יוֹרוּךָ ["they shall show thee"] in vss. 10 and 11 is a clear indication), then it follows that the latter must be supreme over the secular one, and the reference to the *judge who shall be in these days* in vss. 9 and 12 cannot be original; while an ordinance which implied a royal court of appeal in Jerusalem would be meaningless. Ch. xvii. 14–20, the section containing the so-called "law of the king," is involved in the gravest material difficulties. The beginning obviously shows literary dependence on 1 Sam. viii. 3 ff.; as an example of what a king should not be, Solomon seems clearly to be intended here: vs. 18, according to which the king on ascending the throne is to prepare a copy of the law-book preserved among the priests and Levites, implies the appended passage xxxi. 8 ff.; in vs. 16 there occurs again a suspicious plural, and an injunction such as that in vs. 15 would hardly be intelligible in pre-exilic times. This passage also must be regarded as a later insertion. The same verdict must hold good for xviii. 14–22. On the fact that xix. 1 connects well and closely with xviii. 13 I do not lay any particular stress; but a speech of Moses of so deliberately personal a character, with its historical reminiscence of the period of the Desert-journey, is not congruous with the rest of the legislative division, and relapses rather into the tone and manner of the farewell-discourses—and here again occurs in vs. 15 (and 18) the tell-tale plural! A similar verdict to that reached respecting xvii. 8–13 applies to xix. 16–20, where the plural in vs. 12 already suggests revision. In this case also a spiritual and secular tribunal jostle each other. Since the phrase לִפְנֵי יהוה ("before Jahve"), vs. 17, is certainly original, it follows that D must have reclaimed this case also for the jurisdiction of the spiritual tribunal. On the other hand, in ch. xx., vss. 2–4 are an insertion (the plural again only here), because in vss. 5–9 no trace occurs of the priests. The question with reference to the difficulties inherent in the subject-matter of xx. 1–9 is by no means easy of solution. That war could not be waged on such principles is obvious; but, on the other hand, injunctions on the subject of waging war generally—such as meet us in ch. xx. and the substantially and closely related passages, xxi. 10–14, xxiii. 10–15—are only really intelligible in connexion with the time of Israel's independent national existence, and the point up to which theoretic speculation can ignore the actual requirements and conditions of life can never be determined *a priori* beforehand. In xx. 18 we again meet with a plural, and vss. 15–18 throughout give the impression of being an addition to vss. 10–14. That ch. xxi.–xxv. are marked by an altogether different character from that of ch. xii.–xx. and xxvi. has long been recognised. Here we are confronted with quite new ideas, such as קְהַל יהוה ("congregation of J."), בֵּית יהוה ("house of J."), and repeatedly the

וּקְנִים ("elders"), who are never mentioned elsewhere. The manner, also, of the legislation is different, it is more casuistic in character, and almost exclusively confines itself to regulating the conditions of ordinary civic justice. To exhibit an arrangement of the subject-matter is difficult; the method actually employed fails to justify itself even by the loosest logical collocation—*cf.*, *e.g.*, the way in which xxii. 6–8 is interjected between xxii. 5 and 9, or xxiv. 7–9 [1] between xxiv. 6 and 10. If the Book of the Covenant, Ex. xxi.–xxiii., is also a *corpus juris civilis*, civil laws can equally well have stood in this *Book of the Covenant*, and certain details in xxi.–xxv. have good literary attestation, such as xxiii. 2 ff. by Lam. i. 10, xxiv. 4 by Jer. iii. 1, xxiv. 10 by 2 Kings xiv. 6; but that the section ch. xxi.–xxv. as a whole belonged to D is more than improbable. Injunctions such as those about the treatment of the "chance" bird's nest, or that a battlement should be constructed round the roof of the house, are not adapted to occupy a position among the fundamental laws of a state; about such things the circles from which D sprang can hardly have troubled themselves; they had at heart larger and more important matters. Thus ch. xxi.–xxv. must at least be regarded as having been worked over. Against the genuineness of xxvi. 1–15 nothing can be advanced. Consequently—reserving further analysis—in the original Deuteronomy of 621 there may have stood the following: ch. xii. 1–xiii. 1 in an essentially shorter

---

[1] Here again vss. 8–9, as xviii. 15 ff., are open to suspicion owing to the occurrence of historical reminiscence of the Desert-journey and the presence of the plural.

form: xiii. 2–19; xiv. 3, 21aa*, 21b?; xiv. 22–xv. 3; xv. 7–23; xvi. 1–8*, 9–20; xvi. 21–xvii. 7 (but in other places): xvii. 8–13*; xviii. 1–13; xix. 1–15, 16–20*, 21; xx. (minus, however, vss. 2–4 and 15–18); xxi.–xxv. (in part); and xxvi. 1–15.

3. But in determining the *contents of D*, must we not go beyond *the legislative* sections, ch. xii.–xxvi.? The impression produced upon Josiah by the reading of the book was obviously a powerful and terrifying one, and 2 Kings xxii. 16 and 19 expressly mentions the evil and misfortune which Jahve, in accordance with the words of the book that has been discovered, will bring upon Jerusalem. This seems to point clearly enough to ch. xxviii., where, in fact, the heaviest and most fearful curses are threatened on the non-observance of this law. It is true that ch. xxviii. in its present form cannot be attributed to D; such a conclusion is forbidden by the manifold and close dependence that is exhibited on Jeremianic turns of speech, as well as by the point of view that is taken, which barely considers the possibility of securing the blessing at all, but assumes absolutely that the law will not be observed. Yet it is possible to extract from this inordinately long and prolix chapter a shorter form,—perhaps vss. 1–25*, 43–45 —through which a curse fully analogous with the blessing of vss. 1–14 is secured (Staerk), and nothing precludes this passage being ascribed to D; in fact, the ending of the corpus of law embodied in Lev. xvii.–xxv. with ch. xxvi. offers an exact parallel. If, however, the necessity of such a conclusion should appear after all to be questionable, yet at any rate an introduction at the beginning was indispensable: a

ARRANGEMENT OF DEUTERONOMY

complete and independent writing such as that which was handed to King Josiah can hardly have begun with ch. xii. As the speaker in ch. xii.–xxvi. is unquestionably Moses, and the situation implied is that immediately preceding the crossing of the Jordan, this must have been explicitly stated, and the reader in this way prepared. This requirement, as a matter of fact, is satisfied by the opening chapters of Deut. i.–xi., which contain Moses' "farewell discourses." But quite apart from the inordinate length of the preface in comparison with the bulk of the treatise itself which these chapters would produce, they are divided by the two essentially identical superscriptions in ch. i. 1–5 and iv. 45–49 into two speeches, ch. i. 6–iv. 40 and v.–xi., which are clearly distinguished from and parallel to each other; while the insoluble contradiction that exists between ch. i. 25, ii. 14–16 and v. 3, vii. 19, ix. 2–3, 23–24, xi. 2–7 precludes their composition by a single hand. As the second farewell discourse, ch. v.–xi., both in tone and expression, is clearly allied to D in the closest way, and stands in an essentially nearer relation thereto than does the first discourse, it has been derived from the author of the original Deuteronomy, ch. i. 6–iv. 10 being regarded as the introduction of an editor of D who intended to replace the preceding books of the Pentateuch by a recapitulation of their contents. In the natural course it would then be necessary to proceed further and attempt to classify the several (and in part disparate) passages, now embodied in ch. xxvii.–xxxi., in their mutual relationship, and to determine their relation to the two farewell discourses; and this more especially because it was ch. xxviii. (though in a shorter original form) which equally with ch. v.–xi. was claimed for D. As a matter of fact, this classification and distribution of the material seemed to be successfully attained to within a few outstanding minor details. But Steuernagel and Staerk, in obviously independent agreement with each other, and arguing on the basis of a strongly marked separation of the passages in question throughout into "plural" and "singular" speeches (according as Israel is addressed as *thou* or *you*), and supporting their results by a minute examination and demonstration of the coherence of the plural and singular passages respectively—which Steuernagel has further confirmed by a number of acute observations on the linguistic usage,—have reached the conclusion that a clear division into two distinct parts is unattainable; these chapters owe their present form rather to a highly complex literary process. Details may be disputed; this main result must be regarded as proved. But in like manner I too feel bound to hold fast unreservedly to the opinion that ch. v.–xi. cannot have been the indispensable introduction to D from the very first, because in that case the origin of ch. i.–iv. remains inexplicable; the problem how to account for the juxtaposition of ch. i.–iv. and v.–xi. can only be solved on the hypothesis of two distinct and separate editions of D, which form the basis of the present Deut.

4. D—thus certainly the kernel of Deut. xii.–xxvi., with an introduction and conclusion—was demonstrably promulgated in 621, but *when did it originate, and who is its author?* Here it cannot be disputed

ARRANGEMENT OF DEUTERONOMY

that the book itself purports to have been written by the man who led Israel to the other side of Jordan up to the time immediately prior to the crossing of that river, *i.e.* by Moses; and this holds good even if ch. xviii. 14-22 is not accepted as original: because everywhere throughout the passage over the Jordan and the conquest of West Palestine are placed in the future—though it is the immediate future—and an anonymous contemporary of Moses is, in any case, quite out of the question. But every unprejudiced consideration of the subject shows that this claim is an impossible one, and is opposed to all the historical circumstances of the case. That this book was something quite unique, its contents something absolutely new, appears clearly enough from the account in 2 Kings xxii.: how can the circumstance of such a book remaining concealed for a period of 700 years be explained—especially as this book, to an extent that is quite without parallel elsewhere, is a Lawbook marked by a decidedly reforming aim, no mere theoretic speculation, but having in view the definite object of transforming the whole religious life in accordance with its own requirements? How could it possibly, in the economy of the Solomonic Temple, have lain there for centuries, unnoticed, and then be rapturously welcomed as a testament of Moses? The actual contents of the Law-book also exclude the possibility of a high—or at any rate the highest—antiquity. To the *maççebôth* and *ashērîm* which it bans as heathenish and everywhere peremptorily consigns to destruction Hosea and Isaiah took no exception; while the requirement that the whole religious life of Israel should be concentrated in the Solomonic

Temple at Jerusalem presupposes the disappearance of the Ten Tribes and the prophetic teaching of Isaiah about the central significance and inviolability of Mount Zion. On the whole, both in contents and character this legislation is essentially prophetic, and can only be understood as a deposit and crystallisation of prophetic views and hopes. Its origin must be looked for in the circles of the pious whom the reaction under Manasseh had taught to cling only the more closely and intimately to the Jahve of the prophets—in other words, within the circles of the prophetic party, which must also have succeeded in gaining influence over the priests: for in fact Deut. represents a compromise and alliance between prophecy and priesthood, which resulted, however, in benefiting the latter only. In any case D cannot have been composed long before its publication, because from the very first it was calculated for this particular end; how long or short the interval that preceded may have been can never certainly be stated.

5. Such being the case, D would thus, according to our view, seem to be a *literary fraud*, or at any rate a *deliberate mystification*; nor would this result in any essential respect be modified by pushing back its origination to the time of Manasseh, in order to allow Hilkiah and Shaphan, instead of the last deceivers, to be the first deceived. Our duty is unflinchingly to face this question and to come to a conclusion about it, and, as will immediately appear, on a more minute inspection the matter assumes an essentially different complexion. It has long been noticed that the Deuteronomic legislation stands in a specially

ARRANGEMENT OF DEUTERONOMY

close relation with the collection of laws which we read in Ex. xxi.–xxiii., and which, after Ex. xxiv. 7, is called *The Book of the Covenant*: in fact, the relation between the two is so close a one that D can without inaccuracy be described as a revised or amplified Book of the Covenant. The Book of the Covenant, it is generally allowed, belongs to E, and Kuenen has proposed the brilliant hypothesis that in the connected work of E the Book of the Covenant was originally placed not in conjunction with the revelation at Horeb but with the death of Moses before the passage over the Jordan, and thus stood in this documentary source in exactly the same position where in our present Pentateuch we read Deut. (*cf.* below, § xiii. 8). That the author of D was cognisant of the Book of the Covenant is a fact beyond dispute, as also that the Book of the Covenant had been traditionally handed down to him through E as Mosaic, composed and promulgated by Moses himself. Holzinger and Staerk have independently conjectured that the speech (in its original form proceeding from E) which we now read in Josh. xxiv., and which is designed to form an introduction to a concluding covenant immediately following it, originally stood before the Book of the Covenant; and Staerk further points out the remarkably close relation in which Deut. vii. 12-24 stands to Ex. xxiii. 23-30, and thus reaches the hypothesis that D originally consisted of an introductory speech corresponding to Josh. xxiv. (fragments of which may have been preserved in Deut. ii. and iii.), the kernel of ch. xii.–xxvi., with the passage ch. vii. 12-24 as conclusion, and at first had been designed to form a part of the source E, and to replace in the latter the Book of the Covenant. Whether this hypothesis about the Book of the Covenant and D's literary relation to it be accepted or not, it is certain that D is dependent upon the Book of the Covenant and in close connexion with it; and if the author recast a collection of legislation, traditionally handed down to him as Mosaic, in the form of a freely composed speech of Moses, he only did what all historical writers have done, and to speak of his work as a literary fraud is out of the question; indeed, D cannot even rightly be described as pseudepigraphic.

6. The hypercriticism of a G. d'Eichthal ("Mélanges de critique biblique," 1886) and of a M. Vernes ("Une nouvelle hypothèse sur la composition du Deutéronome," 1887), which deny all connexion between the Reformation of Josiah and Deut., explaining the latter as a production of the post-exilic period, and vagaries such as the contention that the Law-book found in the reign of Josiah was the so-called Second Decalogue (Ex. xxxiv.),[1] may be passed over without further remark. On the other hand, energetic efforts have also recently been made from the critical side to secure a higher antiquity for D: these take as their starting-point the account in 2 Kings xviii. 4, narrating that as early as the time of Hezekiah a reformation of the cultus similar to that of Josiah was undertaken, and in this way they at the same time succeed in reinstating the narrative of 2 Kings xxii. about the "finding" of the book. Steuernagel conceives Deut. to have originated thus:

[1] S. A. Fries, "Die Gesetzesschrift des Königs Josia," Deutsche Uebersetzung, 1903.

Under Hezekiah a groundwork of law was committed to writing for the purposes of his reformation of the cultus; and from this, with the assistance of legal material from other quarters, at the beginning of the reign of Manasseh two nearly contemporary revised editions were prepared, a plural (*D pl*) and a singular (*D sg*) one; and to these, in addition to the revised legal groundwork, ch. v.–xi.† and xxviii.†, xxx. 15, 19*b*–20, xxxi. 9*aa*, 10, 11*b* belonged. Not long afterwards an interested reader got the two revised editions written out together by a scribe on a single roll; and it was this written-out exemplar—of which the place of disposal had been forgotten—that was really found by accident in the Temple in 621. The theoretic possibility of this hypothesis cannot indeed be denied, but this only makes its practical improbability the more evident, so that the modification of it proposed by Erbt must be considered a distinct improvement. W. Erbt ("Die Sicherstellung des Monotheismus durch die Gesetzgebung im vorexilischen Juda," 1903) allows the "Reform-Law of Hezekiah," which is essentially identical with Steuernagel's *D pl*, to have been committed to writing in the year 625, as the basis of the first measures which, according to 2 Chron. xxxiv. 3–7, Josiah took in hand in the twelfth year of his reign; and afterwards Steuernagel's *D sg* he regards as the "Reform-Law of Josiah" in the year 620. But even so thorough a conservative as Baudissin (§ 34, p. 112[1]) assumes a sceptical attitude towards the account in 2 Kings xviii. 4, and declines to accept that in 2 Chron. xxxiv. 3–7, remarking: "It could not have been any long

[1] Of the work cited § 2, 7 above.

time before this finding (of the book) that the Deuteronomic law was committed to writing." On the narrative of 2 Kings xxii., which in its groundwork and main features is unassailable, another acute and brilliant reconstruction, that of Cullen, which proceeds mainly on literary considerations, is also wrecked. According to this scholar, the Book of the Covenant of the year 621 possessed no legislative character at all, but consisted only of a speech of Moses with the מִצְוָה ("command") to serve Jahve alone; it is constructed out of ch. vi.–xi.†, xxvi.†, and xxviii.†, and to these, for rounding off the result, some further passages from ch. iv., v., xxvii., xxix., xxx., and xxxii., and also Ex. xxiv. 4–8, were added. On the other hand, the actual book of the תורה ("law"), ch. xii.–xxv., is really (on his view) a product of the Reformation, hurriedly written down in the press of circumstances, and without any careful revision. According to Klostermann[1] also the Deuteronomic Book of the Covenant was in character not so much a law-book as a collection of materials for one that came into existence but got lost—this collection being (afterwards) piously put together so as to form an edifying whole.

7. When D once became the fundamental law of the kingdom, it is obvious that it would be multiplied in numerous exemplars. It was in this connexion that the *Deuteronomic Redaction* of the book made itself influential, to which we must ascribe all those Deuteronomic passages and sections which cannot have been derived from D itself. This literary

[1] "Neue kirchl. Zeitschr.," xiii. 677 ff. (1902); xiv. 266 ff., 359 ff., 693 ff. (1903).

process, at the background of which lies a twofold edition of D, had already begun in pre-exilic times; that it was a highly complex one, extending over a long period of time, has been shown by Steuernagel and Staerk: to attempt to follow it in detail through all its stages would be a useless task.

8. A certain number of passages in Deut. still remain which *cannot be attributed to this Deuteronomic Redaction*, and which call for special treatment:—(a) Ch. iv. 41-43. This passage, which stands in complete isolation, is altogether dependent upon Deut. xix. 1-10, not on Numb. xxxv. 10-34; at the same time, it was written with Numb. xxxv. and Josh. xx. in view, and is intended to assert that the three free cities which are contemplated as in theory constituted in Deut. xix. 8-10 are not to be identified with those which had been definitely fixed and appointed by Moses in the country East of the Jordan, but meant three additional ones in West Palestine. The risk of being in error as to this result, owing to the Deuteronomic colouring of ch. iv. 41-43, is minimised by the fact that in Josh. xx. the most recent redaction—carried out even after the time of the LXX.—has enlarged and amplified an unadulterated passage coming straight from the Foundation-Writing ("Grundschrift") by the addition of expressions and phrases taken from Deut. xix. 1-10. (b) Ch. x. 6-7. The two verses, which narrate the death of Aaron at Moserah, clearly break the connexion between vs. 5 and vs. 8, and as according to P (Numb. xx. 23-29, xxxiii. 38-39) Aaron died on Mount Hor, while J has absolutely no knowledge of Aaron at all, they can only be derived from E: they

would have their appropriate place in Numb. xxi. Probably their original position was there, and they may, perhaps, have been removed from the neighbourhood of Numb. xx. and placed here, in order to preserve them in their integrity. (*c*) Ch. xxvii. 4–8. The passage offers a twofold difficulty. First of all, vss. 5–7 intrude between vss. 4 and 8 in a harsh and disturbing way, such as no original narrator could ever have been guilty of: it would be tempting here also, on account of the close dependence upon Ex. xx. 25, to regard E as the groundwork.[1] Further, vss. 4 and 8 are obviously doublets of vss. 2–3, and indicate Ebal as the place where the erection of the whitewashed stones of the Law is to take place, a statement which would be very strange in the mouth of a Deuteronomic author, and points even more clearly to E, though we are no longer able to indicate the organic position of this characteristic touch in the original continuous text of that source. (*d*) Ch. xxvii. 11–26. The method of action here prescribed produces a strong impression of antiquity, and the way in which in the performance of it (xxvii. 12) Levi appears in exactly the same manner as any other secular tribe, as well as the circumstance that the scene of such an all-important and sacred procedure is laid at Sichem, are equally noteworthy. It might be natural to think of E as proximate source. But the passage xxvii. 15–26 extracts its twelve curses not from Deut., but from the whole Pentateuch promiscuously, and is of quite recent origin; moreover, the account of the procedure

---

[1] According to Budde, "Z.A.T.W.," xi. 228 (1891), vss. 6 and 7 seem to have been excerpted from "exactly between Ex. xx. 25 and 26."

given in Josh. viii. 30–35—which, however, does not fully coincide with the prescriptions of Deut.—is shown to be a later addition by the fact that in the LXX. it has been inserted in another position in the Book of Joshua; in addition, it already presupposes Deut. xxvii. 1–8 in its present form, which it approximates to in a harmonistic way. (*e*) Ch. xxxi. 1–8, which is purely Deuteronomic, is obviously intended to join on Deut. to the Book of Joshua immediately following. (*f*) Ch. xxxi. 14–15, 23 is a doublet of vss. 1–8 ; it forms an introduction to Joshua, and clearly is derived from E (*cf.* above, § 8, 2). In D there was no occasion to point forward to Joshua. Thus the passages (*a*) to (*f*) above, all belong to the redaction of the complete Pentateuch. (*g*) Ch. xxxi. 16–30* forms the introduction, which has been very considerably worked over, to the Song in ch. xxxii., and can best be discussed in connexion with it (*cf.* below, § 13, 5).

§ 10. THE LITERARY IMPLICATIONS OF DEUTERONOMY

LITERATURE: W. H. Kosters, *De historie-beschouwing van den Deuteronomist*, etc., 1868 ; A. Kayser, *Das vorexilische Buch der Urgeschichte Israels*, 1874, pp. 122–146.

1. Having found in Deut. a definitely fixed point, we shall proceed from that and investigate the question, *What written sources of the Pentateuch are already known and presupposed in Deuteronomy*, that are thus older than itself? If it should prove that Deut. absolutely ignores one or the other of these sources, it would not indeed be proved by this

circumstance that they were not extant at the time of Deut., but still a strong presumption for such a conclusion would be created. It is especially fortunate for this investigation that Deut. ch. i.–xi. are parallel in subject-matter to the books of Exodus and Numbers: under such circumstances points of contact are unavoidable, and consequently an abundance of relevant material is forthcoming.

2. We begin with Deut. ch. xii.–xxvi. xii. 3 = Ex. xxxiv. 13, xxiii. 24*b*; xiii. 6 and 11 = Ex. xx. 2; xiii. 13–19 = Ex. xxxiv. 15, xxii. 19; xiii. 18 = Gen. xxiv. 7, xxvi. 9 J, l. 24, Numb. xiv. 23 E: Numb. xiv. 30 P has another expression recalling Ez.; xiv. 21*b* = Ex. xxiii. 19, xxxiv. 26; xv. 1–6 = Ex. xxiii. 11 against Lev. xxv. 1–7, where שמט does not occur; xv. 12–18 is clearly a transformed and developed version of Ex. xxi. 2–6; xvi. 16 = Ex. xxiii. 14–17, xxxiv. 20*b*, 23; xvi. 19 = Ex. xxiii. 8; xviii. 3 flatly contradicts Ex. xxix. 27–28, Lev. vii. 31–34, Numb. xviii. 18 P.; xviii. 10 = Ex. xxii. 17; מְכַשֵּׁף does not occur at all in Lev. xix. 26, 31, xx. 6, 27 P; xviii. 16 = Ex. xx. 18–19 E; xix. 1–13 is clearly a transformed version of Ex. xxi. 12–14, and contradicts in phraseology and actual contents Numb. xxxv. 10–34 P; xix. 21 = Ex. xxi. 24; xx. 17 הַחֲרִים only again Numb. xxi. 2 and 3 J; xxi. 4 עָרַף = Ex. xxxiv. 20 and only again Ex. xiii. 13 J; xxii. 1–4 reminds of Ex. xxiii. 4–5; xxii. 12 is substantially = Numb. xv. 38 P, but in phraseology altogether different; xxii. 28–29, *cf.* Ex. xxii. 15–16; xxiii. 5–6 = Numb. xxii. 5 E against Numb. xxxi. 16 P; xxiii. 11 substantially = Lev. xv. 16–17 P, but is different in expression, while the word מִקְרֶה ("chance"), in connexion with the case in

question, is found in the extremely old account given in 1 Sam. xx. 26; xxiii. 20 diverges from Ex. xxii. 24 as from Lev. xxv. 36 in expression; xxiii. 24 substantially = Numb. xxx. 3, 7, 9: *cf.* Lev. v. 4 P, but with different phraseology; xxiv. 7 = Ex. xxi. 16; xxiv. 8 is so general in expression that a formal dependence on Lev. xiii. P cannot be proved; xxiv. 9 = Numb. xii. 10 E; xxiv. 12–13 = Ex. xxii. 25–26; xxiv. 17, *cf.* Ex. xxii. 20–21, the phrase, הִטָּה מִשְׁפָּט ("wrest judgment") outside Deut. only again Ex. xxiii. 6; xxv. 17–19 = Ex. xvii. 8–16 E; xxvi. 3 and 15, see xiii. 18; xxvi. 5 עָצוּם וָרָב ("mighty and populous") = Ex. i. 7 and 9 J; xxvi. 6 וַיָּרֵעוּ ("evil entreated") = Numb. xx. 15 E, elsewhere again Gen. xxxi. 7 E; Gen. xix. 7, 9, xliii. 6, xliv. 5, Ex. v. 22, 23, Numb. xi. 11, xvi. 15 J: never in P in this sense: xxvi. 6 וַיְעַנּוּנוּ ("afflicted us"), Ex. i. 11, 12 עִנָּה ("afflict") E; xxvi. 7 = Ex. iii. 7, 9 E against Ex. ii. 23 P, עָמָל ("toil") only again Gen. xli. 51 E; xxvi. 8 בְּיָד חֲזָקָה ("with a strong hand"), Ex. iii. 19, vi. 1 J; xxvi. 9 אֶרֶץ זָבַת חָלָב וּדְבַשׁ ("a land flowing with milk and honey") only in J E and Lev. xx. 24: never in P.

Especially instructive is a whole series of points of contact between Deut. and Lev. xvii. – xxv. Ch. xii. 16, 23, 24 = Lev. xvii. 10–14, xix. 26; xiii. = Lev. xix. 4; xvi. 1–17 = Lev. xxiii.; xviii. 10a = Lev. xviii. 21, xx. 2; xxii. 22 = Lev. xx. 10; xxxiii. 1 = Lev. xviii. 8, xx. 11; xxiv. 14–15 = Lev. xix. 13; xxiv. 19–22 = Lev. xix. 9–10; xxv. 13–16 = Lev. xix. 35–36; the passages already dealt with, xv. 1–6, xviii. 10, xxiii. 20, should also be compared. Everywhere parallels in substance occur, but throughout a divergent formulation. Only Deut. xxii. 9–11 has two characteristic expressions in common with Lev. xix. 19; but this single passage is not sufficient to prove a dependence of Deut. on Lev. xvii.–xxv.

3. Deut. ch. i.–xi. also yield a rich collection and an even clearer result. i. 7 = Gen. xv. 18 J, Ex. xxiii. 31 E, against Numb. xxxiv. 8 P; i. 8, see on xiii. 18; i. 9–18 = Ex. xviii. 13–26 E; i. 24 = Numb. xiii. 23–24 E, against vs. 21 P; i. 28 = Numb. xiii. 28 J; i. 34–36 = Numb. xiv. 22–24 E, against vs. 30 P; i. 39a is = Numb. xiv. 31 P, but this half-verse is wanting in the LXX., and is at least superfluous by the side of 39b; i. 40 = Numb. xiv. 25 E; i. 41–44 = Numb. xiv. 40–45 E; i. 45, *cf*. Numb. xiv. 1b J; ii. 1 = Numb. xxi. 4 E; ii. 3–8 is substantially = Numb. xx. 14–21 E, and was written in obvious verbal dependence upon this passage, though the circumstance narrated presents a somewhat different turn of events; ii. 9–37 is substantially and (to some extent) verbally = Numb. xxi. 12–32 E; ii. 34 וַנַּחֲרֵם ("and we banned"), see on xx. 17; iii. 1–11 = Numb. xxi. 31–35 E; iii. 15 = Numb. xxxii. 39 J, against vss. 1–32 P; iii. 18–20 = Numb. xxxii. 16–32, which in its present form is marked by a strong admixture of elements derived from J E and P, but in Deut. expressions characteristic of P, such as חֲלוּץ צָבָא ("armed for war") and אֲחֻזָּה ("possession"), are wanting; iii. 23–28 is in substance = Numb. xxvii. 12–23 P, but nowhere is there any trace of direct contact or dependence—in fact iii. 27 flatly contradicts Numb. xxvii. 12 and Deut. xxxiv. 1a P: *cf*. on the other hand Numb. xxi. 20 E and Deut. xxxiv. 1b J; iv. 3 = Numb. xxv. 3, 5 E against P; iv. 10–38 and

LITERARY IMPLICATIONS OF DEUTERONOMY

v. 2–30 = Ex. xx.–xxxiv. J E ; v. 4 פָּנִים בְּפָנִים ("face to face"), cf. Ex. xxxiii. 11 E : מִתּוֹךְ הָאֵשׁ ("from the midst of the fire"), cf. Ex. xix. 18 J ; v. 5a = Ex. xix. 9 J ; v. 5b = Ex. xix. 12 E, 21, 24 J ; v. 6–18 essentially = Ex. xx. 2–17 E ; v. 19 = Ex. xxxi. 18 E ; v. 20–25 = Ex. xx. 18–21 E ; vi. 3, see on xxvi. 9 ; vi. 8 = Ex. xiii. 9, 16 J ; vi. 10, see on i. 8 ; vi. 12 = Ex. xx. 2 E ; vi. 15 = Ex. xx. 5 E ; vi. 16 = Ex. xvii. 2, 7 J, cf. also Numb. xiv. 22 E ; vi. 21, see on xxvi. 8 ; vii. 2, see on ii. 34 ; vii. 3 = Ex. xxxiv. 16, which certainly does not belong to P ; vii. 6, see on xii. 3 ; vii. 9 = Ex. xx. 6 E ; vii. 12–24 is in substance fully and in diction largely parallel to Ex. xxiii. 22–30 (cf. § 9, 5) ; viii. 15 נָחָשׁ שָׂרָף ("fiery serpents") = Numb. xxi. 6 E, and צוּר הַחַלָּמִישׁ ("flinty rock") = Ex. xvii. 6 E with צוּר ("rock") against P, which in Numb. xx. 8–11 employs סֶלַע ("crag") throughout ; ix. 1, see on i. 28 ; ix. 2 בְּנֵי עֲנָקִים ("the sons of the Anakim") = Numb. xiii. 33 E, against P's אַנְשֵׁי מִדּוֹת ("men of great stature") vs. 32 ; ix. 5, cf. Gen. xv. 16 E ; ix. 8–21, 25–29 = Ex. xxxii. E ; ix. 22 תַּבְעֵרָה ("Taberah") Numb. xi. 1–3 E, קִבְרוֹת הַתַּאֲוָה ("Kibroth-hataavah") Numb. xi. 34 J ; with regard to מַסָּה ("Massah"), see on vi. 16 ; x. 1–5, 8–11 = Ex. xxxiii. and xxxiv. J E, vs. 8 glances back to Ex. xxxii. 26–29 E ; x. 22 = Gen. xv. 5 E, xxvi. 4 J ; xi. 6 only Dathan Abiram, as in J, against Korah P ; xi. 24, see on i. 7 ; xi. 30 אֵלוֹנֵי מוֹרֶה ("terebinths of Moreh") = Gen. xii. 6 J.

4. The result of this comparison is as definite as it is surprising. Of legal documents, Deut. is certainly acquainted with and makes use of the so-called "Book of the Covenant," Ex. xxi.–xxiii., as

well as the two Decalogues, Ex. xx. 2–17 and xxxiv. 10–26, all from J E. With the priestly legislation (P) no acquaintance is shown, and no influence from it is traceable. Either Deut. flatly contradicts the legislative directions of P, or, where a parallelism in subject-matter comes to view, as is particularly the case with Lev. xvii.–xxv., the phraseology and method of expression are so divergent that even then there can be no question of a literary dependence of Deut. on P, although the legislation of the latter source should, on totally different grounds, be shown to be older. We are led to the same conclusions by a comparative study of the historical passages : here also there is *throughout dependence on and the closest connexion with J E, but on P not a trace of such*; where both accounts diverge to some extent from each other—even if it be in relatively unimportant details — Deut. also follows J E against P. In only three points does Deut. show details for which we can adduce no parallel from J E : i. 23, the spies number twelve = Numb. xiii. 2–17 P ; x. 22, the fact that Jacob journeyed to Egypt with seventy souls = Gen. xlvi. 27, Ex. i. 5 P ; and x. 3, acacia-wood as the material for the Ark = Ex. xxv. 10 P. But E also knew of an ark, Numb. x. 33–36, xiv. 44, and the ark of Ex. xxv. could hardly be described curtly as an "ark of wood"; the number seventy as that of the souls who migrated with Jacob was not a pure invention of P's, because in Gen. xlvi. 8–27 he only succeeds in bringing the required number together after much effort and difficulty, and direct contact with P in the case of the number of the spies who were sent out would only be demonstrable if J E had preserved the tradition of another number than the number twelve. Thus in these cases only matters are in question which in the Pentateuch as it is now extant we read of solely in P, which, however, are never contradicted by J E, and about which it cannot be shown that they may not have had a place also in J E: in view of the overwhelming weight of the evidence of the other factors of the case, we must rather conclude that these details originally had a place in J E, and that in our present Pentateuch, in the process of working P into the whole, they have been struck out. In any case one result reached stands beyond all dispute, viz. that Deut. was acquainted equally with J and E, and we now proceed to deal with these two documentary sources.

Special Introduction

CHAPTER IV

BOOK I.—HISTORICAL BOOKS—*continued*

§ 11. THE JAHVISTIC-ELOHISTIC HISTORY

1. When we interrogate *the contents* of the former work (J) for information *about the time of its origin*, so much is clear, viz. that in dealing with it we are not carried up beyond the years of the early monarchy. Features such as the relation of the twin brothers Esau and Jacob—which really belong to the substance and essence of the ancestral legend—could only have taken shape first during or after the reign of David, and have been transferred to the historic Israel respectively, although they were of prehistoric origin: the mould and form in which the tradition is cast, agreeing as these do in the shape in which they are given to us in J and E, cannot possibly be older than the time of David; and as a certain time for the oral development of the tradition and its familiarisation in the consciousness of the people must be allowed for before it could have found literary embodiment in works of such classical beauty as J, the oldest written recitals of the primitive history that have been preserved to us will not have emanated directly from the earliest time immediately subsequent to

David. Deut., which was acquainted with and used J and E equally, will form the *terminus ad quem*.

2. In order now to ascertain the absolute age of these two written sources, we must first discover whether we can succeed in *definitely determining their relative age*. And that, in fact, is possible even though the very obvious inference is not universally acknowledged. The two writings stand in a very close relation to each other, deal with the same matter in essentially the same way, and present a compact unity as opposed to P. But in details certain divergences and differences appear which make a conclusion as to their relative age possible. The relation of the first connected narrative of E, Gen. xx. 1–17, to the Jahvistic parallel Gen. xii. 10–20 is highly instructive on both sides. In the latter we have a strongly realistic, altogether human history, in E a legend in which the whole apparatus of marvel, with visions and direct divine interpositions, is brought to bear on the scene, and that too on an occasion where it is introduced with very little propriety. Altogether, E is fond of importing, in place of the purely human pragmatism of J, supernatural intermediary causes, and invests his narration in its external features with a more directly religious character: Abraham is a prophet who makes intercession with God (Gen. xx. 7); already Jacob is anxious to abolish the *strange gods* of his wives (Gen. xxxv. 4); the birth of Issachar and Joseph, which J associates with the love-apples of Reuben (Gen. xxx. 14–16), is in E purely an act of God's grace (vss. 17, 18, 22b^a, 23); the extraordinary fertility of Jacob's flocks is, according to J, brought about by manipulation with

peeled rods (Gen. xxx. 28-43), while according to E it is a marvel effected by an angel and revealed in a dream (Gen. xxxi. 9-12); in J (Ex. xxxiv. 1-27) Moses himself hews and inscribes the two tables of the Law, and by this fact his forty days' stay in the mountain is explained, while in E (xxxi. 18) he receives the tables already prepared and inscribed by the finger of God, so that the forty days' retirement is not rightly understood. That the Decalogue of J, too, (Ex. xxxiv.) is far more ancient in character than that of E in Ex. xx. needs only to be stated to be immediately evident. Furthermore, where in E, in such cases as Gen. xxi. 17, xxii. 11, angels speak down from heaven with men, this feature also marks a more recent and developed stage of religious reflection, as against J, in whose work angels move about on earth in human form and speak and act like men (Gen. xvi. 7, xviii.-xix.; Numb. xxii. 22-24); even Jahve Himself is spoken of by J in an anthropomorphic and anthropopathical manner such as only the most pronounced religious naïveté could suggest; on the other hand, it is a clear indication of theological speculation when in E (Ex. iii. 13-15) the divine name יהוה (Jahve) is revealed for the first time to Moses, which J has used quite innocently from the very first. So then we can only join Wellhausen, H. Schultz, E. Meyer, Stade, Kuenen, Holzinger, Wildeboer, Kautzsch, and Gunkel in their verdict, and agree with them in regarding J as the relatively older of the two sources; by this it is not intended to deny that the tradition of E also exhibits very much that is ancient and original.

The Work of the Elohist

3. Our next task is to subject the younger work to a close scrutiny, in order to reach in this way the approximate *terminus ad quem* for the older. As regards the work of E it is, at the outset, generally conceded that it emanates from the northern kingdom, and that *its author was an Ephraimite*. Joseph is regarded by him as the royal figure among his brothers, the darling of his father and of Jahve; by Joseph's side Reuben—not Judah—appears as the tribal leader among the brethren; the ancient holy places of Joseph, Bethel, Shechem, and—a spot especially resorted to as a place of pilgrimage by northern Israelites—the much-visited town of Beersheba (Amos v. 5, viii. 14; 1 Kings xix. 3), form the central points and principal scenes of his narratives; in direct opposition to J, he brings Abraham, not to the specifically Judaean or rather Calebite town of Hebron, but to Beersheba, and this is true of Jacob also if Gen. xxxvii. 14 in this form originates from J. Ephraim is the true heir of the promises and prerogatives of Joseph; the Ephraimite Joshua is from the first Moses' servant and companion; E alone mentions the graves of Deborah and Rachel, as well as that of Joseph (and of Joshua, too, as we can here add), as time-honoured shrines, and the way in which, in opposition to J, the covenant concluded between Laban and Jacob is described points clearly to the war of the kingdom of Israel with the Damascenes. Thus if E, as is generally admitted, belongs to the northern kingdom, we have a *terminus ad quem* for his work in the year

722, and the whole manner of his recital, the strongly marked national sentiment and the naïve joy—dashed by no shadow of misfortune—which he unaffectedly displays in the supremacy of Joseph and his kingdom, must lead us to conclude that this great history came into existence in a relatively prosperous period of the kingdom of Israel. / As the influence of prophetic ideas is clearly perceptible, a time is suggested when this spiritual phenomenon had already become a living power in Israel; and further, as we are precluded by the very fact that E's recital is not the most ancient from putting it too far back, all these considerations are met and satisfied by a date within the last glorious period of Israel's history in the long and brilliant reign of Jeroboam II., *i.e.* about 750; and this conclusion also agrees with the verdict of Stade and Kuenen.

4. But in connexion with this work there is still to be settled the further question, whether *we are to regard it, as we have it, as a literary unity.* It is Kuenen's merit to have been the first to raise this problem with respect to the whole extent of E, and to pursue the investigation of it in detail: he comes in this connexion (*cf.* § 13, 25 and 26)[1] to the conclusion that an edition of E for Judah (E^2) was produced in the seventh century, because the original form of the work (E^1) could not continue to satisfy the needs and necessities of that time, which were the result of gradual changes. That the preparation of this E^2 proceeded from a Judaean quarter is a conclusion that need not be accepted altogether, because the whole of Ephraim was not carried into exile in 722, and there is no reason that forces us

[1] For the work cited, *cf.* § 2, 7 above.

to suppose that all higher life and aspiration was completely extinguished among those who remained behind in the land; I should regard it as much more natural to look for the origin of E^2 among such circles. Kuenen next reclaims for E^2 the entire first Decalogue, together with those parts of the historical narrative which belong to and depend upon it in Ex. xix.–xxiv. and the story (inseparably connected with these chapters) of the golden calf (Ex. xxxii. 1–xxxiii. 6). We may proceed on the basis of the latter passage. In this account there obviously comes to view a prophetic rejection—delivered by Moses himself—of the cultus of Ephraim, that of the "calves of Bethel and Dan": such, however, could hardly be looked for from the same narrator who tells with such holy joy of divine appearances in those venerable spots which were later proscribed by the prophets—who, in particular, carries back the foundation of the sanctuary at Bethel to a theophany, and in Bethel clearly recognises the central sanctuary of Jacob, to which the whole of Israel is liable for tithes of all that Jahve gives it. If, moreover, the words of Ex. xxxii. 34*b* be regarded as pointing to the Assyrian Exile as a punishment for the calf-worship of Samaria, then this one feature, at any rate, must belong to a revision, which would be later than 722. That the account of the golden calf stands in inseparable connexion with the legislation of the first Decalogue is obvious, and this, consequently, cannot belong to E^1: if we reflect that not one of the older prophets who were zealous against idol-worship appeals to the Decalogue, and that the only trace of any acquaintance with this Decalogue to be found in the older literature (Hos. iv. 2), by reason of its different arrangement and designation of the sins mentioned, proves nothing, we shall find it possible to pronounce Kuenen's view a not unjustifiable one. But in addition to this yet further criteria are available. That the departure from Horeb to the Promised Land was to be regarded as a punishment, and the sanctuary of the Ark a mere substitute, for the reason that Israel was not yet ripe for the pure knowledge of God demanded by the Decalogue, can never have been the meaning of the original tradition, which recognised in the Ark the visible pledge of Jahve's helpful and gracious presence, and in the guidance to Canaan saw a mark of goodwill on the part of the mighty, wonder-working God of the nation. By assigning this part of the narrative to E^2 we further secure the advantage that the highly characteristic and ancient fragments Ex. xxiv. 1–2 and 9–11, where all indications argue for their belonging to E, while in the existing history of the legislation they cannot be fitted in at all, are reserved for E^1; these, with Ex. xxxiii. 7–11 and possibly also xix. 13b, are the only passages preserved from E^1 in Ex. xix.–xxxiv. Staerk, however, would include in E^1 a Decalogue as a revelation at Horeb, and thinks this can be distinguished in Ex. xxii. 27–28, xxiii. 14–16, 10–12; while O. Meisner ("Der Dekalog," Diss., 1893) looks for the Horeb-"words" of E^1 in Ex. xxiii. 14–19 (*cf.* on this point also § 13, 8, below). Further, Kuenen ascribes to E^2 Numb. xi. 14, 16–17, 24b–30 and ch. xii. in its present form. The narrative Numb. xi. 14 f. stands out of logical connexion with its immediate context, and, besides, its relation with

Ex. xviii. is involved in considerable difficulties—all the greater if (as appears to follow from Deut. i.) Ex. xviii., vs. 5 of which transports us to the background of xix. 2*b*, was originally placed at the departure from Horeb, and thus exactly in the position occupied by Numb. xi. The seventy elders are derived from Ex. xxiv. 1-2, 9-11 E^1, and dependence also on Ex. xviii. is clear; *cf.* Numb. xi. 14 with Ex. xviii. 18*b*, 22*b*. Thus in Numb. xi. 14 ff. we have a specifically prophetic parallel narrative to, or rather new exposition of, Ex. xviii. E^1—an assumption that solves all difficulties. Numb. xii. also is not a uniform narrative. After Miriam and Aaron have reproached Moses *because of the Cushite woman whom he had married*, one hardly looks for a dissension on the question whether Moses alone possesses the prophetic spirit : thus vss. 2-8 also are to be assigned to E^2, and in them and Numb. xi. 14 ff. we have "two interrelated stages in the course of prophetism." Further, Kuenen shows that the passage Numb. xxi. 32-35 (which Wellhausen had recognised already as a "later addition") is at least a development from E^1, even if possibly it does not depend upon E^2: it owes its existence to the view that the whole of the country east of the Jordan had already been conquered by Moses, while in E^1 only the tribes of Reuben and Gad are concerned (*cf.* § 14, 2). I should prefer to claim further for E^2 the form of the narrative in Gen. xxxiv., which is derived [1] from E. This narrative can hardly be harmonised with Gen. xlviii. 21-22 (which certainly belongs to E^1), while, on the other hand, the question of intercourse

[1] "Z.A.T.W.," xi. 1 ff. (1891).

and intermarriage of Israelites with heathen certainly was one of great practical significance for those northern Israelites who had not been carried into exile, and whose land was deluged with foreign colonists. One is tempted also, in spite of Josh. xxiv. 2, to assign Gen. xxxv. 1-4 to E², since it hardly accords with the original character of the tradition that the wives of Jacob, who in E (ch. xxx.) give names to their sons like genuinely pious women of Israel, should be represented as downright heathens. In agreement with these results is the assertion of Lagarde ("Mitteil.," iii. 226-220)—based upon the consistent use of אלהים (Elohim) and the Egyptian names occurring in Gen. xli.—that E belongs "to the seventh century" and was a contemporary of Psametichus I. (664-610); in that case the story of Joseph would have been revised by E². Thus we reach the result that E¹ was written down in the time of Jeroboam II., *circa* 750, and that about a century later this work, either by a Judaean or by a North-Israelite who had remained behind in the land, was revised on the basis of the development of theological views that had taken place owing to the work of the great writing prophets.

The Work of the Jahvist

LITERATURE: E. Schrader, *Studien*, 1863 (§ 6, 4); E. Meyer, *Z.A.T.W.*, i. 117 ff. (1881), v. 36 ff. (1885); K. Budde, *Die biblische Urgeschichte*, 1883; C. Bruston, *Les quatre sources des lois de l'Exode* (in *Revue de théol. et phil.*, 1883), and *Les deux Jéhovistes* (*ibid.*, 1885); B. Stade, *Das Kainzeichen*, *Z.A.T.W.*, xiv. 250 ff. (1894); and *Der Turmbau zu Babel*, xv. 157 ff. (1895).

5. In the case of this source *the question of its*

derivation is especially matter of controversy. Men of such eminence as Schrader and Kuenen attribute J equally with E to the northern kingdom; but the opinion held by Ewald, Dillmann, Wellhausen, E. Meyer, Stade, Budde, Kittel, Driver, Holzinger, Gunkel, and Baudissin, viz. that it belonged rather to the kingdom of Judah, seems to be preferable. When it is remembered that [J, in evident opposition to E, makes Abraham, and perhaps Jacob also, dwell in Hebron instead of Beersheba; that, in the story of Joseph, Judah, and not Reuben, appears as the spokesman of the brothers; that the (as it appears) specifically North-Israelitish figure of Aaron is entirely foreign to this documentary source; that the Ephraimite Joshua is so much in the background in it that critics like E. Meyer and Stade are able altogether to deny his appearance in J at all,—all this seems to point to the Judaean origin of this documentary source.[The Ephraimitic native background of the most important of the patriarchal narratives asserts itself even in J; its presence, however, is not due to insertion by the Jahvist with any special purpose in view, but belongs essentially to the tradition, and such a passage as Gen. xxxviii. was not written to make mock of Judah (Reuss), but from special interest in this tribe.

6. Before we proceed to determine the age of J, the *question of its literary unity* must first here be considered. Investigations on this subject are still in process of being made: still, in spite of O. Gruppe,[1] thus much can be said to be established, that the answer to the question, Is J a literary unity? is an

[1] "Z.A.T.W.," viii. 135 ff. (1889).

unqualified negative. The first impelling factors in this direction came from the contents of the Biblical history of primaeval origins: here Schrader and Wellhausen noticed contradictions in detail which made it impossible to continue the defence of its literary unity. Gen. iv. 16*b* stands in sharp contrast with the immediately preceding verses 11-16*a*, and these again in one equally glaring with iii. 17, because Cain is here threatened as a punishment with the discontinuance of what in iii. 17 is spoken of as a curse for mankind; the undoubtedly parallel passages iv. 7 and iii. 16, iv. 15 and iv. 24 do not give the impression of being the actual repetitions of the same writer, but rather that of being due to imitation; iv. 26 cannot have been written by an author who already in iv. 1 employs the name Jahve without the slightest hesitation; xi. 1-9 does not agree with ix. 19, where that which in the former passage can only be understood as the consequence of a special retributive interposition of Jahve, appears as an ordinary process of nature requiring no explanation; the Noah of ix. 20-27, the father of the three sons, Shem, Japheth, and Canaan, *i.e.* the tribal father of three definite and distinct peoples, is not the Noah of ix. 18-19, who, through his three sons, Shem, Ham, and Japheth, is the ancestral father of the whole of post-diluvian mankind. And this brings us to the most important and most profound and far-reaching difference in the primaeval history; we can still detect in it clear traces of a tradition which has no knowledge of the Deluge, which derives the three classes of the entire human race from the sons of Lamech (iv. 20–22), which traces back all נְפִילִים ("Nephilim")—

THE JAHVISTIC-ELOHISTIC HISTORY 87

even those still existing in historic times (Numb. xiii. 33)—to the marriage of the sons of God with the daughters of men (vi. 4). As all the passages adduced are undoubtedly Jahvistic, while nowhere does any trace of E occur, this narrator apparently having possessed no primaeval history, no course remains but to give up the unity of J.

7. The original formation of the *primaeval history*, as it now lies before us in this documentary source, has been most thoroughly treated by Budde, who adopts and develops the investigations of Schrader and Wellhausen; it results in the discrimination of three *strata* of narrative. The oldest and most original, J^1, embraces Gen. ii. 4*b*–8, 9*, 16, 17*, 18, 19*, 20*, 22–25; iii. 5–19, 21; vi. 3; iii. 22; iv. 1*, 2*b*β, 16*b*, 17*, 18–21, 22*, 23–24; vi. 1, 2*, 4*; x. 9*; xi. 1–9 .... ix. 20*, 21, 22*, 23–25, 26*, 27. It has no knowledge of a Deluge, and regards Cain as the ancestral father of mankind subsequent to Paradise; Noah in it is the ancestor of Israel and of his next tribal relatives, the Phoenicians and Canaanites. By the side of J^1 stands a later narration, J^2, in part preserved only in fragments. Its central feature is the Deluge. Seth is the only son of the original pair, and Seth's descendant in the ninth generation is Noah, who appears here as the hero of the Deluge and the ancestral father of post-diluvian mankind: these facts are enumerated in a table of the peoples. A genealogy of seven generations then leads from Shem to Terah, the father of Abraham. A younger hand, J^3, has worked up these two strata together and harmonistically adjusted them; he has independently formed the account of Cain's fratricide as a

connecting-link by which the Cainite table of J^1 and the Sethite table of J^2 should be united to one another. The story of Paradise exhibits certain developments which cannot be traced back to J^3, but are entirely new compositions proceeding from the Jahvistic school. Such was the extraordinarily acute and brilliantly executed reconstruction of Budde; it at once won enthusiastic assent, and at last it seemed possible to indulge the hope that the problem of the origin and formation of J had thus been really solved, until Stade came forward with a very different view. Stade also distinguishes in the Jahvistic narrative of the primaeval history of mankind three strata, but defines them and their relation to each other in a way altogether different from that of Budde. According to Stade, ch. ii., iii., xi. 1-9 compose the first stratum. "Here we are confronted with myths, which have travelled from Babylonia and Assyria to Palestine, and have gained entrance into and acceptance in the Jahvistic cycle of legends." The second stratum consists of iv. 25 f., 17 ff. (exclusive, however, of the Song of Lamech), ix. 20 ff., and perhaps x. 9, and also the torso vi. 1-2. It gives a list of the first men up to Noah, and that also in the form of a tabular list of the line of Seth, and further of Palestinian mankind descending from Noah. Everywhere and throughout the standpoint assumed is in Palestine, and of all the Jahvistic material that precedes ch. xii. this produces the impression of greatest antiquity. The third stratum is formed by the Jahvistic elements of the Deluge-myth. This third stratum was worked up by a redactor into the existing Jahvistic Book, which had been formed by the union of the two former strata, the latter being essentially transformed by the process. The same redactor inserted the story of Cain and Abel, and probably also the Song of Lamech. In the story of Cain and Abel Stade sees a genuine folk-legend, a natural product of the popular way of regarding things; Cain, as Ewald had already conjectured, is the representative of the nomadic tribe of the Kenites, who lived in the desert south of Israel. Still another solution of the problem is propounded by Gunkel. He points out in the accounts of Paradise and of the Building of the Tower (which have hitherto been regarded as literary unities throughout), as also in the Jahvistic table of the nations, the existence of a double thread of narrative, and so reaches the conclusion that two Jahvistic primaeval histories were in existence, of which one consisted of passages from the Paradise-narrative, Seth's genealogy, Noah's vineyard-planting, a table of the nations in connexion with Canaan, Japheth, and Shem, and passages from the legend of the Building of the Tower; the other of passages from the Paradise-narrative, Cain's genealogy, the marriage of the Angels, the Deluge, a table of the nations in connexion with Shem, Ham, and Japheth, and passages from the legend of the Building of the Tower. The narrative of Cain's fratricide appears to belong to neither of these two sources, but to have been inserted by a compiler into the whole history; it is a primaeval legend, but the figure of Cain in it hardly represents the Kenites. Gunkel, in his investigation, proceeds from what is certainly the right point of view, viz. "that in the oral tradition and finally in the collected forms of it each individual legend stands independently on its own basis, and thus circumstantial inconsistencies and contradictions do not necessarily prove difference of sources."

8. *Outside the primaeval history*, it has hitherto been supposed only secondary accretions are to be assumed generally in the main body of J: Gunkel, however, has pointed out the existence of a double thread of Jahvistic narrative in the history of Abraham, while in the history of Joseph the undoubtedly Jahvistic passages ch. xxxviii. and xlix. likewise stand outside the general framework. As belonging to neither of the two principal strata of narrative the following are to be distinguished: xiii. 14–17; xviii. 17–19, 22b–33a; in xix. the episode of Lot's wife, and the Zoar-incident; xxii. 20–24; xxv. 1–6; xxvi. 3b–5 (here, however, clear traces occur of Deuteronomic phraseology, so that we have not to deal with a purely Jahvistic passage); xxxii. 10–13; and xxxvi. so far as it does not belong to P, viz. the important section vss. 31–39. In Exodus and Numbers no purely internal Jahvistic developments have up to the present been certainly indicated. The combination and union of these Jahvistic strata with our present J is really to be regarded as an "internal Jahvistic" process, which lies behind the working up of J with the other Pentateuchal sources; outside the primaeval history, the insertion of xii. 10–20 into the context of the narrative xii.–xiii. affords a specially striking and characteristic example of this branch of editorial activity.

9. As regards *the time of the origin and formation of J*, we have in Gen. ix. 25 an absolutely certain *terminus a quo* for the oldest stratum: this passage

THE JAHVISTIC-ELOHISTIC HISTORY 91

could at the earliest only have been applied to historic Israel and the historical Canaanites during or immediately after the reign of Solomon. The *terminus ad quem* is given by the time at which E arose, *circa* 750. If J was a Judaean, on the ground of considerations analogous to those which led us to assign E to the reign of Jeroboam II., the earliest possible date for his work would be the reign of Jehoshaphat, *i.e. circa* 850 ; moreover, the good relations then existing between Judah and Israel would afford a very important incentive. Gen. xxvii. 40*b* offers no real obstacle. For in Gen. xxvii. a detailed and certain articulation of the sources is not even possible at all, and further, the words in question give the impression of being a later prosaic addition. In the case of the more recent stratum of J it will be more prudent to give up any attempt at fixing the chronology. As a lower time-limit for purely Jahvistic developments and amplifications we have Deut., the influence of which no author writing subsequently could ignore. Thus J must have arisen between 850 and 625.

Special Introduction

CHAPTER V

BOOK I.—HISTORICAL BOOKS—*continued*

§ 12. THE PRIESTLY WRITING

LITERATURE: Th. Nöldeke (see § 6, 4); F. W. L. George, *Die älteren jüdischen Feste mit einer Kritik der Gesetzgebung des Pentateuchs* (1835); Vatke (*cf.* § 2, 5); Graf and Kayser (§ 2,7); Wellhausen (§§ 2,7; 6,4). Criticism based on contents and subject-matter: J. W. Colenso, *Pentateuch and Book of Joshua critically examined*, 7 vols. (1861–1879). From the point of view of the history of religion: R. Smend, *Lehrbuch der A.T.lichen Religionsgeschichte*, 2nd ed. (1899, §§ 17 and 42). From the point of view of the history of the language: F. Giesebrecht, *Der Sprachgebrauch des hexateuchischen Elohisten* (*Z.A.T.W.*, i. 177 ff., 1881); different conclusions are reached in V. Ryssel, *De Elohistae Pentateuchi sermone Diss.* (1878), and S. R. Driver, *On some Alleged Linguistic Affinities of the Elohist* (*Journal of Philology*, xi. 201 ff., 1882). Of scientific opponents of the "modern critical" view (apart from the works of Introduction adduced in § 2, 7) the following call for mention: D. Hoffmann in a series of essays in the *Magazin für die Wissenschaft des Judentums*, 1879 and 1880; A. Dillmann (see § 5, Literature) especially: *Num., Deut. and Josh.* (1886), pp. 593–690; F. Delitzsch, *Pentateuchkritische Studien* (12 essays in *Z.W.L.*, i., 1880), and *Urmosaisches im Pentateuch* (6 essays, *ibid.*, iii., 1882); K. Bredenkamp, *Gesetz und Propheten* (1881); E. C. Bissell, *The Pentateuch, its Origin and Structure*, etc. (1885); W. H. Green, *The Hebrew Feasts*, etc. (1885), and *The Higher Criticism of the Pentateuch* (1895); R. Kittel (see § 5, Literature); W. W. Baudissin, *Die Geschichte des A.T.lichen*

Priestertums (1889); A. Klostermann (see § 6, 5); J. Halévy, *Recherches bibliques* (2 vols., 1895, 1901); A. van Hoonacker, *La sacerdoce lévitique dans la loi* (1899); R. Schaefer, *Das Passah-Mazzoth-Fest*, etc. (1900). On F. Hommel, *Die altisraelitische Ueberlieferung in inschriftlicher Beleuchtung* (1897), *cf.* the remarks in the Preface to the last (German) edition of the present work.

1. P is sharply and clearly differentiated from all the rest of the documentary Sources. In the vast majority of cases no serious doubt can arise as to *what really belongs to it*. Style and phraseology, linguistic usage and ideas are everywhere so markedly similar, the same interests are everywhere served and the same ends so studiously pursued—whether it be a piece of simple historic narrative or a section purely legal in character that is in question—that the impression is produced that we are dealing with a single complete unit. But on closer inspection it will appear that the *unity is one of spirit only*, that it is *not a literary unit* that lies before us; in fact, the history of the origin and formation of P is compli- cated to a quite unusual degree. The penetrating investigations of Wellhausen and Kuenen have re- sulted in showing that, in addition to older priestly categories (P^1 in Kuenen, P^h in Holzinger), a larger priestly writing (in character and content partly narrative, partly legislative) was composed which forms the kernel and skeleton of P (P^2 Kuenen, P^g Holzinger). About this kernel later developments have become attached and grown up, partly amplify- ing and partly enriching P^2; to indicate these younger and most recent elements I propose to employ the general designation P^x (Holzinger P^s), since the division into P^3, P^4, P^5 is useless and cannot be carried

through in detail. The criteria for dividing the kernel from later formations and developments are the same as elsewhere: inconsistencies and obscurities in the composition. In the face of such facts as that, according to Ex. xxix. 7, 29, Lev. iv. 3, 5, 16, vi. 13, 15, viii. 12, xvi. 22, xxi. 10, 12, Numb. xxxv. 25, only Aaron and the High Priest for the time being, while on the other hand, according to Ex. xxviii. 41, xxx. 30, xl. 15, Lev. vii. 36, x. 7, Numb. iii. 3, the whole number of priests were anointed; and again, that according to Numb. iv. 3 ff. the Levites became liable for Temple-service at the age of thirty, while, on the other hand, according to ch. viii. 24 they were already liable at the age of twenty-five; or again, that according to Lev. iv. 6–7, in the case of a sin on the part of the High Priest (and in vs. 17 in the same way of the whole community), sprinkling with the blood of the sin-offering is to be made seven times on the veil in the Holy Place, but according to Ex. xxix. 12, Lev. viii. 15, ix. 9, on the horns of the altar of burnt-offering; or again, that Lev. iv. 14 prescribes in the case of a sin on the part of the whole community a bullock, while Lev. ix. 3, Numb. xv. 24 enjoin only a he-goat as a sin-offering; or again, that Ex. xxvii.–xxix. and Lev. viii.–ix. are acquainted only with the altar of burnt-offering simply as הַמִּזְבֵּחַ, and in Lev. x. and xvi., Numb. xvi. and xvii. the incense-offering on censers is introduced, while in Ex. xxx. 1–10 a golden incense-altar suddenly appears, and in Ex. xxxv.–xl. a מִזְבַּח הָעֹלָה ("altar of burnt-offering") and מִזְבַּח הַקְּטֹרֶת ("altar of incense") are distinguished—in the face of such facts as these the literary unity of P cannot possibly be maintained. Such phenomena, too, as the sandwiching of Lev. i.–vii. between Ex. xl. and Lev. viii., of Lev. xi.–xv. between ch. x. and xvi., and the position of such passages as Numb. xv. and xix., xxviii.–xxx., are hardly compatible with the work of an author who has a definite aim in view and is writing connectedly.

2. I now proceed to give a summary survey of P^x. In GENESIS there must be assigned to this element ch. xlvi. 8–27, a laborious but inconsistent attempt to provide the seventy souls referred to in Ex. i. 5 (P^2) with names, which can only be brought into agreement with the latter if, against Gen. xlvi. 8, Dina is included in the reckoning, and, in opposition to the words and sense of Ex. i. 5, Jacob himself is counted with the יֹצְאֵי יֶרֶךְ יַעֲקֹב ("those that came out of the loins of Jacob").

In EXODUS there are the following:—Ch. vi. 13–30: The immediate continuation of vi. 12 is vii. 1. The genealogy, which is borrowed from Numb. xxvi., and embellished with additions after the manner of the chronicler, and which is inserted very awkwardly and abruptly, is intended to prepare the way for Aaron's sudden appearance in vii. 1. Ch. xii. 14–20 and 43–50: Here a lapse from the historical situation of the moment is evident such as the original conception cannot be credited with. Ch. xxviii. 41 is certainly to be assigned to this element, because according to this passage Aaron and his sons are to be anointed. Besides this, the following passages in ch. xxv.–xxix. are also to be claimed for P^x, viz. xxvii. 20–21, xxviii. 41–43, xxix. 21, 27–30, 36–42 (on vss. 38–42 *cf.* subdivision 12 of this section below). Ch. xxx.

and xxxi., the whole: xxx. 1–10, the altar of incense; 11–16, an allusion to Numb. i. 22–23, Aaron and his sons anointed; 17–21 and 34–38 "are already condemned by their context"; xxxi. 1–21 presupposes xxv.–xxix. + xxx.; with it vss. 12–17, which also evince language of a striking character, stand in close connexion, since the original meaning is that even work on the Tabernacle was to be suspended by the Sabbath-rest. Ch. xxxiv. vss. 29–35 according to Kuenen, vss. 32–35 according to Baentsch. Ch. xxxv.–xl., the whole. These chapters presuppose ch. xxv.–xxxi. as a complete unit; moreover, the Greek text has an order in many respects different, omits xxxvii. 25–39 entirely, and has been translated by a different hand.

In LEVITICUS ch. i.–vii. similarly stand, as has already been remarked, in an altogether misplaced position. Here again the motive at work for so placing them is easy to recognise. In ch. viii. and ix. sacrificial rites were carried out on the occasion of the consecration of Aaron and the Tabernacle; hence it appeared fitting and proper to have this preceded by a sacrificial Tora (law of sacrifices). This sacrificial Tora originally constituted an independent corpus, which, however, was not formed all at once or written down by a single hand; ch. i.–v. are in opposition to vi.–vii., which deal with the same material largely in a different way. Moreover, neither of the single groups is itself uniform: ch. ii., where the singular address in vss. 4–10, 13–17 is a striking feature, originally stood without doubt after ch. iii.; in ch. iv.–v., which mark an altogether new start, vss. 1–6 and 15–16, 21–26, with their clear definition and nice separation of sin- and trespass-offerings, form the oldest kernel. In ch. vi.–vii., vi. 12–16 and vii. 22–27 are certainly secondary: for the rest, directions as to the priests' share in the prescribed sacrifices generally are a prominent feature. As to the relation of these individual elements to P^2 nothing certain can be said; undoubtedly ch. i.–vii. as a whole belong to P^x, for ch. iv. in vss. 7 and 18 shows acquaintance with the altar of incense and heightens the demands of P^2 (*cf.* sub-section 1 above), and ch. vi. 1 ff. presupposes the evening burnt-offering, Ex. xxix. 38 ff. Ch. viii. also must be regarded as having been worked over; for an anointing of the Tabernacle and the vessels (vss. 10–11) was not commanded in Ex. xxix., and the ordering of the sacrifices in vss. 16, 20, 26 closely accords in its special directions with ch. i.–vii., against Ex. xxix. In ch. x., vss. 6–7 exhibit Aaron and his sons anointed, and vss. 8–11 introduce a very rare introductory formula, while 16–20 bring to view a correction of ix. 15 on the basis of a combination of iv. 18 with vi. 23. On ch. xi.–xv. a similar verdict must be given as on ch. i.–vii. They disjoin ch. x. and xvi. and show themselves dependent on the sacrificial Tora of i.–vii. These chapters, too, are not uniform: xi. 24–40 and xiv. 33–53 are certainly accretions, and probably also xiii. 47–59 and xiv. 21–32, while xii. 2 glances back to xv. 19. Ch. xvii.–xxvi. will be dealt with in detail later: ch. xxvii. is a supplement which clearly continues xvii.–xxv., and was written down by the same hand which inserted that section; still, the possibility of an older groundwork is not excluded.

In NUMBERS the analysis of P is beset with great

difficulties. Ch. i.–ii., the relation of which to xxvi. in any case offers a difficult problem, have at the least been subjected to a drastic revision; the following are certainly of a secondary character: ch. iii. 1–4 (Aaron and his sons anointed); ch. iii. 40–51 (a casuistic enlargement of the thought of vss. 11–13 characterised in part by peculiar expressions); ch. iv. in conjunction with iii. 5–39, which also, like the secondary stratum in ch. xvi., sets in a strong light the gulf separating Levites and Aaronites; ch. v.–vi., which go back to Lev. i.–vii., xi.–xv.; and ch. vii., which in vs. 1 already shows signs of dependence on Lev. viii. 10–11 and produces chronological difficulties. The only exception in this chapter is vs. 89, which appears to be a stray fragment out of P^2; ch. viii. 1–3 may also be such. On the other hand, ch. viii. 5–22 brings to view a mechanically enlarged and (in a purely theoretic way) subtly refined treatment of the sacrificial idea in connexion with the Levites (note מֵי הַחַטָּאת, "water of expiation," vs. 7, ἅπαξ λεγόμενον); while vss. 23–26 exhibit a heightened form of ch. iv., which is itself of a secondary character; and ch. ix. 1–14 is an example of a casuistic supplement, invested, like Lev. xxiv. 10–16, with a historical character, and equally productive of chronological difficulties. Ch. xv. and xix. do not stand in connexion; xv., which is a collection of legal enactments, is in substance reminiscent of Lev. i.–vii., and in expression in many respects of Lev. xvii.–xxv.; ch. xix. 1–13, the law of the red heifer and about defilement contracted from a corpse, with vss. 14–22 as an explanatory supplement, is specially peculiar—it is only referred to again in xxxi. 23.

Against assigning the narrative passage xxv. 6–19 to P^2 grave doubts also suggest themselves; at the least, drastic revision must be assumed. The same holds good of ch. xxvi., which in its present form cannot be derived from P^2. The establishment of a census with a view to the forthcoming division of the land can be understood; but vs. 4*b* is concerned with setting forth an enumeration of those who journeyed out of Egypt, who, however, according to vs. 64 f. are already all dead, and the enumeration itself nowhere takes account of ch. i. Consequently P^2 gave an enumeration of the children of Israel only, and that too in connexion with the regulation of all relationships at Sinai. Ch. xxvi.—whose secondary character in this case would as a consequence be shared by xxvii. 1–11 and xxxvi. 1–12—has been developed out of xxxiii. 54. Ch. xxviii.–xxx., again, are additions of a legal kind. xxviii.–xxix., which in thorough formal consistency even surpass Lev. i.–vii. and xxiii., occupy their present position because their directions could only be introduced first in Canaan; xxx., which in its phraseology has much that is peculiar and shows fewer indications of P's distinguishing characteristics, is a later supplement, which could not have been suitably introduced earlier. Finally, ch. xxxi. is in substance very strange and startling, and recalls such compilatory elaborations as Ex. xxxviii. 21–31 and Numb. vii.; it also presupposes ch. xxii.–xxv. (J E + P) in their present form; it was, however, designed from the very first to occupy its present position. At the most it might be possible, on the ground of xxxii. 4*a*, to raise the question whether P^2 may not have given some account of a warlike collision between Israel and Midian—but note the variants of the LXX. in xxxii. 4*a*! Ch. xxxiii. 1–49 also does not belong to P², while ch. xxxiii. 50–xxxiv. 15 has only been worked over. Further, the law about the Levitical cities does not fit into the limits of P², and can only be a later supplement.

3. *The share of Pˣ in Lev. xvi. and Numb. xvi.* requires a detailed discussion. Lev. xvi. in particular raises considerable difficulties; the close connexion it has with Lev. ix. and x., and certain definite criteria (Aaron only anointed, and the incense-offering in censers), argue in favour of P²; but militating against this is the fact that Neh. viii. and ix. is silent about the יום כפורים (Day of Atonement), and in fact leaves no room for such an observance. Benzinger has now shown ("Z.A.T.W.," ix. 65 ff., 1889) that only the following passages belong to P² as a continuation of Lev. x., viz. vss. 1–3, 4*, 6, 12–13, 34*b*, a prescription as to how a priest may be able to enter the holy place without dying. Bertholet adds convincingly vss. 23 and 24*. The rest of the chapter consists of directions about the Day of Atonement. Benzinger was of opinion that from this body of material vss. 29–34*a* might in the same way be retained for P⁹; but this result is also irreconcilable with Neh. viii., and consequently the Day of Atonement belongs entirely to Pˣ; vss. 29–34*a* are the first step towards it, and, as is attested by Lev. xxiii. 26–32 and Numb. xxix. 7–11, the peculiar rite with the two goats is younger still. In Numb. xvi. a transformation of P² has also been effected, with a special purpose in view, by Pˣ. Wellhausen long ago had correctly recognised that in Numb. xvi. three different accounts

have been fused together: (1) revolt of the Reubenites Dathan and Abiram against the supreme command of Moses; (2) protest of laity against the priesthood of the tribe of Levi, on the ground of the common priesthood of all Israelites; (3) protest of the Levites against the Aaronites, they also claiming the priesthood. Wellhausen claimed (3) for P; but Kuenen ("Th.T.," xii., 139 ff., 1878) has shown that (2) preferably belongs to P^2, to whom Korah (Numb. xxvii. 3) is a non-Levite; while (3) gives a revision by P^x, the purpose of which is parallel with Numb. iv. Thus the following belong to P^x: vss. $1a\beta$, $7b$–11, 16–18 and the passage which cannot be separated therefrom, xvii. 1–5.

4. Accordingly P^2, or the *kernel of the Priestly Writing*, may be exhibited as follows:—It includes all that belongs to P from Gen. i. to Ex. xxiv., apart from Gen. xlvi. 8–27 and Ex. vi. 13–30, xii. 14–20, 43–50. Then Ex. xxv.–xxix.†, and following these chapters a short notice about the carrying out of what is enjoined in them. Lev. viii.†; ix.; x. 1–5, 12–15; xvi. 1-3, 4*, 6, 12–13, 23, 24*, 34b. Numb. i.–ii.†; iii. 5–39; vii. 79–viii. 3 ?; ix. 15–x. 28; xiii. and xiv. (so far as they belong to P); xvi. $1a\alpha$, 2*, 3–7a $15a\beta$, 19–23, 24*, $27a\alpha$, 32b, 35; xvii. 6–xviii. 32; xx. 1–13†, 22*, 23–29; xxi. 10, 11*; xxii. 1; xxvii. 15–23, xxxii. $1a\alpha$, 2b, 4a, 18–19, 28–30; xxxiii. 50, 51, 54; xxxiv. 1–15†, 16–29; xxxv. 9–34. Deut. xxxii. 48–52; xxxiv. 1a, 8–9. The plan and character of this Writing is so far clear. It gives a history of Israel, but a history that is exclusively sacred, its aim being " to prove the historical origin of certain religious institutions in a past of hoary antiquity "

(Wurster in "Z.A.T.W.," iv. 112, 1884). Sabbath, dietary laws, circumcision, Passover, sanctuary, priests, sacrifices, Levites and their service, revenues of the clergy, legitimation of the Aaronite High Priesthood,—around such points as these its subject-matter is grouped, and on them the history in P^2 is pivoted: "by the hand of History and through History the religious blessings enjoyed by the nation were to maintain and preserve their sanctions. On this account P in its original form is nothing less than a priest's manual, but it is also, and was intended to be, a people's book, the history of Israel's worship in the form of a sacred history" (*op. cit.*, p. 118).

5. In approaching the question as to *the time of the composition and formation of P^2*, we come to the most serious and burning problem of modern Old Testament science. From the outset, when a beginning was made in following up the rational analysis of the Pentateuch, it was assumed that P was the oldest documentary Source, as an axiom that required no proof: it was just in P above all else, it was believed, that Moses and the spirit of Moses could be recognised most clearly. And this assumption was not without a certain amount of justification. What was commonly termed "Mosaism"—that which, for example, was for the Apostle Paul identified with Μωυσῆς and ὁ νόμος—all reverts to P, and finds in this source its presentment and most complete embodiment. And with this estimate of it the form also seemed to correspond. Everywhere throughout, the legislation is set forth from the standpoint of desert conditions of life, with an Israel living in the *camp*; and even the simple,

artless method of the representation which avails itself of such devices as the chronological scheme and genealogies, seemed to argue the most venerable antiquity, as the annalistic does, in fact, usually precede the pragmatic form of historical narration. It must, therefore, be regarded as an act of courage and a great critical achievement on his part when Ewald brought up the original formation of the "Book of Origins" to the reign of Solomon, and this became the prevailing "critical" view. But in this matter some very obvious considerations had been allowed to be forgotten. The desert-standpoint might, after all, only be the literary dress with which the author invested his work, such as had been universally recognised to be the case in Deut. since the time of De Wette (1805); and in fact the chronological - genealogical method of presenting history appears for the first time in the literature of Israel in the Chronicler, by whose side P stands in close relation, while, in the examples of historical composition that are certainly old and most ancient, at the most only insignificant tendencies towards such a method occasionally occur. And above all, one important question was ignored, in the omission to ask when and where can we show this supposed "Mosaism" actually in practice, having regard to the fact that as early as 1805 J. S. Vater (*cf.* § 6, 2) had already recognised the practical and literary inoperativeness of the Pentateuch in the pre-exilic period as a serious problem. How could such a fact be accounted for as, for example, that Malachi—as to whose post-exilic origin there can be no doubt whatever, and who everywhere

shows himself to be a kindred spirit with P —
is dependent solely on Deut., and betrays not
the slightest trace of an acquaintance with P?
(*cf.* § 38, 2). The first to give expression to the
view that the Law is younger than the Prophets,
and the Psalms younger than both, was Reuss, in
1834; the credit of being its literary initiators must
be given to George († 1873) and Vatke, who nearly
simultaneously, in the year 1835, arrived at the
conclusion that P does not belong to the beginning
but to the end of Israel's religious-historical development. George showed in a really striking way that,
according to internal evidence, the legislation of the
Pentateuch can only have developed in the following
order: Book of the Covenant, Deuteronomy, P.
But these results remained for thirty years unheeded,
until Graf again undertook the investigation of the
subject on a broader basis, and likewise reached the
result—which asserted and vindicated itself from all
sides—that the legislation of P is a product of the
post-exilic period; at the same time, Graf, however,
believed it possible to maintain the purely narrative
portion of P as being the oldest documentary Source.
Shortly before his death he gave up this serious error,
and allowed the historical portion to follow suit in this respect with the legislative (Merx, "Archiv," i. 466-477).
In 1869 and 1870 appeared Kuenen's "Religion of
Israel"—a work of fundamental importance,—in
1874 Kayser's careful and thorough investigations,
and finally in 1878 the (for Germany) epoch-making
"Geschichte Israels" of Wellhausen, whose good
fortune it has been to muster under his banner an
ever-growing number of adherents. The old view

THE PRIESTLY WRITING 105

which regarded P as the most ancient documentary Source has now been given up practically on all sides: all the more eagerly, however, is the attempt now being made by a certain number of investigators to secure at least a pre-exilic date for P.

6. *We can with certainty prove the existence of P from 444 onwards.* In the year 458 (*cf.* § 21, 8), Ezra, the teacher of the Law, came *with the Law of God in his hand* from Babylonia to Palestine, to visit Judah and Jerusalem, and to organise and regulate the conditions there prevailing on the basis of this Law. Later, in the person of the governor Nehemiah he found a powerful and sympathetic colleague who threw the weight of secular authority into the movement for the attainment of these ends, and the "Book of the Law of Moses" was publicly read in a great assembly of the people held at the earliest in the month of October 444. The result was terror and consternation, and, by a solemn covenant subscribed with the names of its leading and influential persons, the community bound itself to the observance of this Law (Neh. viii.–x). That the "Book of the Law of Moses" in question was identical with or contained P is absolutely certain; Neh. viii. 15 is = Lev. xxiii. 40; Neh. viii. 18 = Lev. xxiii. 36, against Deut. xvi. 13–15; Neh. x. 36–40 = Neh. xviii. 12–32; the arrangement of worship set forth in Neh. x. 34 is altogether that of P, the Temple-tax (x. 32) is mentioned only in P (Ex. xxx. 11–16), the insistence on the law of the Sabbath (x. 31) is similarly characteristic of P (Gen. ii. 3; Ex. xvi. 22–34, xxxi. 12–17; Numb. xv. 32–36); an express prohibition of intermarriage is not found anywhere in P (yet *cf.*

Gen. xxvi. 35, xxviii. 1–9 ; Numb. xxv. 6–15). After 444, familiarity with it and its effective operation can be shown at every point ; the entire work of the Chronicler can only be understood as a picture of the pre-exilic history of Israel, as it must have happened if P had been the fundamental law of Mosaism ; and we know well enough that P was peculiarly the Law of Judaism. The similarity of the circumstances under which P was published with those of the publication of Deut. (2 Kings xxii.–xxiii.) immediately strikes one. If we may from similar circumstances argue similar conclusions, we must suppose that P also did not originate long before 444 or 458. We shall now have carefully to sift all the evidence, direct and indirect, that is available for determining the age of this Writing.

7. And first of all there is to be considered *the position it occupies with reference to Deuteronomy.* Deut. was made public by the priest Hilkiah. If P at that time really formed the programme of the priests, and is to be regarded as the expression of their final wishes and aims, why was the experiment not made with P ? In circumstances where they could trust themselves to institute a measure of such far-reaching importance and vast comprehensiveness as the suspension of the whole of the ancient shrines outside of Jerusalem, they certainly had no need to be modest in their demands. But every unprejudiced consideration and examination of the matter must reach the conclusion that P is rather a development of D, and depends upon it throughout. What D requires as something absolutely novel— the centralisation of worship, completely purged

from idolatrous associations and purely spiritual, in the one legitimate sanctuary, administered by the one legitimate priesthood of Levi—all this is presupposed in P, and carried back as the fundamental element in the religion of Israel to the remotest past; of a suspicion that it was at any time otherwise, or could be otherwise, there is not in P a trace. The Tabernacle, about which the entire pre-exilic literature does not utter a single word—for 1 Sam. ii. 22b is lacking in the LXX., and 1 Kings viii. 4 is the work of one of the latest redactors, and stands in a passage which is overgrown with interpolations and glosses,—is purely a projection of the Deuteronomic central sanctuary, *i.e.* the Solomonic Temple, into the Mosaic past, after having been (with a somewhat contemptible display of acumen) made movable: that the fixed Temple is involuntarily visible in the Tabernacle is shown by the fact that in connexion with it reckoning is made according to the points of the compass, an indication according to orientation being nowhere given. In the pre-Deuteronomic period absolutely nothing was known of the requirements of P; priests are royal officials, appointed and removed by the king, not only in Israel but in Judah; that sacrifice might not be made at any and every time and place, that only those belonging to the tribe of Levi might perform the sacrifice, and that everything in connexion with the sacrifices depends especially upon ritual—of all this the most pious of the kings and prophets have not a suspicion. The prophets rejecting as they do the cultus as not being of main and primary importance, such passages as Is. i. 13-14, Amos v. 21-23 are hardly comprehensible if the legislation of P had been known to these men and their hearers as divinely commanded and as binding law; and how could Jeremiah have given utterance to such a remark as vii. 22 if the books of Ex., Lev., and Numb. had been lying before him in their present form? The release of the cultus from its natural basis, for which the way was prepared in D, is so consistently carried out in P that in the latter it has become a purely legal *opus operatum*. Where we are able to compare individual prescriptions of D and P together, there is everywhere evident in P a heightening of the enactment, and it is significant that in the most recent strata of P this heightening process is always carried still further. To interpret P as older than D is to make both incomprehensible.

8. Possibly of even greater significance and importance is *the relation of P to Ezekiel*. Vatke, in his classical Introductory work[1] (pp. 534–542), had already indicated this prophet as the connecting-link between D and P. The subterfuge that P might have remained unknown to the prophet, or could have been ignored by him, as being a private document of the priests, is already involved in difficulties when confronted by Jeremiah, and in the case of Ezekiel cannot avail at all; for Ezekiel was himself a member of the Jerusalem priesthood, and P would have corresponded (if that were possible) even better to his ideal than his own Tora-programme. How can such a circumstance possibly be explained as that a Jerusalem priest puts forth a prospective Tora of his own which completely ignores P, in all points lags far behind

[1] *Cf.* § 2, 7 above.

the latter's demands, and reaches out to and aims at the future, instead of adapting itself to the already (*existing*) complete and finished system? Why is it that Ezra demands in the cultus so much less than Numb. xxviii. and xxix.? Where has the High Priest—who in P is the centre of the theocracy— been left in Ezekiel? Where is the Day of Atonement of Lev. xvi.?. How is Ezekiel's direction about the land which is to be reserved for priests and Levites to be conceived of by the side of the forty-eight Levitical cities of Numb. xxxv.? Here, again, an unbiassed view can only recognise in P a development of the ideas of Ezekiel. There are, however, two points in which the dependence of P on Ezekiel admits of exact proof, one of a literary character, the other a matter of substance and content. The word רָקִיעַ, which is frequent in P in the sense of *heaven*, occurs (with the exception of Ps. xix. 2, cl. 1, and Dan. xii. 3) only again in Ezekiel. The process by which a word which etymologically signifies *pavimentum*[1] could reach the meaning *heaven* is made quite clear from Ezek. i. 22, 25. The evidence of Ezek. xliv. 9–16 is unanswerable. While D still maintains the theoretic equality in right and privilege of all Levites, the "Levites" in this passage, as a punishment for their service in the worship at the high places, are degraded to the position of Temple-servants, *i.e.* to the status of inferior clergy, and the priesthood is assigned ex-

---

[1] רָקִיעַ (lit. "that which is beaten out") = *extended surface, solid expanse, firmament* (of heaven); the Second Isaiah consequently uses the root רקע only of the creation of the earth, xlii. 5, xliv. 24; and so also Ps. cxxxvi. 6.

clusively to the family of Zadok officiating in Jerusalem : as P carries this characteristic distinction —which we see originating in Ezekiel as something specifically new—right back to the Mosaic past, and makes it the foundation of his entire hierarchical system, he can only be dependent on Ezekiel, and therefore younger than the latter. *Cf.* the excellent and comprehensive discussion of the whole matter by M. Kamrath ("J. pr. Th.," xvii. 585 ff., 1891).

9. As the time when P arose the Babylonian Exile is suggested in the most definite way by a particular point of critical importance. In P *circumcision* is treated as the sign of a covenant and the seal denoting membership in the nation of Israel, and consequently has a sacramental character attributed to it. Such a way of regarding things could only have been reached in an environment and under conditions where Jew and circumcised were co-incident terms as much as non-Jew and uncircumcised. This state of affairs first arose in the Babylonian Exile, for circumcision was unknown to the Babylonians, while in pre-exilic times it is only the Philistines who appear as "uncircumcised" (עֲרֵלִים).

10. Just as pre-exilic practice shows no knowledge of or acquaintance with P (and this is conceded more or less even by those who maintain its pre-exilic authorship), so also *pre-exilic literature* is equally at fault. "The traces of the so-called 'Grundschrift' of the Hexateuch in the pre-exilic prophets," the existence of which K. Marti ("J. pr. Th.," vi. 127 ff., 308 ff., 1880) attempted to show (though he himself has for long regarded the position as no longer a tenable one), are, in relation to the extent and

importance of the things compared on both sides, of the most meagre description, and could convince no unprejudiced eye. In this connexion special emphasis must be laid on the absolute lack of acquaintance shown by D of P, which has already been pointed out (§ 10); to admit so absolutely latent an existence of P as this fact necessitates practically amounts to nothing, while the supposition itself encounters material difficulties that are insuperable. That P cannot have been the first literary embodiment of the oldest traditions of Israel is sufficiently evident from its general character: by anyone who considers attentively the history from Abraham to the call of Moses according to P, as it is printed by Wellhausen in his " Prol.," 2nd ed. (pp. 346–351), it must be conceded that a narrative of this character could only have been written by one who was able to assume on the part of his readers complete familiarity with the whole range and essential content of the material he is using. It has also been shown by Giesbrecht that P, judged by linguistic standards, belongs to the latest period of Hebrew literature: even if some few of Giesbrecht's examples be doubtful, the general result is so conclusively demonstrated and so incontrovertibly established that no detailed refutation of it has so far been even attempted.

11. Lastly, the evidence of the *chronology*—which assumes a position of quite central importance in P, and furnishes the entire framework for his historical representation—would be absolutely decisive if the brilliant discovery of J. Oppert ("G.G.N.," 1877, 201–223) should prove to be sound, viz. that at the basis of the "chronology of Genesis" there lies the

chronology of the Babylonian primaeval history, reduced in accordance with a definite system. For so intimate an acquaintance with the innermost core of the Babylonian tradition could only have been acquired by a Jew in Babylonia itself, and even then not at a time when the Jew was the despised thrall of the Babylonian world-empire, but only when both Jews and Babylonians had become equally the dependents of the Persians. The proofs adduced by Oppert are brilliant enough almost to be convincing; but the whole matter is itself too obscure to justify me in attaching decisive importance to this particular point.

12. In this way we should reach, *as the time when P was formed*, the century from 570 (end of Ezekiel's prophetic activity) to 458 (arrival of Ezra in Jerusalem). In order to define the matter more exactly it is necessary to ask, what was the writing that Ezra brought with him and probably read? Was it simply P^2, or this work already expanded? The definition of the extent of P^2 which has been set forth above is sufficient to negative the former alternative: a work of such brevity and meagreness as P^2 could not possibly have been adequate to serve as the law-book of a community, and Neh. viii. 15 shows in abundance clear cases of direct reference to Lev. xxiii., which only in a very qualified way, if at all, belongs to P^2. That at the very least P^1 had by this time been united with P^2 must, therefore, be regarded as certain. It might be supposed that Ezra himself undertook the task of combining these writings together, whether it was accomplished while still in Babylon, before 458, or in Jerusalem between

THE PRIESTLY WRITING

458 and 444; but Ezra's procedure "will in every way be more psychologically explicable if . . . he had taken no share in the redaction of his corpus" (Holzinger, "Pent.," 453). Whether J E D also had at this time been united with P—whether, in other words, Ezra's "Book of the Law of Moses" was identical with our Pentateuch—is doubtful, and highly improbable, for what Ezra was interested in was the successful establishment of P, and practically to envelop and bury P in the mass of the other documentary sources was not the way best calculated to secure the object he had in view. On the other hand, P itself contains elements that are clearly of later date than Ezra. Such a case as that of Ex. xxx. 13, where, in opposition to Neh. x. 33, the Temple-tax is fixed at a half-shekel, is clearly the expression of later practice, and the fact that Neh. x. 38 is silent about the tithe of the herd which is expressly demanded in Lev. xxvii. 32–33 is not accidental; by the side of Neh. viii. there is no room for Lev. xvi. in its present form—Kuenen, indeed, on the basis of a comparison of Neh. x. 34 with Ezek. xlvi. 13–15, supposes that the elevation of the תָּמִיד ("continual offering") and of the two burnt-offerings to a position of importance first took place after the time of Ezra, as Ezra in his own memoirs speaks only of the מִנְחַת הָעֶרֶב ("the evening meal-offering"), Ezra ix. 4–5; in this case Ex. xxix. 38–42 would have to be separated from P². The differences adduced between Neh. and Pˣ are all the more weighty because Neh. x. also proves to be a constituent part of the memoirs of Ezra (*cf.* § 21, 5). Thus Pˣ mainly is to be regarded as younger than

Ezra, a conclusion which is an eminently reasonable one: if P became by Ezra's agency a binding lawbook, then innovating additions to it from time to time would imperatively be required, partly by the exigencies of a living and growing practice, partly to meet cases which the original legislator had not foreseen. If, however, P^2 had not preserved its original form and character entirely without admixture by 458, but had already been subjected to recension, we cannot assign its origin to a time immediately preceding this date, and should be justified in assuming that P^2 was written by a priestly author in Babylonia *circa* 500, who lived in a circle where Ezekiel's views were influential, and who developed these views still further. In P we possess a work which is rather the product of an entire school than of a single individual, and it is by no means an accident that this school took its rise in Babylonia. The exiles who returned in 537, in the depressed circumstances in which they found themselves, and the hard struggle for existence in which they were involved, were perpetually concerned with problems of immediate practical importance, while unbroken quiet and relatively favourable external circumstances afforded those who remained in Babylonia the zest and leisure for theoretic speculation and for the systematic formulation of religious thought. These grounds for determining the formation of P are spoken of even by so cautious and reserved a scholar as Driver as "cogent," and though König still believes it possible to hold fast by a date previous to 536, and consequently speaks only of an "exilic date," this difference is not a radical one. Care should be taken to guard against grave self-deception, as, *e.g.*, to suppose that having proved that the legislation of P contains *material of great antiquity and originality* is equivalent to showing *its ancient character as a literary product.* It is one of the strange ironies of fate that this legislation, whose aim was to spiritualise as far as possible the religion of Israel, harked back to just the most pagan elements in it: circumcision, dietary laws, prescriptions about clean and unclean, sacrifices allied with an exactly defined and to some extent magic-working ritual, together with a mystical and mechanical conception of sin— all these are things that the religion of Israel shares with nature-religion; the legislation of P is therefore a reversion to an older stage of religious development, which Prophetism had already surpassed. But it was not the appearance of these elements in themselves that proved so fateful in the history of religion, but the value and the position given to them in the system, and the fact that they now assume the chief place in the religion of Israel and form its essence and distinguishing characteristic—a view which we never meet with prior to P, and which first gained currency through P. I hope the time is not far distant when the account of P's formation given by the "modern-critical" school will enjoy the same general approval as the critical view of Deut. now meets with: it is just as firmly grounded and just as certain in its method and results in the one case as in the other. And much that is of great importance depends upon this issue. For it is no slight matter that is herein involved — nothing less than this, whether it is to be made possible for us at all to understand the religious history of Israel, whether God, who always and everywhere reveals Himself and works in history, has also revealed Himself and worked in the same way in history's greatest and most significant phase, the history of Israel's religion. We may conclude with an earnest application of the words of the Apostle, and say that God is not a God of disorder; and we may give up panic cries about Darwinism in theology if we make it our endeavour to discern and to show forth in the history of revelation a higher order and a profound organic life. The natural and the naturalistic are of two kinds; would it really be unworthy of God if the process could be shown to proceed naturally? And in conclusion, is it not just the natural that is the greatest marvel?

Special Introduction

CHAPTER VI

BOOK I.—HISTORICAL BOOKS—*continued*

§§ 13, 14. *Special Passages of the Pentateuch. The Pentateuch as a Whole.*

§ 13. SPECIAL PASSAGES OF THE PENTATEUCH

1. *The Blessing of Jacob, Gen. xlix. 1b–27*

LITERATURE: L. Diestel, 1853; J. N. P. Land, *Disputatio de carmine J*, Leiden, 1858; E. J. Fripp, *Note on Gen. xlix. 24b–26* (*Z.A.T.W.*, xi. 262 ff., 1891).

In the literary form of a spiritual testament bequeathed by the dying Tribal Father to his twelve sons, there are here set forth solemn utterances on the fate and characterisations of the twelve tribes of Israel, which to a large extent depend on word-plays upon the names of the tribes in question. As the historical events to which clear reference is made—the fall of Reuben and the dispersion of Simeon and Levi—glance back to passages which are certainly Jahvistic (Gen. xxxiv., so far as it belongs to J, and xxxv. 22), it is probable that J already contained this Blessing in his work. In that case we should have 850 as a time-limit for its formation, and in agreement with this conclusion there is the fact that the

"Blessing of Moses" in Deut. xxxiii., which is in many respects very similar, is decidedly younger. The Blessing gives the impression of being the uniform embodiment of a single conception, the object of which is in a similar manner to celebrate all twelve tribes in song: yet the utterances do not all reflect the same period and the same set of conditions, and are also surprisingly different in length and arrangement. As the longer pieces divide into single loosely connected sentences, we must conclude with Gunkel that songs of this kind had been sung by the singers of Israel from the earliest time, but that the individual utterances were transformed according to circumstances and tribes. The oracle about Judah in its present form is inconceivable before the time of David, and Gen. xlix. in its traditional form certainly emanates from a Judaic pen, and from the time of Judah's supremacy over Israel. The oracle about Joseph also does not point down from a time when the division of the kingdom had taken place, because נָזִיר, vs. 26, does not necessarily mean *Prince*, and the original connexion of the whole passage vss. 24*b*–26 (identical as it is with Deut. xxx. 13–16) with this Blessing is disputed on good grounds; moreover, the Aramaeans of Damascus would hardly have been characterised as *archers*.

2. *The Red-Sea Song, Ex. xv.* 1–18

After the happy and eventful passage through the Red Sea, Moses and the children of Israel (it was thought) must have sung a song, which we read in Ex. xv. That this song was composed contemporaneously with that event is quite inconceivable, for it presupposes the settlement of Israel in Canaan, and, indeed, according to the actual wording of vs. 17b, the existence of the Solomonic Temple; thus, as it lies before us, it is "the true Passover-song" of Ewald, so far as it is in that case stamped unmistakably with a liturgical character. If the song were really old, as vss. 20 and 21 belong certainly to E, it was bound to be attributed to J. Ewald was willing to suppose the existence in it of a genuinely Mosaic kernel, which he thinks it possible to discover in vss. 1–3 and 18, and Kautzsch ("Abriss," 138) calls attention to the representation in xiv. 24 ff., where echoes of the poetical form of the narrative that is to follow are still audible; but none of the characteristic expressions and idiomatic turns of Ex. xv. 1–18 meet us in Ex. xiv. At the same time also this Song gives the impression of being a literary unity throughout, which it is not easy to reconcile with a supposed working over of an older basis. As vs. 1 is identical with vs. 21, and the latter undoubtedly belongs to the genuinely older tradition, it is by far the most probable view to regard the former verse as a later extension of vs. 21, which extension, on account of its psalm-like style, can lay claim to no great antiquity. The absolute *terminus ad quem* is afforded by Neh. ix. 11 from Ezra's memoirs (§ 21, 5), where Ex. xv. 5 is quoted. Sievers[1] regards the original Song as ending with vs. 12, and on metrical grounds considers vss. 14–18 to be the work of a more recent continuator.

---

[1] In p. 409 of the work referred to in § 4A, 6 above.

3. The Little Songs in Numb. xxi.

LITERATURE: F. Delitzsch, Z.W.L., iii. 337 ff., 449 ff., 561 ff., 1882; E. Meyer, Z.A.T.W., v. 36 ff., 1885; J. Wellhausen, Skizzen und Vorarbeiten, ii., 2nd ed., 343, 1889; K. Budde, P.Jb., lxxxii. 491 ff., 1895.

In Numb. xxi. we have in vss. 14b–15, 17b–18, and 27b–30 some song-fragments as the source of which vs. 14 quotes ספר מלחמות יהוה ("Book of the Wars of Jahve"). The Songs—obscure and mutilated and (in the traditional text) obviously corrupt as they are—give the impression of being thoroughly ancient and popular in character: as the whole passage in which they occur certainly emanates from E, they are at least as old as 750. The first fragment, which merely contains some geographical data, cannot be determined absolutely; the second, the so-called "Song of the Well," is either to be construed literally, for which Budde adduces a very interesting original form, or, with Wellhausen, metaphorically of the conquest of the Moabite town of Beer. The longer third Song, as E. Meyer ("Z.A.T.W." i. 130 f.; 1881) was the first to recognise, was originally only a glorification of a victory of Israel over Moab, and was already incomprehensible to E, and, as the insertion undoubtedly made by him of the words לְמֶלֶךְ אֱמֹרִי סִיחוֹן ("unto Sihon king of the Amorites") in vs. 29 suggests, was applied to events of the Mosaic age. In the "Book of the Wars of Jahve" above mentioned, from which all the song-fragments in question certainly emanated, we must recognise a collection of songs of war and victory: as the collection was used by E, it will have been compiled in the kingdom of Israel, some considerable time before E. Stade ("G.V.I.," i. 521) refers the original events alluded to to the war between Israel and Moab during the dynasty of Omri: that would point to the first half of the ninth century.

4. *The Oracles of Balaam, Numb. xxiii. and xxiv.*

LITERATURE :. H. Oort, *Disputatio de Num. xxii.–xxiv.*, 1860; F. Delitzsch, *Z.W.L.*, ix. 119 ff., 1881; J. Wellhausen, *Skizzen und Vorarbeiten*, ii., 2nd ed., 346–351, 1889; A. von Gall, *Zusammensetzung und Herkunft der Bileamperikope, Numb. xxii.–xxiv.*, 1900.

In the history of Balaam we find four longer and three shorter oracles, which are placed in the mouth of the seer Balaam; these require independent treatment. A cursory glance already reveals that ch. xxiii. and xxiv. 1–19 are parallel narratives, and on comparing specially xxiii. 21 and 22 with xxiv. 7 and 8 the mutual independence of these passages must appear to be excluded. As ch. xxii. already shows clear traces of a double narrative from J and E, these chapters (xxiii.–xxiv.) have been apportioned to the same two documentary sources, in which case, with Dillmann, ch. xxiii. is to be assigned to E, and xxiv. to J; notice the specifically theocratic colouring of xxiii. 9, 21, 23, and, on the other hand, in xxiv. 17–19 the clear indication of the dominion and achievements of David. On account of the significant features in which both chapters agree, side by side with the strongly marked divergence by which they are distinguished, we are driven to the supposition that two Balaam-oracles had become traditional at an early period, which were then set forth by J as well as by E, each in his own manner, unless indeed this divergent form had itself been transmitted to them, so that in ch. xxiv. we may have perhaps the Judaic, and in ch. xxiii. the Ephraimitic impress stamped upon the old traditional Balaam-oracles—for Wellhausen has convincingly shown that J also originally possessed a full and independent Balaam-history. The three short oracles xxiv. 20–24 are clearly of later growth: vs. 22 presupposes the Assyrian, vs. 24 the Greek period; and in close connexion with these also the intrinsically colourless oracle vs. 20, which glances back to vs. 7, must be pronounced not original. Recently Gall has explained the four longer oracles as post-exilic products of the messianic-eschatological expectation of later Judaism, and it may be conceded that still more recent retouches have been taken up into them: but Balaam-oracles are categorically desiderated by the narrative both in J and E, and that the poetry of early Israel was capable of clothing clear thoughts in clear words is sufficiently evident from the indubitable examples afforded by those parts of the Song of Deborah, of the Blessing of Jacob and the Blessing of Moses, which have been preserved in their textual purity and integrity.

5. *The Song of Moses, Deut. xxxii.*

LITERATURE: H. Ewald, *Jb. W.*, viii. 41 ff., 1857; W. Volck, *Mosis canticum cygneum*, 1861; A. Kamphausen, 1862; A. Klostermann, *Das Lied Moses und das Dtn.* (*St. Kr.*, xliv. 249 ff., 1871, and xlv. 236 ff., 1872); B. Stade, *Z.A.T.W.*, v. 297 ff., 1885; M. Loehr, *Protest. Monatsch.*, vii. 1 ff., 1903.

This longest of the poetical passages of the Pentateuch purports to be what has been described as "the swan-song of Moses," in which the Lawgiver, foreseeing the apostasy of the future, calls Heaven and Earth to witness against his people. As a perpetual warning for all future generations, the Song is to be learnt by heart, and not allowed to be forgotten out of the mouth of their seed. On the subject of this poem criticism has notably gone astray in the past. That it could not have been composed by Moses himself was soon seen; but as it already occupied a position in Deut., it was regarded as being older than that book, and that being so, only one really rational date remained: its author must have been a North-Israelite of the time when the overthrow of the kingdom of the Ten Tribes took place. Thus Ewald and especially Kamphausen. But even then a patient investigation of Deut. xxxi. must have proved disconcerting. This chapter displays secondary characteristics throughout; on vss. 1–8 and 14–15, 23, see § 9, 7. Between the connected vss. 15 and 23, vss. 16–22, forming the first introduction to this Song, are inserted, and this, in a form drastically worked over, is continued in vss. 24–30. Thus this Song need not, to say the least, have belonged originally to Deut., and we can attempt to fix its chronological setting on the basis of internal criteria. It is now abundantly clear that the Song, though marked by many peculiarities in expression, yet cannot claim any originality in thought: it is largely a compendium of the prophetic theology, steeped from end to end in reminiscences of the older prophets. There is a whole series of quite striking ones of Hosea, and some less remarkable of Isaiah and Micah: on the other hand, a considerable number of Jeremianic expressions and words occur, which Kamphausen (p. 296 f.) has collected, and which prove beyond a doubt that the Song belongs to a time subsequent to Jeremiah: here I adduce the following examples: vss. 4 and 21, *cf.* Jer. ii. 5; vss. 6 and 28, *cf.* Jer. iv. 22 and v. 21; vs. 21, *cf.* Jer. ii. 11; vss. 37 and 38, *cf.* Jer. ii. 28. Further, the Song is stamped throughout with a Deuteronomic impress, גֹּדֶל ("greatness"), predicated of God, and הִכְעִים ("vex," "provoke to anger") are purely Deuteronomic words; in vs. 7 the question to the father ("ask thy father") and in vs. 27 the reference to enemies are purely Deuteronomic turns of expression. Even specifically Deutero-Isaianic characteristics reveal themselves: *cf.* vss. 12 and 39, God alone and none "with Him," and in vs. 31 the very heathen to decide between Jahve and the gods. Such a passage as vs. 8, according to the undoubtedly correct reading of the LXX., cannot be old; אֵיד ("calamity"), תַּהְפֻּכוֹת ("perversities"), and כִּפֶּר ("atone") are quite modern words: we can hardly assign the Song to an earlier period than the end of the Babylonian Exile, if we should not, indeed, come down to a still lower date. Deut. xxxi. 16–22 was in this case designed for the insertion of the Song as a supplement to the already complete Deut. Steuernagel rejects from the Song as younger accretions vss. 5, 6, 7*b*, 17, 18, 29–31, and Löhr adds to these vss. 11, 14, 15*a*β, 16, 22, 24, 25*b*, 32*a*, 36–39, and 43*b*α, and replaces before vs. 43*a* a stichus according to the LXX., which displays vs. 43 enlarged to a full eight-lined stanza.

6. The Blessing of Moses, Deut. xxxiii.

LITERATURE: K. H. Graf, 1857; W. Volk, 1853, and in the Festschrift für A. von Oettingen, 1898, pp. 196-219; G. I. van der Fleier, *Deut. xxxiii.*, Leiden, 1895.

On passing from Deut. xxxii. immediately to ch. xxxiii., one feels oneself plunged into quite another world, and it is perhaps due to this fact that the two passages should have been regarded as equally ancient. In Deut. xxxiii., vss. 6-25, the special utterances appropriate to the tribes, at once stand out distinctly from the rest. Here everything breathes high antiquity and fresh and vigorous power; Steuernagel is only able to separate vss. 9b and 10; in any case vss. 8-11 raise the presumption that the poet was himself a priest. This Blessing of Moses calls to mind the Blessing of Jacob, Gen. xlix., but is clearly later than the latter, and in fact dependent on it. Simeon has vanished, Reuben has all but died out, and Levi has become the priestly tribe, but has by no means secured for itself a settled and recognised position, but is hard pressed to struggle for its existence. From vs. 7, the true sense of which was first understood by Graf, the conclusion is clear that its author was a North-Israelite: the rapturous delineation of Joseph in vs. 17 seems to point to the period of Jeroboam II., and the blessing over Gad in vs. 20 clearly reflects the difficulties and dangers of the position of this tribe—which were, however, successfully overcome — during the Syrian wars. Everything combines to suggest that this Song is to be attributed to a North-Israelite of the first half of the eighth century, and, moreover, all probability supports the supposition that E already admitted this composition into his work; even the superscription ch. xxxiii. 1 may have emanated from E, *cf.* לִפְנֵי מוֹתוֹ ("before his death"), Gen. xxvii. 7, 10, L. 16 E. Ch. xxxiii. 1 would link itself on immediately with xxxi. 23; xxxi. 14, 15, 23, even if they have been revised under Deuteronomic influence, appear to rest upon an Elohistic groundwork, and in any case E was bound to narrate the institution and consecration of Joshua. It is also particularly notable that the story in Ex. xxxii. 25-29, which obviously is closely connected with Deut. xxxiii. 9, and has grown out of it, is embodied in a narrative that throughout belongs to E. The opening and closing verses of the Song, vss. 2-5 and 26-29, are regarded by Steuernagel as a connected post-exilic psalm, in which the composition has been given its setting that it might receive the personal "Mosaic" note.

7. *Genesis xiv.*

LITERATURE: Th. Nöldeke, *Die Ungeschichtlichkeit der Erzählung Gen. xiv.* (*Untersuchungen*, 1869,[1] pp. 156-172); E. Meyer, *Geschichte des Altertums*, i. 1883, §136. For the extensive special Assyriological literature on the subject, see the commentaries on Genesis.

Among the purely narrative parts of the Pentateuch, Gen. xiv. calls for special treatment. This passage falls altogether outside the boundaries of the rest of the patriarchal story, and introduces Abraham into a setting of world-history with a far wider and more extensive outlook. Abraham is called *the Hebrew*, and appears as confederate of the Amorite chieftains; all through we meet with peoples who had long since vanished, and names that had been forgotten, and

[1] *Cf.* §6, 5 above.

the precision of the narrative in small details seems to argue a historical tradition; and thus Ewald thought it possible to recognise in Gen. xiv. a genuine fragment of an ancient Canaanite historical work, and with this opinion Kittel ("History of the Hebrews," vol. i.) and Klostermann ("G.V.I.," 1896) agree. But this view altogether misapprehends the character of the narrative, in which Abraham is regarded not merely as an episode, but as the principal feature—the whole can only have been written with direct reference to Abraham and for his glorification, its object being to wreathe the head of the tribal ancestor of Israel with the laurel of the conquering hero for a halo. Especially strange is the fact that the passage cannot be assigned to any documentary source of the Pentateuch: like its own Melchizedek it stands therein ἀπάτωρ, ἀμήτωρ, ἀγενεαλόγητος. It presupposes the whole Pentateuch, and is more especially dependent on P, as the use of רכוש, נֶפֶשׁ, and יְלִידֵי בַיִת sufficiently shows. When in addition to this we consider the unhistorical character of the contents of the narrative, which has been shown incontrovertibly by Nöldeke, we are forced to the conviction that we have here to deal with a quite late product of free poetical fancy and literary reflection: the antiquarian names and indications have been gathered together partly from incidental allusions in the O.T., partly have been freely invented, and it is highly probable that even in the 316 servants of Abraham nothing more is involved than a "Gematria" of the name אליעזר ("Eliezer"). The fact that the names of the four foreign kings have been authenticated from the inscriptions is, of course, no proof of the historicity of the content of the narrative, with its material impossibilities, but is evidence for its having originated in Babylonia, where a Jew with literary interests could obtain names and dates from the old Mesopotamian history in abundance; and the last link in the chain may be said to be joined, if it really be the case that "during the Persian or rather Seleucid period in Babylonia an epos with Hammurabi, Kudur-Laghamar, Eriaku, and Tudchul as the principal figures appears to have been current" (H. Zimmern, "Th. R.," i. 322, 1898). In Gen. xiv. we have a very late addition, inserted into the already completed Pentateuch, and composed in the style of the Midrash and of Chronicles, the aim of which is made apparent in the episode of Melchizedek. The latter, therefore, can neither be isolated from the context, nor can the name and person of Melchizedek rest upon an older tradition. The view that E may have given an account in this place of some warlike intervention of Abraham on behalf of his nephew Lot (Dillmann, Kittel) contributes nothing of any solid value: such a narrative (supposing it to have existed) would have "left behind nothing but the vague impression that it might once have been there" (Holzinger).

8. *The Book of the Covenant, Ex. xxi.–xxiii.*

LITERATURE: J. W. Rothstein, *Das Bundesbuch und die religionsgeschichtliche Entwicklung Israels*, 1888; K. Budde, Z.A.T.W., xi. 99 ff., 1891; B. Baentsch, 1892; W. Staerk, *Das Deuteronomium* (see § 9), 29–57.

The two Decalogues, Ex. xx. 2–17 and xxxiv. 10–26, need not be gone into in detail. It is sufficient to recall the fact that Ex. xx. 2–17 belongs to E^2, xxxiv. 10–26 to J; the decisive word on these two noteworthy passages must be spoken by Biblical theology. On the other hand, a larger body of legislation which falls within Exodus, the so-called " Book of the Covenant " (= Bb) requires special treatment here. By this name Ex. xxiv. 7 designates a book on the basis of which Moses concluded a covenant between Jahve and Israel. It is generally conceded that by the designation in question the section comprised in Ex. xxi.–xxiii. is intended. In these chapters we have a collection of laws which deal in great detail with civic life, and briefly also with the cultus in its main features: they conclude with a parenetic ending which promises as a reward for the conscientious observance of these laws a successful conquest of the Promised Land. As in the case of Deut., a number of passages here also strike us in which the address suddenly changes to the plural; and all these cases involve material difficulties as well. Ch. xxii. 20*b* and 21 dissever vss. 20*a* and 22; after separation from vs. 23, vs. 22 closes parallel with vs. 26: vs. 24*b* following 24*a* is at least superfluous; vs. 30 is out of accord with the tenor of the rest of the Book of the Covenant, and cannot be reconciled on material grounds with xxi. 34, 35, 36, xxii. 10, 12; xxiii. 9*b* is specifically Deuteronomic, as also is xxii. 20*b*. On other grounds the following passages must be regarded as strange: xxiii. 9*a* compared with xxii. 20, and xxiii. 7*a* compared with 1*a*; xxiii. 4–5 intrudes disturbingly between xxiii. 3 and 6, and in its terms even goes beyond Deut. xxii. 1–4; xxiii. 17–19 is an appendix out of the Second Decalogue, ch. xxxiv. 23, 25, 26, as a comparison of vs. 17 with vs. 14 and of vs. 19a with xxii. 28a already demonstrates; vss. 15–16 also have been amplified out of xxxiv. 18, 20bβ ?, and 22 ; cf. esp. xxiii. 15b with xxxiv. 20bβ ("Z.A.T.W.," xi. 217, 1891). But after separating the passages which are certainly secondary, the original form of Bb is not yet made available. Side by side with these additions there are traces of abridgments, as when the enactments of the marriage-law are restricted to xxii. 15–16; the arrangement appears to be much confused, and the tone and formulation of particular prescriptions is marked by much divergence: there are partly enactments in the third person, which for the most part regulate questions of civil right in sharp and precise casuistic, after the manner of pure jurisprudence (ch. xxi. 2–xxii. 16†), and in some cases questions of criminal law, with pointed brevity (ch. xxi. 12, 15–17, xxii. 18–19, as well as [in spite of its divergent formulation] vs. 17); partly admonitions in the second person of a specifically religious and moral character (ch. xxii. 20–xxiii. 16†), and in this category is also to be included ch. xx. 22–26, which cannot well be separated from Bb. The data thus adduced make it altogether improbable that in Bb we have a uniform collection of laws written by a single hand. When we proceed to make an attempt to attain clear results as to Bb, it is an exceedingly fortunate circumstance that we are able to assign it with tolerably complete certainty to one documentary source. The opening (xx. 22–26) and concluding verses (xxiii. 20–33), and the account of the conclusion of a covenant, completed on the basis of this book (xxiv. 3-8), so clearly bear the characteristic marks of E, that the question of its belonging to the latter source is placed beyond any doubt: the laws themselves, also, display in their formulation to a large extent an unquestionable relationship with E. But with the recognition of this fact the real problems only begin. The most felicitous solution of these has been proposed by Baentsch, who modifies Kuenen's hypothesis already mentioned (see § 9, 5). Baentsch distinguishes in Bb (1) *mišpaṭim*, xxi. 2–xxii. 19†; (2) a series of injunctions concerning the cultus, xx. 22-26*, xxii. 28-29, xxiii. 10-16*; (3) a number of moral commands, xxii. 20-26*, xxiii. 1-9*. The injunctions concerning the cultus show such a relationship with the so-called Second Decalogue (Ex. xxxiv.) that it is clear they form the Elohistic parallel—here also clearly somewhat younger—to the Jahvistic Sinai-*debarim* ("Sinai-words") there set forth. We have in them the Horeb-*debarim* of E, and on the basis of these Horeb-*debarim* Moses mediates the covenant between Jahve and Israel narrated in Ex. xxiv. 3-8. The passages of Ex. xxxiv. which in Bb have no parallel have then been appended in xxiii. 17-19 (*cf.* § 14, 1). The *mišpaṭim*, to which the moral commandments form the appendix, have no place at all within the limits of the Horeb-legislation. They are primarily a personal instruction to Moses for the purposes of judicial decisions, which he then promulgated, before his death, in the plains of Moab, as binding for Israel. In these *mišpaṭim*, which reveal striking parallels with the recently discovered Code of Hammurabi, we have clearly a deposit of old Israelitish customary law: its codification may go back to the priesthood of Bethel (Wildeboer). In order to make room for Deut., these laws were transplanted to Horeb, and placed bodily in the midst of the Horeb-*debarim*; moreover, the secondary elements of Bb, and especially the redaction of the concluding verses, xxiii. 20–23, are stamped with a Deuteronomic character.

9. *Leviticus xvii.–xxvi.*

LITERATURE: A. Klostermann, *Beiträge zur Entstehungsgeschichte des Pentateuchs* (*Z.L.T.*, xxxviii. 401, 1877); L. Horst, *Leviticus xvii.–xxvi. und Hezekiel*, 1881; P. Wurster, *Zur Charakteristik und Geschichte des Priesterkodex und des Heiligkeitsgesetzes* (*Z.A.T.W.*, iv. 122 ff., 1884); B. Baentsch, *Das Heiligkeits-Gesetz Lev. xvii.–xxvi.*, 1893.

This corpus of legislation also requires to be subjected to a special and detailed examination. It reveals an undeniable relationship with P, and many phrases and expressions characteristic of P occur in it; but at the same time it has so much that diverges from P, and such a strongly marked character of its own, and approximates in the general impression it produces so unmistakably to Deut., that it cannot without further question and qualification be derived from P. Our attention is primarily arrested by a long parenetic speech (ch. xxvi. 3–45) in which blessing and curse are prospectively set forth, according as Israel walks in Jahve's statutes or not. This passage in its whole plan and structure is so strikingly similar to Deut. xxviii. that it can only have been designed for a similar purpose, viz. to form the conclusion to a longer connected corpus of law: it is, moreover, followed by a formal subscription, vs. 46, exactly like Deut. xxviii. 69 (*cf.* also Ex. xxiii. 20–33). The whole section xxvi. 3–45 is distinguished by a specially strongly marked literary individuality, and its characteristic expressions and phraseology are only again to be met with within the Pentateuch in ch. xvii.–xxv.; there can be no doubt, therefore, that these ten chapters originally formed an independent whole, for which Klostermann has proposed the excellent designation "Law of Holiness" (= H). On examining this corpus more closely some notable phenomena become apparent: redundancy of expression, as in xvii. 10–14, xxii. 31–33; repetitions, such as xvii. 10–14 and xix. 26*a*, xix. 4*a* and xxvi. 1*a*, xix. 30 and xxvi. 2*a*, xix. 31 and xx. 6, 27; formal doublets, as xxiv. 17–18 and 21, and the larger passages xviii. and xx.; ch. xix. also is marked by much that is peculiar. All these considerations, taken in conjunction with the fact that the characteristic peculiarities of xxvi. 3–45 are of far less frequent occurrence in the actual laws than in their framework, suggest that H is a collection of various laws, already fixed in writing, which was compiled by the author of ch. xxvi. 1–45: the presence of marks characteristic of P would then be explained in this way, that H was worked into P, and this occasioned its being revised. The whole problem has been most minutely investigated by Baentsch, who reaches the following results :—Ch. xvii. has been revised in a particularly thorough way in accordance with P, but the kernel of it is to be claimed for H. The festival-calendar of ch. xxiii. belongs almost entirely to P; only vss. 9–22† and 39–43 can be regarded as fragments of the festival-legislation of H. Ch. xxiv. 1-9 is to be assigned to P throughout; H, however, had prescriptions in this place on the subject of holy oil and holy bread; vss. 15-22 belong to H throughout, the historical framework being due to a younger hand. In the specially difficult and complicated ch. xxv. there belong to H the law about the sabbatical year and a series of humanitarian precepts, general in character, and having no reference to the year of jubilee. A more recent stratum of H has then inserted the law about the year of jubilee, but purely as *restitutio in integrum*, while the transference of the functions of the sabbatical year to the year of jubilee is due to a revision which depends upon P. In ch. xxvi. was preserved originally an independent homiletical discourse which later became, by the process of revision, the conclusion of H. In detail the elements of H are to be grouped as follows, according to Baentsch: (1) ch. xviii.-xx., xxiii.-xxv. so far as it belongs to H. This is the oldest stratum (H^1), but had already been subjected to redaction and revision on the basis of older series of laws; (2) ch. xxi.-xxii. (H^2), in the same way worked up into collected form out of existing subject-matter; (3) ch. xvii. so far as it belongs to H (H^3). These three strata were then united together, and ch. xxvi. in a revised form inserted, this process taking place towards the end of the Babylonian Exile, which situation ch. xxvi. clearly reflects. Bertholet will only discriminate twelve distinct passages in ch. xvii.-xxv., and makes no attempt at more definite dating, although he thinks ch. xviii.† is clearly younger than ch. xx.†, and in ch. xxv. the stratum which deals with the year of jubilee is younger than the one that deals with the sabbatical year.

A distinct and separate problem is furnished by the question of *the relation of H to Ezekiel*. This is of so close and intimate a character that Graf, Kayser, and Horst have accepted the view that the prophet was himself the author or redactor of H. Such a supposition, however, is opposed by the presence of undeniable material differences that exist between them, above all by the fact that H includes within its purview the High Priest, of whom Ezekiel still has no knowledge. According to Baentsch, ch. xxvi.—an "anthology out of Ezekiel"—H^3 and H^2 are dependent on and younger than the prophet: on the other hand, the reverse relation is affirmed for H^1. The proofs advanced by Baentsch for this view do not appear to me to be convincing, especially for the reason that Ezekiel is already acquainted with H^1 in its present combined form, which is itself the product of redaction. The conclusion that H as a whole is younger than Ezekiel may be described as absolutely certain. H is related to P^2 "as a first step."; "matters are here not yet so far or so fixedly developed" as in P^2, and for this reason Kuenen denotes it with the symbol P^1, and sees in it one of the older collections of laws of a priestly character, which served the author of P^2 as a basis and starting-point; it must quite early have been worked up into P^2, because already in the time of Ezra, in the "Book of the Law of Moses," Neh. viii. 14-18, the prescription about the Feast of Tabernacles, which is derived from P^1 (Lev. xxiii. 39-44), stands in conjunction with the prescription of P^2, which (Lev. xxiii. 36; Numb.

xxix. 35) extends the Feast to a length of eight days. In the less strongly marked element of H, which is rather an aggregation of individual laws than a systematically co-ordinated corpus, the question may be raised whether it may not originally have included passages outside of Lev. xvii.–xxvi. In this way it has, in fact, been thought possible to detect in Lev. xi.–xv., i.–vii., Numb. v.,[1] vi., ix., xv., xix. equally constituent elements of H. Baentsch concedes this absolutely only in the case of Lev. xi. 43–45, which formed the conclusion (originally following ch. xx. 25) to some brief directions of a general character about procedure with regard to clean and unclean animals, and "with well-grounded assurance" in the case also of Numb. xv. 37–41; the other sections adduced he regards as belonging to P^1, *i.e.* they are older than P^2, but a closer literary connexion with H cannot be shown to exist.

§ 14. THE PENTATEUCH AS A WHOLE AND ITS FORMATION

Having completed our analysis of the Pentateuch, we pass on to the synthesis, and proceed to ask how out of these individual documentary sources and pieces the Pentateuch received its formation as a whole. As we shall see, this literary process was accomplished in three principal stages.

1. *The Union of J and E.*—It was Nöldeke who first expressed the view in so many words—though Knobel was already on the way towards recognising

---

[1] But *cf.* on the subject of this Tora of the "offering of jealousy" Stade in "Z.A.T.W.," xvi. 166, ff., 1895.

it—that these two documentary sources did not find their way into our Pentateuch "as two independent works," but had already been united together before this took place. Subsequently Wellhausen subjected the process by which this was accomplished, for the first time, to a minute investigation: he sees in it the work of a "Jehovist." The latter makes use of the divine name יהוה, and has throughout made J the basis and foundation of his compilation; only to E²—the author most akin and in time standing nearest to himself—does he allow J to be subordinated, as in Gen. xxxiv., Ex. xix.–xxxiv. We designate this redactor by the symbol Rj. His work is primarily a fusion of sections entirely blended out of J and E: as, however, J and E, in spite of a considerable family likeness, differ from each other in not unimportant respects, this redactor must have assimilated the two collections of material and eliminated contradictions that were too glaring, and it is for this reason that Kuenen calls him the "harmoniser of J and E"; besides this, he has not hesitated on occasion to introduce insertions and amplifications into his subject-matter, which are immediately distinguishable from their context by their advanced prophetic-theological standpoint. Generally his method is to work with a tolerable amount of independence, and his position as regards his material is a comparatively free one. In GENESIS xv., where the first trace of E is met with, he appears to have intervened directly; from him xvi. 9–10 emanates, also, with a view to reconcile J with E, ch. xxi., and further also xx. 18. Ch. xxii. he has subjected to a drastic revision. The passage vss. 14*b*–18 is by him, and in the story itself he has in vs. 2 obliterated all traces of the original *locale* and transferred the incident to Jerusalem, whence it follows that Rj was a Judaean. In ch. xxvi. he has introduced vss. 15 and 18 in order to reconcile the context with ch. xxi. E; xxviii. 14 also illustrates his method. As no trace of P is present in the sections in question, the drastic revision of xxx. 31–xxxi. 3 and xxxi. 47–54 will be his work: Wellhausen ascribes to him also xxxii. 10–13 and the "modest expression" designating Jerusalem ("tower of Eder") which occurs in xxxv. 21; also xxxii. 33 may possibly emanate from him. If the history of Joseph displays throughout a certain breadth of representation, this will be traceable, equally with the additions xxxix. 1*ba*, 20*aγ*, xl. 3*b*, 15*bβ* and the revision of xlv. 19 and 21 (?), to Rj.

In EXODUS he has in ch. i.–xviii. very deftly woven the two sources together, and where necessary assimilated them by means of such additions as אַחַר שִׁלּוּחֶיהָ ("after sending her away"), ch. xviii. 2. His interventions in the sections of the legislation ch. xix.–xxxiv. are highly significant. In xix. 23 we are at once confronted with a characteristic instance of his harmonising method. He has throughout these chapters made E—which at that time seems not to have contained the Decalogue (xx. 2–17)—the basis of the compilation, and filled this out with J; xx. 17–19 was inserted from the Second Decalogue of J, in order that it might be possible to represent it as a repetition of the *Horeb-debarim* of E, while xxxii.–xxxiv. were moulded essentially into their present form (xxxii. 8–14 already presupposes Deut. ix. 8 ff.). In NUMBERS xi. the peculiar combination of the quail-feeding of J with the outpouring of the spirit on the seventy elders of E^2—which resulted in the transposition of Ex. xviii. to its present place (*cf.* § 11, 4)—is certainly the work of Rj, as well as the admirably effected fusion of the two Balaam-stories, xxii.-xxiv. His hand can also be detected in xiv. 11-21, which is throughout dependent on JE, displays a remarkable affinity with the other sections which have been framed by Rj, and immediately terminates in a fragment derived from E. In DEUTERONOMY no trace of his work is discoverable.

Referring to this redactor, Holzinger remarks that the method of the "Jehovist" revision is altogether different in different parts of the Pentateuch: in the case of Genesis it is predominantly compilatory, combining J and E, but leaving their elements intact; in Ex. i.-xi., Numb. xxii.-xxiv. the narrative is, with considerable skill, to some extent "composed" on the basis of the sources; in the account of the wilderness-period and the law-giving drastic revision is evident, and the unity of the representation and the orderly sequence of the narrative have been allowed to suffer. Holzinger in consequence would look upon Rj not as the designation of a person, but only as denoting a literary process characterised merely by certain uniformity. The features observed by Holzinger are undeniably present, and the inference deduced from them is, to say the least, very attractive. The *terminus a quo* for this literary process is furnished by E^2, thus giving a date *circa* 650; regarding its conclusion, it is noteworthy that, in spite of much affinity of spirit, no literary influence from Deut. is apparent: both may be regarded as members of the same school, but the two stages of it to which they respectively belong are everywhere kept sharply distinct. The independent works J and E were, of course, still preserved in their distinctive forms even subsequent to the process of fusion above described, as may be inferred from the fact which E. Meyer[1] was the first to recognise, and which was afterwards demonstrated in detail by Dillmann, viz. that E still lay before the Deuteronomic authors in the form of an independent writing. They associate themselves, that is to say, so closely and thoroughly with E—even to such minute points as the use of חֹרֵב ("Horeb") as the name of the mountain of the law-giving, of אֱמֹרִי ("Amorite") as the designation of the original Canaanite inhabitants, the description of Joshua as מְשָׁרֵת ("minister") of Moses, the use of הַצִּרְעָה ("the hornet") to indicate something that creates *panic terror*; and also in points where E and J diverge (*e.g.* the spies come to the wady Eschol, Balaam is from Mesopotamia, the tables of the Law written by Jahve)—that it is hard to see how they can possibly have distilled all these specific characteristics of E out J E.

2. *The union of J E with D.*—Once Deut. had become a canonical law-book, and was regarded as the work of Moses, it must soon have been incorporated into the great national history. This was effected by a second redactor who all the time lives and moves in a world of ideas and modes of expression that belong to Deut., and who is therefore termed Rd. In GENESIS only one clear trace of his work is visible, in xxvi. 5. In EXODUS, iv. 21–23 is apparently by him, as it can be derived neither from J nor E.

[1] "Z.A.T.W.," i. 123, 1881, v. 42–52, 1885.

In the story of the Egyptian plagues, x. 2 at any rate has a Deuteronomic tinge, also viii. 18*b*, ix. 29*b* are certainly additions made by this redactor's hand, while in ix. 14-16 he has intervened rather more decisively. Ch. xii. 21-27, xiii. 3-16, which belong to J, and xv. 26, belonging to E, have been subjected to drastic revision, as well as the Jahvistic account of the manna in xvi., where vss. 4 and 28 in particular have quite a Deuteronomic sound. But the most distinct traces of his handiwork are to be seen in the truly disastrous confusion in which Ex. xix.-xxxiv. in its present form is involved.[1] In order to make room for Deut. he has violently transposed the *mišpaṭim* from the *Arboth Moab* ("Plains of Moab") into the Horeb-*debarim* of E (*cf.* § 13, 8), and thus composed the "Book of the Covenant," (Ex. xx. 22-xxiii. 33); but he has also subjected the Decalogue of ch. xxxiv. to drastic revision, and the present form of the Decalogue proper (ch. xx. 2-17), as well as its unfortunate position before xx. 18-21, may equally be traced back to him. In addition, xix. 3*b*-8 is specifically Deuteronomic. In NUMBERS, x. 33 and xiv. 44 reveal in the expression *Ark of the Covenant* a clear trace of Deuteronomic phraseology: the following passages, also, which have a connexion of their own with each other, viz. xxi. 23-35,[2] xxxii. 33$a\beta$* and 40, as well as the transposition of xxxii. 39, 41-42 (J) to its present place, can best be traced

---

[1] On this point see esp. B. Klopfer, "Z.A.T.W.," xvii. 197 ff., 1897; C. Steuernagel, "St. Kr.," lxxii. 319 ff., 1899; and C. Bruston, "Les quatres sources de la législation du Sinai," "Rev. de Théol. et Philos.," 1899.

[2] This passage has already been discussed in § 11, 4, above.

back to Rd. In DEUTERONOMY, xxxi. 1-8 certainly emanates from him, as well as vss. 14-15 and 23, based upon an Elohistic groundwork; by this means it was intended to unite Deut. with the Book of Joshua; the concluding comment (xxxiv. 10-12) is also most naturally derived from him. On the other hand, it may well be asked whether the composition of our existing Deut. out of the various elements of the Deuteronomic ordered resources is due to the same hand, and whether Rd should not be understood to refer less to an individual writer than to a stage of redactional activity. The beginning of this redactional activity can hardly be placed earlier than the Babylonian Exile: the last stage of it would be marked by the insertion of the "Song of Moses" (Deut. xxxii. 1-43), with xxxi. 16-22, 24-30† as introduction and xxxii. 44 as postscript. This insertion is certainly older than the union of J E D with P.

3. *The Union of J E D with P.* — We have already seen (§ 12, 12) how altogether improbable it is that Ezra should have brought P with him in a form already united with J E D. When P, however, had been publicly proclaimed and solemnly acknowledged and accepted, he must have taken steps to get it annexed to the larger national history and law-book, which had already for a long time held an assured position. This union was effected by a third redactor, Rp, in whose eyes P is the holy code *par excellence*, and who consequently both in phraseology and ideas occupies exactly the same standpoint as P, and in cases of divergent views or representation almost without exception gives the latter the preference:

any mutilation of P by the hand of Rp can only be looked upon as a curiosity of the rarest kind. The task confronting this redactor was of the most comprehensive and difficult kind, and therefore it is not to be wondered at that his handiwork has left behind the clearest traces. As a whole, he performed his work with a considerable amount of piety, even as regards J E D. That in the case of matters which he could not recount twice over—such as, perhaps, the building of the Ark, or the death of Abraham—he struck out the sections of J E D corresponding to P is easily conceivable under such circumstances: all the same, however, he has truthfully preserved and inserted into some suitable place divergent features of the parallel accounts, thus often violently dislocating J E D, but still, as far as possible, preserving its contents. To specify these displacements and deletions in detail would lead us too far afield. What is difficult to determine is the redactor's relation to P^x—whether, viz., the more and most recent elements of P were added by Rp, or at some time before or after his activity : I will indicate the problem involved in each case.

We have seen (§ 12, 12) that P^1 had already been united with P^2 by the time of Rp. In GENESIS, ii. 4a, which, if original, was the superscription to ch. i., has been placed by Rp at the end, or else it was written independently by him, in reliance upon parallel passages, as an introduction to J. In ch. v. he has worked in details out of the Jahvistic Sethite-table. By him vi. 7 has been filled out, vii. 3a and 8–9 inserted, and vss. 7, 22a, and 23a enlarged in accordance with P. In ch. x. he has in vs. 21

added כָּל־בְּנֵי ("all the sons of") and the whole of vs. 24; also the number of the names, designedly worked up to seventy, is certainly his work. In ch. xv., where very probably Rj had already intervened, vss. 13-15 and 19-21 (a very complete but also unhistorical enumeration of the original Canaanitish population) emanate from him, and in addition xxvii. 46 as a connecting-link with xxvi. 35. By the same hand the conclusion of ch. xxiv. has been somewhat ruthlessly transposed in order to reconcile J with P. In ch. xxxiv., where circumcision is in question, he has revised the contents in the sense and in accordance with the linguistic usage of P; in ch. xxxv. he has added vs. $19b\beta$, and freely rewritten vss. $6a$, 9-15, having, out of regard to J E, removed vss. $6a$, 11, 12, $13a$, 15 down from xxviii. 9, and blended them with a second divine revelation to Jacob on the return-journey, vss. 9-10 (Gunkel). Ch. xxxv. 1-5 has been wholly corrected by him: the framework is throughout that of P, but the divergent names have been inserted by Rp out of J. In the following passages there is some uncertainty as to how far Rp's hand is to be recognised: xxxvii. 14, fixing Jacob's *locale* at Hebron?; xliii. 14, אֵל שַׁדַּי ("God Almighty"); xlvi. $1a\beta$ in connexion with xxxvii. 14?; xlvi. 8-27, Rp or P^x?; xlvii. 30, בִּקְבוּרָתָם ("in their burying-place"); xlviii. 7*?; xlix. $28a$; xlix. 31 altered out of regard to J E; according to P, Rachel also was certainly buried in the Cave of Machpelah. In Exodus iv. Rp has inserted vss. 9 and $14a\beta$-16, and revised vss. 27-30, as well as added "Aaron" everywhere in ch. v.-x.; the whole passage vi. 13-30 emanates from him or P^x. In ch. vi. 6-9 he also seems to have meddled: there, in the midst of a purely priestly context, correspondences distinctly Deuteronomic occur which can only have been interspersed by Rp; for though Rp depends primarily and essentially on P, yet, as being the real composer of our present Pentateuch, he can on occasion take up particular expressions and turns of speech from the rest of the Pentateuchal sources also. The question as to xii. 40–42 is a very difficult one. Only the fact that redaction is present in the passage is sure; in vs. 42*a* Budde ("Z.A.T.W.," xi. 200, 1891) recognises a passage from J. In ch. xvi. we meet with one of the rare cases where Rp has displaced a narrative of P out of regard to J E. Following vss. 9 and 34, the story of the manna, which P combined with the episode of the feeding with quails, can only have been narrated by him after the divine revelation at Sinai; the transposition of his account to its present place was the work of Rp, who at the same time arranged vss. 6–7 before 9–12, revised vs. 10, and wrote vss. 8 and 36. In ch. xvii. Rp has abruptly introduced the Jahvistic fragment about the miraculous supply of wells (at Rephidim), in order to make room for P in Numb. xx. In addition there proceeds from him the recurring expression לְחֹת הָעֵדֻת ("tables of the testimony"), xxxi. 18, xxxiv. 29, and he it was who in ch. xxxiii. struck out the Elohistic account of the preparation of the Ark. On the other hand, xx. 11 is not an addition of Rp, but an original feature of E^2 (see Budde, "Bibl. Urgesch," 493–495). With regard to the rest of Ex., the whole of Lev., and Numb. i.–x. the only question that arises in each case is whether Rp or P^x is the redactor. In NUMBERS xi. Rp has appended vss. 7–9 with the object of recalling once more, after the long intervening interval, the manna of Ex. xvi.; the delineation is a combination of Ex. xvi. 13–14 (J) with vs. 13 (P). The expressions לְמִשְׁפְּחוֹתָיו ("throughout their families"), xi. 10, and בְּמִדְבַּר פָּארָן ("in the wilderness of Paran"), xii. 16*b*, also point to Rp. In xiv. 27–38 he has considerably enlarged the much shorter divine speech as given in P. In ch. xvi. only P² side by side with J lay before him, so that the revision by Pˣ and the closely dependent interpolation of xvii. 1–5 and xxvi. 11 would have to be placed later than Rp; xvii. 27–28, however, either comes directly from or has been transposed by him. In xx. 1–13 we have an instance in which Rp has purposely mutilated P, with the object of removing a narrative from the latter which was a stumbling-block to him (see "Z.A.T.W.," xi. 20 ff., 1891); xxi. 4*aa* again is also by him, and xxvi. 9–10, which presupposes the composite text of Numb. xvi. (J + P²) due to him. The elders of Midian, xxii. 4–7, are younger than Rp, since they stand in close connexion with ch. xxxi. and xxv. 16–18, which narrative can only have been formed by a combination of xxv., in the form given to it by Rp, with xxii.–xxiv. In ch. xxxii. P has been fused indissolubly with J E; here Rp seems to have proceeded in a specially independent manner, possibly because (as in the case of xiv., of which xxxii. especially reminds us) Rj had already worked on it beforehand, and because even younger hands than Rj have been actively engaged on this chapter. The itinerary xxxiii. 1–49 was composed at the earliest by Rp, because it builds on P and J E; originally it was supposed there must have been forty stations corresponding to the forty years of the desert-journey. In xxxiii. 50–56 Rp may have intervened in the same way; he certainly inserted xxxvi. 13 as conclusion and at the same time introduction to Deut. In DEUTERONOMY traces of this redactor's handiwork naturally are of the slightest, but even here they are not altogether absent; he has made the first superscription, i. 1–5, conformable with P, although, in the presence of the terribly corrupt condition of the first two verses, his share in the process cannot be determined exactly; he inserted iv. 41–43, and he it is who must have transplanted also x. 6–7 from Numb. xxi. to its present position. *Cf.* § 9, 7. On the other hand, he has left ch. xii.–xxvi. quite intact. He may have had some share in that very complicated production, ch. xxvii.; at any rate, vss. 15–26 presuppose the entire Pentateuchal legislation, esp. H by the side of D; it may, however, be even younger than Rp. In xxxi. 19 the latter may perhaps have altered an original כְּתָב לְךָ (sing.) into כִּתְבוּ לָכֶם (pl.), and in xxxii. 44 have inserted Joshua or Hosea; the phrase אֲשֶׁר עַל־פְּנֵי יְרֵחוֹ ("that is over against Jericho"), xxxii. 49, has been appended from J.

4. Thus Rp is practically the author of the Pentateuch as it now lies before us, and he must have undertaken this work of his not so very long after the public proclamation of P, somewhere, perhaps, between the years 440 and 400. But in this connexion also the possibility—nay, even the probability—has to be taken into account that the work may have been performed not by a single individual but by the Jerusalem-circle of the Scribes.

As P did not reach its close with Ezra, neither did the Pentateuch with the work of Rp. We have above already repeatedly referred to the possibility of *still younger hands having been at work*, and we have seen (*cf.* § 13, 7) that a whole section like Gen. xiv. was inserted by way of supplement into the already completed text of the Pentateuch. In this connexion it is especially passages from P^x that are in question. A fixed landmark is provided by Chronicles, which regards enactments derived from P^x as Mosaic Tora; *cf.* 2 Chron. xxiv. 6–9 with Ex. xxx. 13, and 2 Chron. xxxi. 6 with Lev. xxvii. 32–33; to the fourth century we might well also assign Numb. xxiv. 20–24, at least vs. 24, which contains a clear allusion to the Macedonian Power. But we are obliged to descend even lower, into the third century; for the Hebrew text was revised and glossed after the time of the LXX. A highly significant example of this is to be seen in the long section Ex. xxxv.–xl., which in the time of the LXX. at any rate was no fixed constituent element of the Pentateuch (*cf.* § 12, 2); in Deut. i. 39a we have already (§ 10, 3) detected a characteristic addition, which is absent in the LXX. text. - It is clear from the LXX. that not only was the text furnished with glosses but also edited, as is proved by Gen. xlvii. 4–6, where our Hebrew text has reached a more advanced stage of redaction than the LXX. These, however, are but the last convulsive movements before complete torpor sets in: this later scholastic activity had no real and decisive importance, and therefore it does not fall to us to follow it up in all its details.

Special Introduction

CHAPTER VII

BOOK I.—HISTORICAL BOOKS—*continued*

§§ 15, 16. *Joshua and Judges*

§ 15. THE BOOK OF JOSHUA

LITERATURE: In general the same as for the Pentateuch or Hexateuch. Special treatises: J. S. Black, *The Book of J.*, 1891; J. Hollenberg, *Die deuteronomischen Bestandteile des Buches Josua* (*St. Kr.*, xlvii. 462 ff., 1874), and *Die alexandrinische Uebersetzung des Buches Josua*, 1876, and *Zur Textkritik des Buches Josua und des Buches der Richter* (*Z.A.T.W.*, i. 27 ff., 1881); K. Budde, *Richter und Josua* (*Z.A.T.W.*, vii. 93 ff., 1887); E. Albers, *Die Quellenberichte in Josua i.–xii*, 1891.

1. *The contents of the Book of Joshua* form the necessary development and completion of the Pentateuch. No historical narrative could break off with the death of Moses and leave Israel standing on the threshold of the Promised Land; that Jahve really did lead the people into the land which He had sworn to give to their fathers, and to reach which they had striven through a long, toilsome, and painful desert-march, is the indispensable conclusion desiderated for the history of the patriarchs as well as of Moses. In accordance with its contents, the Book of Joshua is divisible into two sharply distinguished parts:

ch. i.–xii., the history of the conquest of Western Palestine, and ch. xiii.–xxiv., the history of the division of the conquered land and its settlement. Ch. i.: after the death of Moses, Joshua receives the divine command to cross the Jordan, makes all arrangements, and reminds the two and a half tribes whose land had been assigned on the east of Jordan of the promise given by them to Moses. Ch. ii.: Jericho having been reconnoitred by the spies, there follows in ch. iii. the wonderful passage of the Jordan, and, ch. iv., Israel takes up fixed quarters in Gilgal. Ch. v.: Joshua there circumcises the Israelites, keeps the Passover, and receives an apparition of the commander of the heavenly host. Ch. vi.: Jericho is miraculously taken, banned, and destroyed. Ch. vii.: Achan's sacrilegious offence against the ban, and its punishment. Ch. viii.: the conquest and destruction of Ai. An altar is erected on Ebal, and the law read. Ch. ix.: the crafty covenant of the Gibeonites with Israel. Ch. x.: battle at Gibeon. Marvellous victory over five kings of Southern Canaan, and conquest of the entire south. Ch. xi.: Jabin of Hazor and his allies defeated at the Sea of Merom, and the whole of Northern Palestine conquered. Ch. xii.: list of thirty-one kings *whom the children of Israel slew and whose land they conquered.* Ch. xiii.: Joshua is commissioned to apportion the land west of the Jordan among the nine and a half tribes. Next, the region assigned to the two and a half tribes east of the Jordan is exactly defined. Ch. xiv.: bestowal of Hebron upon Caleb. Ch. xv.: the district assigned to the tribe of Judah, of Ephraim (ch. xvi.) and Manasseh (ch. xvii.). Ch. xviii.: erection of the sanctuary at

Shiloh, and assembly therein. The rest of the land is surveyed, divided into seven portions, and allotted. The territory assigned to Benjamin. Ch. xix.: the territory assigned to Simeon, Zebulun, Issachar, Asher, Naphtali, and Dan. Joshua obtains Timnath-serah. Ch. xx.: appointment of six cities of refuge, and (ch. xxi.) of forty-eight levitical cities and their distribution among the individual families of the tribe of Levi. Concluding remark. Ch. xxii.: the East-Jordan tribes are dismissed. Dispute on account of the altar erected by them at the Jordan. Ch. xxiii.: exhortation of the aged Joshua to all Israel. Ch. xxiv.: meeting at Shechem. Farewell speech of Joshua and solemn engagement by the people to cling to Jahve. Joseph's bones buried in Shechem. Joshua and Eleazar die.

2. Such close relations existing between Joshua and the preceding books, we should expect *a priori* to find here again *in the Book of Joshua the same writers of documentary sources* who have so far narrated to us the history and fortunes of Israel, and this expectation is not doomed to disappointment. Joshua and the Pentateuch are so inseparably linked together that it is now for the most part customary to speak of a Hexateuch. Still, from a literary point of view, Joshua displays an essentially different physiognomy from that of the Pentateuch, and so it appears to be the only right course to consider the former as a whole by itself, and to regard Joshua more particularly as an appendix to it, and in developing this method to adduce only those points in which Joshua diverges from the Pentateuch. The divergence, in fact, arises from a difference in the

extent and degree to which the admixture of the sources has been carried, and from a different method employed in composing them; in such a book as this, where purely narrative sections alone are in question, where legislative passages—which in and by themselves offered fewer opportunities for redaction, and the content of which could hardly be called in question—were not present to resist the action of the editorial and literary forces at work, the revision of the material of the sources effected by the redactors resulted in nothing less than a new compilation, which obscures the process of detecting and separating the original elements. The analysis has to contend with far greater difficulties, and cannot therefore exhibit results which are as firmly assured as in the Pentateuch.

3. *In chapters i.-xii.* an especially striking feature is the almost complete withdrawal of P; only three fragments can be traced back with certainty to this source, viz. iv. 19, v. 10–12, and ix. 15*b*, 17–21, 27*a*, and only the last of these affords any ground for supposing that P also narrated in some detail the history of Joshua. With P, Rp also retires into the background; it has been supposed that the only clear trace of his work exists in iv. 13, where expressions characteristic of P occur; it is not easy to believe, however, that the whole verse was written directly by P, and the present form of ix. 23 and 27 certainly emanates from Rp; the remaining incidental traces of P's linguistic usage, such as אֲרוֹן הָעֵדוּת ("ark of the testimony"), iv. 16, or עַד־עֶצֶם הַיּוֹם הַזֶּה ("to this very day"), x. 27, may very well have slipped into the text later. Josh. i.-xii. in its whole character is through-

out rather marked by Deuteronomic features, and therefore to be traced back to Rd: Albers, Steuernagel, and Holzinger distinguish a double Deuteronomic redaction. At the outset ch. i., even though it rests on a basis derived from E, is specifically Deuteronomic, and in none of the eleven chapters immediately following is the Deuteronomic element absent, although it is not again so pronounced. The narrative itself everywhere bears traces of composition and compilation; these are especially clear in ch. iii., iv., vi., viii., and x., but also are evident in ch. ii., v., vii., ix., and xi. The distribution of the material to J and E, and perhaps even to J^2 and E^2, has not so far reached any generally recognised results, and if ch. xxiv. really should have stood originally in another position (*cf.* § 9, 5), that would be a fact of the greatest significance and importance in the question as to the separation of E in Josh. i.–xii. The important passage x. 12–14—important on account of its reference to the old ספר הישר ("Book of Jashar")[1]—is assigned with a fair amount of unanimity to J. In ch. xii. the question may be asked whether the enumeration of the vanquished kings is derived from Rd, or already comes out of J E, emanating perhaps from J^2; in its present form the chapter is essentially Deuteronomic in character. The noteworthy passage v. 13–15, which Kuenen reckons among the "younger sections," is by Albers and Holzinger claimed for J, by Steuernagel for E as an organic member in the body of the history of the conquest of Jericho. Ch. viii. 30–35 in its present form must be attributed to the youngest diorthosis of all (*cf.* § 9, 7).

[1] *Cf.* §§ 17, 12*b*, and 18, 2*a*.

4. *Chapters xiii.–xxiv.* so far display an essentially different character that P is here predominant, or at any rate reveals strong traces of his presence: in this section of the book, where such matters as number and arrangement, statistical enumerations and lists are in question, P was completely in his element. But it is not P exclusively who has specified the territories of the individual tribes, with their boundaries. It has been shown by Wellhausen that within ch. xiii.–xxi. there are traces of a representation which in some way is derived out of J E. These passages are as follows: xv. 4*b*, 12*b**, xvi. 1–3, xvii. 5, 8–9, 10*b*, xviii. 2–10; and further in the superscriptions xix. 1, 10, 17. In particular cases also confusion or overloading is often apparent, which suggests two accounts worked up together; ch. xvi. and xvii. especially are in such disorder that Wellhausen has assumed here the interference (by way of insertion) "of a hostile Samaritan redactor." As to the *provenance* of this second account of the allotment of the land which has been worked up into P nothing more definite and certain can be said: in any case it is pre-Deuteronomic, because the purely Deuteronomic passage xxiii. 4 (*cf.* also xiii. 6) clearly indicates an apportionment of the land west of the Jordan. On the other hand, some indubitable fragments of J have been preserved in these chapters which stand out against their context in the sharpest contrast, and produce an essentially different picture, on the whole, of the settlement of Canaan: ch. xiii. 13, xv. 13–19, 63, xvi. 10, xvii. 11–18, and xix. 47–48 LXX. To E xix. 49–50 can be traced back with a fair amount of certainty. The passage xiii. 21*b*–22, which glances

back to Numb. xxxi., was inserted quite late. In the same way, as may be inferred from the LXX., the "Deuteronomic additions" in ch. xx. belong to the latest diorthosis. In ch. xxii.–xxiv., xxiv., with the exception of some small Deuteronomic retouches, is certainly derived from E; xxii. 1–6 and xxiii. are purely Deuteronomic; xxii. 9–34 has P's manner, but is certainly to be attributed to P^x. P also, of course, must have given an account of the death of Joshua; possibly a trace of this written source is preserved in the statement of age given in xxiv. 29*b*.

5. *The Book of Joshua was disjoined from the Pentateuch* at a comparatively early period, in the case of P well before the time of Ezra (*cf.* Holzinger, "Pent.," 501). It is especially significant that Rp deals with P here with much greater freedom than in the Pentateuch: even in ch. xiii.–xxiv., where P plays a prominent part, he has remodelled the material and adapted the representation of the latter in accordance with J E, has transposed xviii. 1, which in P must have stood before xiv. 1, has altered the position of xvi. and xvii., and in xix. has either varied, or else altogether affixed, the ordinal numbers in the superscriptions. That Joshua subsequently underwent a process of development independently of the Pentateuch is shown by a number of textual differences. Thus, for example, the use of the form הוא in writing for the feminine as well as the masculine, which is regular in the Pentateuch, and also of הָאֵל for הָאֵלֶּה, which were formerly regarded as "archaisms," never occurs in Joshua. Some other differences have been collected by Kuenen (§ 16, 14). That the later diorthosis was at least as intensely active in Joshua

as in the Pentateuch is proved by the LXX.; on this point *cf.* Hollenberg.

§ 16. THE BOOK OF JUDGES

LITERATURE: *Commentaries:* G. Studer, 1842, 2nd ed.; E. Bertheau, *K.E.H.*, 1883, 2nd ed.; G. F. Moore, 1895; K. Budde, *K.H.C.A.T.*, 1897; W. Nowack, *H.K.A.T.*, 1902.
Monographs, Essays, etc.: B. Stade, *Zur Entstehungsgeschichte des vordeuteronomischen Richterbuches, Z.A.T.W.*, i. 339 ff., 1881; K. Budde, *Die Bücher Richter und Samuel, ihre Quellen und ihr Aufbau*, 1890; R. Kittel, *History of the Hebrews*, ii., 1896, § 30, and *Die pentateuchischen Urkunden in den Büchern Richter und Samuel, St. Kr.*, lxv. 44 ff., 1892; W. Frankenberg, *Die Komposition des deuteronomischen Richterbuches*, Diss., 1895 (on i. 1–ii. 5); E. Meyer, *Z.A.T.W.*, i. 167 ff., 1881: R. Kittel, *History of the Hebrews*, i. § 26. On ch. iii. 12–30: H. Winckler, *Alttestamentliche Untersuchungen*, 1892, 55 ff. On the Song of Deborah: G. Hilliger, 1867; A. Müller in *Königsberger Studien*, 1887, pp. 1–21; G. A. Cooke, *The History and Song of Deborah*, 1892; K. Niebuhr, *Versuch einer Rekonstellation des Deboraliedes*, 1893; H. Grimme, *Z.D.M.G.*, l. 572 ff., 1896; J. Marquart, *Fundamente israelitischer und judischer Geschichte*, 1896, 1–10; J. Ruben, *Jewish Quarterly Review*, x. 541–558, 1898; A. Segond, 1900; J. Rothstein, *Z.D.M.G.*, lvi. 175 ff., 437 ff., 697 ff., 1902, lvii. 81 ff., 344 ff., 1903. On ch. vi.–ix.: W. Böhme, *Z.A.T.W.*, v. 251 ff., 1885. On ch. xiv.–xv.: B. Stade, *Z.A.T.W.*, iv. 250 ff., 1884; A. van Doorninck, *Th. T.*, xxviii. 14 ff., 1894. On ch. xxi.: W. Böhme, *Z.A.T.W.*, v. 30 ff., 1885. On the chronology: Th. Nöldeke, *Untersuchungen* (*cf.* § 13, 7 above), pp. 173–198. On the criticism of the text: A. van Doorninck, *Bijdrage tot de tekstkritiek van Ri i.–xvi.*, 1879; J. Hollenberg, *Z.A.T.W.*, i. 97 ff., 1881 (*cf.* § 15 above); G. F. Moore, *S.B.O.T.*, 1900 (English transl., 1898). On the LXX. of Judg. i.–v., *cf.* P. de Lagarde, *Septuagintastudien*, i. 1–72, 1891.

1. Joshua is followed in our canon by a book which narrates the history of the people of Israel from the

THE BOOK OF JUDGES

death of Joshua to the birth of Samuel. It is designated "Book of Judges" (שֹׁפְטִים) according to the supporters of the developed historical tradition. Ch. i. gives a survey of the results of the conquest of Palestine, and specifies in particular all those parts of the land which Israel at first was unable to annex. Ch. ii. 1–5: the angel of Jahve blames them in consequence. Ch. ii. 6–iii. 6: the general characteristics of the whole period as one of regular alternation between apostasy, punishment by foreign foes, repentance, deliverance by a judge, and again apostasy. Ch. iii. 7–31: the history of Othniel, Ehud, and Shamgar. Ch. iv.–v.: Deborah and Barak. Ch. vi.–ix.: Gideon-Jerubbaal and his son Abimelech. Ch. x. 1–5: Tola and Jair. Ch. x. 6–xii. 7: Jephthah. Ch. xii. 8–15: Ibzan, Elon, Abdon. Ch. xiii.–xvi.: Samson. Ch. xvii.–xviii.: private sanctuary of Micah in the hill-country of Ephraim, and migration of the tribe of Dan from Zorah and Eshtaol to Dan. Ch. xix.–xxi.: outrage at Gibeah. Disciplinary measures against the tribe of Benjamin, and the tribe's rehabilitation.

2. There are thus *twelve men* who are the subjects of narrative in the Book of Judges, and with whose careers it deals in rather diverse fashion: in the case of several, detailed accounts are given, in other cases only brief notices, and so the distinction is made between "greater" and "minor" judges. They form, however, in this book a closely connected chronological series: one might almost say they follow one another in legitimate succession: the first, Othniel, is the son of a contemporary of Joshua; the twelfth, Samson, belongs to the time of the Philistine

domination, which was finally and completely shaken off by the exertions of the first two kings. That this enumeration of the judges as twelve has a close connexion with the coincident number of the tribes is a surmise that naturally suggests itself; for it cannot be regarded as accidental here that, with the exception of the priestly tribe of Levi, of the two tribes Reuben and Simeon which disappeared at an early period, and of the tribe of Asher, always quite insignificant, each tribe is represented by at least one judge: Judah by Othniel, Benjamin by Ehud, West-Manasseh by Gideon, East-Manasseh by Jair, Issachar by Tola, Zebulun by Elon, Naphtali by Barak, Ephraim by Abdon, Gad by Jephthah, and Dan by Samson.

3. If we regard the *Book of Judges as a literary production*, it will be seen that its real kernel is the history of the twelve judges, ch. iii. 7–xvi. 21. From this central portion, however, it is impossible to separate ch. ii. 6–iii. 6, for in this section we immediately recognise the introduction to the history of the judges: ii. 11–19 to some extent sets forth the programme the realisation of which the following narratives serve to illustrate. Now this passage is Deuteronomic in character through and through: its whole point of view and all its individual expressions are verifiable in Deut. and the sections dependent on it. When we examine the particular histories in their relation to this programme, we find that at the outset the first of the judges, Othniel, has been constructed entirely out of expressions and phrases derived from the introductory section; when we further reflect that the events here narrated are

absolutely impossible to have taken place in fact—the attempt of Graetz, approved by Klostermann, to explain the Mesopotamian Cushan-rishathaim of iii. 8, 10 as identifiable with the third Edomite[1] king, Chushan the Temanite, mentioned in Gen. xxxvi. 34, misses the point of the whole story, which consists in this, that it is the Judaean judge who accomplishes the greatest achievement of all—we are driven to the conclusion that the Deuteronomic author of the introductory section, who was certainly a Judaean, was himself the creator of the "model judge" Othniel, in order to get the tribe of Judah represented at the very beginning by a judge: the name and personality of the latter were provided by the ancient passage Josh. xv. 17; the Mesopotamian king "Negro of double-wickedness"[2] has been freely invented, in reliance on Gen. x. 8 (*cf.* also Jer. xiii. 23), and stands in the same category as מְרָתַיִם ("Land of *Double-rebellion*") as a name of Babylon in Jer. l. 21. As regards the rest of the judges, no trace of this Deuteronomic hand is visible in the case of Shamgar, Tola, Jair, Ibzan, Elon, and Abdon; in the case of the five greater judges, Ehud, Deborah-Barak, Gideon, Jephthah, and Samson, only at the beginning and end of the respective accounts: iii. 12–15, 30; iv. 1–3, 23–24; vi. 1–2*a*, 6*b*; viii. 28, 33–35; x. 6–8; xi. 33*b*; xii. 7; xiii. 1; xv. 20. Hence we may conclude that the author of the introductory section, whom we will call Rd, borrowed the five last-mentioned narratives from some other source, made them subservient to his theological pragmatism, and to some extent gave them a frame-

---

[1] אדם for ארם.   [2] = Cushan-rishathaim.

work and setting in the latter. Our next task, therefore, should be to explore the history of the five greater judges to its sources.

  4. The story of Ehud, the first great judge (iii. 12-30), is in itself entirely of a popular kind, and gives evidence throughout of the presence of genuinely old tradition. It offers many points of difficulty, which Winckler has attempted to remove by distributing it into two parallel accounts, that are not in entire agreement: but his solution has not met with general acceptance, and even the adherents of the two-source theory do not attempt a clear and precise separation of the material. On the other hand, the second great story in Judges, that of Deborah-Barak, is clearly composite. In this composite narrative the first element that detaches itself is the precious Song, v. 2–31a. This is indeed in parts very difficult and obscure, undoubtedly in consequence of textual corruption, but on the whole and as a whole is quite intelligible. In moving and brilliant poetical pictures it brings us into the midst of men and things, and makes us live through events to the accompaniment of fear and anxiety, of joy and triumph: at the same time it displays a number of quite special features such as only a contemporary and eye-witness of the events narrated could have known. This powerful and unalloyed poetical effusion obviously originated while the impression of the actual events was still fresh and vivid. The tradition which (vs. 1) makes Deborah in person the poetess rests, indeed, upon a misunderstanding of vs. 7, where the term שקמתי ("I arose") was without doubt originally intended for the 3rd pers. perf. fem., unless with Budde the whole

THE BOOK OF JUDGES 161

half-verse is to be struck out, as having itself originated out of the erroneous view mentioned. The "Song of Deborah"—it will keep this name notwithstanding—is the oldest and most important source we have for the history of the people of Israel: if it survived the centuries and was handed down orally, this fact in itself enables us to see how profound and ineradicable was the impression which the events here sung of made upon Israel. When we pass from the Song to the prose-narrative in ch. iv., which obviously purports to give an account of the same events, a whole series of differences at once strikes us. While, according to v. 15, both Deborah and Barak belong undoubtedly to the tribe of Issachar, in iv. 5 Deborah—no doubt through confusion with the similarly named nurse of Rebecca, Gen. xxxv. 8—is living at Bethel, in the hill-country of Ephraim, and Barak (iv. 6) at Kadesh-Naphtali. According to iv. 10 only Zebulun and Naphtali, according to v. 14-18, however, six tribes, viz. besides those already mentioned also Ephraim, Manasseh, Benjamin, and above all Issachar, fought the great decisive battle. Still more important, almost, is the difference in reference to Sisera: in the Song the latter is clearly the leading person and stands at the head of a coalition of kings of Canaan, while in ch. iv. he appears only as commander-in-chief of King Jabin of Hazor. Differences of secondary importance may here be left out of account. This King Jabin of Hazor, however, has a double in Josh. xi., where an account is given how the whole of Israel, under the leadership of Joshua, smote a King Jabin of Hazor and the North-Palestinian kings allied with him at the Sea of Merom, and destroyed Hazor—a fact which proves that an independent tradition about Jabin, having no connexion with Sisera at all, was extant. On a closer examination of Judg. iv. we notice obscurities and material impossibilities in the narrative, especially an inextricable confusion in the geographical data. All this leads us to suppose that in the chapter in question two accounts have been confused together which originally had nothing to do with one another: (1) a history of Jabin, according to which the tribes of Zebulun and Naphtali, under the leadership of a Barak of Kadesh-Naphtali, smote King Jabin of Hazor in the neighbourhood of that town, and by so doing ensured respect for their own tribal territory as against the Canaanites; Heber the Kenite also, who encamps at the oak Zaananim in Kadesh, belongs to this Jabin-tradition—the prosaic אֵשֶׁת חֶבֶר הַקֵּינִי ("wife of Heber the Kenite") of v. 24, which at the same time destroys the parallelism, to use A. Müller's words, is "a gloss as late as it is cheap," and unquestionably is to be struck out. This Jabin-history is not consistent with Josh. xi., is rather the original of the latter, and stands in exactly the same relation to it as Judg. i. 1–20 to Josh. x.: the achievements of individual tribes are magnified into the achievements of Israel as a whole. (2) A history of Sisera. Sisera, with 900 iron chariots, is smitten at Kishon by Israel under the leadership of Barak and Deborah, and in the flight killed by a woman. This narrative has many features which have not been derived from the Song, but give evidence of the existence of an independent tradition. On the number of the chariots I do not wish to lay any stress, but that Harosethhaggoyim is mentioned as the residence of Sisera, and that the Israelites should have delivered their attack from the ancient holy (Deut. xxxiii. 19) Mount Tabor, are assuredly points of the highest value and verisimilitude. Whether the difference regarding the manner of Sisera's death owes its origin to a misunderstanding of the Song may under these circumstances be doubted. The blending of the two accounts in Judg. iv. is so close that the task of detaching and restoring them to their original form is no longer possible of accomplishment: Rd had them before him already united in their present form. The possibility of such a blending and confusion is easily explicable from the similarity of the names of the two leaders, Barak of Kadesh-Naphtali and Barak of Issachar. The name is no longer verifiable elsewhere in the O.T., but was also current among the Carthaginians.

5. It has long been seen that the *history of Gideon* also is composed of two quite different individual accounts: ch. viii. 4–27 proceeds on altogether different premises from those of ch. vi. 2–viii. 3. According to viii. 4–27, the Midianite kings Zebah and Zalmunna (who had slain some brothers of his in an expedition) are pursued by Gideon, who crosses the Jordan with 300 yeomen of his clan Abiezer, bent upon exacting blood-revenge from them, and overtakes and captures them on the border of the Arabian desert; according to vi. 2–viii. 3, Gideon is designated by a divine call to be the deliverer of all Israel from the ravages of the regularly recurring Midianite inroads, falls on their camp on Mount Gilboa and scatters them in confusion, while the

Ephraimites, who have been summoned by him for that purpose, bar the fords of the Jordan to the fugitives, and capture and slay the two Midianite kings Oreb and Zeeb. Ch. vii. 25b and viii. 10b are harmonistic additions intended to bring the two accounts into accord. But the narrative in vi. 2–viii. 3 is itself not uniform in structure. In ch. vi. Budde was the first to recognise and distinguish as a younger narration vss. 7–10, 25–32, 36–40. The binding link between vss. 10 and 25 has been worked into vss. 11–24. As ch. vii. and viii. are clearly doublets —since Gideon's special act of deliverance both times consists in a night-surprise of the Midianite camp— the relation to this double narrative of the two accounts which have been united together in ch. vi. must be determined. Here ch. vii. shows itself throughout to be younger, ch. viii. more ancient, and therefore vii. 1–viii. 3 must be regarded as the continuation, united by vi. 33, of the younger narration, while the older main narrative vi. 2b–6a, 11–24†, 34 details the preliminary history to viii. 4–27. According to viii. 3, Gideon in the younger narration also only effected the act of deliverance with the aid of his clan Abiezer; consequently vi. 35 and vii. 2–8 are not to be looked upon as harmonistic adjustments of the two narratives, but as a younger accretion. In vii. 16–21 trumpets, pitchers, and torches carried in the hands of Gideon's warriors form an incredible combination. Winckler and Frankenberg independently of each other have solved these difficulties by the help of the narrative in viii. 4–27, which in vs. 11b gives a strikingly brief account of Gideon's special achievement: the 300 trumpets belong to ch. vii., and at the blast of these the enemy turn against and slaughter each other; the pitchers and torches belong to ch. viii. But the narrative in viii. 4–27 has not only suffered by such abbreviation in the process of being worked up into combination with ch. vi.–vii. Vss. 22 and 23, although they fit very well and naturally into the account, on material grounds arouse the gravest suspicions. According to ch. ix., Gideon, if not in name yet in fact, has assumed a royal overlordship; but while the repudiation of a human kingship as incompatible with the God-willed form of the theocracy is, it is true, demonstrably traceable as early as the time of the prophet Hosea, its occurrence in so entirely ancient a narrative as this would be exceedingly strange and bizarre. Vs. $27a\beta$ quite certainly contradicts the original tenor of the account, which can only have valued it highly, as a proof of Gideon's disinterestedness and piety, that he did not retain the captured gold for his own use, but devoted it to the purpose of an ephod, and thus sanctified Jahve. Altogether, the conclusion of ch. viii. offers still further stumbling-blocks. To Rd vss. 28 and 33–35 are certainly traceable, but they cannot be understood as forming a transition-passage to ch. ix.: viii. 33, it is admitted, is clearly derived from ix. 4, and viii. 35 coincides in substance with ix. (16–18), but not in such a way as to introduce but rather to take the place of it. The transition from viii. to ix. is formed rather by viii. 29–32. Here vs. 29 is singularly out of place on material grounds; after vs. 27 it follows in a suspiciously halting manner; Budde— rightly, without a doubt—regards it as the continuation and close of viii. 3. In vss. 30 and 33 we encounter expressions which belong decidedly to the language of P, and also other more recent phraseology: the explanation of such facts as these can best be discussed in considering Judges as a whole.

From the history of Gideon it is impossible to separate that of his son Abimelech, of which we have an account in ch. ix., one of the most valuable and precious relics of old Hebrew historiography that has come down to us. The chapter is by no means a literary unit, but is burdened with difficulties and obscurities. The pioneer-investigations of Winckler have here also helped on the two-source theory to victory, and furnished proof that both the Gideon-narratives were provided with a corresponding Abimelech-history. No trace of Rd occurs in ch. ix.

6. In the *history of Jephthah* (ch. x. 17–xii. 7) likewise inconsistencies and strange features in the substance of the narrative had long been remarked; but Holzinger[1] was the first to take up the two-source theory in connexion with it in earnest, and to distinguish two Jephthah-narratives. According to one, Jephthah was a fugitive in exile, summoned to Gilead to act as leader in freeing the land from the oppression of the Ammonites, which he succeeds in accomplishing: on the Ephraimites, when they would oppress Gilead, he inflicts a severe defeat. According to the other account, Jephthah lives at Mizpah in Gilead. In a war with the Moabites he himself suffers grievously, despatches an embassy to the Moabite king in vain, and then makes the fatal vow in case of securing victory: he actually vanquishes

[1] *Ap.* Budde, "K.H.C.A.T.," *cf.* the Preface.

the Moabites and absolves his vow by the sacrifice of his only child. The hand which worked up the two narratives together retains the victory over the Ammonites only, because successful struggles with the Moabites had already been fought by Ehud. In this way all difficulties are satisfactorily solved; but *cf.* on xi. 12–28 R. Smend in "Z.A.T.W.," xxii. 129 ff., 1902. The objection which has been raised from different sides against xii. 1–6 is groundless.

The *history of Samson* gives no grounds for suspicion. It is true ch. xiii. and xiv. have clearly been revised, but the whole story, at least as far as ch. xiv.–xvi. are concerned, is stamped throughout with a uniform character and is obviously the production of a single pen: to the question of the relation of xv. 20 to xvi. 31 it will be necessary to return later.

7. As the result of our investigation so far we obtain *a Deuteronomic Book of Judges* to which the following sections certainly belonged: the prologue ii. 11–19, followed by the histories of Othniel, Ehud, Deborah-Barak, Gideon, Jephthah, and Samson, and it is clear that this work forms the groundwork of Judges. The question now arises whether the "minor" judges occupied a place in this Deuteronomic historical work. It is at once obvious that the sections which deal with the five minor judges, ch. x. 1–5, xii. 8–15, were written by a single hand: we have already seen that no certain traces of Rd are present in them; above all the religious pragmatism of Rd, to which the greater judges have been subordinated, is absent. Further, it is to be observed that these minor judges immediately follow on

Abimelech, in the history of whom we were unable to discover any trace of Rd, for which, indeed, Rd has provided a substitute in the words (viii. 33-35) written by him. The chronology is altogether striking. By the side of its religious pragmatism the most distinctive feature in the Deuteronomic framework is the chronological scheme, rigorously followed throughout, which (in the case of the six judges certainly accepted by Rd) first of all details the years of the oppression from which the judge delivered Israel, and then the time for which Israel's freedom lasted : in the case of the first four this is given in the formula *And the land had rest . . . years*; in the case of Jephthah and Samson, *He judged Israel . . . years*. In the case of the minor judges, as to whom no information is given at all that they delivered Israel out of any particular danger, details as to the years of oppression are, of course, lacking: they only receive a notice as to their magisterial activity according to the formula *And he judged Israel . . . years.* That the chronology of Judges is an artificially adjusted one may be inferred from the fact that among the judges are included some who are certainly not historical personages, but personifications, *heroes eponymi* : the regular recurrence also of the numbers 20, 40, and 80 must arouse suspicion. The key to the whole chronological system is given by 1 Kings vi. 1, according to which between the Exodus from Egypt and the building of Solomon's Temple 480 years elapsed. These 480 years are made up of 12 times the number 40, which according to Hebrew ideas was the average age of a generation, so that in this way 12 generations intervene between the Exodus and the building of the Temple. And thereby the minor judges are made impossible for the chronological scheme. The 12 generations are composed of Moses, Joshua, Othniel, Ehud, Barak, Gideon, Jephthah, Samson, Eli, Samuel, Saul, David, so that no room is left for any further links. We are brought also to the same result by counting again the individual numbers given in each case: $40 + ? + 40 + 80 + 40 + 40 + 6 + 20 + 40 + 20 + ? + 40 = 366 + ?$ Added to this there are still to be reckoned the first 3 years of Solomon and the 71 years of oppression during the period of the judges, yielding a total of exactly 440 years; the 40 years still missing are to be divided between Joshua and Saul, about the length of whose official reigns we possess no direct information. That in the chronology of Judges, according to the view of the matter taken by Rd, the years of oppression are not included in the reckoning of the period of office in the case of the respective judges, but are to be counted separately, is shown by the case of Jephthah, where 6 years of office as judge stand side by side with 18 years of oppression. If, now, the numbers of the minor judges are included, in any case a total considerably too high results. It is one of Wellhausen's most brilliant observations to have detected that the number of the years of office in the case of the five minor judges ($23 + 22 + 7 + 10 + 8 = 70$) nearly coincides with the years of oppression in the case of the first five greater judges ($8 + 18 + 20 + 7 + 18 = 71$): the one missing year is furnished by assuming that the fourth year of Solomon was included in the reckoning. When all this is taken into account, it cannot be doubted that the five minor judges were inserted by way of supplement into the already complete scheme of the Deuteronomic Book of Judges, and take the place chronologically of its interregna: according to this view of the matter the years of foreign domination and of the usurper Abimelech, who received no call from Jahve, do not come into the reckoning. The object of the insertion of the five minor judges is quite clear: they were intended, as Abimelech, x. 1, is expressly reckoned in with them, to bring up the number of the judges to twelve. But it is now necessary to inquire: from what source has this post-Deuteronomic hand taken them? That the accounts here set forth are ancient, and (rightly interpreted) of high historic value, cannot be doubted; but on examining more closely the genealogies of Chronicles—certainly the youngest historical work of the O.T.—we shall find there a mass of isolated data of an antiquarian and genealogical character which show a remarkably close likeness with the notices of the minor judges; there is thus no guarantee that the sections in Judges referred to are of any great literary age. In reference to the selection of the five minor judges, it cannot well be accidental that three of them belong to just those tribes which had not so far been represented by a judge: viz. Tola–Issachar, Jair–East-Manasseh, and Elon–Zebulun; and it is from a similar consideration that I explain also the strange circumstance that in the case of the two remaining judges it is not the tribe but only the native place that is detailed, all the more strangely in the case of Ibzan, as there are two Bethlehems, and here it should have been stated

THE BOOK OF JUDGES

distinctly whether that in Judah or Zebulun was meant. But these two tribes (Judah and Zebulun) were already represented by Othniel and Elon; and as Abdon was buried at Pireathon in the land of Ephraim, he belongs to Ephraim, which tribe was likewise supposed, on the ground of the erroneous details given in iv. 5, to be represented by Deborah. By no means all the questions which meet us in connexion with the minor judges are thus, indeed, disposed of—their sequence and position in Judges are not explained, nor the calculation of their years of office, which produce here a particularly natural and "historical" impression. With thus much, however, we must be content.

The account of Shamgar (iii. 31), which undoubtedly comes from another hand, has intentionally been left out of the present discussion.

8. We must now attempt to settle the question of *the nature and origin of the sources used by Rd.* It is natural to think at once in such a connexion of the sources of the Pentateuch. After the precedent set by J. J. Stählein [1] as long ago as 1843, Schrader, in De Wette ("Einleitung," 8th ed.), made the attempt to distribute the material of the whole of Judges between the theocratic narrator E, the prophetic narrator J, and the Deuteronomist, and incidentally adduced many excellent observations and striking parallels. That E at any rate intended to continue the historical narrative beyond Joshua may be inferred from the whole tenor of the farewell discourse of Joshua, which all through points onward

[1] "Untersuchungen über den Pentateuch, die Bücher Josua, Richter, Samuels und der Könige."

to the future, and would also suggest itself even more distinctly from Josh. xxiv. 21 = Judg. ii. 7, if only this verse belonged to the original material of E ; but the circumstance that it occupies a different position in the LXX. at once awakens suspicion, besides which it is purely Deuteronomic in character, being a continuation of the Deuteronomic accretion at the end of Judg. ii. 6 compared with Josh. xxiv. 28, and descended from Judges to Joshua. Investigation on this point has rather fastened on a passage which so far we have not discussed, viz. i. 1–ii. 5. This shows itself to be an immediate continuation of Josh. xxiv. ; but on closer inspection it is clear that it forms a parallel to the narratives of the Book of Joshua, in which the course of the conquest and settlement of West Palestine are exhibited in an essentially different manner from that in the latter book, namely, as effected by individual tribes issuing from the common camp at Gilgal. Now E. Meyer has shown convincingly that this passage—with the exception of some revision and the later addition ii. 1b – 5, already recognised as such by Wellhausen—originates from J, and further, that this written source is a continuation of the original elements of ii. 23–iii. 3 : if, however, J narrated that Jahve did not hastily drive out the Canaanites before Israel in order that Israel might learn the art of waging war from them and at their expense, he must also certainly have narrated a corresponding history of the actual conflicts, and this can only be preserved to us in Judges. The presence of his hand in vi. 11–24 and xiii. 2–24 was clearly demonstrated subsequently by Böhme, after Stade had already pointed out the close connexion of the first Gideon-account with the history of Samson. The case is similar with E. Of this author also a clear trace has been discovered by E. Meyer in ii. 22, where the Canaanites are represented not to have been exterminated completely by Joshua for this reason, to *prove Israel*, whether they remain true to Jahve's commandments. Still more important is the result arrived at by Stade, that in the remarkable passage x. 6–16 likewise unmistakable fragments of E are present, which Budde has distinguished as two transition-passages, worked up together, the one intended to introduce a history of the Ammonite, the other of the Philistine oppression (*cf.* § 17, 4); they already display altogether the theological pragmatism of Rd, which therefore, in the last resort, is derived from E. The two-source theory having triumphed along the whole line, the histories of the greater judges must, in consequence, be distributed between J and E; to J the following belong: ch. i.†, ii. 1*a* (according to the LXX. with the reading *Bethel* instead of בֹּכִים [" Bochim " = " weepers "]; that the Hebrew text at a comparatively late date understood Bethel as the place of this weeping assembly is proved by the secondary and late composition ch. xx. and xxi., where the repeated tearful assemblages at Bethel are borrowed and repeated from ii. 1–5), 5*b*, 23*a*, iii. 2–3, the main narrative of the Ehud-story; the narrative of Jabin worked into ch. iv.; the main narrative in vi. and viii. 4–27, as well as a history of Abimelech; the narrative about the Ammonites in xi. and xii. 1–6; and finally the history of Samson. To E the following belong: i. 1*aa*, ii. 13, 20–22*a*,

iii. 5–6, a history of Ehud; the history of Sisera worked into iv., in which connexion I call attention to the marvellous character of the victory in iv. 15, compared with Josh. x. 10 and 1 Sam. vii. 10 (in all three passages notice the phrase וַיָּהָם יהוה, "and J. discomfited"); the Song of Deborah, which only E can have contained; the younger narration in vi., vii. 1–viii. 3†, viii. 29, as well as a history of Abimelech with a transitional introduction in x. 6–16, which must then, of course, have had Moabites instead of Ammonites; and the history of Jephthah, with the victory over Moab and the sacrifice of the daughter.

9. Before we consider the origin of Judges as a whole, we must discuss the remarkable appendix in ch. xvii.–xxi. The two narratives united in this composition nowhere show any trace of Rd, their chronology is not particularly defined, but in the observation, recurring four times (xvii. 6, xviii. 1, xix. 1, xxi. 25), that *in those days there was no king in Israel* the period of the judges is expressly indicated. From this purely redactional formula— in which we must, with Kuenen, recognise a pre-exilic hand — it necessarily follows that in these chapters we are on comparatively old ground, and the narrative without the slightest doubt belongs to the most precious and ancient of the accounts of the history of Israel that have been preserved to us.

As long ago as 1835 Vatke[1] (p. 268, remark) realised "that this section contains two narratives contradicting each other in details," and Budde later

---

[1] *Cf.* § 2, 5 above.

THE BOOK OF JUDGES 175

attempted to separate them completely, although, owing to the close union and intimate relation of the two accounts, it is no longer possible to effect this with certainty. According to one of these, the Ephraimite Micah prepared for himself an ephod and teraphim, and hired a Levite to be *a father and a priest*; the latter is persuaded by 600 Danites to accompany them and be their *father and priest*. After this Laish is conquered, and Micah's idol is set up there to form the tribal sanctuary. According to the other version, Micah made himself a *pesel* ("graven image") and *masseka* ("molten image"), and hired a young Levite as priest, whom he regards as a son. The Danites steal *pesel* and *masseka*, and prevail on Jonathan, a descendant of Moses, to be their tribal priest, and in his family the priestly office in Dan descends. The former of these accounts is assigned by Budde with certainty to E; in the second there is at least nothing that would absolutely preclude its being derived from J.

Matters are much more involved in the case of the second complete narrative of the appendix, ch. xix.–xxi., which must still be described as an unsolved riddle. Here indeed literary difficulties are also present no less than those concerned with real criticism. That the tribe of Benjamin had been almost wholly destroyed in the time of the judges, in view of the fact it was the first to give Israel a national monarchy, is inconceivable; the manner in which Israel appears and acts in ch. xx. and xxi. as *a community* is unexampled in really old tradition. Further, there is the fact that in the two chapters just mentioned expressions unmistakably belonging to the Priestly Code occur, and indeed the whole narrative throughout exhibits the manner of the stories in P^x (such as Numb. xxxi.) and Chronicles. Wellhausen, moreover, has pertinently directed attention to the remarkable points of contact it shows with the story of the origin of the Benjamite kingdom: the outrage takes place at Gibeah, the town of Saul; the fatally outraged concubine comes from Bethlehem, the city of David; the town of Jabesh-Gilead, by the rescue of which Saul wins for himself the crown, is banned; and Shiloh also, the central sanctuary of the pre-monarchical period, plays an important rôle: the parallelism of Judg. xix. 29 with 1 Sam. xi. 7 is obvious. So Wellhausen believes that in the formation of this story "Judaean hatred against the hegemony of Benjamin in the pre-Davidic period has played a part." But to look upon it as being altogether a later invention does not seem possible. Moreover, in ch. xix. especially the picture is too well drawn and original to be so regarded; xx. 3b–10 and xxi. 15–23 give the impression of being ancient, and the passages Hos. ix. 9 and x. 9 cannot be rejected *a limine*: further, we have seen that the redactional formula by which this section is bound together with ch. xvii.–xviii. must be pre-exilic. As the narrative shows clear indications of a composite character, the question may be asked whether it is not possible in some way to extract an older kernel from it. In ch. xix. Budde has distinguished two thoroughly old accounts, which indeed have been largely revised; one disappears from vs. 16 onwards; in the case of the main account a good deal argues for its being derived from J. In ch. xx. and

xxi. the assembly at Mizpah is an old feature, as also is the triumph over Gibeah and Benjamin by stratagem, and the restoration of the tribe by the allowance of the rape of maidens at the harvest-festival in Shiloh, while all the rest belongs to an altogether later version, which is clearly dependent on P. If, however, an older kernel underlies the narrative, there is much that favours the view of Nöldeke, mentioned by Budde, which "regards this narrative as the precipitate of Benjamin's ruin by the war between David and the son of Saul, and its resurrection in the reign of David."

10. In considering the question of *the origin of the Book of Judges in its present form*, we have to distinguish three principal stages, which run completely parallel with the stages which mark the development of the Pentateuch: these are:

(*a*) The union of J and E by Rj. The latter has added in i. 1–ii. 5, in order to harmonise the account with E, ii. 1*b*–5*a*; from him originate ii. 20–iii. 6 in its present form, the union of J and E in the history of the greater judges, as well as the present form of xvii.–xviii., and of xix. substantially, especially the redactional remark, which binds the two accounts together, xvii. 6 with parallels. From him also will be derived the time-sequence of the five greater judges, and the direct junction of xvii.–xviii. on to xvi., so that, with the exception of the Deuteronomic framework with Othniel, and of the six minor judges and some little revision which is quite late, our present Book of Judges lay substantially complete before Rj.

(*b*) Then out of this material Rd produced his

Deuteronomic Book of Judges. He subordinated the substance of it to his theological pragmatism, which already had its prototype in E, and more especially removed those narrative-portions which were not compatible with it. In this way he eliminated i. 1–ii. 5 and xvii.–xxi., further the story of Abimelech, and, as Budde has inferred very acutely from the presence of the Deuteronomic framework in xv. 20, also the conclusion of the Samson-story. The union of the book with what precedes he effected by taking over the account of the death of Joshua, ii. 6–9. The insertion of vi. 35 and vii. 2–8 may already have been brought about by him. Above all, however, he is responsible for the addition of the rigorously and consistently applied chronological scheme. His work thus consisted of ii. 6–19†, iii. 7–30, iv. 1–viii. 29, viii. 33–35, and his share (no longer definitely ascertainable) in x. 6–16, xi. 1–xxi. 7, and xiii.–xv. To predicate a double Deuteronomic redaction, of which the first was only a meagre revision of the work of Rj, and which left but few traces behind (Budde), does not seem to me necessary.

(c) This Deuteronomic Book of Judges was then enlarged, principally from the work of Rj, by a later hand dependent on P, whom we therefore term Rp, and who added from this source all the passages which had been rejected by Rd, not without some occasional interpolations of his own. The first trace of Rp's handiwork can be detected in the phrase נֶאֶסְפוּ אֶל־אֲבוֹתָיו ("were gathered to their fathers"), ii. 10; he also wrote viii. 30–32, in x. 6–16 has amalgamated the framework of Rd with elements derived from E, wrote x. 17–18, and revised xi. 1–2; from him likewise certainly originates the final form of xix.–xxi. More especially he has brought up the number of the judges to twelve, having appended the five minor judges in x. and xii., and fitted them into the completed chronological scheme of Rd in the manner above described.

(d) But the work of Rp did not bring the Book of Judges to a complete end. Later, exception was taken to the fact that Abimelech had been counted among the judges; in order to remove this objection, while still retaining the number twelve complete, the last hand of all added in iii. 31 the judge who owes his origin to a misunderstanding of v. 6— Shamgar ben Anath—who stands altogether outside the purview both of Rd and Rp, and must therefore, in spite of the characteristic notice about him, be regarded as a very late addition to the already completed Book of Judges; and this conclusion is confirmed by the fact that in the LXX. his position was subsequent to xvi. 31.

Special Introduction

CHAPTER VIII

BOOK I.—HISTORICAL BOOKS—*continued*

§§ 17, 18. Samuel and Kings

§ 17. THE BOOKS OF SAMUEL

LITERATURE: *Commentaries*: O. Thenius, *K.E.H.*, 1864, 2nd ed.; M. Loehr, 1898, 3rd ed.; H. P. Smith, 1899; K. Budde, *K.H.C.A.T.*, 1902; W. Nowack, *H.K.A.T.*, 1902.
Monographs and Essays: On i., ii. 1–10, P. Haupt, *Z.D.M.G.*, lviii. 617 ff., 1904. On the criticism of the sources: C. H. Cornill, *Z.W.L.*, vi., 113 ff., 1885, and *Königsberger Studien*, 1887, 25–59, and *Z.A.T.W.*, x. 96 ff., 1890; K. Budde, as cited in § 16 above, and *Z.A.T.W.*, viii. 123 ff., 1888; R. Kittel, *History of the Hebrews*, ii. § 31, and *St. Kr.*, lxv. 44 ff., 1892 (*cf.* also § 16 above).
On the criticism of the text: J. Wellhausen, *Der Text der Bücher Samuelis*, 1871; A. Klostermann, *S.Z.*, 1887; S. R. Driver, *Notes on the Hebrew Text of the Books of Samuel*, 1890; E. Nestle, *Marginalien und Materialen*, 1893, pp. 13–23; K. Budde, *S.B.O.T.*, 1894.

1. Judges is followed in the Hebrew canon by the *Book of Samuel*, so called after the "King-maker" Samuel: the Hebrew canon reckons it as one book. The LXX. comprehends it with the following Book of Kings under the general title βασιλειῶν, *i.e.* history of the period of the kings, and divides this large work into four books. By means of the LXX. and Vulgate

this division—which in the case of Samuel may be termed a natural and happy one—came to be generally adopted in the Christian Church, and since the appearance of the great Bomberg Bible of 1517 it has also been followed in the printed editions of the Hebrew text.

Contents of 1 and 2 Samuel

Bk. i. ch. i.–iii., history of Samuel's youth; iv.–vii. 1, disastrous battle at Ebenezer: capture of the Ark of the Covenant by the Philistines, and its further fortunes; vii. 2–17, Samuel's marvellous victory by prayer over the Philistines: he judges the whole of Israel all the days of his life; viii.–x., the elders demand from Samuel a king: the Benjamite Saul, who had become accidentally known to him, is chosen in Mizpah by sacred lot, and proclaimed; xi., a deed of deliverance accomplished against the Ammonites, and renewal of the kingdom; xii., Samuel solemnly resigns the office of judge; xiii.–xiv., the first Philistine war, and survey of the achievements and family of Saul; xv., war against Amalek, and rejection of Saul by Samuel; xvi., David, anointed by Samuel, comes from Bethlehem to the court of Saul; xvii., combat with Goliath; xviii.–xx., David's relations with Saul, Jonathan, and Michal; he finally takes to flight; xxi., David with Abimelech in Nob, and with Achish in Gath; xxii., David in Judah as leader of a band of 400 men: punishment of the priesthood of Nob; xxiii., David in Keilah: the wilderness of Ziph: David betrayed by the Ziphites, and only saved by an inroad of the Philistines; xxiv., David spares Saul's life in the cave of Engedi; xxv., David with

Nabal and Abigail; xxvi., betrayed by the Ziphites, he spares Saul's life; xxvii., he escapes to the Philistine king Achish of Gath, who assigns him the town of Ziklag; xxviii., war between Israel and the Philistines: witch of Endor; xxix.–xxx., David, sent away by the lords of the Philistines, avenges on the Amalekites the plundering of Ziklag; xxxi., battle on Mount Gilboa: death of Saul.

Bk. ii. ch. i., David learns of Saul's death: lamentation over Saul and Jonathan; ii., David at Hebron tribal king of Judah: Ishbaal, Saul's surviving son, is raised to the throne by Abner in Mahanaim: conflicts between Ishbaal and David: victory of Joab over Abner at the pool of Gibeon; iii., David's family at Hebron: Abner deserts Ishbaal, comes over to David, and is murdered by Joab; iv., Ishbaal murdered; v., David king over all Israel: captures Jerusalem: further family accounts: victories over the Philistines; vi., transference of the Ark of the Covenant to Jerusalem; vii., David wishes to build a temple: oracle of Nathan regarding the eternal duration of the House of David; viii., survey of David's military exploits, and state officials; ix., Jonathan's son Meribaal; x.–xii., Syro-Ammonite war, and David's grave lapse into sin; xiii., Amnon and Tamar: Absalom murders Amnon and flees; xiv., Absalom recalled; xv.–xviii., Absalom's rebellion and end; xix., return of David to Jerusalem. Contention between Judah and Israel; xx., rebellion of the Benjamite Sheba ben Bichri: list of ministers; xxi. 1–14, Gibeon and the seven sons of Saul; vss. 15–22, particular exploits during the Philistine wars; xxii. = Ps. xviii.; xxiii. 1–7, David's last words; vss.

8–39, list of David's heroes; xxiv., numbering of the people and pestilence: altar on the threshing-floor of Araunah.

1 Samuel i.–xv.

2. 1 Sam. xv. forms a turning-point in the subject-matter: the history of Saul, so far as he alone is concerned, is at an end. God has abandoned him, and a successor appears on the scene. It has long been recognised that in 1 Sam. i.–xv. it is not a uniform narrative but a combination of different accounts that comes to view; the guiding principle for threading the labyrinth was long ago discovered by Gramberg, but it is due to Wellhausen's incisive and far-reaching criticism that it has become a commonplace of Biblical science that the passages ix. 1–x. 16, xi., xiii.–xiv. are to be separated from their context and regarded as a closely knit narrative, in fact *the oldest narrative* extant about the origin of the Israelitish monarchy; especially important is the proof that, in spite of some inconsistency in the representation of Saul given in these chapters (in ix. he appears as a dependent son of the family, in xi. and xiii. as a fully equipped warrior, and father of a heroic son), xi. 1 (or more exactly x. 27*b*, as in the LXX.) forms the continuation of x. 16. As the result of an accidental meeting with the seer Samuel, the Benjamite Saul, prompted by him, summons, a month later, a levy *en masse* of Israel for the relief of the town of Jabesh-Gilead, besieged by the Ammonites, and, after gaining a victory, is proclaimed king in Gilgal by the acclamations of the exultant people; he thereupon immediately prosecutes the war against

the hereditary foe, the Philistines, in order to free Israel from the yoke of these uncircumcised, which weighs heavily upon them: this war, waged with varying fortunes, occupies the principal part of Saul's life and reign. In this account xiii. 19–23 primarily is to be regarded as a legendary embellishment. With a people so entirely destitute of arms Saul could not have relieved Jabesh nor have been able to fight the battle of Michmash, and further, xiii. 23 is the immediate continuation of vs. 18. In the same way xiii. 1—a verse which in its traditional form is quite meaningless—is a later insertion; it is lacking in the LXX.: it was intended to fit Saul into the chronological scheme applied by Rd in Judges, although no clear recollection of the age and length of reign of this first king of Israel any longer remained. More important, however, is the passage xiii. 7*b*–15*a*, which likewise shows itself to be not original, and most grievously disturbs the inner connexion of the narrative with which we are concerned; with it also must be removed a verse which prepares the way for it—x. 8—and which stands equally out of relation with its context. Here, however, we have to deal not with a mere embellishment, but with a formal correction of the original narrative. In its main features xv. is similar; there also it is at Gilgal, on the occasion of a sacrifice, that his rejection by God is announced to Saul through Samuel; but in details the two narratives fundamentally diverge to such an extent that xiii. 7*b*–15*a* cannot be regarded as a secondary composition due to imitation of xv.; in it we must recognise rather a self-contained parallel tradition, not dependent on the latter, the insertion of which Budde rightly attributes to the special history of the oldest source.¹ Ch. xi. 8*b* is also shown to be a later addition by the enormous numbers given ; the original writer may, however, have given a probable estimate of the numbers. In the same way ix. 9 is purely a gloss, which, moreover, would be expected properly to follow vs. 11.

3. What remains, after separating these passages, in ch. i.–xv. appears to form a connected whole, which is plainly distinguished from the stratum just discussed, especially by this fact, that Samuel occupies the centre of interest and is the principal figure. Ch. i.–iii. narrate the story of his youth, and how he comes to the sanctuary at Shiloh ; the priestly family of Eli there installed is godless and vicious, and on this account its ruin is announced. The fulfilment of this is recounted in ch. iv., which was united in the closest way with ch. iii. by a transitional introduction, still extant in the LXX. ; ch. v.–vii. depict the wonderful events connected with the Ark of the Covenant, when it had been captured by the Philistines. After its retrocession Israel returns to Jahve, and Samuel gains a wonderful victory by prayer over the Philistines, which breaks their supremacy, and then judges Israel. But when the prophet grows old Israel demands a king, whom Samuel gives them by lot, and thereupon solemnly resigns his office of judge. Meanwhile the newly appointed king at the outset does not stand the first test of obedience, and therefore Samuel announces to

¹ Budde regards xiii. 7*b*–15*a* as an addition to the Judaic document (= J²), to the main body of which (J¹) the oldest account of the origin of the kingship belongs.—Tr.

him his rejection by God. Such is the narrative given to us in vii. 2–viii. 22, x. 17–27a, xii., xv. But the middle section, vii.–xii., creates difficulties. The history of Samuel's youth, which accredits him simply as a prophet, does not lead us at once to expect to find him here as judge; much more important, however, is the disagreement with respect to xv. In vii.–xii. the sharpest repudiation of human kingship is manifested, as being equivalent to apostasy from Jahve as the sole Ruler and King in Israel: no trace of such a view occurs in xv. Moreover, the Samuel of xv. is simply a prophet, who works only by his word and by the power of a personality sustained by the spirit of Jahve—a representation which agrees with i.–iii. Conversely, however, xv. 1 presupposes the anointing of Saul by Samuel, and the latter as the true founder of the kingdom; the author of xv. must thus have recounted the same circumstances as those detailed in viii. and x. 17–27a, only in another light and from another point of view. The choice of the king by means of the lot cast by Samuel, and the exultant greeting of the chosen one by the people (x. 19b–24, 26b, 27a), may be derived from him without further question, and he will be responsible for the elders approaching Samuel with the request for a king, as in viii. 4; between vii. 1 and viii. 4 he must have narrated the consequences of the unfortunate battle described in iv., and by this means have made clear the motive which induced the elders in their necessity to pray for a king as leader and emancipator: Wellhausen, by a comparison of Jer. xix. 3 and 1 Sam. iii. 11, and by referring to Jer. vii. 12–15, has made it highly probable that the prophet Jeremiah still read this now deleted passage in this place. E was shown by me to be the source of the last-named stratum of tradition, and this conclusion has been accepted and further developed by Budde; E certainly gave a recital of the anointing of Saul by Samuel in place of x. 22; it must have been struck out after x. 1 subsequent to the union of E with the older source. Beyond this, leaving out of account some slight occasional revision, iv. 18*b*, with the closely connected vs. 15, is an addition of the sort already spoken of in xiii. 1, and ii. 22*b*β (which is lacking in the LXX.) is a much later insertion, dependent on P^x: and this is the case above all in ii. 27–36; this purely Deuteronomic passage, which also destroys the entire effect of ch. iii., in vs. 25 clearly has Zadok in view, whom Solomon appointed in the place of the scion of Eli's house, Abiathar, while vs. 36 can best be explained from the circumstances which followed Josiah's reformation of the cultus. The subject of " Hannah's Song," ii. 1 – 10, will be discussed separately.

4. The source of vii., viii., and xii. still remains to be ascertained. As it rejects the principle of monarchy, this stratum of the narrative was regarded as embodying a Deuteronomic accretion, quite late and destitute of value. The proof first adduced by myself, against Wellhausen, Stade, and Kuenen, that vii.–xii.† form an independent parallel account, older than Jeremiah, who (Jer. xv. 1) clearly alludes to ch. vii. and xii. here, has won acceptance. It has been handed down to us in a form worked up into the narrative of E, and by the dominating position

it assigns to Samuel is also in substance connected in the closest possible way with E, who forms the necessary link between this account and the oldest stratum of tradition: the unknown seer of a remote country town in ch. ix. must first have become the celebrated and revered prophet of ch. i.–iii. and xv., before he could have grown to the proportions of the judge over all Israel. Afterwards it was convincingly proved by Budde that the literary form of this younger stratum throughout is marked by the characteristic features of E; it would therefore belong to E^2, and the older representation to E^1. To assign the whole of the history of Samuel in i.–xv. to E^2, as is now done by Budde, does not seem to me a possible course to accept; in xv. only the passage vss. 24–31—doubts as to which were first raised by Stade ("G.V.I.," i., 2nd ed., 221)—would fall to this source. On the other hand, I now feel compelled to recognise in vii.–xii. traces of E^1, as the latter must also, of course, have given an account of the origin of the monarchy; if vii.–xii. at least is to be assigned as a whole to E^2, it would be necessary with Loehr to distinguish vii. 2–viii. 9, x. 17–19a, viii. 11–22ba, x. 19c–24, xii., x. 25b–27 as the original form. Ch. vii. and xii., which altogether proceed from E^2, have to a considerable extent been retouched by a Deuteronomic hand, but with regard to the respective relationship in style and spirit of E^2 and Deuteronomy it is not possible with absolute certainty to set forth the exact distinction, and to separate between them. The union of this Elohistic history of Samuel with the Elohistic Book of Judges has been detected by Budde in the transitional introduction to the history of the Philistine oppression, which now exists in a worked-up form in Judg. x. 6–16 (*cf.* § 16, 8 above).

5. If all that remains in i.–xv. emanates from E, it is natural to think of J as the source for the older stratum of tradition in ix. 1–x. 16, xi., xiii., and xiv. That J must at least have recounted the history of the two first Israelitish kings may without ambiguity be deduced from Judg. xiii. 5, which directly refers to Saul, and also from Judg. iii. 2, which takes its standpoint on the assured position of power and authority that had been attained by David. This step forward has been taken by Budde. In that case xiii. 7*b*–15*a* and its pioneer-verse, x. 8, would have to be ascribed to J^2 or J^3, and the working up of this material, and its harmonistic accommodation to E, as it lies before us in its present form, would have to be assigned to a redactor Rj. In this process J and E did not remain intact. In E, out of regard to J, Rj has struck out the Elohistic account of the anointing of Saul by Samuel which followed x. 24, and in vs. 25 made some compensation for his proceeding by the addition of a few words, which are shown not to be following a source by the fact that they do not accord with viii. 11–18; they have been imitated, indeed, from Josh. xxiv. 26. Further, he has placed ch. xii., which originally must have followed immediately on x. 24 or 25, after xi., and perhaps disintegrated the choice of the king by lot into two incidents. In J the beginning is cut away, which must have introduced Samuel (*cf.* ix. 14) and also have given some account of Jonathan (*cf.* xiii. 2), and which formed the connexion with the history of Samson; a remnant of this is embedded in iv.–vi., where Stade (" G.V.I.," i.,

2nd ed., 201, remark 3) was the first to detect a double strand of narrative. In addition, ix. 2b seems to have been taken over from x. 23, and also the gloss ix. 9 was certainly written by Rj (*cf.* the phrase לְכוּ וְנֵלְכָה, "come let us go," with xi. 14), as well as the addition x. 16b (notice הַמְּלוּכָה, "the kingdom," as in x. 25, xi. 14). In xi. Rj's intervention is more far-reaching. Here, in the first place, Samuel has been inserted right through, and also the immense numbers in vs. 8b may be credited to Rj; more especially, however, he has inserted in its entirety vss. 12-14; vs. 12 harks back to x. 27a, vs. 13 is modelled on xiv. 45 (*cf.* also 2 Sam. xix. 25), while vs. 14 is a naïve harmonistic accommodation to x. 19-24, of the same character as Gen. xxvi. 15 and 18, Ex. xix. 23 Rj. But an important passage has still to be separated from the older narrative, viz. xiv. 47-51, which, although the events there narrated could not possibly be regarded as historical in the strict sense, yet hitherto has been accepted by all critics as following a source, and thus has proved an insuperable obstacle to the further following up of the narrative set forth in ch. ix.-xiv. In this connexion Budde was the first to point out that the wording of these verses accords throughout with that of the Deuteronomic framework; they have clearly been added by a later Deuteronomic hand, for whom Saul was only legitimate king until his rejection by God had been announced, which, in consequence of xiv. 46, was looked upon as having happened towards the end of his reign, and in this place it was desired to insert a final panegyric, as the king was after all the one who had been chosen by the holy lot and solemnly anointed by the great prophet. On the other hand, xiv. 52 is due to the source, and forms the immediate continuation of vs. 46 and the transitional introduction to the appearance of David: that a source should have narrated with such circumstantiality merely a fragment out of the history of Saul, and then have left off, is as improbable as it is impossible.

1 Samuel xvi.–2 Samuel viii.

6. Before we enter upon the analysis of the sources of this section, there is a preliminary question to settle which for the purposes of this discussion is of profound and far-reaching importance, viz. the question of the *relation of the Hebrew text in ch. xvii. and xviii.* to the LXX. As is well known, the LXX. in Samuel often very markedly diverges from the Hebrew text, which in many places has been handed down in an obviously corrupt and very bad condition. In the case of ch. xvii. and xviii. the divergence of the two recensions is especially marked. The LXX. presents this chapter in an essentially shortened form. In xvii. the following verses are not represented in the LXX.: vss. 12–31, 41, 50, in 51 the expression וַיִּשְׁלָפָהּ מִתַּעְרָהּ, 55–58; in xviiii., vss. 1–6aα, 8b, 10–11, 12b, 17–19, 21b, 26b, in 27 the expression וַיְמַלְאוּם לַמֶּלֶךְ, 20b–30 Now it cannot be denied that these passages stand in glaring contradiction and opposition to their context, and everywhere break the connexion, so that the supposition easily suggests itself that the LXX. may have resorted to a harmonistic criticism here and have struck out the offending passages on account of these disagreements. But I have shown ("Königsberger Studien," 25–30) that this solution of

the problem does not hold good. Many passages are wanting in the LXX. in cases where no reasonable ground for, or harmonistic interest in, their elimination is perceptible at all: in addition, the text of the LXX. gives an excellent and unbroken connexion which does not need the rejected passages for its elucidation either as a whole or in part—which, indeed, in xvii. 34 (where David not *is* but *was* his father's shepherd) directly contradicts them. As the most important point of all, there is further the additional fact that the passages that are wanting in the LXX. from the first word to the last stand in connexion among themselves and form a continuous narrative, so that no other explanation is possible than to recognise in them fragments of a further independent source-narrative which was worked up into the Hebrew recension, but found no acceptance in the Alexandrian: the cogency of this demonstration has been expressly acknowledged by Stade ("G.V.I.," i., 2nd ed., 226, remark).[1] When Budde objects that the reading in xvi. 19, which is also followed by the LXX., אֲשֶׁר בַּצֹּאן ("who is with the sheep"), can only be a harmonistic accommodation to ch. xvii. in the form it has in the Hebrew text, he overlooks xvi. 1–13 and 2 Sam. vii. 8, in which passages (also read by the LXX.) David similarly is summoned from the flock. A harper is also met with in the campaign described in 2 Kings iii. 15; and that two sources quite independent of each other should assign the reason of David's coming to Saul as due to his musical gift is thoroughly natural, as this obviously was a persistent feature in the Hebrew tradition: in the oldest passage

---

[1] *Cf.* also W. R. Smith, "O.T.J.C.," 2nd ed., additional note A, pp. 431–433.

where he is mentioned at all outside the historical books (Amos vi. 2) David still appears as a musician. Therefore, for the purpose of the critical analysis of the sources we can only deal with ch. xvii. and xviii. in the form handed down by the LXX.

7. On the basis of the results secured with respect to ch. i.–xv. we now proceed to the analysis of ch. xvi.–xxii. Here the connected passage xvi. 14–23 at once proves to be the immediate continuation of xiv. 12, and should therefore similarly be assigned to J: only the words אֲשֶׁר בַּצֹּאן ("who is with the sheep") are a harmonistic accommodation to another and younger tradition. On account of the fundamental disagreement between xvii. 39 and xvi. 18, 21, ch. xvii. and xviii. (LXX.) cannot be the continuation of xvi. 14–23, but must be connected with xv., *i.e.* with E; and their whole manner and diction argues in favour of this conclusion. In this case E must between xv. and xvii. have given an account narrating how David, on account of his musical gifts, was brought to the court of Saul, who had been stricken with melancholia. Ch. xix. 1–10*ba* forms the immediate continuation to ch. xviii.; here only vss. 2–3 and 7*a* are accommodations, and therefore to be separated from their context. The passage vss. 11–17 has been claimed by Budde for E in the same way, and to accept it as such would essentially simplify the analysis; but material and circumstantial considerations weigh too heavily in the opposite direction: as it does not fit into the connexion of the other sources, and both before and after ch. xx. is equally impossible, we must recognise in it a by-product of the tradition, As in the case of xix. 11–17, so also

the continuation in xix. 18–xx. 1a does not allow of being accommodated organically to either of the two main authorities. But while xix. 11–17 is marked by a thoroughly ancient and popular character, and is of inestimable value to us as a unique disclosure regarding the economy of the תְּרָפִים ("Teraphim"), in xix. 18 ff. we have merely a prophetic legend, entirely destitute of value, of the sort exemplified in 1 Kings xiii. or 2 Kings i. On the other hand, it connects with the passage xvi. 1–13, with which it shares the same lofty atmosphere and general character, and in particular has the common feature of the direct personal association of David with Saul. Side by side with xvi. 1–13, xix. 11–17, and xix. 18–xx. 1a the passage xxi. 11–16 ranges itself: its original object may have been to supplant and suppress the parallel narrative in xxvii. (Kuenen). Ch. xx. 1b–xxi. 1 disagrees with xvii.–xix. in all points, and, as it assumes that David is the regular domestic companion of the king, reverts to xvi. 21: the high antiquity of the whole narrative likewise argues its derivation from J, which in that case must have recounted between xvi. 23 and xx. 1b the same matter substantially as is now embodied in xvii.–xix.; a residuum may still survive in xviii. 6–8: there traces of amplification are perceptible, and if xxix. 5 is original, J also must have presented the ominous song of the women. Ch. xx. 40–42 has been rejected by Wellhausen on material and aesthetic grounds; similarly vs. 19a and the words וַיְהִי בַבֹּקֶר ("and it came to pass in the morning") in vs. 35 are to be struck out as attempts at assimilation with xix. 1–7, and vss. 4–17 have undoubtedly been revised. Ch. xxi. 2–10, on account of the mention of Goliath's sword, has without protest been claimed for E ; xxi. 2 is the immediate continua- of xix. 10*ba*. Ch. xxii., which diverges from xxi. 2–10 in not unimportant respects, on the other hand belongs to J ; but vs. 5 is a later addition, and in vss. 10 and 13 the appending of the sword is a harmonistic assimila- tion with xxi. 2–10. Only vs. 19, which verbally coincides with xv. 3, will have been taken from the account of E, which, of course, recounted so important a historic event as the execution of the descendants of Eli.

8. In ch. xxiii.–xxxi. the controversial problems are the relation of xxiii. 19–xxiv. 23 to xxvi., and the origin of the passage xxviii. 3–25. Ch. xxiii. 19–xxiv. 23 and xxvi. are obviously doublets, of which xxvi. throughout gives the impression of being the more ancient and original: if a passage from the beginning of ch. xxvi. has been worked up redactionally in its entirety into xxiii. 19–24 (Budde), everything in xxvi. would argue for its derivation from J, and xxiii. 19–xxiv. 23† would point to E. Ch. xxiv. 14 is rejected by Wellhausen as a gloss, and in vss. 5–8 it is necessary to effect a transposition, as follows: 5*a*, 7, 8*a*, 5*b*, 6, 8*b*. Ch. xxiii. 1–14*a* belongs substantially to J—according to Budde, however, it contains traces of a parallel account out of E ; xxiii. 14*b*–18 is an Elohistic parallel (drastically revised) to ch. xx. J. Ch. xxv.–xxxi. would exhibit a continuous and unbroken narrative out of J, if xxviii. 3–25 did not intrude in a highly disturbing fashion. Partly on this account, partly because the spirit which speaks in response to the exorcism is the spirit of the Samuel of ch. xv., it has

generally been ascribed to the author of xv.; but Budde has demonstrated the presence of J's style and phraseology right through, and has removed the last lingering doubt on this score by assuming that the passage, on account of Deut. xviii. 11, was sacrificed to the exigencies of the Deuteronomic redaction, and was later replaced, but unskilfully, out of its proper position: in view of the union of J and E which had then already taken place, some reference back to ch. xv. was unavoidable. In J the passage would stand naturally between xxx. and xxxi., and in favour of this is the somewhat fragmentary and obviously damaged beginning of xxxi.

That 2 Sam. i.–v. belongs to the same source is generally admitted; only iii. 2–5 and v. 4–16 will have stood originally in another place: iii. 6b is the immediate continuation of vs. 1, and v. 17 of v. 3; but the Chronicler must have read these chapters entirely in the form in which they now lie before us, and in particular ch. iii. with iii. 2–5 inserted, as appears clearly enough from 1 Chron. xiv. 3–7. Ch. ii. 10a, like 1 Sam. iv. 18a and xiii. 1, is an accommodation to the Deuteronomic chronological framework; both data are clearly erroneous, in fact; ii. 11 also comes in too early. In the same way iii. 30 gives rise to suspicion, and iv. 4 may originally have stood after ix. 3, so that iv. 4b followed immediately on ix. 3. The "Song of the Bow," i. 17–27, will be discussed separately. Only i. 1–16 is problematical; but the difficulties are resolved if, with Budde, we regard vss. 5–10 and 13–16 as transferred from the parallel account of E. Ch. vi. has been taken by Wellhausen in conjunction with ch. ix.–xx., and can therefore be passed by here without further observation. Ch. vii. both in style and phraseology so markedly diverges from all that precedes that it must be dealt with by itself. It clearly presupposes the present union of v. and vi., and in its content is penetrated through and through with a prophetic-messianic character, so that the question is, whether this chapter is the root of messianic prophecy or one of the latter's offshoots. Everything argues the latter alternative; it can hardly have been written before the time of Isaiah. On the other hand, the ruin of the nation and its dynasty lies altogether outside of its horizon, and so we shall assign this passage—which, vs. 13*b* having already been detected by Wellhausen to be an interpolation, must be pre-Deuteronomic—to the seventh century, and shall have to derive it from a younger Jahvistic or Elohistic (Budde) hand. Finally, ch. viii. produces the impression in all respects of being a concluding panegyric. In the form of a short statistical survey, David's military exploits and victories are mentioned, and at the end a list of his chief officers is given. It had long been remarked that in content this survey coincides substantially with x.-xii.; with this fact in view, ch. viii., regarded as belonging to a source, must again have presented an insuperable obstacle to the analysis. Budde, however, has now shown that this passage, like 1 Sam. xiv. 47-51, is the work of a redactor, originally intended to take the place of ch. ix.-xx., the contents of which it was thought well to suppress in the interests of David, exactly as Judg. viii. 33-35 was designed to take the place of the history of Abimelech. For the rest, ch. viii. is not to be set down at too late a date; it has at least utilised good old historic material: vss. 7-10, 13, 14a, and 16-18 may be regarded as following a source, and Wellhausen's conjecture that iii. 2-5 and v. 13-16 originally belonged to this context is very attractive; *cf.* in particular also viii. 18.

2 Samuel ix.–xxiv.

9. That ch. ix.–xx. are inseparably bound together and form a material and literary unit may be regarded as generally admitted: Wellhausen includes with this ch. vi. in addition. Now that the dividing barrier has been removed with ch. viii., nothing precludes this section being derived from the same hand as i.–v., *i.e.* from J. It forms the culminating point of Hebrew historiography: the characterisation of all the individual personalities is drawn with such marvellous psychological delicacy and consummate skill, the narrative is so clear and vivid, that the presence of an eye-witness suggests itself: Duhm has conjectured that the memoirs of the deposed priest Abiathar underlie this part of the history. But at any rate these chapters belong, so far as their literary features are concerned, to J, and in their traditional form were written down by him; and I will only indicate here a few significant expressions which regularly pervade all the material that is discriminated as belonging to J: *to find favour in the sight of*, 1 Sam. xvi. 22, xx. 3, 29, xxv. 8, xxvii. 5, 2 Sam. xiv. 22, xv. 25, xvi. 4; *to become stinking* ("be had in abomination with"), 1 Sam. xiii. 4, xxvii. 12, 2 Sam. x. 6, xvi. 21; the peculiar oath-formula, 1 Sam. xiv. 44, xx. 13, xxv. 22, 2 Sam. iii. 9, 35, xix. 14 (1 Kings ii. 23); *not*

one hair of the head shall fall to the ground, 1 Sam. xiv. 45, 2 Sam. xiv. 11 (1 Kings i. 52). These precious chapters, with the exception of some small amount of revision, have survived substantially intact. Ch. xii. 10-12 gives the impression of having been inserted later, in order to bring out in clearer definition the pragmatic coherence of the narrative; Schwally ("Z.A.T.W.," xii. 153 ff., 1892) regards the whole passage xii. 1-15*a* as "having been interpolated . . . into the old source," and xii. 15*b* would certainly quite appropriately join on to xi. 27 without a break. Doubts of a historical character have been expressed by Winckler ("Geschichte Isr. in Einzeldarstellungen," i. 139-144, 1895) regarding x. 15-19*a*.

10. Ch. xxi.-xxiv. occupy a peculiar position in every respect, somewhat analogous to that of the supplements in Judges. But while in the latter the connexion is still of too close a character for the interposition of the supplements to prove embarrassing, in this case, on the other hand, 1 Kings i. 1 forms the immediate continuation of 2 Sam. xx. 26, and even is derived, as will appear, from the same source. Moreover, these four final chapters internally display many strange features. It is, for instance, quite clear that xxi. 1-14 closely connects with xxiv., xxi. 15-22 likewise with xxiii. 8-39, while the two poetic pieces which stand in the middle are themselves homogeneous. Thus a double interpolation has taken place in a section which is itself an interpolation. When we proceed to inquire as to the *provenance* of the individual passages, xxi. 1-14 is claimed by Budde —correctly, without a doubt—for J, and, judged by

its contents also, this narrative (in which only vs. 7 is an addition, and vs. 2*b* an interpolated explanatory remark) belongs to J; it is the preparation preliminary to introducing ix. 5, is clearly echoed in xvi. 7-8, and can only have occurred at the beginning of David's reign, when this crime of Saul's, which is not mentioned elsewhere, was still freshly remembered. Ch. xxiv. also belongs to the same period: the desire for a census of the people is most easily understood if it is referred to the beginning of David's reign over all Israel; and the erection of the altar on the threshing floor of Araunah, in my view, precedes the transference of the Ark of the Covenant to Mount Zion. But in its literary features xxiv. is not so simple; the narrative has at least been subjected to drastic revision, if it is not actually a fusion of two parallel accounts: a fundamental form of it in some shape may here be claimed as belonging to J. Ch. xxi. 15-22 and xxiii. 8-39 both in tone and contents exhibit striking points of contact with v. 17-25, and may actually have been the immediate continuation of v. 25; still, they at the same time have so many markedly peculiar features that the conjecture that an ancient book of heroes may have been utilised in their composition at any rate deserves consideration. The two poetical pieces will have to be dealt with separately. If, however, the prose supplements are also derived from J, their position between 2 Sam. xx. and 1 Kings i. is still more difficult to understand: it can only be explained with the aid of Budde's assumption that ch. ix.-xx. were cut out by a Deuteronomic hand and replaced by ch. viii. This same hand would then have retained the two narratives xxi. and xxiv., for the sake of their theocratic character, out of the old narrative material, and have inserted them as an important supplement to his concluding panegyric: the restorer of the rejected material allowed these chapters to remain at the end of the book, and inserted ix.–xx. between viii. and xxi. The addition of xxi. 15–22 and xxiii. 8–39 then represents a still later stage, that of the two poetical pieces the latest of all.

11. In this way, then, with the exception of the three poetical pieces, ch. vii. and viii., and isolated traces of E in ch. i., and perhaps also in ch. xxiv., the whole of 2 Sam. emanates from J, and we therefore obtain for Samuel a similar result as in Judges. With the exception of a small residuum, the contents can be apportioned between J and E, and in this connexion it is noteworthy that with the death of Saul E suddenly disappears, and thus Rj will be substantially the author of Samuel. The latter then experienced later much the same fortunes as Judges, only in this case the later developments cannot be so exactly shown as in the latter book, and, in particular, the Deuteronomic redaction has not been carried out so thoroughly as in Judges, because the matters dealt with in Samuel were too well known and too familiar to the popular consciousness to allow of any radical transformations being effected. Thus the work of Rd restricts itself to slight revision of particular passages, and to a very cautious extension of the chronological thread, and this redactor has only ventured to reject stumbling-blocks like 1 Sam. xxviii. 3–25, 2 Sam. ix.–xx., and perhaps also—as Budde infers from the absence in it of Deuteronomic

traces—1 Sam. xv.; these eliminated pieces—which, as in the case of Judges, are for us at once the most important and valuable—were subsequently by good fortune replaced by a later hand. A time-limit for the fixing of the present form of Samuel is furnished by Chronicles.

Poetical Pieces in the Books of Samuel

12. If we disregard the few short words in 2 Sam. iii. 33*b*, 34*a*, there occur in Samuel four independent poetical pieces, which require special discussion. These are:

(*a*) *The Song of Hannah*, 1 Sam. ii. 1–10.—This Song does not belong to the old contents of Samuel, for the LXX. exhibits it in a somewhat divergent form, and one that has been enlarged from Jer. ix. 22–23, while its equivalent of the words וַיִּשְׁתַּחוּ שָׁם לַיהוה ("and he worshipped J. there"), i. 28, is placed after ii. 10. It is a psalm, like other songs of the psalter, which only a literal interpretation of the metaphorical phrase in vs. 5 can have placed in the mouth of the mother of Samuel. The psalm, the literary character of which does not suggest an early date for its composition, clearly has one distich too many: consequently vs. 10*b* is explained for the most part—and this is the case even with Klostermann—as "a later embellishment" by which the king is got rid of; but the words, as forming a conclusion, cannot well be dispensed with, and it will be better to strike out the distich 8*b*, which is not read by the LXX., and which is not in harmony with the general tone of the Song as a whole and disturbs the connexion between vss. 8*a* and 9. The "king" in 10*b* is, of course, intended in a messianic sense; the possibility of the Song having originated in the period of the monarchy cannot seriously be taken into account.

(b) *The "Song of the Bow,"* 2 Sam. i. 19–27—a dirge over the death of Saul and Jonathan inspired by the deepest feeling, and especially in the reference to the personal loss of Jonathan of convincing psychological truth. The superscription, vss. 17–18, which has certainly suffered textual corruption, ascribes its composition to David, and appeals to the ancient collection of songs, which has already been cited in Josh. x. 13, known as the ספר הישר ("Book of Jashar"), which will come up for discussion definitely and finally in § 18, 2a below. There is not the slightest ground for doubting the authenticity of the Song—both external and internal criteria support it in the most decisive way—so that this poem is recognised even by "advanced" critics as being a genuine survival of David's poetic activity. The text is at many points corrupt, and the entire absence of religious motive is worthy of note.

(c) *2 Sam. xxii.*—a longer hymn which, with the exception of variants which all tradition necessarily involves, is identical with Ps. xviii. For this reason this poem, as being doubly attested, is widely regarded as the only certainly authentic psalm. But there can be no question of authenticity when it is remembered that specifically Deuteronomic expressions occur in it. Independently of each other, both Loehr and Budde simultaneously made the observation that the second half of this long poem is marked by a different character from that of the first, in which Loehr also considers vss. 8–16 to be interpolated. In the first part a pious devotee of the Law is the speaker, in the second a warlike king, who can only be understood to be either David or Alexander Jannaeus. The first half—which, according to Budde, extends to vs. 25, according to Loehr to vs. 31 (I also include in it vss. 26–29 and 31)—has the manner of a psalm with a representative character, in which the community gives expression to the hope that as a reward for its piety and devotion to the Law it will be delivered from all enemies and from all need. Budde thinks this poem, with the superadded inscription למנצח לעבד יהוה לדוד (Ps. xviii. 1, but not 2 Sam. xxii. 1; *cf.* also Ps. xxxvi. 1), stood in the psalter, was taken thence and by revision into its present form was accommodated to the situation required for 2 Sam. xxii., and in this form then found its way back into the psalter; but it seems to me easier to suppose that the first half was already in existence, but not yet admitted into the psalter, and that the whole poem was taken into the psalter from Samuel.

(*d*) *2 Sam. xxiii. 1–7*—the so-called *last words of David*, couched in sententious, enigmatic language. This piece also is an outcome of messianic thought, and is in no case older than Isaiah. The dependence of vs. 1 on the Balaam-oracles is obvious, and the eschatological ideas embodied in vss. 6–7 of a punishment of the godless by hell fire are first verifiable only at a quite late period. We must, therefore, recognise in these "words" a wholly recent מָשָׁל ("oracle"), artificially impressed with an archaic character, of which the author and time of composition naturally can no longer be ascertained. The "last words" were no doubt inserted in Samuel at the same time as the psalm, when xxi. 15–22 (in which an account of grave personal danger involving David is given for the last time) already occupied its present position: according to H. P. Smith they are to be regarded as forming a conscious counterpart to Deut. xxxii. and xxxiii.; *cf.* 2 Sam. xxii. 1 with Deut. xxxi. 30, and 2 Sam. xxiii. 1*a* with Deut. xxxiii. 1. From the absence of these two passages in Chronicles Budde infers that they were first inserted in Sam. after the time of the Chronicler, who in 1 Chron. xvi. only with great effort succeeds in compiling a Davidic psalm, and this conclusion must be accepted if 2 Sam. xxii. is really derived, even only as regards its groundwork, from the actually existent psalter: but this view is by no means yet placed beyond doubt, and the "psalm" above mentioned hardly stood in Chronicles from the very beginning; *cf.* § 41, 10 below.

§ 18. The Books of Kings

Literature : *Commentaries :* O. Thenius, *K.E.H.*, 1873, 2nd ed.; A. Klostermann, *S.Z.*, 1887; I. Benzinger, *K.H.C.A.T.*, 1899; R. Kittel, *H.K.A.T.*, 1900, and *History of the Hebrews*, 2 vols, 1895–6, §§ 32 and 51; C. F. Burney, *Notes on Heb. Text of Kings*, 1903.

Essays, Monographs, etc.: A series of essays of B. Stade in *Z.A.T.W.* on 1 K. v.–vii., vol. iii 129 ff., 1883; *cf.* also vol. xxi. 145 ff., 1901; on 1 K. xxii. 48 f., vol. v. 188, 1885; on 2 K. viii. 21–24, vol. xxi. 337 ff, 1901; on 2 K. x.–xiv., vol. v. 275 ff., 1885; on 2 K. xv.–xxi., vol. vi. 156 ff., 1886; F. Schwally, *Zur Quellenkritik der historischen Bücher*, *Z.A.T.W.*, xii. 157 ff., 1892 (on 1 K. vii. 41–45, xx. 13 ff., 30, xxii. 19–25); H. Winckler, *Beiträge zur Quellenscheidung der Königsbücher* in *alttestamentliche Untersuchungen*, 1892, 1–54 On the history of Elijah : G. Rösch, *St. Kr.*, lxv. 551 ff., 1892; H. Gunkel, *P. Jb.*, lxxxvii. 18 ff., 1897. On the chronology : J. Wellhausen, *Jd. Th.*, xx. 601 ff., 1875; A.

Kamphausen, *Z.A.T.W.*, iii. 193 ff., and *Die Chronologie der hebräischen Könige*, 1883; H. Winckler, *op. cit.*, 77-96; F. Rühl, *Deutsche Zeitschrift für Geschichtswissenschaft*, xii. 44 ff., 1894.

On the criticism of the text: B. Stade and F. Schwally, *S.B.O.T.*, 1904. On the LXX., J. Silberstein, *Z.A.T.W.*, xiii. 1 ff., 1893, xiv. 1 ff., 1894; A. Rahlfs, *Septuaginta-Studien*, 1 Heft, 1904.

1. Kings also is reckoned in the Hebrew canon as one book; in the LXX., on the other hand, as third and fourth βασιλειῶν; and all that was remarked above (§ 17, 1) in the case of Samuel holds good here.

1 K. i.–ii. gives a narrative of the last days of David, the complications about the succession, and Solomon's ascent of the throne. Ch. iii.–xi.: reign of Solomon. Ch. xii. 1–24: the division of the kingdom. 1 K. xii. 25–2 K. xvii. 6: history of Israel and Judah from the division of the kingdom to the downfall of Israel. 2 K. xvii. 7–41: concluding discussion as to the downfall of the kingdom of Israel, and notice concerning the further fortunes of the land. 2 K. xviii.–xxv.: history of Judah from the capture of Samaria to the destruction of Jerusalem and the Babylonian Exile.

Regarding the *first section*, 1 K. i.–ii., we can be very brief, because it clearly forms the immediate continuation and necessary conclusion of the history of David in 2 Sam., and is derived from the same author. Ch. ii. 27, containing a reference to the secondary passage 1 Sam. ii. 27–36, can only be a supplement, and ii. 1–9 must also be objected to: for vss. 2–4 are purely Deuteronomic in character, and strong reasons exist for supposing that vss. 5–9 also did not stand in ch. ii. from the first. Vss.

10–12 are the formal conclusion, as it occurs at the end of all the royal reigns in Kings.

2. In *chapters iii.–xi.* we can distinguish three strata: (*a*) A series of narratives and short notices which are obviously intended to subserve the glorification of Solomon, but yet do not conceal the shady side of his reign: we must proceed substantially on the basis they afford if we are to secure a picture of the real historical Solomon. These consist of the following: iv. 2–19 and v. 7–8, which form one connected passage; v. 16, 20, 22–25, 29–28; 31–32, vi. 37–38; a short account of Solomon's buildings; a short account of the consecration of the Temple, here more particularly in its original form consisting of viii. 2a and viii. 12–13 LXX.; ix. 11b–21, 24–27; x. 16–20, 28–29; xi. 7a, 14–28, 40; and here also we must add ch. iii.†, which indeed, as it stands at present, has in its first half been subjected to drastic revision. The most obvious course is to think of J as the source, for J's historical work can never have ended at ii. 46. Ch. viii. 12–13 points directly to J. The LXX. exhibits this passage in a somewhat divergent form after vs. 53, and concludes it with the words οὐκ ἰδοὺ αὕτη γέγραπται ἐν βιβλίῳ τῆς ᾠδῆς;[1] in which a scribal error of הַשִּׁיר for הַיָּשָׁר has been recognised. Thus here also the ספר הַיָּשָׁר ("Book of Jashar") would be cited, as in Josh. x. 11, 2 Sam. i. 16 J; and if besides David's "Song of the Bow" this unquestionably authentic utterance of Solomon on the consecration of the Temple also stood in this book, the conclusion is obvious that this collection of songs—whose title[2] is

---

[1] "Is it not written in the book of Song?"
[2] Herder explains it "Book of the Valiant" or "of the Heroes."

connected in some way with the name יְשֻׁרוּן ("Jeshurun") as a designation of Israel (*cf.* Numb. xxiii. 10) was a Judaean work of the time of the monarchy (*cf.* H. Franke, "Ueber Bedeutung, Inhalt und Alter des Sepher Hajjaschar," Diss., 1887).

(*b*) Embellishments of a more legendary character, which especially bring out into prominence Solomon's wisdom and riches: viz. iv. 20?, v. 2, 3, 6, 9–15, 21, 26, 29, 30; ix. 22, 23, 28; x. 1–15, 21–27; these passages also are undoubtedly of Judaic origin. (*c*) A Deuteronomic stratum, consisting partly of mere revision, partly of work of an independent character. Thus ch. iii. 1–15 and v. 17–19 have been subjected to drastic Deuteronomic revision, while viii. 15–53, Solomon's prayer at the consecration of the Temple (which will be discussed separately later), is purely Deuteronomic, and ix. 1–9 is a Deuteronomic parallel to iii. 5–14, clearly assuming its standpoint already in the Exile, and xi. 1–13, with the exception of vs. 7*a*, is also Deuteronomic in character. Ch. xi. 29–39, which intrudes in a disturbing manner into xi. 14–40—a section in other respects quite homogeneous —is in its present form decisively Deuteronomic, but seems to have made use of an older groundwork. Ch. xi. 41–44 constitutes the conclusion of the history of Solomon in set form such as the Book of Kings regularly employs to conclude the histories of all the kings: it will be necessary to return to this point later. In the chronological notice vs. 42 and the important verse vi. 1 we recognise the same hand which has manufactured the chronological framework in Judges and continued it through Samuel. Isolated traces of a post-Deuteronomic revision, dependent on

P, occur in viii. 1–11, and when in v. 4 (Heb. = iv. 24 E.V.) Solomon's empire is described as the *region beyond the river*, in such language we recognise the point of view of the official Persian nomenclature as exhibited in Ezra iv. 11 and elsewhere. This verse at the earliest can only have been written in the Babylonian Exile.

3. No king's career is dealt with in such detail as that of Solomon; with i. 12 there begins a *comprehensive recital of the whole history of the monarchy* from the division of the kingdom to the destruction of Jerusalem. This is a thoroughly uniform work, so that it is possible to speak of it more definitely as of a historical book by one author. First of all the purely statistical information is given about each king in stereotyped formula: in the case of the kings of Judah, the age of each on ascending the throne, the duration of his reign, the name of his mother, his death and burial; in the case of the Israelite kings, merely the length of the reign, and the king's death; in addition to the information dealing with the ascending of the throne in the case of the kings of Judah, there is added the corresponding reign-year of the contemporary king of Israel, and *vice versâ*. In spite of some few divergences, which for the most part have been caused by some material consideration, it is certain that this scheme everywhere proceeds from the same hand. In the eyes of its author, however, the most important matter in this history is the theocratic verdict which he deals out to every king, even to Zimri, who reigned altogether only seven days. His standpoint here is radically Deuteronomic: by the requirements

of Deut. which he reiterates, and even verbally quotes (2 K. xiv. 6 = Deut. xxiv. 16), all the kings are measured. In general the author with full deliberation made it his aim to present an exclusively church history of Israel: for details as to the profane history he refers the inquisitive reader, at the end of each reign, to a large historical work, the "Chronicles of the Kings of Judah" or "of Israel." Even in the few and scattered larger narratives that he has admitted into the book, it is a theocratic interest that everywhere predominates: such cases consist either of stories in which prophets play the principal rôle, or they are accounts about the Temple and the affairs of the cultus. As regards the relation of these embodied larger passages to the formal statistical scheme of the individual kings, there can be no doubt that it was the author of these formulas who himself included the larger passages: they have been completely adapted to this framework, often pass over into it quite imperceptibly, and without the latter would in many cases be quite unintelligible. Thus 1 K. xvii. presupposes for its right understanding xvi. 30–33, 2 K. ix. similarly viii. 28–29, just as, conversely, 2 K. xi. 1 resumes ix. 27–28 and x. 12–14.

4. Our next task must be to determine the relation of the Book of Kings to the דִּבְרֵי הַיָּמִים that is so often cited up to the time of Jehoiachim. As was the case in all civilised states of the ancient East, in Israel also, from the beginning of the monarchy onwards, *official annals* will have been kept, in which the achievements of the kings and personal details about them were described. If these annals, perhaps just on account of their official character, did not

altogether coincide exactly with historic truth, still they were certainly loyal to the tradition of facts, and in particular in the chronology, which was naturally reckoned according to the years of the reign of the individual kings, absolutely trustworthy: in any case such, if preserved, would form a historical source of unequalled and altogether inestimable value. The question now is whether, in the דברי הימים so constantly referred to by our author, we have to recognise the old official royal annals of Israel and Judah. This question is rightly answered by the majority of scholars in the negative. More especially in the kingdom of Israel, with its constantly changing dynasties and usurpers, it is equally improbable and impossible that the new monarch simply continued the annals of his predecessor, so that these royal annals would in themselves have formed a ready-made and continuous "book"; and it is still more improbable that the lucky stealer of a throne should himself have gravely given an official narrative of the קשר ("conspiracy") which brought him to the throne, for the guidance of future stealers of thrones —and yet it is the fact that twice, viz. in 1 K. xvi. 20 in the case of the king of a week's reign, Zimri, and in 2 K. xv. 15 in the case of Shallum, who was king for a month, express reference is made respecting the קֶשֶׁר אֲשֶׁר קָשָׁר ("conspiracy which he conspired") to the ספר דברי הימים ("Book of the Annals"), though here indeed, as the matter in question in both cases concerns only quite ephemeral pretenders, the stigmatising process may quite well have come from the annals of their fortunate successors (*cf.* the Behistun-inscription of Darius I.). It is also very questionable whether these official inventories were accessible, as a matter of course, to any and every one who cared to look into and use them. We shall rather have to accept the view that the דברי הימים to which our author refers "belong not to the documentary class, but to that of historical literature" (Kuenen, § 24, 8), if indeed they may be said, so far as they are still extant, to have issued from the documents at all. The annals of the kings of Judah and the annals of the kings of Israel were two distinct works; then we shall also have to accept the ספר דברי שלמה as a third distinct writing. This annalistic work is adduced by the author less as a source than as a means of supplementing his own body of information: for matters falling within the domain of political history—which he excluded from his treatment of the theme on principle—the author refers to the annals. Still, his statistical material, and consequently the data as to age on ascending the throne, duration of reign, name of the mother, he undoubtedly did derive from these sources. It has been shown, especially by Kamphausen and Rühl, that the chronological notices in Kings are essentially historical. Regarding the time and place of composition, the character and aims of the representation, as well as the authors of these annalistic works, we can, of course, form no idea which even approximates to definiteness or certainty: in the same way we are debarred by lack of knowledge from saying whether the short historical notices and dates which are incidentally scattered about by the author—such as 2 K. viii. 22, xiv. 7, xvi. 6 (in all these passages the phrase עד היום הזה, "to this day"), or 1 K. xii. 25,

xv. 23*b*, xvi. 21, 24; 2 K. xv. 5, 35*b*, xviii. 8, and similar passages—also proceed from the same quarter; but this after all is the most natural supposition.

5. We now address ourselves to the question as to *the origin of the more extensive narrative-pieces* which the author has admitted into his scheme and adapted to it, and first of all we will discuss 1 K. xii.–xvi. Here our attention is at once arrested by xii. 1–20, an extraordinarily vivid picture of the council of Shechem and the division of the kingdom resulting from it. The narrative by no means ranges itself against the Ten Tribes, and it draws quite a false picture of Rehoboam, whom it depicts as an inexperienced and hasty young man (*cf.* xiv. 21); it recalls, moreover, xi. 29–39, and shows literary dependence on 2 Sam. xx. 1 K. xii. 16 can only be understood as an imitation of 2 Sam. xx. 1. It is, doubtless, of Ephraimitic origin: both here and in the kernel of xi. 29–30, which is closely related to 1 Sam. xv., it would be natural to regard E as the source; and in the same way with regard to the groundwork of xiv. 1–18. This passage in its present form has been subjected to a penetrating Deuteronomic revision, but is distinguished by its marked superiority to such prophet-legends as that contained in the chapter immediately preceding it (xiii.); in this case decidedly an older kernel underlies the narrative. The reviser is certainly our author himself; *cf.* xvi. 1–4 and xxi. 20–24. Ch. xiii., which embodies a prophetic legend of a highly grotesque sort, demands special treatment. We have good grounds for not crediting this to the account of the author of Kings, but we must rather look upon it

as a quite late production, written in the style of the miraculous stories in Chronicles and Daniel. In 2 K. xxiii.—a chapter which itself is not old—the reference in vss. 16-18 to the narrative we are discussing has been appended later and contradicts its immediate context, while 1 K. xiii 32 and 33, which verses are transitional to xiii., exhibit a clear trace of the "Grundschrift" (P). Wellhausen has made the very attractive conjecture that a reminiscence of the prophecy of judgment uttered by the Judaean prophet Amos at Bethel in the reign of Jeroboam II. lies at the basis of the narrative (*cf.* § 20, 9 below). On xiv. 25-28 and xv. 16-22, see paragraph 7 of this section.

6. The proper central core of Kings is formed by the group of chapters 1 K. xvii.–2 K. x., from which 2 K. xiii. 14-21 cannot be disjoined. These chapters—which belong to the best and most valuable narrative-passages in the O.T.—give an account of the history of the two great prophets Elijah and Elisha, and afford us a far-reaching view into the secular history of those disturbed and stormy times. Here, first of all, must be rejected 2 K. i. 2*b*-16, a prophetic legend marked by the same spirit as 1 K. xiii. and 1 Sam. xix. 18-24; it obviously emanates from an altogether later period. The remaining material of the narrative is, however, not uniform nor by one hand. More especially the four chapters 1 K. xvii.-xix. and xxi. are marked off in this way, and perhaps, also, 2 K. i. 2-4, 7*a*, which are simply prophetic stories of Elijah without any direct outlook on political history. This history of Elijah, in spite of many doubtful features, may be

regarded as a literary unit; only xxi. at all events has been drastically revised, and xix. abridged at the conclusion in the interest of the parallel narratives of Elisha. The verbal quotation in xviii. 31*b* from Gen. xxxv. 10 (P) is, of course, a gloss, which even forced its way into the LXX.; *cf.* the similar passage, which is quite late, in 2 K. xvii. 39*b*. The stories of Elisha form a more extensive group, from which the narrative of Elijah's ascension to heaven, which introduces them, is not to be separated, 2 K. ii.–viii. 15, xiii. 14–21. They present less a history of Elisha than "a series of anecdotal narratives," which do not exhibit any literary uniformity. Ch. v. disagrees in material respects with vi. 8–vii. 20; v. 27 in particular points with viii. 4–5, while viii. 7–15 runs parallel with ch. v. throughout. On the other hand, ch. ii., iv., vi. 1–7, and viii. 1–6 appear to stand in close connexion with one another, as vi. 8–vii. 20 does with xiii. 14–21 and also with iii., the close connexion of which latter with the Elisha-stories has been shown by Kittel and Benzinger. They are not derived from the living tradition, but are of literary origin: the composite character of vi. 24–vii. 20 was first detected by Winckler ("Gesch. Isr.," i. 135), that of iv. 8–37 by Benzinger. By the side of these prophetic legends 1 K. xx., xxii., 2 K. ix. 1–27 stand as a special group by themselves. Here the prophets indeed play a part, but the political history is the main feature; they are therefore of inestimable value as sources for the history, although they have not been preserved intact: in particular Stade has proved that in ch. x. vss. 12–16 are of a secondary character. The four sources (at least) which in a united form lie before us in these prophetic histories, although they make reference at many points to the king of Judah, and in 2 K. iii. 14 even accord him a certain privileged position, still, as a whole, are undoubtedly of Ephraimitic origin, and as a whole, too, are older than the writing prophets; thus they must have been written between 850 and 750: no attempt to identify their original source with E will succeed.

7. Side by side with this precious collection of Ephraimitic accounts we now encounter a *number of detailed Judaean histories*, viz. 2 K. xi. 1–xii. 17, xvi. 10–18, xviii.–xx., xxii.–xxiii. Here the unmistakable points of contact of ch. xxii. with xii. are at once noticeable, and Wellhausen consequently derives the three passages, xi.–xii., xvi., and xxii.–xxiii. (which have this in common, that they deal with the Temple and the cultus), from a single source, which in that case must have been of comparatively modern date. But this view is incompatible with the impression produced by ch. xii. and xvi.: it is difficult to regard these narratives as post-Deuteronomic; this, however, is obviously true of ch. xxii., and we shall thus better explain the striking points of contact with ch. xii. already referred to, if, with Kuenen, we regard them as resulting from dependence upon the latter passage (xxii.). The narrative in 2 K. xxii. and xxiii., which at many points has undergone revision (*cf.* Stade, "G.V.I.," i. 647–655), was undoubtedly written by the author of Kings himself. From the older "Temple-history" we may well derive the detailed description of the Temple and its furniture in 1 K. vi. and vii., for it is improbable that the old history of Solomon gave a full and thorough account of these

matters. Also 1 K. xiv. 25–28 and xv. 16–22, as well as 2 K. xiv. 8–11 and xviii. 14–16, will be derived from the same Temple-history; *cf.* especially 1 K. xiv. 27 f. with 2 K. xi. 4, 7, 11, 19. On ch. xviii. 17–xx. 19, which recurs in exactly the same form in Isaiah xxxvi.–xxxix., a detailed discussion will be found in § 24, 17 below. In ch. xi., as Stade has shown, vss. 13–18a are a fragment of a parallel account which has been worked up into the chapter.

8. Having brought the analysis of the Book of Kings to an end, we have still to settle the question as to *when the Deuteronomic author wrote*. If only one author were really in question, he would have to be placed very late, for 2 K. xxv. 27–30 brings us down to a date below 561. On this account K. H. Graf ("Geschichtliche Bücher," p. 110) explains vss. 22–30 as a later addition; but, as Kuenen rightly remarks, there appears to be no ground for such a view, either in the form or substance of the verses. Wellhausen long ago called attention to 1 K. iii. 2 and 3. Both verses are Deuteronomic in character, but cannot have proceeded from one hand, because they contradict each other, and are mutually exclusive. Here clearly two distinct Deuteronomic hands must be recognised. The same dualism, however, occurs also in 2 K. xvii., which chapter has long been regarded as being in a quite peculiar sense the work of the author of Kings. In vss. 19–20 and 34b–41 later additions were already recognised by Wellhausen. According to the penetrating investigations of Stade, vss. 7–17 and 29–34a [1] are to be rejected also, while on the other hand vs. 41 is to be retained, the

[1] Here in particular שֹׁמְרֹנִים in vs. 29 is suspicious.

result being that vss. 18, 21–28, and 41 survive as the original nucleus. Kuenen pursued the investigation still further, and showed that some of the Deuteronomic passages maintain the pre-exilic standpoint, and do not yet take into account the downfall of Judah and Jerusalem, while others, again, already presuppose these events. To the latter series, in spite of Kuenen's warm protest, 1 K. viii. 15–53 also belongs, for it is throughout dependent on Deut. xxviii.; on Biblical-theological grounds it cannot be regarded as pre-exilic, because its idea of God and its representation of the Temple at Jerusalem as a house of prayer for all peoples are specifically Deutero-Isaianic, and, as its different position in the LXX. shows, the passage itself was inserted into the text comparatively late. At the most a nucleus might possibly be pre-exilic, which, however, in that case must have been revised out of all recognition. In this way Kuenen comes to distinguish a Rd^1 and Rd^2. Rd^1 is the author of Kings proper, and in particular is the originator of the characteristic scheme for the survey of each royal reign which runs through the whole book; his active life would be assigned to the reign of Jehoiachim († 600). Everything up to 2 K. xxiv., which is not expressly to be attributed to Rd^2, or to still younger hands, belongs to him. From Rd^2 must be derived 1 K. iii. 3 and 15 certainly, v. 4–5, viii. 15–53,[1] ix. 1–9, xv. 4–5, xvi. 7, 12–13, 2 K. xiii. 4–6, 23, xvii. 7–17 certainly (the complete dependence of this last on Jeremiah was rightly seen long ago by Thenius;

[1] This section, however, in exactly the same way as 2 K. xvii., shows traces of still later revision.

vss. 19–20 and 29–34a form a later, vss. 34b–40 the latest supplement of all), xxi. 11–15, xxii. 15–20, xxiii. 26–27, xxiv. 2–4, and, of course, the whole of the remainder of the book. This redactor would then in xxiv. 5–9 and 18 have imitated the scheme of Rd^1. Kuenen would also ascribe to him the two stories of prophets in 1 K. xiii. and 2 K. i.; but neither of these displays the least Deuteronomic character, and will therefore have to be regarded as still more recent. On the other hand, it is in the highest degree probable that Rd^2 has interposed in the scheme of Rd^1 and everywhere appended the synchronistic notices; according to Rühl, indeed, the existence of two synchronists is to be assumed. It is obvious that the synchronistic notices are not authentic, because nobody in Judah reckoned according to the years of the kings of Israel, and *vice versâ*. They can thus have only been calculated artificially, and hardly by Rd^1, because at many points they are in the sharpest disagreement with the historical narratives. On the other hand, they cannot have been inserted by way of supplement, because the somewhat strange arrangement of the accounts of the individual reigns corresponds to the synchronistic notices; the king who first entered on his reign is first finished with altogether, and then those who came to the throne after him in order. Thus, for example, the scheme of Jehoshaphat's reign (1 K. xxii. 41–51) is placed after the death of Ahab, because he began to reign after Ahab, although in the history of Ahab he had already been repeatedly mentioned. All these considerations combine to indicate that the synchronistic notices are derived from Rd^2, who is thus responsible for the present arrangement and sequence in Kings. In accordance with 2 K. xxv. 30, he can have written at the earliest in the second half of the Babylonian Exile. To him also we shall then owe the chronological notice in 1 K. vi. 1, which hardly comes from Rd¹.

9. If we disregard such quite recent passages as 1 K. xiii. and 2 K. i., not many traces of *a later diorthosis* occur in the Hebrew text: לְקֹדֶשׁ הַקֳּדָשִׁים ("even for the most holy place") in 1 K. vi. 16 is a gloss dependent upon P, and similarly in 1 K. xviii. 31*b*; in 1 K. viii. 1–11 the Tabernacle has been transferred into the text from P, and in other respects the section has been subjected to revision; in 1 K. xii. 32 and 33 the definition of the Feast of Tabernacles in accordance with the calendar-date shows the influence of P, and in 1 K. vii. 48 the מִזְבַּח הַזָּהָב ("the golden altar"), standing in the interpolated¹ passage vii. 48–50, is even derived from P^x. But in comparison with the whole extent of Kings these are but evanescent and trifling details which cannot affect its general Deuteronomic character. On the other hand, a comparison of the LXX. reveals that quite late and on a fairly extensive scale Kings was still the object of diorthosis: more especially the succession and arrangement of particular constituent elements—which to some extent were only held together in a very loose connexion—were still subject to variation, and had not been brought to any fixed and conclusive result in the third century. Still more significant than this, however, is the existence of a series of extensive doublets in the LXX., following 1 K. ii. 35 and 46 and

¹ Stade.

xii. 24; these are denominated by Benzinger S^2, and go back to a different recension of the material that has been worked up into the Hebrew text. Winckler was the first to recognise the high importance of these variants as to some extent offering a more original form of text against the Hebrew recension, and in any case serving to control the latter.

Special Introduction

CHAPTER IX

BOOK I.—HISTORICAL BOOKS—*continued*

§§ 19, 20. *Exilic Books and Chronicles*

§ 19. The Exilic Book of the History of the People of Israel

1. Long ago Spinoza recognised that the historical books of the O.T., as they now lie before us, form a large connected work of history, narrating the history of the People of Israel from the creation of the world to the destruction of Jerusalem, and subordinating the whole of the material embodied in it to a far-reaching religious pragmatism. This one-sided but yet decidedly elaborate method of dealing with the entire past history of the peculiar people falls within the period of the Babylonian Exile; and it was just at that time that the conditions, both external and psychological, were present which would be favourable to a process of this intellectual and spiritual character. The downfall of the state and nation stimulated interest in the vanished past; the contemplation of ancient greatness helped to maintain a brave front—to be reminded of the past contributed to prevent extinction in the present and conduced to self-preservation for the future. In such a view of the past,

however, it was above all things necessary that explanation should be given how it could have come about that Jahve gave up His people, His land, His Temple to the heathen: the essential problem was thus to vindicate the theodicy. And this was effected by showing that things were bound to come to this pass. The basis for this theodicy was provided by the views and ideas of the prophets, and the crystallisation of these as seen in Deuteronomy. Every misfortune that Israel encounters is punishment for sin, and especially for idolatry: at bottom it is the sin of Jeroboam that has condemned Israel, and the sin of Manasseh—in spite of the radical amendment and conversion which succeeded it—can only be expiated by the downfall of Judah. Thus arose this prophetic representation of the history of Israel, which really turns the historian into a retrospective prophet. But this history-writing we are considering has not only a theoretic and retrospective side, but also an eminently practical and prospective one. There is a firm and deep-seated hope in the nation's restoration — a consummation which was guaranteed by Jahve's word given through His prophets. Under such circumstances this prophetic history of the past was bound to be regarded as a warning and as setting a standard for the future. The new Israel that is rising out of the grave of the Exile must avoid the sins and failings of old Israel, through which the latter fell. In this way, then, we can understand how it was that in the Babylonian Exile a far-reaching activity in literary historical production could have been developed, by men, too, the most diverse, but animated by the same tendency and the same spirit; for it was no single hand that composed and edited the whole vast work.

2. This Deuteronomic revision makes itself felt in the different books in very different degrees of strength: it completely dominates the representation in Joshua, Judges, and Kings, while in the Pentateuch and Samuel it appears rather more occasionally, and in Genesis, *e.g.*, leaves only one single clearly demonstrable trace. But it has also in its treatment of the material made use of a certain amount of criticism, has not always reproduced the given material without abbreviation, and has rejected passages which appeared to it doubtful and threatened to impair the edifying character of the historical representation, such as we have already had examples of in Samuel and Judges. Although we have here the work of a whole school, we are still obliged to assume a final redaction of a uniform Deuteronomic character, and can ascribe to this particularly the few isolated additions in Samuel, by which the epoch of that book is intended to be organically fitted into the chronological scheme of Judges and Kings, in this way superficially investing the course of the history with the appearance of unbroken continuity, and stamping the representation with a connected character. Thus the Deuteronomic Exilic Book of the History of the People of Israel contained in the Hexateuch $JE + D$ (in the form which Rd had given to it), the Deuteronomic Book of Judges (*cf.* § 16, 10*b*), Samuel, without 1 Sam. xv., xxviii. 3-25, 2 Sam. ix.-xx. and xxi. 15-xxiii. 39, and Kings substantially in the form in which it now lies before us, only without 1 K. xiii. and 2 K. 1.

3. This work later underwent varied fortunes. By

the appearance of P on the scene the Hexateuch was totally transformed; P also exercised a certain influence on the other books, but by good fortune only in a very slight degree. To what results a systematic revision of the whole pre-exilic history of Israel on the basis of P leads we shall see in the next section (§ 20), and here it need only be said how immeasurable our loss would have been if Chronicles had succeeded in displacing and suppressing altogether Judges, Samuel, and Kings, or if these books had survived only in a form produced by such a revision: the possibility would then have been denied to us of forming even an approximate picture of the actual course of the pre-exilic history of the People of Israel. In one point only can we rejoice that the final Deuteronomic redaction was departed from, in so far as the passages were again inserted in Judges and Samuel which that redaction had rejected—a circumstance which at the same time affords proof that the earlier form of Rd's material still maintained its existence up to a comparatively late period side by side with his revision.

§ 20. The Book of Chronicles

LITERATURE : *Commentaries:* E. Bertheau, *K.E.H.*, 1874, 2nd ed.; H. Bennett, 1894; W. E. Barnes, 1900; I. Benzinger, *K.H.C.A.T.*, 1901 ; R. Kittel, *H.K.A.T.*, 1902, and *History of the Hebrews*, ii. § 52. *Monographs, Essays, etc.:* W. Bacher, *Der Name der Bücher der Chronik in der Septuaginta, Z.A.T.W.*, xv. 305 ff., 1895; K. Budde, *Bemerkungen zum "Midrasch des Buches der Könige," Z.A.T.W.*, xii. 37 ff., 1892.
On the question of its trustworthiness: De Wette, *Beiträge*, i., 1806 (*cf.* § 2, 5 above); C. P. W. Gramberg, *Die Chronik nach ihrem geschichtlichen Charakter und ihrer Glaubwürdigkeit neu*

geprüft, 1823; K. F. Keil, *Apologetischer Versuch über die Chronik*, 1833; F. Movers, *Kritische Untersuchungen über die biblische Chronik*, 1834; K. H. Graf, *Geschichtliche Bücher*, 1866 (*cf.* § 2, 7 above), pp. 114–247; J. Wellhausen, *Prolegomena*, 2nd ed., pp. 177–239; H. Winckler (*cf.* § 18 above), pp. 157–167.

On the criticism of the text: R. Kittel, *S.B.O.T.*, 1895.

1. By the side of the Exilic Book of the History of the People of Israel, which has engaged our attention in § 19, there appears a historical work which the Hebrew canon designates דִּבְרֵי הַיָּמִים, and which, just as Samuel and Kings, is counted as one book. The twofold division παραλειπομένων α' and β' is derived from the LXX. The title παραλειπόμενα ("things left over") characterises "Chronicles" as a complement of the older canonical books of history, adding and supplementing what has been omitted from them. Long ago Jerome, who retained the Greek designation *Paralipomenon*, wrote these words in the Prologus Galeatus: *Quod significantius Chronicon totius divinae historiae possumus appellare;*[1] and so Luther designated it as *Erstes und zweite Buch der Chronika*.

Contents of 1 and 2 Chronicles

2. The *contents* of Chronicles run parallel to the historical books from Genesis to 2 Kings.

1 Chron. i.–ix.: genealogical register, with short notices incidentally scattered within it—i., from Adam to Israel, thence (vss. 35–54) Esau–Edom; ii., the tribe of Judah; iii., the House of David; iv., again Judah and Simeon; v. 1–26, Reuben, Gad,

[1] "Which we may term more significantly the Chronicle of the whole of the sacred history."

and East-Manasseh; v. 27-vi. 28, Levi; vi. 39-66, the Levitical cities; vii., Issachar, Benjamin, Naphtali, West-Manasseh, Ephraim, Asher; viii., again Benjamin and the House of Saul; ix. 1-34, list of the inhabitants of Jerusalem arranged as Judaeans, Benjamites, priests, Levites, and doorkeepers, and list of the duties of the individual Levites; ix. 35-44 is a verbal repetition of viii. 29-38. 1 Chron. x.-xxix.: history of David—x., death of Saul; xi., David anointed at Hebron, and the capture of Jerusalem: list of David's heroes; xii., list of those who resorted to David at Ziklag and at Hebron; xiii., the holy Ark brought from Kirjath-Jearim to the house of Obed-Edom; xiv., building of the palace, family notices, victory over the Philistines; xv.-xvi., transportation of the Ark to Mount Zion; xvii., the oracle of Nathan; xviii., survey of David's military exploits and officials; xix. 1-xx. 3, the Syro-Ammonite war; xx. 4-8, conflicts with the Philistines; xxi., numbering of the people; xxii., preparations for building the Temple, and commission to Solomon; xxiii., list of the Levites and their service in the Temple; xxiv., arrangement of the twenty-four classes of priests; xxv., organisation of the Temple-music among twenty-four classes of Levites; xxv., doorkeepers and treasurers: administrators of the external business of the Temple; xxvii., military commanders, princes of tribes, officials of David; xxviii., Solomon proclaimed as successor, receives the pattern of the Temple, and gold for its vessels; surrender of the treasures collected for the building of the Temple; free-will offerings.

2 Chron. i.-ix., history of Solomon. x. 1-xi. 4, the

division of the kingdom. xi. 5–xxxvi. 21, history of Judah from the division of the kingdom to the destruction of Jerusalem. xxxvi. 22–23, Cyrus gives permission for the return from Babylon to Jerusalem and for the rebuilding of the Temple therein.

3. This conclusion of the book indicates its origin, at the earliest, in the Persian period. And 1 Chron. xxix. 7—where for the period of David a calculation is made in darics, the Persian coinage introduced by Darius I.—makes it clear that the writing does not fall within the beginnings of that period. But we are obliged to come down still further. For if the genealogy of the Davidic family in 1 Chron. iii. 19–24 is (according to what is probably the original text of this highly corrupt passage) brought down in its eleventh member to Zerubbabel,[1] we are thereby carried, with absolute certainty, into the Greek period—perhaps the first half of the third century—and must assign the composition of Chronicles to that epoch.

4. If the Chronicler wrote at so late a date, he must naturally have been acquainted with *the older canonical books of history*. And in fact there occur in his work a large number of parallel texts to these, which show verbal, or almost complete verbal, agreement.

1 CHRON. x. 1–12 = 1 SAM. xxxi. ; xi. 1–3, 4–9 = 2 SAM. v. 1–3, 6–10 ; xi. 10–41a = xxiii. 8–39 ; xiii. = vi. 1–11 ; xiv. 1–16 = v. 11–25 ; xv. 25–29 = vi. 12–16 ; xvi. 1–3, 43 = vi. 17–19, 20a ; xvii., xviii., xix. = vii., viii., x. ; xx. 1 = xi. 1 ; xx. 2–3 = xii. 30, 31 ; xx. 4–8 = xxi. 18–22 ; xxi. 1–27 = xxiv ; xxix. 27 = 1 KINGS ii. 11.

---

[1] But *cf.* on this point W. Rothstein's "Des Genealogie des Königs-Jojachin," 1902.

THE BOOK OF CHRONICLES

2 Chron. i. 3–13 = 1 Kings iii. 4–15; i. 14–17 = x. 26–29; ii. 2–17 = v. 16–30; iii. 1–v. 1 = vi., vii. 13–51; v. 2–vii. 10 = viii.; vii. 11–viii. 2 = ix. 1–14; viii. 4–18 = ix. 17b–28; ix. 1–28 = x. 1–28a; ix. 30–31 = xi. 42–43; x. 1–xi. 4 = xii. 1–24; xii. 2–4, 9–11 = xiv. 25–28; xii. 15b–16 = xiv. 30–31; xiii. 1–2, 23a = xv. 1–2, 8; xiv. 1–2 = xv. 11–12; xv. 16–18 = xv. 11–15; xvi. 1–6 = xv. 17–22; xvi. 12–xvii. 1a = xv. 23b–24; xviii. 2–34 = xxii. 1–36a; xx. 31–xxi. 1 = xxii. 41–51; xxi. 5–10 = 2 Kings viii. 17–22; xxii. 2–6 = viii. 26–29; xxii. 10–xxiii. 21 = xi.; xxiv. 1–14, 23–26, 27b = xii. 1–14, 19, 21–22; xxv. 1–4, 11, 17–24, 25–28 = xiv. 2–6, 7a, 8–14, 17–20; xxvi. 1–2 = xiv. 21–22; xxvi. 3–4, 21, 23 = xv. 2–3, 5, 7; xxvii. 1–3a, 9 = xv. 33–35, 38; xxviii. 1–4, 16, 17, 21, 22–24, 27 = xvi. 2–5, 6, 7, 8, 10–18, 20; xxix. 1–2 = xviii. 2–3; xxxii. 1–24 = xviii. 13–xx. 19 very much shortened; xxxii. 33 = xx. 21; xxxiii. 1–10a, 20–22, 24–25 = xxi. 1–10a, 18–21, 23–24; xxxiv. 1–2, 8–28 = xxii.; xxxiv. 29–32, 33 = xxiii. 1–3, 4–20; xxxv. 1–19, 20–24 = xxiii. 21–23, 29–30a; xxxvi. 1, 2, 3–4, 5 = xxiii. 30b, 31b, 33–34, 36a + 37a; xxxvi. 6a, 8, 9, 10 = xxiv. 1a, 5 + 6b, 8a + 9a, 10–17; xxxvi. 11–21 = xxiv. 18–xxv. 21 radically abbreviated. In the edition of the text by Kittel the relation of the Chronicler to the parallel literature is very ingeniously made clear to the eye.

That our canonical books of Samuel and Kings lay before the Chronicler—directly or indirectly—is shown by the mechanical adoption on his part of phraseology which in the original falls back upon and is determined by passages which the Chronicler has not admitted into his text. 1 Chron. xiv. 3–7 is verbally = 2 Sam. v. 13–16, although the parallel passage which the עוֹד recalls, viz. 2 Sam. iii. 2–5, has not been embodied by the Chronicler, and it is hardly possible to see a reference in it to 1 Chron. iii. 1–4. The remark, verbally transferred from 2 Sam. xi. 1, וְדָוִיד יֹשֵׁב בִּירוּשָׁלָםִ ("but David tarried at Jerusalem"), is suspended in 1 Chron. xx. 1 completely in the air, and is in palpable opposition to vs. 2. In the same way 2 Chron. x. 15 verbally = 1 Kings xii. 15, although the Chronicler has passed over 1 Kings xi. 29–39 ; and 2 Chron. vii. 21 can only be understood as an attempt to secure a tolerable sense for the textual error עֶלְיוֹן, which the Chronicler with the LXX. must have read already in 1 Kings ix. 8. Thus even the textual errors of his exemplar we find repeated in the Chronicler, although it is true, on the other hand, that in many cases he shows better readings than the parallel texts—which is intelligible enough, because the earlier historical books were more read, and therefore more largely multiplied, than Chronicles, in the case of which, consequently, one main reason for the growth of textual corruption was non-existent.

5. But in spite of all this material, and even, to a considerable extent, verbal parallelism, it cannot be denied that the picture as a whole which the Chronicler produces of Israel's past is one that completely diverges from and is absolutely unlike the picture in Samuel and Kings. And this brings us to the cardinal question as to the *trustworthiness* of the Chronicler. By everyone who looks at the matter with unprejudiced eyes and who has the historic instinct it must be regarded as settled. The first thing that strikes one is the Chronicler's fondness for large numbers:

like a regular "seven-figure champion,"[1] he flings about his hundred thousands and millions in this way wherever the bare attempt to give concrete representation to the things described is sufficient to demonstrate their utter impossibility. Further, he altogether omits much which stands in his original material, while conversely he proffers a very great deal of which nothing can be read in the former. And in both instances, in the omissions as well as in the additions, a very definitely marked and evident aim reveals itself. In Chron. we possess the latest and most pronounced outcome of that transformation of the History of Israel into Church History for which the way was first prepared by Deut. and the Deuteronomic writers. The favoured representatives of the national history are saints, and the history must be thoroughly edifying, and in particular exhibit the pragmatism of a righteous rule of God: must show that every misfortune is punishment for sin, and all prosperity the reward of piety, and conversely, also, that all piety must realise its reward, and all sin its punishment. And, too, the piety and dogmas of the Chronicler are throughout those of P: "the traditional material is refracted through a strange and foreign medium, the spirit of post-exilic Judaism" (Wellhausen). Whatever does not fit in with this religious pragmatism is passed over in silence. Thus of God-rejected Saul we are told nothing but his death, which serves as an introduction to David's ascent of the throne; in the same way the seven years of Ishbaal's reign are passed over in silence, as well as all the many weaknesses and

[1] "Messer milione," lit. "measurer by millions."

failings of David, and the deplorable occurrences in his family; all the doubtful features of Solomon's reign are ignored, even so comparatively innocent a piece of information as that given in 1 Kings ix. 16–17a; with the death of Solomon there exists, as far as the Chronicler is concerned, only Judah, as being the home of the Temple and the legitimate worship; the heretical kingdom of Israel is simply ignored, or, if mentioned at all, appears merely to prove the occasion of, or punish, eventual sins on the part of the Judaean kings. Or where the expedient of silence is not resorted to the tradition is remodelled, and here the Chronicler seems, in cases where we are able to check him, not to go in direct opposition to his original material, as, *e.g.*, 2 Chron. viii. 2 compared with 1 Kings ix. 10–14, or 2 Chron. xx. 35–37 compared with 1 Kings xxii. 48–50. How regard for P leads to alterations in the original material can be seen by a comparison of 2 Chron. xxiv. with 2 Kings xxi., or even by so small a detail as is involved in 2 Chron. xxxiv. 15 and 18 compared with 2 Kings xxii. 8 and 10, which are quite characteristic examples. All that the Chronicler himself contributes independently serves pragmatic ends throughout: thus reason must be given why the pious Asa became diseased in his feet; how it was that the heretical Joash of Israel could conquer and take captive Amaziah, who is pictured as a pious monarch; how the pious Uzziah became afflicted with leprosy, and the pious Josiah could fall in battle against the heathen Necho; how, on the other hand, it came to pass that the arch-sinner and miscreant Manasseh could enjoy unmolested the longest reign of all the Davidic princes, and die in peace. And this aim can be shown to be present all through. According to the verdicts given in the Book of Kings the history of the individual kings is construed, or modified in such a way as to suit these. And in all this transformation of the old tradition the Chronicler is actuated by good faith throughout: he has corrected in it what, according to his honest convictions, must have been clearly false. Some 2000 years before the "Grafian school" he rightly perceived that the old historical books and the Pentateuch are mutually exclusive. Either the representation of the historical books is correct, in which case the Pentateuch cannot be the basis of Mosaism and of the religion of Israel; or the Pentateuchal Law is Mosaic, and in that case the representation of the historical books cannot be correct. As in the Chronicler's eyes, of course, the authenticity of the Tora was placed beyond the reach of doubt, he was only able to adopt the second alternative, and consequently corrected the historical books: he has expounded the history as it must have been on the assumption that the entire Pentateuch was the basis of Mosaism, and has acted in good faith throughout, as also in one case, which has nothing to do with the particular object he had in view, he has corrected the tradition in good faith. Having regard to the well-known narrative in 1 Sam. xvii., 2 Sam. xxi. 19 could not possibly be correct, but must rest upon an error of the tradition, and to rectify this must have appeared to the Chronicler the plain duty of a cautious narrator.

6. At the same time, by such facts as these sentence is passed on the *material value* of that which is peculiarly the Chronicler's own. If any result is

marked by a clearly discernible dominating objective, it cannot be accorded any historical value. The representation of the Chronicler and that of the older historical books are mutually exclusive, and, such being the case, it is only the representation of the older historical books that can possibly be as a whole the correct one—and all the more so because we can indicate the prism which has produced the peculiar refraction that is visible in the Chronicler's work. This does not of necessity absolutely exclude the possibility that among the material exhibited by the Chronicler alone some one or other valid and useful detail may occur; more especially in cases where the tendency-aim is not obviously present the particular detail in question should be tested carefully and without prejudice: with reference to 1 Chron. xi. 10–47 compared with 2 Sam. xxiii. 8–39, so eminent a critic as Kuenen (*op. cit.*, § 30, 11) held the view that the source from which 2 Sam. xxiii. was derived still lay before the Chronicler, and more especially the genealogies in 1 Chron. i.–ix.—the text of which is in a wretched state — emphatically demand most careful sifting. But a narrator whose untrustworthiness has been demonstrated in all cases where he can be controlled, in cases where no such means of checking him exist has at least a very strong presumption against him. And though even such a historian as Winckler can regard a comparatively large number of the details peculiar to the Chronicler as historical, yet the whole picture drawn by the latter is and remains completely unhistorical.

7. One point in the material peculiar to the Chronicler remains still to be indicated specially:

this is the *conspicuous interest he displays in the Levites*, which is far more pronounced than in the case of the priests, and, among matters affecting the Levites, especially *in the Temple-music*. He deals with the entire musical-liturgical side of the cultus with obvious relish and with marked expert knowledge. From this fact it has been inferred—without doubt correctly—that he was himself to be found in this circle, and was thus a Levitical Temple-musician.

8. We have so far dealt with the material peculiar to the Chronicler as being his own intellectual property. This, however, brings us, unprompted, to the question of *possible sources* for the material that diverges from the older historical books, and this question must be raised all the more urgently because the Chronicler himself is repeatedly appealing to sources. Only in the cases of Joram (2 Chron. xxi.), Ahaziah (xxii.), Athaliah (xxiii.), Amon (xxxiii.), Jehoahaz, Jehoiachin, and Zedekiah (xxxvi.) are such references to sources wanting, and it may be remarked generally that Kings also, in the cases of Ahaziah, Athaliah, Jehoahaz, Jehoiachin, and Zedekiah, has omitted the reference—otherwise usual —to "the Chronicles of the Kings of Judah." Among the sources adduced by the Chronicler we can distinguish two classes, historical and prophetic.

(*a*) *Historical Sources.*—For the history of David reference is made in 1 Chron. xxvii. 24 to דִּבְרֵי הַיָּמִים לַמֶּלֶךְ דָּוִיד, and in the very obscure passage xxiii. 27 to דברי דויד הָאַחֲרוֹנִים. In the case of Asa there is cited a ספר המלכים ליהודה וישראל; in the cases of Amaziah (xxv. 26), Ahaz (xxviii. 26), and Hezekiah (xxxii. 32), a "ספר מַלְכֵי יה" וישר"; in the cases of

Jotham (xxvii. 7), Josiah (xxxv. 27), and Jehoiakim (xxxvi. 8), perhaps also 1 Chron. ix. 1, a "ויה "מלכי יש" ס"; in the case of Jehoshaphat (xx. 34), and, according to the Massoretic accentuation, also in 1 Chron. ix. 1, a "ס" "מלכי יש"; in the case of Manasseh (xxxiii. 18), "דברי מלכי יש"; and, finally, in the case of Joash (xxiv. 27), a מדרש ספל המלכים.

(b) *Prophetic Sources.*—In the case of David (1 Chron. xxix. 29) he appeals to דברי שמואל הָרֹאֶה, to דברי נתן הנביא, and to דברי גד הַחֹזֶה; in the case of Solomon (2 Chron. ix. 29), to דברי נתן הנביא, to נבואת אֲחִיָּה הַשִּׁילוֹנִי and to חֲזוּת יעדי החוזה; in the case of Rehoboam (xii. 15), to דברי שמעיה הנביא ועדי החוזה; in the case of Abijah (xiii. 22), to a מִדְרָשׁ הנביא עדו; in the case of Jehoshaphat (xx. 34), to דברי יהוא בֶן־חֲנָנִי אֲשֶׁר הֹעֲלָה עַל־סֵפֶר מַלְכֵי יִשְׂרָאֵל; in the case of Uzziah (xxvi. 22) and Hezekiah (xxxii. 32), to יְשַׁעְיָהוּ (חָזוֹן) בֶן־אָמוֹץ הַנָּבִיא; and in the case of Manasseh (xxxiii. 19), to דברי חוֹזָי, which is palpably corrupt: the LXX. gives דברי החוזים in place of it.

9. We will deal first of all with the *historical sources*. That the Chronicler in the composition of his work made use of written records is clear from the genealogies with which he opens his work: he cannot purely have invented these. The material which he independently presents, that goes beyond Kings, exhibits a varied character. As we come across in his work detached notices and data which have no clear connexion with his special aim, such as 2 Chron. xxxii. 30, 33, xxxiii. 14, and similar passages, Kittel in his edition of the text has coloured these dark red. They are quite similar in character with the detached data and notices that occur in

Kings, and in such cases the sources used in Kings must either directly or indirectly have still lain before the Chronicler (*cf.* paragraph 6 of this section on 1 Chron. xi. 10-47). Perhaps by his *Book of Kings* he means these materials: at any rate our canonical Book of Kings cannot be intended by this term, as a comparison of 2 Chron. xxvii. with 2 Kings xv. 32-36, is sufficient to show. On the other hand, all that subserves his special purpose and that helps to invest the whole historical picture with its totally altered physiognomy must be judged differently. In this we are dealing with a very free treatment and exposition of old traditional material, the object of which is not so much to narrate history as to conduce to religious edification. And of this 2 Chron. xxiv. 27 affords us a significant indication. Here the Chronicler cites a מדרש ספר המלכים. As all these features are appropriate to Midrash in the technical sense of the term, we must suppose that already before the time of the Chronicler the history of the period of the Israelitish kings had been expounded in the style of the Midrash—we have already met with narratives of such a character: in Gen. ch. xiv.; in Samuel, 1 Sam. xvi. 1-13 and xix. 18-24; in Kings, 1 Kings xiii. and 2 Kings i. The Midrashic work used by the Chronicler was not written by a single hand: in the history of Asa 2 Chron. xiv. 1-4 and xv. 1-19, in the history of Jehoshaphat 2 Chron. xvii. 7-9 and xix. 4-11, are clearly doublets; 2 Chron. xxx. also (of the Passover of Hezekiah) gives the impression, when compared with the account of Josiah's Passover in xxxv. 1-19, of being an exaggerated imitation. All the same, the

Midrash lay before the Chronicler already in the form of a collected work.

10. In the case of the *prophetic sources* the fact that all the prophets whose names are here adduced appear also in Kings or Samuel, while in the historical narrative of the Chronicler a whole collection of prophets emerges whose names the Book of Kings does not hand down, produces a favourable impression. As especially characteristic I call attention to the fact that in the case of Manasseh, in whose reign no prophet comes up for mention in Kings, reference only is made in 2 Chron. xxxiii. 19 in quite a general way to *Words of the Seers*. Even the prophet who is mentioned three times as יעדו or עדו (Iddo) is no exception to this rule, because Josephus is already aware that the man of God is meant about whom 1 Kings xiii. gives so detailed a narrative without mentioning his name; and, as 2 Chron. ix. 29 shows, this was also undoubtedly the opinion of the Chronicler (*cf.* on this point Budde,[1] p. 50 f.). To judge by the manner in which the citation is made in 2 Chron. xx. 34, xxvi. 22, xxxii. 32, it might be concluded that these histories of the prophets—one of which (2 Chron. xiii. 22) is adduced under the title מדרש הנביא עדו ("Midrash of the prophet Iddo")—simply formed part of the great midrashic work already referred to, just as Samuel and Kings contain the history of prophets on an extensive scale, and from this it might be possible to explain the fact that in the cases of Solomon, Rehoboam, and Abijah only prophetic sources are adduced, and not historical ones at all. Still, there may also have been a special

---

[1] In the work cited at the head of this section, under "Literature."

collection of narratives of a midrashic character about the prophets, which perhaps bore the general title דברי החזים (2 Chron. xxxiii. 19, LXX.).

11. All this very extensive material has been excerpted by the Chronicler and worked up by him; the uniform colouring of the language, with its strongly marked individuality, and the specifically Levitical-musical colouring of the narrative are to be regarded as entirely his intellectual property. This makes not the smallest difference to the whole matter: the picture drawn by the Chronicler is in no respect historical, although he does deduce it from "sources," for, assuming their existence, the sources themselves were already untrustworthy and unhistorical; but it may for many be some sort of satisfaction not to be obliged to lay the blame for what, in modern language, would be called the falsification of history in Chronicles on the author of the Biblical Book of Chronicles personally.

Special Introduction

CHAPTER X.

BOOK I.—HISTORICAL BOOKS—*continued*

§§ 21, 22, 23. *Ezra and Nehemiah*; *Ruth and Esther*.

§ 21. EZRA AND NEHEMIAH

LITERATURE: *Commentaries*: E. Bertheau, *K.E.H.*, 1862; V. Ryssel, 2nd ed., 1887; C. Siegfried, *H.K.A.T.*, 1901; A. Bertholet, *K.H.C.A.T.*, 1902.

Monographs, Essays, etc.: B. Stade, *G.V.I.*, ii. 95–193; E. Schrader, *Die Dauer des zweiten Tempelbäues*, etc., *St. Kr.*, xl., 460 ff., 1867; R. Smend, *Die Listen der Bücher Esra und Nehemia*, 1881; E. Nestle (as cited in § 17 above), pp. 29–31, and *St. Kr.*, lii. 515 ff., 1879; A. van Hoonacker, *Néhémie et Esdras, nouvelle hypothèse*, etc., 1890; *Zorobabel et le second temple*, 1882, and *Nouvelles études sur la restauration juive après l'exil de Babylone*, 1896; W. H. Kosters, *Het herstel van Israel in het Perzische Tijdvak*, 1894 (German translation by A. Basedow, 1895); A. Kuenen, *Gesammelte Abhandlungen* (*cf.* § 2, 7 above), pp. 212 ff., and 370 ff.; J. Wellhausen, *G.G.N.*, 1895, 166 ff.; E. Meyer, *Die Entstehung des Judenthums*, 1896; J. Marquart (*cf.* § 16 above), pp. 28–68; Ch. C. Torrey, *The Composition and Historical Value of Ezra-Neh.*, supplement to *Z.A.T.W.*, 1896; E. Sellin, *Serubbabel*, 1898, and *Studien zur Entstehungsgeschichte der jüdischen Gemeinde*, ii., 1901; J. Geissler, *Die literarischen Beziehungen der Esramemorien*, 1899; J Nikel, *Die Wiederherstellung des jüdischen Gemeinwesens nach dem babylonischen Exil*, 1900; J.

EZRA AND NEHEMIAH

Fischer, *Die chronologischen Fragen in den Büchern Esr. Neh.*, 1903. On the criticism of the text: H. Guthe, *S.B.O.T.*, 1896.

1. The two books, which in our Bible are named after *Ezra* and *Nehemiah*, in the Hebrew canon form a single book, as appears from the Talmud, from the Massoretic subscription that follows Neh. xiii. 31, and from the absence of such after Ezra x. 44. The LXX. also counts it as one Book of Ezra; Jerome, who divides it, at any rate designates Nehemiah the Second Book of Ezra. We also shall consider and treat the book as a single unit. Its contents are purely historical.

Contents of Ezra-Nehemiah

Ezra i.–vi.: *Return and building of the Temple*—i., after the capture of Babylon in 538 Cyrus grants permission for the return, and gives back the Temple-vessels; ii., list of those who return, and their free-will offerings for the building of the Temple; iii., in October 537 the altar of the Solomonic Temple is again erected, and the Feast of Tabernacles solemnised. In May 536 the foundation-stone of the Temple is laid, and a beginning made with the work of building; iv., the *adversaries of Judah and Benjamin* bring about a prohibition by Cyrus of the building of the Temple. Correspondence between Rehum, Shimshai, and their companions, and King Artaxerxes (Artaḥšaštha); v. 1–5, in the second year of Darius (520), at the instance of the prophets Haggai and Zechariah, the building of the Temple is resumed; v. 6–vi. 12, correspondence between the satrap Tatnai and Darius; vi. 13-32, completion of the Temple on the 3rd of March 515, and solemn dedication of the same. Ezra vii.-x.: *Ezra's first appearance on the scene*—vii., in the April of 458 Ezra, *the teacher of the Law*, is despatched by Artaxerxes from Babylonia to Jerusalem as royal commissioner; viii., list of the heads of families who journey with him. Arrival in Jerusalem; ix., steps against the foreign wives. Ezra's penitential prayer; x., assembly of the people summoned for the 20th of December 458. A commission chosen to deal with the affairs connected with the mixed marriages. With an enumeration of the *men who had married strange women* the narrative abruptly breaks off.

Neh. i.-xiii. 3: *Nehemiah's first governorship*—i., Nehemiah, the Jewish cupbearer of King Artaxerxes, learns in December 445 that *the walls of Jerusalem are broken down and the gates thereof burned with fire*; ii., Nehemiah gets himself named in April 444 Persian governor in Jerusalem. Night ride round the ruined walls; iii., division of the work of building among the individual families. Scorn of enemies; iv., Nehemiah's regulations for the protection of the building of the walls; v., Nehemiah carries through a remission of debts; vi., further intrigues of opponents. The building of the wall completed, after fifty-two days' work, on the 25th of September 444; vii., measures for safeguarding Jerusalem. Repetition of the list given in Ezra ii.; viii.-x., in October 444 reading of the *Book of the Law of Moses* and solemn engagement to observe the same; xi., every tenth man selected to be an inhabitant of Jerusalem. List of the heads of families in Jerusalem and in the cities of Judah and Benjamin; xii. 1–26, list of the priests and Levites; vss. 27–43, dedication of the walls of Jerusalem; vss. 44–47, installation of overseers over the Temple-chambers; xiii. 1–3, separation of all foreigners. Neh. xiii. 4–31: *various notices respecting Nehemiah's second governorship from 433 onward.* From this rapid survey of its contents it is already apparent that in Ezra-Nehemiah we do not really possess a connected historical work, but various accounts of particular events which were especially important and significant for the history of the people and the theocracy.

2. If we now consider *the book as such*, the first thing that strikes us is that Ezra iv. 7–vi. 18 and vii. 12–26 are written in the Aramaic language, and not only so, but in a peculiar idiom of Aramaic which is characteristically distinguished from that of the Book of Daniel. Other differences, however, are still more important. Ezra and Nehemiah sometimes speak themselves in the first person, sometimes they are made the subjects of the narrative in the third person. Such passages with the first person ("I") occur in Ezra vii. 27–ix. 15, in Neh. i. 1–vii. 5, then again in xii. 31, where, however, the whole passage xii. 27–43 is closely and inseparably bound together, and finally xiii. 4–31. If in these "I" passages there really lie before us authentic memoranda, memoirs of the two eminent men named, then they will prove to be documents of an importance such as hardly anything else in the literature of Israel has for us—to be used with caution indeed, which is doubly demanded in the case of memoirs, but, on the other hand, calculated to bring us in the most

complete and immediate way face to face with the actual events, to let us to a certain extent see into the heart of things. Our next task must, therefore, be to come to a decision on this point.

3. First of all, then, with reference to *the "I" passage Ezra vii. 27–ix. 15*, there is manifest throughout it the same hand and the same spirit; it so clearly lives and moves in the events, and gives us so profound an insight into the thoughts and moods of the narrator, that not the slightest doubt can arise as to the authenticity of this fragment of the memoirs: only viii. 35–36 stands out from its context and exhibits a different manner of expression and representation.

The passage begins with thanks to God for an imperial firman which (vii. 12–26) immediately follows. Objection has been taken to its specifically Jewish colouring, but E. Meyer has conclusively shown its genuineness in this form: it is derived from the memoirs of Ezra. Only vss. 1–11 are an introductory "orientation," written by another hand; for Ezra would hardly have praised himself in the manner vs. 6 does, and, further, from a comparison of the genealogy in vss. 1–5 with 1 Chron. v. 21–40, it is clear that the Seraiah who is here described as the father of Ezra is rather the last principal priest of the Solomonic Temple, who was executed by Nebuchadnezzar, so that the genealogy only intends to assert that Ezra belonged to the high-priestly family. Also the jejune account, anticipating the contents of ch. viii., which is given in vss. 7–9, clearly points to another and external hand—one that makes use of and is dependent upon the memoirs of Ezra. That these memoirs suddenly break off at ix. 15 can also only be due to the interposition of a strange hand: the events of the next thirteen years were clearly of too dismal a character to make it desirable to perpetuate the memory of them. From all this it follows that we have here the authentic memoirs of Ezra, which, however, have simply been used as a source by another author, and only so far embodied as it suited this writer to utilise them. A more extensive fragment of these memoirs will meet us in Neh. ix. 6–x. 40.

4. In Nehemiah the "I" passages are far more extensive. At the outset, ch. i. 1–vii. 5 speak throughout in the first person, and are of indubitable authenticity. This long piece has a far more individual colouring than the fragment of Ezra's memoirs, and from it the personality of the writer emerges still more distinctly. And, moreover, this personality is one of the most engaging and congenial to be met with in the whole course of Israelitish history; it is that of a man who does not, indeed, shrink from using the power that has been conferred upon him, but who, without the suspicion of selfish motive—nay, even to the extent of renouncing his own personal rights and claims—devotes himself with a holy enthusiasm entirely to the service of a great idea, and does everything in his power for it and its realisation. From v. 14 it follows that the memoirs can only have been formulated at a considerably later period. Considerable objection has been taken to the datum given in vi. 15, which as regards its form also gives rise to suspicion, and it is, in fact, not altogether easy to conceive that every-

thing narrated in ch. ii.–vi. could have happened in fifty-two days; but the superhuman exertion of all force and strength at command, coupled with the extremely skilful division of labour and work, make it appear quite possible, and constitute a splendid proof showing how far the enthusiasm and energy of Nehemiah carried along the whole community with him. From what authority Josephus ("Ant.," xi. 5, 8) derives the statement that the building of the walls lasted two years and eight months cannot be ascertained.

When we proceed beyond vii. 5, the section vii. 6–73a attaches itself so naturally and easily on to vii. 5 that this important document also must certainly be regarded as having stood from the very first in the memoirs of Nehemiah. That ch. vii. 73b–x. 40 breaks the connexion, while xi. 1 forms the continuation of vii. 73a, is generally conceded; but as to the meaning and character of the list in ch. xi. no consensus of opinion has been attained. As ch. xi. seems to be the completion of vii. 4–5, it is usually considered to be an account of the ways and means employed by Nehemiah to increase the population of Jerusalem and to make the city defensible; but long ago Ewald ("G.V.I.," iv., 3rd ed., 206, remark[1]) rightly saw that this list—which partly recurs in 1 Chron. ix. 3–17—is rather the immediate continuation of ch. vii., and refers to the measures taken by Zerubbabel, which Nehemiah clearly resumed. Thus this chapter also, although it has not been preserved intact, will have stood in the memoirs of Nehemiah. The continuation, it is true, has not been preserved to us: what

[1] E.T., v. 159, note.

it was that God put in Nehemiah's heart, and for what purpose he assembled the nobles and leaders of the people, with a view to remedying the evil of Jerusalem's sparse population (vii. 4–5), is not told us. The list of priests and Levites that immediately follows in xii. 1–26 cannot have been extracted from the memoirs of Nehemiah, because it carries on the priestly genealogy far below Nehemiah's time, viz. as far as *the reign of Darius the Persian, i.e.* Darius III. Codomannus; the Jaddua mentioned there as the last member is known from Josephus to have been a contemporary of Alexander the Great. On the other hand, xii. 27–43 is again an extract from the memoirs (even though it has been subjected to revision, as Ewald[1] also rightly perceived), and likewise also the passage xiii. 4–31, which, it is true, refers to a period twelve years later. The section xii. 44–xiii. 3 certainly proceeds from the same hand which revised xii. 27–43 and inserted the lists in xii. 1–26. Thus the examination of the Book of Nehemiah produces, with regard to these memoirs, quite the same result as in the case of Ezra; so far as they are preserved they are undoubtedly authentic, but have only been preserved to us by another hand, which used them as sources and made excerpts from them.

5. We now direct our attention first of all to the two passages which take up and interrupt the memoirs of Ezra and Nehemiah—*Ezra x. and Neh. viii.–x.* In both, the representation is so vivid and graphic, and yields features of so detailed a character, that we may be tempted to regard them as due to an eye-witness. This would be precluded if the Johanan

[1] *Op. cit.*, 205, remark 9 (= " Prophets of the O.T.," v. 158, note 7).

ben Eliashib, after whom (Ezra x. 6) a chamber in the Temple is called, were the son or grandson of the Eliashib who in the year 433, according to Neh. xiii. 4, held the High Priesthood; see Neh. xii. 22 and 23 (on which verses Kuenen, p. 239, should be compared). But everything suggests the indirect expression of an eye-witness. For as both passages were clearly written by the same hand, the most obvious inference is to think of the writer to whom we owe the selection and preservation of the memoirs: the imperceptible way in which the memoirs glide into the narrative we are considering, and the latter into the memoirs, is an argument in favour of this view. This author has partly taken over the memoirs directly, partly on the basis of them has produced a representation of his own, so that the intuitive insight and detail that mark his narrative go back indirectly to the memoirs. But Stade has detected that Neh. ix. 6–x. 40 has been taken over directly from the memoirs of Ezra. It must be pronounced as *a priori* probable that Ezra narrated, as well as the first attempt to carry, so also the final triumph of his cause. And for this view there exist positive grounds. Ch. ix. 6 begins in the LXX. with the words καὶ εἶπεν Ἐσδρας—and quite rightly so, because this prayer can only be conceived of as spoken by a single person, and it is twin-brother of Ezra ix. Further, we find the communicative form of the narrative with "we" recurring in Neh. x., just as it is characteristic of Ezra viii. As the most weighty proof I add here the divergences from P^1—already spoken of above in § 12, 12—which occur in Neh. x., and which become the more inexplicable the later the date is at which the passage is placed: only their traditional place in the memoirs of Ezra could have preserved them at all. The sections Ezra x. and Neh. vii. 73b–ix. 5 have thus been composed on the basis of the memoirs by an author living after Ezra and Nehemiah, in whom we can place implicit faith as regards what is narrated by him.

6. There still remains Ezra i.–vi. to form an estimate of. Here the first thing that strikes us is that the opening verses i. 1–3aα are almost verbally the same as, and are obviously identical with, the concluding verses of Chronicles (2 Chron. xxxvi. 22–23). Hence the conclusion was long ago deduced that the Book of Ezra-Nehemiah is the continuation of Chronicles, and originally formed in conjunction with it one continuous historical work, so that the Chronicler would thus be the final author also of Ezra-Nehemiah. And this opinion is, in fact, supported both by external and internal grounds. Wherever in Ezra-Nehemiah older sources are not present in the composition, style, spirit, point of view, and mode of expression are altogether those of the Chronicler—there is the same rigorously legalistic, Levitical character, with special predilection for the musical side of the cultus, the same joy in lists and large numbers, the same colouring of the representation in agreement with the language of the later Psalms. Ch. i. and iii. bear this manner of the Chronicler on their face; ch. ii. = Neh. vii., and thus is borrowed from the memoirs of Nehemiah. There is still the question as to the origin and character of the Aramaic passage iv. 7–vi. 18 to be settled. Here suspicion might be aroused by the circumstance that the last verses of the Aramaic passage (vi. 16–18) cannot be

separated in substance from vi. 19–22, and, in the same way as these latter, must have been written by the Chronicler himself, who naturally had as much command of the Aramaic language as of the Hebrew. But the purely narrative section v. 1–vi. 15 is marked by so peculiar a character, and one that diverges so much from the manner of the Chronicler, that there can be no doubt that the Chronicler here made use of a special source written in Aramaic. This Aramaic source contained in particular a rich store of documents and authoritative pieces whose genuineness has been placed by E. Meyer beyond the reach of doubt, and shows itself throughout extremely well informed exactly in those points which have given occasion for doubt and hesitation, as has been convincingly proved especially by Stade. In using this Aramaic source, however, the Chronicler was unfortunate enough to misunderstand the matter detailed in iv. 6 and the document embodied in iv. 7–23, and has assigned them a false position: the correspondence between Rehum and Artaxerxes belongs, as Bertheau already rightly perceived, to the period between Ezra x. and Neh. i. In order to fit them into connexion with his narrative, the Chronicler then wrote vs. 24. Still, we have every reason to be grateful to him for his misunderstanding, because it is only by reason of it that this highly interesting passage has been preserved to us. It is certain that the latter is derived from the Aramaic source of the Chronicler, and this being so it cannot have been written earlier than *circà* 450, but rests upon extremely good information.

7. Accordingly, we have to conceive *the origin of*

the Book of Ezra-Nehemiah as follows. The author of the book in its present form is the Chronicler. He made use of:

(*a*) An Aramaic source written not earlier than 450, which contained the history of the building of the Temple and the walls, together with a considerable amount of original documentary evidence; and this is to be regarded as thoroughly trustworthy. From it Ezra iv. 8–22, v. 1–vi. 16 have been taken verbally.

(*b*) The memoirs of Ezra and Nehemiah, which, however, no longer lay before the Chronicler in their original form, but worked up into the writing of a later author. For proof of this appeal is usually made to the fact that the relation of Ezra ii. 1–iii. 1 to Neh. vii. 6–viii. 1*a* shows how Neh. vii. already lay before the Chronicler in the connected form in which we now read it. This proof is not convincing, because the words in question also fit Ezra iii. 1 well and naturally in the connexion in that place; but all the same I do not doubt the correctness of the supposed fact. From this work the Chronicler borrowed Ezra ii. and the essential nucleus of his book, Ezra vii. 12–Neh. xi. 36, and further also Neh. xii. 27–43 and xiii. 4–31. It is possible that this is identical with the ספר דברי הימים (" book of the Chronicles ") which is adduced in Neh. xii. 23, and according to that passage reached *even until the days of Johanan the son of Eliashib.* It must remain a moot question whether the serious breaks in the narrative which occur after Ezra x. 44 and Neh. xi. 36 are due to the Chronicler, or already existed in his original authority.

(*c*) It is in itself sufficiently obvious that the Chronicler wrote Ezra i., iii. 2–iv. 7, and iv. 24, and has antedated here the laying of the foundation-stone of the Temple, and the beginning of the work of building, in placing these events immediately after the return of the exiles; in view of the unmistakable assertions of Haggai and Zechariah this cannot be right. Further, he wrote Ezra vi. 16–vii. 11, viii. 25–36, and Neh. xii. 1–26, xii. 44–xiii. 3, and may also in details have revised his original authority, as we discovered this in all probability for the section Neh. xii. 27; at any rate, Torrey and Geissler have noted an undoubted literary relationship existing between the memoirs of Ezra and the work of the Chronicler.

(d) The doublets Ezra i. 1–3aa = 2 Chron. xxxvi. 22–23 are easily explained. After the formation of the Chronicler's great historical work, that part of it was first of all received into the canon which was quite new and narrated things and events of which hitherto no account had been available. And with this accords the circumstance that in the Jewish canon Ezra-Nehemiah precedes Chronicles. Later still the rest of the work, which would naturally appeal much to the sympathies of later times, was considered worthy of a place in the canon, and the verses in question were retained here because it was preferred to bring the book to a close with the consoling prospect of vs. 23, rather than with the lugubrious picture of vss. 17–21. In an exactly analogous way Kings is brought to an end, not with the destruction of Jerusalem, but with the pardon of Jehoiachin.

8. Recently the accounts embodied in the Book of Ezra-Nehemiah have been subjected to *a searching*

criticism of their subject-matter. Hoonacker, indeed, regards the circumstances narrated as historical, but thinks that, having regard to a variety of difficulties that are present, the chronological sequence must be reversed, and Ezra's active life placed after that of Nehemiah: the Artaxerxes whose seventh year is mentioned in Ezra vii. 7 ff. is, according to him, not Artaxerxes I. Longimanus, but Artaxerxes II. Mnemon, and Ezra's visit and work of reform consequently fall in the year 398. Kosters, who agrees in one important point with Hoonacker, goes much further than the latter. According to him, a return of exiles in the second year of Cyrus did not take place at all; the building of the Temple and the walls was rather the work of the population that had remained behind in the land (2 Kings xxv. 12), of whom Zerubbabel and Nehemiah were governors; Ezra's visit and work of reform fall in the second governorship of Nehemiah, after the events narrated in Neh. xiii. 4–31. Ezra arrived for the first time after 433; first of all the community was reconstituted by the dissolution of the mixed marriages, and then solemnly bound to the observance of the Law which had been brought with him by Ezra: the first return-journey under Zerubbabel, with all those who joined themselves with him, has been invented by the Chronicler, who reversed the order of events. Finally, according to Torrey, the "I" passages, with the exception of Neh. i.–ii.† and iii. 33–vi. 19†, have been fabricated by the Chronicler, who in them created his masterpiece, and Nehemiah also belongs to the reign of Artaxerxes II. Hoonacker's reconstruction was already rejected and refuted by Kuenen, and Wellhausen has energetically opposed Kosters: since E. Meyer's demonstration of the authenticity of the documents in Ezra iv.–vii., this hypercritical reconstruction has lost all claim to serious consideration, and we may rest assured that in Ezra-Nehemiah we have every reason to recognise an essentially trustworthy recital of the events narrated therein.

§ 22. THE BOOK OF RUTH

LITERATURE: *Commentaries*: E. Bertheau, *K.E.H.*, 1883, 2nd ed.; C. H. H. Wright, 1864; A. Bertholet, *K.H.C.A.T.*, 1898; W. Nowack, *H.K.A.T.*, 1902. *Essays, monographs, etc.*: K. Budde, *Z.A.T.W.*, xii. 43–46, 1892; J. A. Bewer, *St. Kr.*, lxxvi., 328 ff., 502 ff., 1903; L. Kohler, *Th. T.*, xxxviii., 458 ff., 1904.

1. The Book of Ruth contains, in the form of a vivid poetic recital, a charming idyll, mainly consisting of a simple family-history of the Moabitess Ruth, who, however, by the concluding words of the book is assured a position of far-reaching importance and significance: this Moabitess. though by descent a mere heathen, is yet in piety a true daughter of Israel, and was proved worthy of becoming the ancestress of David. In accordance with this, we should have expected to find the book between Judges and Samuel, where as a matter of fact the LXX., Vulgate, and the German and English Bibles have placed it, and where we should have looked to find it all the more readily because the history of Samuel's youth forms a similar idyll. When in spite of this we find it separated from the historical books in the Jewish canon, we are led by this circumstance to assign the origin of this little book to a period when

the collection of the historical books had already been closed.

2. And other grounds still weightier exist which favour a later period as the time of its composition. The time-indication *in the days when the judges judged* (i. 1) presupposes the rigidly fixed chronological system of the Deuteronomic Exilic History of Israel. The language of the book is strongly tinged with Aramaisms, and has many peculiarities which point with convincing and cogent force to the post-exilic period; while, on the other hand, the recital itself is mainly composed of reminiscences of older historical works, especially J. Quite a striking and convincing example is to be seen in Ruth iv. 7 compared with Deut. xxv. 9; here a custom which was current in the times of Deuteronomy is expressly explained as if it were an antiquarian curiosity. The conclusion (iv. 18–22), which displays the schematic arrangement of the genealogies of P, had better be left out of account, because it may have been added later as the completion of vs. 12.

3. The only plausible ground that can be adduced for assigning the composition of the book to an earlier period is the large-hearted candour displayed here in tracing David's descent to a Moabitish ancestress, and on this account many feel compelled to maintain a place for the book in the pre-Deuteronomic period (*cf.* Deut. xxiii. 4), or at any rate before the time of Ezra, when the purity of families and of family-descent was guarded with rigorous care. But these doubts cannot continue with any force in the presence of the material reasons to the contrary that have been adduced, and thus nothing remains but

to see in Ruth a deliberate protest against the strict point of view—a protest intended to show that not bodily descent but the disposition of the heart is the main thing, and that even union with a truly pious heathen woman is blessed by Jahve. If the genealogy at the end was inserted later, we should be obliged to make the author of Ruth a contemporary of Ezra and Nehemiah, who took up, as the starting-point of his polemic, the tradition of a Moabitish ancestress of David—a tradition which could neither be denied nor concealed. In this case, side by side with its generally acknowledged high aesthetic value the little Book of Ruth also possesses an ethico-religious worth at least equally high.

Remark.—Recently Köhler has endeavoured to show that this conception of the character of the book is an erroneous one, for if the supposed polemical tendency does not clearly emerge, then the real heroine of the narrative is not Ruth but Naomi; in this connexion he indicates many obscurities in the narrative which hitherto have been insufficiently appreciated. But generally speaking it is by no means a fault if a polemical or special purpose does not make itself felt too palpably and insistently; and that for the unsophisticated intelligence Ruth is the person who is the central object of the author's delineation is attested by the consensus of more than two thousand years. The one and only object of the entire narrative in ch. i. is to create a situation in which a man of Israel would have been obliged, in accordance with the law of the Levirate-marriage, to espouse a Moabitess.

§ 23. THE BOOK OF ESTHER

LITERATURE: *Commentaries*: E. Bertheau, *K.E.H.*, 1862; V. Ryssel, 2nd ed., 1887; J. W. Haley, 1895; G. Wildeboer, *K.H.C.A.T.*, 1898; C. Siegfried, *K.H.A.T.*, 1901. *Essays, monographs*, etc. on the Feast of Purim: P. de Lagarde,

Purim, etc., 1887; H. Zimmern, *Z.A.T.W.*, xi. 157 ff., 1891; F. Schwally, *Das Leben nach dem Tode*, 1892, § 14; B. Meissner, *Z.D.M.G.*, l. 296 ff., 1896; W. Erbt, *Die Purimsage in der Bibel*, 1900.

1. The Christian expositor of the O.T. would prefer to pass over the Book of Esther altogether, and at any rate does not care to occupy himself with it more than is absolutely necessary; for, valuable as this book is to us as a document for the history of religion, in receiving it into the collection of the sacred writings the framers of the canon committed a serious blunder. All the worst and most unpleasing features of Judaism are here displayed without disguise; and only in Alexandria was it felt absolutely necessary to cover up the ugliest bare places with a couple of religious patches. Moreover, in Palestine also it provoked some opposition, and was not admitted into the canon without warm protest.

2. It is clear that the Book of Esther—which recounts to us how, after Vashti had been repudiated, Esther, the adoptive daughter of the Jewish exile Mordecai, became the consort of the Persian King Ahašveroš (*i.e.* Xerxes), and in this position broke up the plot of Haman, the enemy of the Jews, and procured the Jews a bloody revenge on their opponents—is simply *a historical romance*; this is now fully recognised by all scholars who occupy a position of scientific freedom in investigation; and even though one or other feature of the account should ultimately rest upon a basis of actual fact, such elements have been worked up so freely, and made subservient to the author's special object to such an extent, as to have been deprived of all historical

17

value. The aim of the book is simply to provide an explanation of and to recommend the Feast of Purim: only with respect to ix. 20–32 have doubts of an isagogic nature been raised, but without cogent reason.

3. The question as to *the age and place of origin* of Esther is coincident with the similar question as to the Feast of Purim. The first clear attestation of the latter is met with in 2 Macc. xv. 36, where the Day of Nicanor (13th of Adar) is described as πρὸ μιᾶς ἡμέρας τῆς Μαρδοχαικῆς ἡμέρας ("the day before Mardocheus' Day"). That the Feast of Purim is intended by the descriptive term Μαρδοχαικὴ ἡμέρα ("Mardocheus' Day") here is obvious. But in view of the considerable distance of time that separates 2 Macc. from the events it narrates, it cannot be deduced from this passage that Purim was observed in the age of Judas Maccabaeus: the evidence is proof positive only for the time of the author. Though it is not strictly a proof, yet a very strong presumptive argument for not carrying the origin of Esther and Purim very far back is afforded by the silence of Jesus ben Sira as to Esther and Mordecai in the πατέρων ὕμνος (Ecclus. xliv.–xlix.)—a fact which is not easily explicable if Purim was celebrated, and Esther generally known, in the time of Ben Sira. Although the scene of it is laid in the time and at the court of Xerxes, it is clear that the book itself was not written during the supremacy of the Achaemenidae from the way in which Xerxes and the Persian Empire are spoken of (i. 1), as of things which have long since faded into the domain of historical reminiscences, in referring to which it is

necessary to refresh the reader's memory. The language also, though it carefully abstains from the use of such late characteristic marks as the employment of שׁ for the relative, and obviously exhibits traces of effort to display a purely Hebrew colouring, shows that the book belongs to the latest period of Jewish literature (*cf.*, on this point, Siegfried, "Einleitung," § 3). The fanatical and aggressive hatred that it breathes against all non-Jews is most easily explained as an echo of the religious war against the savage oppression of Antiochus Epiphanes, and Haman's plot (ch. iii. 8-9) is, in fact, the unmistakable counterpart of the designs of Antiochus (1 Macc. i. 41, iii. 34-36): it is not, however, like Daniel, a product of that great and stirring time itself; we must rather accept the view of Kuenen, who assigns it a date towards the end of the Jewish struggle for freedom in 135, when religious enthusiasm in the case of many had weakened into a more worldly feeling, and, in consequence of past events, Jewish national feeling had adopted a rigorously exclusive attitude against everything non-Jewish, while on the other hand, by the wonderful results of the little people's efforts against the forces of the gigantic empire of the Seleucids, national pride must have been deeply stirred and inspired with confidence of victory.

4. But what is the reason for giving the whole story a Persian setting, and why is the word פּוּרִים ("Purim") in ch. iii. 7 and ix. 19 explained from Persian, and that, too, incorrectly, since there is no Persian word *pûr* with the meaning *lot*? All this suggests that we should look for the origin of the

Feast of Purim in Persia; consequently Lagarde explains Purim—to designate which we meet with the names φρουραια and φουρδαια in the oldest Greek tradition—as the transformed and adapted Persian festival of Farwardigân, and in addition he points out the presence of characteristic features of two other high Persian festivals, those of μαγοφονία and of the Feast of the Beardless. Kuenen approves of the conjecture of M. J. de Goeje, who calls attention to the likeness of Esther to Scheherezade, the heroine of the Tales of the Thousand and One Nights, and from this deduces the conclusion that the author of Esther is dependent upon an old Persian tradition of which the form of the Thousand and One Nights is also an embodiment. Such being the case, it is easy to suppose that the author was not a Palestinian at all, but belonged to the numerous Jewish population living in Mesopotamia and Persia. Zimmern maintains a Babylonian origin for the festival, regarding it as a transformed Zagmuk—*i.e.* New Year Festival, when the gods, under the presidency of Marduk, met together in an assembly (*puḥru*) and cast the lots which were to decide the destinies of the next year. Schwally accepts both solutions, and would also postulate the presence of genuine Israelitish elements, which he regards as survivals of a cult of the dead. Meissner points out that the descriptions given by later authors of the Persian feast of Sakaia, which was widespread throughout the whole of the Orient, can only be explained from a mixture of the old Persian Farwardigân with the Babylonian Zagmuk-festival; while P. Jensen[1] recognises the presence

---

[1] *Ap.* Wildeboer, pp. 173 ff.

also of Elamitic ingredients, just as the scene of the story is in fact laid in Susa, the old Elamite capital. That Purim is not of purely Jewish origin may be regarded as certain.

5. It is characteristic of the Judaism of the last years of the pre-Christian period that this book enjoyed *the greatest possible favour;* being preferred even to the Psalms and Prophets, and accorded a position of equal consideration with the Tora. Eloquent evidence of this great popularity is afforded by the fact that we possess three Targums, several Midrashim, and two widely divergent Greek recensions of Esther. Of the three Targums, that printed in the Antwerp Polyglot reproduces the Hebrew text in a fairly literal version, while the two others prove to be Haggadic developments of the traditional material.

Remark.—According to H. Willrich ("Judaica," 1900, pp. 1–28), the story of Esther is to be regarded as a disguised delineation of Egyptian affairs, and the Ahašveroš mentioned in it is the notorious anti-Jewish Ptolemy VII. Physkon (reigned 146–117).

Special Introduction

CHAPTER XI

BOOK II.—B. PROPHETIC BOOKS

LITERATURE: J. G. Eichorn, *Die hebräischen Propheten*, 3 vols., 1816-1819; H. Ewald, *Prophets of the Old Testament*, 5 vols., 1867-1868; A. Kuenen, *De profeten en de profetie onder Israel*, 2 vols., 1875; B. Duhm, *Die Theologie der Propheten*, 1875; W. R. Smith, *The Prophets of Israel and their Place in History*, 1895, 2nd ed.; F. Giesebrecht, *Die Berufsbegabung der alttestamentlichen Propheten*, 1897; F. Hitzig, *Die prophetischen Bücher des A.T. übersetzt*, 1854.

§ 24. ISAIAH

LITERATURE: *Commentaries*: C. Vitringa, 2 vols, 1714, 1720; J. C. Doderlein, 1775; Lowth-Koppe, 4 vols., 1779-1781; W. Gesenius, 3 vols., 1821; F. Hitzig, 1833; F. Delitzsch, *B.C.A.T.*, 1889, 4th ed.; K. Bredenkamp, 1887; A. Dillmann, *K.E.H.*, 1890, 5th ed.; R. Kittel, 1898, 6th ed.: B. Duhm, *H.K.A.T.*, 1902, 2nd ed.; K. Marti, *K.H.C.A.T.*, 1900. *Monographs, Essays, etc.*: T. K. Cheyne, *Introduction to the Book of Isaiah*, 1895 (German translation by J. Boehmer, 1897); F. Giesebrecht, *Beiträge zur Jesaiakritik*, 1890; C. H. Cornill, *Die Komposition des Buches Jesaia*, *Z.A.T.W.*, iv. 83 ff., 1884; H. Guthe, *Das Zukunftsbild des Jesaia*, 1885; H. Hackmann, *Die Zukunftserwartung des Jesaia*, 1893; P. Volz, *Die vorexilische Jahveprophetie und der Messias*, 1897; A. Soerensen, *Juda und die assyrische Weltmacht*, 1885; J. Meinhold, *Jesaia und seine Zeit*, 1898, and *Studien zur israel. Religionsgeschich.*, i. 89-159, 1903.

On the criticism of the text: G. Studer, *J. d. Th.*, iii. 706 ff., 1877; v. 63 ff., 1879, vii. 161 ff., 1881; P. de Lagarde,

Semitica, i. 1–32, 1878; J. Bachmann, *Alttestamentliche Untersuchungen*, 1894, 49–100; T. K. Cheyne, *S.B.O.T.*, 1899. On ch. iii. 16 ff., H. Oort, *Th. T.*, xx., 561 ff., 1886. On ch. iv., B. Stade, *Z.A.T.W.*, iv. 149 ff., 1884. On ch. vii.–ix., K. Bredenkamp, *Vaticinium de Immanuale*, 1880; K. Budde in *Études dédiées à Mr. Leemans*, 1885, 125 ff.; F. Giesebrecht, *St. Kr.*, lxi., 217 ff., 1888; H. Winckler, (see § 18 above), pp. 60–76. On ch xi. 1 ff., G. Beer, *Z.A.T.W.*, xviii., 345 ff., 1898. On ch. xiv. 24–27, B. Stade, *Z.A.T.W.*, vi. 16, 1883; H. Oort, *Th. T.*, xx., 193, 1886. On ch. xv.–xvi., F. Hitzig, *Des Propheten Jona Orakel über Moab*, 1831; H. Oort, *Th. T.*, xxi. 51 ff., 1887; W. W. Baudissin, *St Kr.*, lxi., 509 ff., 1888; On ch. xviii.–xx., B. Stade, *De Isaiae vaticiniis Aethiopicis*, 1873; H. Winckler, pp. 142–156. On xxi. 1–10, P. Kleinert, *St. Kr.*, 1., 167 ff., 1877; F. Buhl, *Z.A.T.W.*, viii., 157 ff., 1888; and B. Stade, *ibid.*, pp. 165 ff. On ch. xxi. 15–17, H. Winckler, pp. 420–425. On ch. xxii. 15–25, A. Kamphausen, *Amer. Journ. of Theology*, v. 43 ff., 1901. On ch. xxiv.–xxvii., R. Smend, *Z.A.T.W.*, iv. 161 ff., 1884; H. Oort, *Th. T.*, xx. 166 ff., 1886; J. Boehmer, *Z.A.T.W.*, xxii., 372, 1902. On ch. xxviii.–xxxiii., M. Brückner, 1897. On ch. xxviii., J. Meinhold, *St. Kr.*, lxvi., 1 ff., 1893. On ch. xxxii.–xxxiii., B. Stade, *Z.A.T.W.*, iv., 256 ff., 1884. On ch. xxxvi.–xxxix., B. Stade, *Z.A.T.W.*, vi. 172 ff., 1886; H. Winckler, pp. 26–49; J. Meinhold, *Die Jesaiaerzählungen, Jes. xxxvi.–xxxix.*, 1898. On ch. xxxvii. 22–32, K. Budde, *Z.A.T.W.*, xii. 31 ff., 1892. On ch. xxxviii. 9–20, A. Klostermann, *St. Kr.*, lvii., 157 ff., 1884. On the Second Isaiah, L. Seinecke, *Der Evangelist des A.T.*, 1870; A. Klostermann, *Z.L.Th.*, xxxvii. 1 ff., 1876; J. Ley, *Historische Erklärung des zweiten Teiles des Jesaia*, 1893; H. Oort, *Kritische anteekeningen*, etc., *Th. T.*, xxv. 461 ff., 1891. Critical edition of the text, Hebrew and German, by A. Klostermann, 1893. For the literature on the Songs of the Servant of Jahve, and on the question of a Trito-Isaiah, see paragraphs 21 and 22 of this section below.

1. In the order of the books which is familiar to us, the Prophetic Writings are opened by Isaiah. A well-born native of Jerusalem—the son of a certain Amoz—Isaiah began his career of prophetic activity

in the death-year of King Uzziah (vi. 1). He was married (viii. 1), and the father of several sons (vii. 3, viii. 3). Although not of royal descent, he appears to have belonged to the higher ranks of society. His influence and activity, sustained as they were not by the possession of any formal office, but merely by the weight of his own personality and the power of his own religious convictions, must have been great and of far-reaching importance, and they lasted for more than a generation. His career coincided with a period of critical importance for Judah, when, after the downfall of Israel, Judah became the sole representative of the faith of Jahve, and when, in the fate of the tiny land, the destinies of the world were mirrored. According to a later legend, which is perhaps referred to already in Heb. xi. 37, he is said to have suffered a martyr's death, at an advanced age, in the reign of Manasseh.

2. *The Book* which bears this prophet's name is divisible into several clearly distinct groups: ch. i.–xii., a collection of discourses which are addressed exclusively to Judah-Jerusalem and Israel; ch. xiii.–xxiii., a series of oracles almost all distinguished by the designation משׂא ("burden," "oracle") and directed to foreign peoples: forming a grandiose conclusion to this section, ch. xxiv.–xxvii. give a picture of the world-judgment and of the final Messianic salvation; ch. xxviii.–xxxiii., a closely knit and connected group of discourses dealing with the straits to which Jerusalem was reduced and its marvellous deliverance, to which are attached ch. xxxiv.–xxxv., containing a threat of woes to Edom as preparatory to the final salvation of Zion; ch. xxxvi.–xxxix. are a historical

section, giving an account of Isaiah's prophetic activity during and after the time of the siege of Jerusalem by the Assyrians; and finally ch. xl.–lxvi. form a larger coherent whole, in which Assyria completely vanishes, and Babylon appears as Israel's oppressor and tyrant.

3. The oldest attestation of the existence of the Book of Isaiah in the form in which it now lies before us is that of Jesus Sir. [Ecclus.] xlviii. 20–25; it was regarded as a unity, the work of the prophet whose name it bears. If we leave out of account some hesitating and ambiguous suggestions made by Aben Ezra, this view was held unbrokenly till in the fourth quarter of the eighteenth century criticism awoke to life. As pioneers of the latter, the names of Döderlein, Koppe, and Eichorn call for mention — its latest phase is represented by Duhm, Hackmann, Cheyne, and Marti, who adopt the most radical methods in separating non-genuine passages, and also set forth the genuine ones as a mosaic made up of fragments which have been worked over throughout, the whole book being regarded as a product of a process of unchecked literary diorthosis, continued through centuries, which Duhm brings down almost to the time of the birth of Christ; "the final redaction of the Book of Isaiah is thus hardly much older than the rise of the K^{e}tib." To pursue the investigation of all such details as these is, of course, not the proper function of a work which professes to be an Outline; we must restrict ourselves to the task of emphasising the principal aspects of the critical treatment, and to estimating the most important of its results.

4. Only the following passages—though even these are regarded as having been more or less revised—are declared to be of undisputed *authenticity*: ch. i., ii. 6–iv. 1, v., vi., vii. 1–viii. 18, ix. 7–x. 4, x. 5–15, xvii. 1–11, xviii., xx., xxii., xxviii.–xxxi. By critics of repute the following also are in part recognised as Isaianic: iv. 2–4, viii. 19–ix. 6, x. 16–xi. 9, xiv. 24–27, 28–32, xv.–xvi., xvii. 12–14, and xxxii. On the other hand, the following have been abandoned as non-genuine practically by all scholars: ii. 2–4, iv. 5–6, xi. 10–xiv. 23, xix., xxi., xxiii.–xxvii., xxxiii.–xxxv., together with the discourses of Isaiah contained in the historical section, ch. xxxvi.–xxxix. Ch. xl.–lxvi. will have to be dealt with separately.

The Genuine Parts of the Book of Isaiah

5. As the prophetic activity of Isaiah embraced a period of time which was only again equalled in the case of Jeremiah, it is specially important in his case to determine *the time of the composition of each individual oracle*; but just in this particular estimates differ widely from each other. The following are fixed by indisputable time-determinations: ch. vi. (death-year of Uzziah, 740? at the latest 736), vii. 1–viii. 18 (Syro-Ephraimitish War, 735–4), and xx. (capture of Ashdod by Sargon, 711); and further, for the oracles which are directed against the still existing kingdom of Israel, the year 722 must be regarded as the *terminus ad quem*. Essential agreement prevails in regarding ch. ix. 7–x. 4, xvii. 1–11, v., ii. 6–iv. 1 as to be assigned to the early period of Isaiah's prophetic career, and in placing ch. xviii., together with xxviii. 7–xxxi., in the time of Sennacherib,

between 705 and 701. Ch. ix. 7–x.4 (where, however, the strophe x. 1–3 is to be cut out, and v. 25–30 to be inserted as conclusion) falls within the time of the outbreak of the Syro-Ephraimitish war, and xvii. 1–11 at the beginning of the latter. As the date of the passages ii. 6–iv. 1, v. 1–23, and x. 1–3 the early period of the reign of Ahaz may be regarded as generally admitted. That the very noteworthy oracle against the faithless household-minister Shebna (xxii. 15–25) is to be assigned to some year before 701—if it cannot be even more exactly determined—seems to be made certain by xxxvi. 3 = 2 Kings xviii. 18. In the case of ch. x. 5–15 and 32 (also xiv. 24–27) the dates assigned waver between the reigns of Sargon and Sennacherib: I still prefer the latter dating, as we are told nothing of any threatened attack on Jerusalem by Sargon. In the case of ch. xiv. 28–32—the authenticity of which is acknowledged even by Cheyne—it is generally conceded that the datum *In the year that King Ahaz died* (vs. 28) is due to an erroneous combination of the contents of this oracle with 2 Kings xviii. 8: the (smiting) *rod* that *is broken* can only designate an Assyrian tyrant, and that being so, we have to choose between Tiglath-Pileser, Shalmanassar, and Sargon; as Sargon was repeatedly at war with the Philistines, everything points to him as the oppressor meant.

Points of special difficulty are involved in ch. xxviii. 1–4 (and 6), xxii. 1–14, and i. In the case of xxviii. 1–6 the difficulty lies in the connexion with what follows. That ch. xxviii. 7–xxxi. reflect the events of 701 is palpable: xxviii. 1–4, however, presupposes the continued existence of Samaria, and by the manner in which it depicts the overthrow of the *proud crown of the drunkards of Ephraim* its delivery before the actual events is made quite certain; at the latest it may have been written in 724. However, the expression וְגַם אֵלֶּה ("but these also") in vs. 7 demands the presence of something of the kind preceding it, so that the present connexion was formulated by Isaiah himself. In the case of xxii. 1–14, on the other hand, the difficulty lies in the actual situation. Does it depict the wild outburst of exultant joy that followed on the unexpected retreat of the Assyrians? The first impression produced by reading it suggests this. But the intense feeling that marks vs. 13 can only have found expression in the presence of the threatened and impending catastrophe, and having regard to this we are compelled — unless we are prepared to disintegrate the passage into two different discourses — to assign the whole to the time of the warlike preparations that preceded the approach of the Assyrians (*cf.* also xxviii. 7–8). Regarding ch. i., it is clear that the chapter is not a connected discourse, written down *uno tenore* and amid similar circumstances and impressions; this is generally admitted, and, in view of the flagrant contradictions that exist between vss. 5–9 and 19–20, cannot indeed be denied. But how to mark off the different parts, and what situations to assign to them — on these points there is no agreement, and to arrive at any seems hardly possible. For vss. 5–9 we have the choice between 734 and 701. Here everything suggests that the date assigned should be 701; vss. 10–17 also would be explicable from the circumstances of Hezekiah's reign (*cf.* xxix. 13); vss. 19–20 might have been spoken about 705. But the attempt to assign vss. 21–31 also to the period about 701 seems to me to be fraught with the gravest difficulties: here it is hardly possible to discover any other assignable date than the time of Ahaz. Only this much is certain, that the whole chapter in its complete traditional form was from the first designed to form the introduction to the Book of Isaiah.

Special Passages of the Book of Isaiah

6. *Ch. ii. 2–4.*—This passage (following on the late superscription ii. 1) begins quite abruptly with וְהָיָה ("and it shall come to pass"), and in what follows has not in any way a suitable conclusion: ii. 5 is certainly corrupt, and with ii. 6 an entirely new section commences. Further, the passage also recurs in Micah iv. 1–3, and this fact compels us to consider the relation of the two passages to each other. At the outset it must be admitted that in Micah the form of the text as a whole is better preserved than in Isaiah. And, moreover, Micah has an additional verse which obviously belongs to the original form of the piece and which provides it with a satisfactory conclusion. Besides, the connexion of the passage in Micah with what precedes, though not without suspicious features, is yet decidedly better than in Isaiah, and the expression עַמִּים רַבִּים ("many peoples") recurs again as a sarcasm in Micah iv. 11, 13, v. 6, 7. Thus one might be tempted to suppose that Micah was really the original author of this oracle, and that Isaiah borrowed it from him. But this conclusion is negatived by the chronology, for

Micah was a considerably younger contemporary of Isaiah, while the discourse in ch. ii.–iv. belongs unquestionably to the oldest part of Isaiah's work. Besides, in the case of deliberate reproduction by Isaiah the omission of Micah iv. 4 can hardly be explained, and (as we shall see) the chapter in question is not derived from Micah at all, and iv. 1–4 in particular is categorically excluded from being Micah's by Jer. xxvi. 19. But neither can Isaiah be the original, although the author of ch. xxxvii. 32 seems already to have regarded it as Isaianic. For not only does Is. ii. 2–4, when compared with Micah iv. 1–4, produce the impression throughout of being a free citation, made from memory, but it cannot be brought into agreement with the theology of Isaiah, in spite of the presence of obvious points of contact with genuinely Isaianic ideas: to secure its authenticity at the expense of emptying the contents of the passage of all significance and reducing it to triviality in the manner desiderated by Duhm would be to pay too high a price. Because the passage is not original to Micah we need not necessarily assume a third written source, common to both; though Hitzig and Ewald have regarded the latter as the work of Joel, such a view is rendered quite impossible to accept on any right view of the age of Joel. The truth rather seems to be that the passage really did belong originally to the Book of Micah, and was excerpted from thence in order to provide a consolatory conclusion to the threats of Is. i. At any rate, the fact that the palpable textual corruption in Is. ii. 5 obviously arose under the influence of Micah iv. 5 shows clearly enough that the Micah-passage has been worked up into Isaiah. In Isaiah we have a free citation made from memory—possibly something different originally stood in this place in Isaiah; if, however, with Lagarde, we emend ii. 5, and read בֵּית יַעֲקֹב לְכוּ וְנִוָּכְחָה יֹאמַר יְהוָה ("O House of Jacob, come and let us plead together, saith J."), it may very well have formed the beginning of an independent discourse.

7. *Ch. ix. 1–6 and xi. 1–8.*—Stade ("G.V.I.," 209 f.) attributed both these oracles to later literary activity, reproducing the prophetic style and tone, and subsequently Hackmann attempted to fortify this view by detailed exposition, and Cheyne, Volz, and Marti have followed in the course thus marked out. But the oracles by no means display the regular features of the post-exilic picture of the Messiah: the יֶלֶד ("child") in ch. ix. does not at all appear as a triumphant warrior and conqueror of the heathen, in spite of the names in vs. 5, which passage Judaism has deflected from its literal meaning (which it finds objectionable) by means of the accentuation. It must be admitted that both oracles are beset with difficulties and occupy a somewhat isolated position among Isaianic utterances; but yet as marking the zenith of Isaianic ideas and thoughts they are conceivable, whereas, if they are the productions of a post-exilic teacher of the Law, they would have to be regarded as an unmixed marvel, and the entire origin and development of the messianic Hope would remain an inexplicable enigma if in Isaiah it is confined and reduced to ch. i. 26.

8. *Ch. xi. 10–xii. 6.*—Ewald categorically denied the Isaianic authorship of ch. xii., and it certainly is

marked by the manner of the later psalm-poetry; still, the connexion of this passage with what precedes is a close and good one. Yet more clearly apparent is the non-genuineness of xi. 10–17, which was detected long ago by Koppe, Rosenmüller, and De Wette: that Jahve gathers the dispersed of Israel and the scattered of Judah from the four ends of the earth and brings them back to Zion by a miracle analogous to that which marked the Exodus from Egypt, and that the messianic salvation then dawns for a united Ephraim and Judah—all this forms a series of representations that clearly point to Ezekiel and Deutero-Isaiah, to the period and circumstances of the Babylonian Exile or even still later. The subjection, too, of the surrounding peoples to Ephraim and Judah by force of arms forms a pointed contrast to the Kingdom of Peace, in which character the messianic time appears in ch. ix. 4–6, xi. 6–8 (*cf.* esp. Giesebrecht, *op. cit.*, 25–32).

9. *Ch. xiii. 2–xiv. 23.*—A מַשָּׂא בָּבֶל ("oracle concerning Babylon") which, by the superscription in xiii. 1, is expressly claimed for Isaiah. Babylon lies within Isaiah's horizon (*cf.* the narrative in ch. xxxix.), and Dejoces of Media was Isaiah's contemporary. But when Jahve Himself summons Media against Babylon for the execution of His wrathful judgment; when in consequence of this everyone turns to his own people and flees to his own land; when the king of Babylon is received into Sheol with malicious scorn as the man who devastated the world, before whom kingdoms trembled, who made the globe a wilderness and destroyed its cities, and did not permit his captives to return home; it is as clear and obvious

as possible that in all this we are transported into the last period of the Babylonian world-empire, when Israel was sighing for freedom from heathen oppression and for return to the home-land, and we are compelled, therefore, to ascribe this passage, which in form is of such high importance and significance, and exhibits such great poetical power, to an unknown prophet of the Babylonian Exile (against the original character, however, of xiv. 1–4*a* and 22–23 some well-founded suspicions have been raised).

10. *Ch. xv. 1–xvi. 12.*—A מַשָּׂא מוֹאָב ("oracle concerning Moab"), designated by the epilogue (xvi. 13–14), as an oracle delivered in time past (מֵאָז) which is freshly applied to the present. This epilogue appears to be guaranteed by xxi. 16 f.; in that case, however, xv. 1–xvi. 12 cannot be an oracle delivered at an earlier time to Isaiah himself—the radically different manner and style of this passage must strike even the least observant eye—but only one adopted by Isaiah from an older prophet. The situation implied in the original oracle likewise seems clear: the lion-like enemy came from the north and forced the fugitive Moabites over the Edomite border, whence they turned to Mount Zion for protection and mediation. This fits in very well with the conquest of Moab by Jeroboam II. of Israel (2 Kings xiv. 25), and Hitzig has explained it definitely as being the work of the prophet Jona ben Amittai of Gath-hepher there mentioned, in which case it would be the oldest written monument of prophetic literature preserved to us, the work of a Judaean prophet contemporary with Jeroboam II. and Uzziah, the latter of whom also, indeed, exercised

overlordship over Edom (2 Kings xiv. 22; *cf.* also vs. 1 *ibid.*). Isaiah would have understood by the lion-like enemies from the north the Assyrians (*cf.* xiv. 31 also), Sargon in fact, so that the address would be contemporaneous with ch. xx. This view still finds champions of repute. But xvi. 13 f. shares the fate of xxi. 16 f., and it is doubtful whether we can conceive xv. 2–xvi. 12 as a prophecy, and as a uniform passage, at all. It seems more probable that at the basis of it there lies a purely descriptive elegy on some grave catastrophe that befell Moab, which was only transformed into a prophecy by revision: more particularly xv. $9a\beta b$, and also xvi. 1, 3–6, have been assailed on cogent grounds. According to xv. 1 the foe comes from the south-east, and in that case only the desert Arabs can be thought of, with whose attack, indeed, Ezekiel (xxv. 10) threatens Moab: we should then be in the fifth century, in the time, known from Malachi and Obadiah, when the pressure of the Nabateans was being felt: the revision, like that of the Book of Obadiah, would be intended to produce an eschatological result. In later times a special animosity seems to have prevailed against Moab (xxv. 10–12): of the history of Moab we know too little to be able to assign specifically a situation for the epilogue; I see no necessity to bring it down to the time of Alexander Jannaeus.

11. *Ch. xix.* must now also be included among the passages which substantially have been given up: the Isaianic kernel still assumed as possible by Cheyne is of the slightest, and can never be grasped clearly. The oracle is directed in opposition to

Egypt, against which Jahve rides on a swift cloud. Egypt is to be given up to a *hard lord*, and will be involved in the most extreme distress and hardship; then, after having learnt to fear Jahve, they will cry unto Him and He will deliver them, whereupon they are to be converted and, in common with Assyria and Israel, serve Jahve. The *maççeba* ("pillar") in vs. 19 appeared of necessity to point to a period before Deut., and the mention of petty kingdoms in Egypt (in vs. 2) to a time before Psamtik (Psammetichus) I. (664–610); consequently, in spite of grave doubts, the genuineness of the oracle was tenaciously held, and in it was seen the latest oracle of Isaiah preserved to us. But the concluding section, with its five Hebrew-speaking cities in Egypt and the fraternisation between Egypt, Assyria, and Israel in common adoration of Jahve, could not be harmonised with the thought-world of the year 700. As, according to Josephus ("Ant.," xiii. 3), Onias in founding his temple at Leontopolis appealed to vs. 19 of this oracle, Hitzig supposed he was the author of vss. 16–25: but that such an insertion could have been adopted at that time into the sacred text of the Palestinian Synagogue is quite impossible, while, on the other hand, its presence in the text is inexplicable before the systematic settlement of Jews in Egypt by Ptolemy Lagus. Duhm has interpreted the oracle in vss. 1–15 as referring to the conquest and terrible punishment of Egypt effected by Artaxerxes III. Ochus in 343, and as a matter of fact the individual features suit that eventful time very well: at that time three dynasties had followed each other in rapid succession, and throne-feuds and uprisings were frequent and provide a somewhat similar situation to that of this chapter.

12. *Ch. xxi.*—This chapter divides into three distinct oracles, clearly distinguished by superscriptions.

(*a*) Vss. 1-10: a highly rhythmical and poetically original *utterance concerning the desert of the sea*, which, moreover, clearly reveals its historical situation. In order to still Israel's sighing, Elam and Media are to march to the rescue. But the speaker is still fearful and afraid: the longed-for night Jahve has turned into terror unto him. Thus he stands, an anxious watchman on his watch-tower, on the lookout, and listens attentively; then he perceives a ghostly night-caravan which cries that Babylon is fallen and its idols cast down to the ground, and this he must needs announce by way of consolation to the people threshed on Jahve's threshing-floor. In all this we are transported in the clearest possible way into the period towards the close of the Babylonian Exile, when the Persians first emerged on to the political horizon, and when the hope was cherished that the strangely sudden rise of this new world-empire would mean the downfall of the hated Babylonian tyrants. The passage is thus substantially contemporaneous with xiii. 2-xiv. 23, though it may be supposed to be somewhat earlier, and in any case is by a different author, as the difference of style in both is too considerable and essential to allow of a common origin. Kleinert's attempt to save the Isaianic authorship of the passage by referring it to the capture of Babylon by Sargon must be regarded as an unfortunate failure.

(*b*) Vss. 11-12 against Dumah, by which term

undoubtedly Edom is intended; and (c) vss. 13–17 against Arabia. Both these oracles are short, enigmatic, obscure, and abrupt, but that in vss. 11–12 particularly is thoroughly rhythmical; they do not exhibit anything of the Isaianic manner, and display such numerous points of contact and similarity with xxi. 1–10 that they must be ascribed to the same author, who, Duhm thinks, was an inhabitant of Palestine. Winckler misplaces all three oracles in the reign of Assurbanipal, "about 648," assigning vss. 1–10 to the period of the uprising of Samassumkin of Babylon, and vss. 11–17 to the time of the wars of Assurbanipal against the Arabians.

13. *Ch. xxiii.*—An *utterance concerning Tyre* which has in view a siege and capture of that city, in consequence of which it is to remain forgotten for seventy years, only to rise up again and to turn over its wealth to *those that dwell before Jahve.* We know of four sieges of Tyre—one of five years' duration by Shalmanassar-Sargon, one by Esarhaddon-Assurbanipal, one of thirteen years' duration by Nebuchadnezzar, and the well-known one by Alexander the Great; only the last resulted in the city's capture. Of these four sieges, the first falls in the time of Isaiah, and those who defend its authenticity consequently refer this oracle—at any rate vss. 1–14—to the siege by Shalmanassar. But Ewald rightly notes here the absence of the full elevation, majesty, and sublime brevity of Isaiah, and therefore thinks of one of the prophet's disciples as the author, but expressly separates vss. 15–18 from the original oracle, explaining these verses as a supplementary piece dating from the beginning of the

Persian period; in disjoining vss. 15–18 most moderns have followed him. I should much prefer to refer vss. 1–14 to the period of the thirteen-year siege of Tyre by Nebuchadnezzar, if only I could feel assured that the passage really from the first had Tyre in view. As, however, Sidon is mentioned in vss. 2, 4, and 12, Duhm's conjecture has much in its favour, according to which in vs. 8 (vs. 5 is a gloss) צר is to be changed into צדן, and the whole passage is to be regarded as an elegy on the awful devastation of Sidon inflicted by Artaxerxes III. Ochus in 348; it was then altered, after the devastation of Tyre by Alexander the Great, into a משא צר ("oracle concerning Tyre"). The supposed Isaianic kernel of vss. 1–14 still retained by Cheyne is just as elusive and impossible to grasp as in ch. xix.

14. *Ch. xxiv.–xxvii.*—A fearful last-judgment on earth and in heaven, which brings the hosts on high and the kings on the earth into captivity to Jahve, and which more especially discharges itself on Moab, ushers in the kingdom of Jahve's majesty upon Mount Zion: all sinners and heathen are extirpated, while at the sound of the great trumpet all the dispersed of Judah are gathered together, and even Israel's dead are summoned back to life once more in order to share in the kingdom of Jahve's majesty. These chapters in their external features have very much that is peculiar: style and diction are laboured and ornate; the frequent use of paronomasia, of rare expressions and peculiar rhetorical devices, is intended to make up for what the discourse lacks in natural power and vigour. The representations and ideas set forth in it are also highly peculiar. From the

standpoint of Biblical theology these chapters are among the most noteworthy passages of the O.T.: on no other section in the prophetic writings is the apocalyptic character so clearly and unmistakably stamped as this. No greater contrast can be imagined than that between these chapters and the undisputed discourses of Isaiah. Consequently their claim to Isaianic authorship has for long and with almost complete unanimity been rejected.

In this connexion, however, the question of their literary unity must first be discussed. A number of lyrical intermezzos stand out in this apocalypse, about the first of which (xxv. 1–5) Ewald rightly perceived that it breaks the connexion between xxiv. 23 and xxv. 6. In this direction Duhm subsequently has gone further in his results, and in xxiv. 1–23, xxv. 6–8, xxvi. 20–21, xxvii. 1, 12–13 obtains a uniform apocalypse which forms the groundwork of ch. xxiv.–xxvii.: he supposes it to have been written in the death-year of Antiochus VII. Sidetes, 128; the lyrical intermezzos, whose *mighty city* is the later Samaria which was destroyed by John Hyrcanus, must then be somewhat later in date. But to me, as to Cheyne, this hypothetical reconstruction seems to be excluded by the history of the canon. Moreover, Boehmer has proposed a new arrangement, which is very plausible, and separates xxiv. 1–23, xxv. 6–8 and xxvi. 9–21, xxvii. 1, 12, 13, as two distinct and independent passages. In any case, in xxiv., xxv. 6–8 only one situation is conceivable. The author was a Palestinian; הָאָרֶץ ("the land") in xxiv. 5 is Judaea, הָהָר הַזֶּה ("this mountain") in xxv. 6, 7, 10 is Mount Zion; moreover, many Jews are living in the west, in *the isles of the sea, i.e.* the Greek Archipelago (xxiv. 14–16), and the offence of Jahve's people is on the whole earth (xxv. 8): the people in its entirety is described as priests and laity (xxiv. 2), and elders are the only persons bearing an official character (xxiv. 23). These are all features which point with certainty to the period following the return from the Babylonian Exile, to the community of the Second Temple, and the whole character of the section suggests that no firm place can be found for it at the beginning of this period. The author is writing obviously while the impression of some vast catastrophe is fresh and vivid, which powerfully fanned into flame the messianic and eschatological hopes of Israel; as this mighty catastrophe comes from the west, as it is from the isles of the sea that the news resounds of Jahve's sovereignty, while by this fact a complete overturn of all existing things is ushered in, it is only possible in such a connexion to think of the triumphant march of Alexander the Great, and the section would thus have as its contemporary historical background the last confused and dreadful times of the Persian supremacy—one need only recall how Ochus acted in Phoenicia and Egypt—and its overthrow by Alexander the Great. With regard to the remaining parts of ch. xxiv.–xxvii. it is impossible to pronounce judgment with equal certainty; Cheyne, however, brings them similarly into the epoch of Alexander the Great.

15. *Ch. xxxii. and xxxiii.*—Ewald on good grounds long ago denied the Isaianic authorship of xxxiii., and attributed it to a disciple of the prophet. This judgment, however, must, with Stade, be extended

also to xxxii., although Duhm is inclined to regard nearly the whole chapter, and Hackmann, though "not without some hesitation," at least vss. 9–20, as authentic. The feeble address to the נָשִׁים שַׁאֲנַנּוֹת ("ye women that are at ease") and the בָּנוֹת בֹּטְחוֹת ("ye careless daughters") in xxxii. 9 ff., which so soon breaks off from its subject, and which also in other respects shows traces of dependence on models from elsewhere, can only with difficulty be derived from the author of iii. 16 ff.; and a definition so prosaically didactic in character as that (xxxii. 6–8) of the כִּילַי and נָבָל ("churl" and "fool"), and of the נָדִיב and שׁוֹעַ ("liberal" and "bountiful"), never occurs in the genuine Isaiah. The chapters are obviously intended to form the conclusion of the genuinely Isaianic group of discourses, ch. xxviii.–xxxi., by drawing a picture of the blessings of the messianic kingdom— an object which is more particularly fulfilled in xxxii. 1–5 and 15–20 throughout. Ch. xxxiii. displays a more apocalyptic character, and may be of still later date than ch. xxxii., but is apparently intended to refer to the events of 701, and thus forms a good conclusion to the whole Sennacherib-group, ch. xxviii. ff.

16. *Ch. xxxiv. and xxxv.*—A connected oracle, the contents of which are transparently clear and intelligible. The final judgment of the world breaks forth, but specially discharges itself upon Edom, as the people banned by Jahve, in vengeance and retaliation, in order to plead the cause of Zion; Edom becomes an eternal desolation, burnt up with pitch and brimstone. Then the wilderness is transformed into a garden through which Jahve's redeemed ones return to Zion, to dwell there in eternal joy. As this

representation belongs to the thought-world of Deutero-Isaiah, and hatred against Edom was fanned into fierce flame to a special degree subsequently to the destruction of Jerusalem, it might seem natural to assign its composition to the period before the return from the Babylonian Exile. But the radically apocalyptic character of the conceptions, and the quite secondary character of the representation set forth, compel us to bring it down to a much later date, although not perhaps as far down as the second century; for whether xxxiv. 16 really refers to a "prophetic canon" is, in the uncertain state of the criticism of the text of that passage, more than doubtful.

17. *Ch. xxxvi.–xxxix.*—A purely historical section which gives an account of the siege of Jerusalem by the Assyrians and of events contemporaneous with it, and of several utterances of Isaiah delivered in connexion with that event. It recurs in almost the same verbal form in 2 Kings xviii. 13–xx. 19, and for the most part in a better recension there; in particular ch. xxxviii. is involved in terrible disorder in Isaiah. The two recensions differ in this respect, that in Isaiah the important and highly significant section preserved in 2 Kings xviii. 14–16 is missing, and in place of it there stands a psalm of Hezekiah (Is. xxxviii. 9–20). Stade has shown that ch. xxxvi. and xxxvii. do not constitute a uniform passage, but consist of two accounts which have been worked up together: viz. (*a*) xxxvi. 1–xxxvii. 9*a*, to which, as conclusion and fulfilment of the utterance in 7*b*, vss. 37*b* and 38 also belong; and (*b*) xxxvii. 9*b*–37*a*. In spite of some divergence in details, both are parallel

accounts of the same events, and of these (*a*) clearly shows itself to be the older by individual historical features, and (*b*) as the younger and throughout legendary in character, and to it (the latter) ch. xxxviii. and xxxix. also belong. But (*a*), as a comparison of xxxvi. 6 with Ezek. xxix. 6 f. shows, must be younger than Ezekiel, and, that being so, (*b*) brings us down to a still later date. Under these circumstances naturally small security exists for the authenticity of the oracles of Isaiah preserved in (*a*) and (*b*); and indeed the longer one (xxxvii. 22 ff.), which only comes into consideration so far, is a later elaboration, composed in dependence on Isaianic words and placed in the mouth of the great prophet, in much the same way as the " Psalm of Hezekiah " (xxxviii. 9–20). This latter also cannot be authentic. There is nothing to mark the author as a king; nothing suggests that his illness comes at a moment of grave anxiety for his land and his people, and that his recovery is a pledge of better times; in fact, on a closer inspection it turns out to be no hymn of thanksgiving at all, but simply a prayer—in vs. 20 the deliverance is still in the future, and is only hoped for. Further, it is hard to conceive how this " psalm " could have been passed over in Kings if it was known in ancient times as an authentic song of Hezekiah. Just as Kings has admitted two prayers of Solomon and all the long prophetic discourses, just as in 2 Kings xix. 15–19 a prayer of Hezekiah has been incorporated, this psalm also might just as easily have been admitted. There is further the fact that in language and thought it exhibits the most striking similarity with Job and the youngest psalms, and thus itself cannot be old.

With regard to the entire section ch. xxxvi.–xxxix., we must suppose that its original position was in Kings, and that on account of the utterances of Isaiah contained in it the section was transferred into the Book of Isaiah to form an appendix to the Isaianic collection of discourses; according to 2 Chron. xxxii. 32, this process seems to have taken place before the time of the Chronicler—and, too, in a freer and in many respects a much briefer manner. In this process it is clear that the highly significant passage in 2 Kings xviii. 14–16 was deliberately passed over, because it stood in pointed contrast to what follows, and because the editor who transferred the section into Isaiah was concerned not so much to write history as to compose an edifying narrative. On the other hand, the "Psalm of Hezekiah," as the terribly bad condition of the text of Is. xxxviii. shows, was only inserted in Isaiah by way of supplement, when this historical section already formed a part of the book. The opinion may be hazarded that it was taken over from the midrash referred to in § 20, 9 above.

Isaiah xl.–lxvi.

18. With ch. xl. begins a longer connected section which without question ranks among the grandest and most outstanding parts of the entire O.T. Superscription it has none, but begins immediately with the cry of consolation: *Comfort ye, comfort ye my people.* Since it appears in our texts as a constituent part of the Book of Isaiah, it has consequently been regarded, even as early as the time of Jesus Sirach, as a work of Isaiah ben Amoz, and gladly would we accord

this brilliant jewel of the prophetic literature of Israel to the mightiest spirit among Israel's prophets. The many undeniable points of contact—both in language and substance—that it shows with Isaiah cannot, however, disguise from us its pervading and essential difference of character. This displays itself externally in the whole method and manner of the composition. While Isaiah overwhelms us with an unfailing and inexhaustible wealth of thoughts and images, we have here two main thoughts and two images which—though indeed amid perpetually fresh turns of expression and gorgeous verbiage — are constantly recurring; while Isaiah is first and foremost a preacher of repentance and a herald of judgment, here consolation is equally prominent; while Isaiah closely associates the final salvation with an ideal descendant of David, here Jacob-Israel and Zion-Jerusalem appear as the upholders and representatives of the future kingdom of God, and the whole representation is dominated by the fundamental idea —wholly strange to Isaiah—of *the Servant of Jahve*. But still more palpable than these dissimilarities in form and in the circle of ideas is the difference of the contemporary historical background. While for Isaiah Assyria is the centre of importance in his treatment of the theme, in these chapters it is Babylon, and, in fact, the destruction of Jerusalem and of the Temple (xliv. 26–28; xlv. 12), the leading captive of the people (xlv. 13), its downfall and loss of liberty (xlii. 22–25; xliii. 8; xlvii. 6), that are throughout not predicted but presupposed, and Babylon is described as the tyrant (xliii. 14; xlvi. 1; xlvii. 5–7; xlviii. 14, 20) in whose dungeons Israel is languishing. It is the latter, the Israel of the Babylonian Exile, who is addressed; to it goes out the prophet's cry of consolation that its military service is at an end and its guilt expiated, and that it is to prepare itself for the exodus from Babylon, for Jahve is coming in might, and eye to eye they shall see how He returns with them to Zion. The occasion for this comforting hopefulness is furnished by the victories of Cyrus, which have brought the downfall of the Babylonian world-empire closely into sight. Cyrus is mentioned by name (xliv. 28; xlv. 1–8), not as though the mention of him were a marvellous and mysterious disclosure, but as a well-known contemporary living personality, to whose achievements it is only necessary to refer, without mentioning his name (xli. 2–4, 25; xlv. 13; xlvi. 11; xlviii. 14–16), in order immediately to be understood by everybody; and in such connexions the fact is often pointed to with great emphasis that these events have taken place *now* in fulfilment of prophecies given long ago (xli. 26–27; xlii. 9; xliv. 8; xlviii. 3–7). When we further take into account occasional indications of later linguistic usage, and allow sufficient weight to the fact that these chapters throughout show themselves dependent on Jeremiah, while no writer from the time of Isaiah till the end of the Babylonian Exile displays the slightest trace of any acquaintance with this highly characteristic and supremely significant spiritual product, the conclusion is not to be evaded that in it we have the work of a prophet of the period towards the end of the Babylonian Exile, which by error or accident was united with the Book of Isaiah ben Amoz. After the perception of this fact had, in cautiously veiled language, been hinted at by Aben Esra, it was first positively enunciated in 1775 by Döderlein, and may now be considered a commonplace of Old Testament Science; the mediating view that a genuinely Isaianic basis existed which was later worked over or interpolated straight away (Klostermann, Bredenkamp) is quite untenable; the phenomena on which the theory is based find a completely satisfactory explanation in another direction.

19. It has been customary to designate this entire group of discourses as *Deutero-Isaiah*, and the first question we must discuss is whether we can ascribe them to a single author. That first of all the section ch. xl.–xlviii., even conceding a certain amount of insertion and working in of alien elements, mainly and on the whole forms a closely coherent and connected piece is evident. Beginning with the cry of consolation, *Comfort ye, comfort ye my people*, and ending with the triumphant outburst, *Come forth from Babylon*, there is exhibited in these chapters so marked a unity of thought and consistency of historic situation in the representation that the contemporary character of their conception and reduction to writing cannot be doubted. And indeed the historic situation is here especially clear: Babylon is still mistress (xlvii. 1) and tyrant of Israel (xliii. 14; xlvii. 5–9; xlviii. 14), but Cyrus has been called by God, to accomplish His decree on Babylon (xli. 25; xlv. 13; xlvi. 11; xlviii. 14, 15). The manner in which, in ch. xlvi. and xlvii., the fate of Babylon is depicted shows clearly enough that the author had not yet lived to see its actual capture by Cyrus; thus the year 538 is the *terminus ad quem*. On the other hand, the menace

of Cyrus hovers so threateningly and fatefully over Babylon, he has achieved such mighty things, trodden down kings and trampled on rulers like clay, that the destruction of the Lydian kingdom in 546 must already lie well behind the author; after the downfall of Croesus, indeed, the overthrow of Babylon — or, at any rate, conflict with it—was only a question of time. The repeated and emphatic mention of the *isles* (xl. 15; xli. 1, 5; xlii. 10, 12) leads us to suppose that the conquest of the whole of Asia Minor, together with the Greek coast-towns and islands, was already a *fait accompli*. How these events must have stirred and fanned the hopes of the Israelites, who had now been languishing in exile within a little of half a century, can easily be seen. Now it seemed that what a Jeremiah and Ezekiel had prophesied was really coming to pass, and the classical interpreter of these moods and feelings is the author of these chapters. That he was living in Babylonia, at any rate at the time when he wrote ch. xl.–xlviii., cannot be doubted : for the whole situation is depicted with a freshness and directness such as only the impressions of an eye-witness can convey (*cf.* also R. Kittel, " Z.A.T.W.," xviii. 161 f., 1898) ; the conjecture that the author wrote in Egypt (Ewald, Bunsen) is quite untenable ; but neither is there any indication that Jerusalem and Palestine (Seinecke) could have been the place of composition, for passages such as xl. 9 are merely personifications and vivid poetic ways of enhancing the reality of the representation: Duhm himself describes northern Phoenicia in this connexion as " a hypothesis of despair."

20. When we pass from ch. xl.–xlviii. to the

following chapters an essential dissimilarity is noticeable. The main thoughts of the former—God the almighty Creator of heaven and earth (xl. 12–14, 22, 26, 28; xliv. 24; xlv. 7, 12, 18; xlviii. 13), the timeless eternal (xli. 4; xliv. 6; xlviii. 12) and only God of prophecy (xl. 21; xlii. 9; xliv. 7–8; xlvi. 9–11; xlviii. 3–7), who thereby authenticates His uniquely true godhead as against the unreal gods of the heathen (xli. 21–29; xlii. 8–9; xliv. 9–13; xlv. 25–29), Jahve God alone (xliii. 10; xliv. 8; xlv. 5–6, 18, 21, 26; xlvi. 9), and the nothingness of idols and idolatry (xl. 18–22; xli. 5–7; xliv. 9–17; xlv. 20; xlvi. 6–7; xlviii. 5); Cyrus as the chosen instrument of Jahve, and the return of the exiles through the desert which has been made passable (xli. 17–20; xlii. 16; xliii. 2–7, 16–21; xlviii. 20–21)—all these disappear wholly or almost wholly from xlix. onward all at once: Zion-Jerusalem and its glory take the position of central importance, and in place of the return from Babylon the gathering in of the Israelites, scattered throughout the world, to Zion is prominently set forth (xlix. 10–12, 22; lvi. 8; lx. 4). Nor are the historical circumstances of the time so clear as in ch. xl.–xlviii.; and it could not fail to be noted that the prevailing mood and spirit had changed. Therefore it was supposed that ch. xlix.–lxvi. were not written down by Deutero-Isaiah consecutively with ch. xl.–xlviii., but only later and under totally changed conditions. But the more thoroughly the investigation was pressed home, the more difficulties accumulated from ch. lvi. on, and thus Duhm in 1892 was led to propound the thesis that *only ch. xlix.–lv. depend on Deutero-Isaiah*, while ch. lvi.–lxvi. are the work of an author writing some eighty years later, the *Trito-Isaiah*. And in fact the difficulties are solved by this hypothesis, and lv. 10–13, with its backward reference to xl. 3–11, rounds off the whole first part with a satisfactory conclusion. In ch. xlix.–lv. also Jerusalem is still destroyed (xlix. 16 ff.; li. 3; lii. 9; lii. 2; liv. 7), and the people are still languishing in exile (xlix. 9, 24–26; li. 13–14); but joy and confidence have increased, the call to return is more urgent, hope in the future more glowing. Deutero-Isaiah clearly wrote ch. xlix.–lv. under the immediate impression produced by the issue of the edict in which Cyrus gave permission to the exiles to return home, and consequently some time later than the composition of ch. xl.–xlviii. To attempt to ascertain who this "Deutero-Isaiah" was, to glean any information as to his name and person, is an idle task: he is and must remain "the Great Unknown."

21. One part of Is. xl.–lv. still remains to be discussed separately: the so-called "*Songs of the Servant of Jahve*." Under this name are embraced xlii. 1–7, xlix. 1–6, l. 4–9, and lii. 13–liii. 12, and the view has been largely held that these must be separated from the context of Deutero-Isaiah, and be explained as independent passages, whether older or younger than Deutero-Isaiah himself. In an essay published in the "Theol. Rundschau" (iii. 409 ff., 1900) I have given a survey, citing the entire literature, of the very complicated history of this critical movement up to the year 1900, and in that connexion I had the pleasure of finding proof that the "full authorship" of Deutero-Isaiah, which was always upheld by me, appears to be winning its way to acceptance; new

publications also that have appeared in the interval by E. Sellin ("Der Knecht Gottes bei Dt.-Jes.," 1901), H. Roy ("Israel und die Welt in Jes. xl.–lv.," 1903), and L. Lane (" St. Kr.," lxxvii. 319 ff., 1904) have not made me wrong (*cf.*, on the other hand, F. Giesebrecht, "Der Knecht Jahves bei Dt.-Jes.," 1902, and A. Zillessen, "Z.A.T.W.," xxiv. 251 ff., 1904). The conclusion will remain that the Songs of the Servant of Jahve form an integral part of Deutero-Isaiah, composed by that author himself, and in the Servant of Jahve in these passages Israel is to be seen, in just the same way as in xli. 8 ff., and in all the Deutero-Isaianic passages outside of the Songs.

22. I have also (*op. cit.*, pp. 416 ff.) cited and discussed the literature on the Trito-Isaiah, ch. lvi.–lxvi., up to the year 1900. That these chapters can only have been written in Palestine after the return from the Exile is obvious; but the social and religious conditions depicted here—unscrupulous and self-seeking *overseers*, rich men who oppress and drain the resources of the poor; the *righteous* and *men of piety* gone, and in their place *apostate children* and godless asserting themselves and boldly practising idolatry, or making a display of hypocritical piety; and looming behind these an oppressed community of *broken spirits* and *crushed hearts*—could not have been represented in this manner immediately after the return of the exiles. The inferior time-limit is furnished by the reformation of Ezra and Nehemiah, and as the circumstances against which that reforming movement was directed, as they are drawn in the Book of Malachi, are in essential agreement with Trito-Isaiah, Duhm places the time of his writing

shortly before the active career of Nehemiah in Jerusalem: the false brethren against whom this author's zeal is kindled are those circles out of which later sprang the Samaritan community, and he is already aware that they are threatening a rival temple. In contents, form, and expression he is essentially dependent on Deutero-Isaiah, and his writing was perhaps from the first regarded as forming a continuation to, or completion of, the latter: ch. lxi.–lxvi. may originally have stood before ch. lvi.–lx. It is true that the majority of scholars who agree in principle with Duhm deny the unity of ch. lvi.–lxvi., and would prefer to see in this section a collection of supplementary pieces to Deutero-Isaiah, of various character, and originating at different times; but there does not seem to me to be any necessity for this view, and I firmly adhere to the theory of a Trito-Isaiah. In any case, the conviction that ch. lvi.–lxvi. are to be dissevered from Deutero-Isaiah and are younger than the latter may now be regarded as the prevailing view.

The Composition of the Book of Isaiah

23. It is obvious that a book which comprehends within itself passages of such different character and emanating from such various periods cannot have originated and come together by pure accident. The lack of orderly arrangement which marks its present form at first gives the impression of a mixed collection thrown together without any definite plan: the task, then, of seeking for some explanation of this is all the more urgent.

Traces of arrangement in groups are soon

ISAIAH

detected: thus ch. vi.–viii. form a book of narratives, xiii.–xxiii. a book of oracles ("massas"), xxviii.–xxxiii. a book of woes; ch. ii.–iv., with its full conclusion, iv. 2-6, produce the impression of being a special collection. The important and significant superscription in ii. 1, taken in conjunction with the final character that distinguishes xi. 10–xii. 6, suggests that ch. ii.–xii. once formed an independent collection; the circumstantial superscription in xiii. 1, also, applied to the whole Book of Oracles ("massas") in xiii.–xxiii., with perhaps xxvii. The problem is rendered more difficult by the fact that of these smaller or larger groups none can be traced back to Isaiah himself, because they all as a whole contain too much non-Isaianic matter. Beyond these groups we cannot penetrate with certainty: still, it is not mere egotistic caprice on my part to suppose that my theory of catchwords having influenced the formation of these groups, and their position with regard to each other—a theory which has almost universally been rejected—at least contains an element of truth. That ch. i. was placed at the beginning of the book to form a prefatory introduction is self-evident, and similarly the historical appendix, drawn from Kings (Is. xxxvi.–xxxix.), was added to the Book of Isaiah (i.–xxxv.), with which at that time ch. xl.–lxvi. cannot have been yet united. For the arrangement of the subject-matter of ch. i.–xxxv.—Judah-Jerusalem; foreign nations; the future of Judah and Jerusalem—Marti refers by way of illustration to the Book of Ezekiel and Jeremiah according to the LXX. This Book of Isaiah with i. 1 as superscription and xxxvi.–xxxix. as an integral constituent part appears, according to 2 Chron. xxxii. 32, to have lain already before the Chronicler: for Jesus Sirach (Ecclus. xlviii. 24) ch. xl.–lxvi. also were inseparably united with it. Here we are confronted with the most difficult problem of the composition of the book, which only the history of the canon can solve. According to trustworthy tradition, the original order of the greater prophets among the Jews was: Jeremiah, Ezekiel, Isaiah, in which there is preserved a reminiscence of the fact that Isaiah as a book is younger than Jeremiah and Ezekiel—in the case of the Minor Prophets also it is clear that the order is designed throughout to be a chronological one. In that case, following Isaiah, as last of the three greater prophets, would have appeared the anonymous book of the Deutero-Isaiah, which was very soon united with the Trito-Isaiah; this was too voluminous and important to be ranked among the Minor Prophets. If, however, Isaiah and Deutero-Isaiah stood in immediate juxtaposition, the step which resulted in uniting them together was rendered all the easier because, in fact, xxxix. 6–7 concluded Proto-Isaiah with a highly significant reference to a catastrophe in the future that is to befall Babylon: in this way the anonymous prophetic book would have been united with that which immediately preceded it, just as the anonymous passage Zech. ix.–xiv. was united with the preceding little Book of Zechariah.

Special Introduction

CHAPTER XII

BOOK II.—PROPHETIC BOOKS—*continued*

§§ 25, 26. *Jeremiah and Ezekiel.*

§ 25. Jeremiah

LITERATURE: *Commentaries:* F. Hitzig, *K.E.H.*, 1866, 2nd ed.; K. H. Graf, 1862; F. Giesebrecht, *H.K.A.T.*, 1893; B. Duhm, *K.H.C.A.T.*, 1901; C. H. Cornill, 1905.

Essays, Monographs, etc.: K. Marti, *Der Proph. Jer. von Anatot*, 1889; W. Erbt, *Jeremia und seine Zeit*, 1902; G. Jacoby, *Glossen zu den neuesten kritischen Aufstellungen über die Komposition des Buches Jer.* (i.-xx.), Diss., 1903; essays by B. Stade in *Z.A.T.W.*: on ch. i. (vol. xxiii. 153 ff., 1903); on iii. 6–16 (vol. iv. 151 ff., 1884); on xxi. and xxiv.-xxix. (vol. xii. 276 ff., 1892); on xxxii. 11–14 (vol. v. 175 ff., 1885). On ch. xxv., xlvi.-li., F. Schwally, *Z.A.T.W.*, viii. 177 ff., 1888; L. H. K. Bleeker, *Jeremia's profetieen tegen de Volkeren*, 1894.

On the text-critical questions: F. Cosse, Diss., 1895; on ch. l.-li., C. W. E. Nägelsbach, *Der Prophet Jeremia und Babylon*, 1850; K. Budde, *Jd. Th.*, xxiii. 428 ff., 529 ff., 1878; on ch. lii., C. H. Cornill, *Z.A.T.W.*, iv., 105 ff., 1884.

On the relation of the Hebrew text to the LXX.: F. C. Movers, *De utriusque recensionis vaticiniorum Jeremiae*, etc., 1837; J. Wichelhaus, *De Jeremiae versione Alexandrina*, 1847; E. Kühl, Dissertation, 1882; G. C. Workman, *The Text of Jeremiah*, 1889; A. W. Streane, *The Double Text of Jeremiah*, 1896.

On the criticism of the text: C. H. Cornill, *S.B.O.T.*, 1895; F. Giesebrecht, *Jeremia's Metrik*, 1905.

1. Jeremiah, in whom Israelitish prophetism found its purest exemplar and attained its highest and completest development, was a native of Anathoth, near Jerusalem (i. 1, xxix. 27), and was the son of a priest named Hilkiah (i. 1), whom many have regarded —certainly wrongly—as identical with the person of that name mentioned in 2 Kings xxii. 4 ff. Jeremiah appears to have resided at Anathoth at a later period also (xi. 21–23), and only to have settled permanently in Jerusalem on taking up his active work as prophet; according to xxxii. 7–15; xxxvii. 12? he cannot have lived in needy circumstances. He received the call and consecration to be a prophet in the thirteenth year of Josiah (i. 2, xxv. 3), *i.e.* 627, at which time he must have been still comparatively young (i. 6). Remaining unmarried (xvi. 1–2) in order to be able to devote his life to his prophetic vocation, he served his office amid perpetual conflict and often in danger of his life, as *a defenced city and an iron pillar and brazen walls against the whole land, the kings of Judah and the princes thereof, the priests and the whole people*, for nearly half a century; only after the destruction of Jerusalem, among the exiles who fled to Egypt after the murder of the Babylonian governor Gedaliah, does all trace of him disappear: according to a quite credible tradition, the great prophet was doomed to give up his mighty soul there, stoned to death by his own countrymen.

2. The *book* traditionally handed down to us under the name of Jeremiah is distinguished from all the rest of the prophetic writings by the prevalence of the biographical element: apart from ch. lii., ch. xix.–xx. 6, xxvi.–xxix., xxxiv., and xxxvi.–

xlv. are purely narrative in character. In these chapters an entirely objective account (only ch. xxvii. lapses strangely into the first-personal form) is given of the prophet's active career and what befell him, and the penetrating and intuitive clearness that mark the delineation, as well as the large number of details that is given, combine to make these sections a historical source of the first rank. It is to be observed, however, that the narrative passages in the other parts of the book, as at the outset the famous vision of the call in ch. i., follow the first-personal form throughout, so that by this fact the literary unity of the book is already rendered doubtful.

3. *Regarding the origin of the book itself* we are, thanks to ch. xxxvi., informed in a circumstantial and detailed manner which is without parallel in the case of any other prophetic writing. According to the narrative of this chapter, Jeremiah for a period of twenty-three years adopted oral methods exclusively in his work, and only in the fourth year of Jehoiachim received the commission to write out all the words which Jahve had hitherto spoken to him; this he did through the good offices of a younger friend and disciple, Baruch, who wrote down the book at the dictation of the prophet. A year afterwards this roll was read at an extraordinary general fast in the Temple, and when it had been cut up and thrown into the fire by Jehoiachim, Jeremiah had it again written out by Baruch, and added to it many like words. It follows from this that we possess no authentic reports from the first half-period of Jeremiah's active ministry, but only a *résumé* given

by himself, in which he had striven to recapitulate its fundamental thoughts and ideas in as brief and impressive a way as possible: as the original written document was read through three times in a single day, it cannot have been very voluminous. The first task of the criticism of Jeremiah would now be to restore this "*original roll*" of the fourth year of Jehoiachim (Stade, "G.V.I.," i. 646, rem. 2), and to attain this end the simplest way appears to be to separate those passages which in point of time precede that date. If we leave out of account the narrative sections, these comprise the following: ch. i., ii.–vi., vii.–x., xi.–xii. 6, xxv.; xviii. will also fall within this time-limit. But a closer study of the groups of discourses adduced shows that they cannot possibly depend, directly or indirectly, in this form on the prophet himself. Ch. iii. 6–18 breaks the connexion between iii. 5 and 19; ix. 22–x. 16, which itself consists of three discourses, dissevers the immediately continuous verses ix. 21 and x. 17 from each other; xii. 4 stands in an altogether unsuitable and impossible place; and here it may at once be observed that similar phenomena occur also in the other parts of the Book of Jeremiah, in the prophetic as well as the historical portions. We are thus compelled to suppose that this original roll was utilised, indeed, in the composition of our existing Book of Jeremiah, but that it has not been preserved in its original form.

4. We now have to attempt *to fix chronologically the remaining passages of the Book of Jeremiah*, with the exception of the oracles against foreign nations. To the time of Jehoiachim the following also belong:

ch. xiii. 15–17, 20–27 ; xiv.–xv., which already presuppose afflictions of longer duration; xvi. 2–xvii. 18, the basis of which is formed by a connected discourse whose content is that in spite of apparent delay the judgment must still come; xx. 7–18 ?, xii. 7–17, to be explained in accordance with 2 Kings xxiv. 2 and xxxv.; of narrative passages, xix. 1–xx. 6, xxvi., xxxvi., xxxv. To the short reign of Jehoiachin, of three months' duration, at the most are to be assigned the sentences on the subject of Jehoiachin himself, which, however, clearly fall in part within a time subsequent to the catastrophe. The remaining portions of the book would then belong to the time of Zedekiah, or after the destruction of Jerusalem. Ch. xvii. 5–8 and 11, by reason of the general character of their contents, cannot be assigned to any definite time and situation.

5. *The narrative passages* were not written by the same hand as those containing the discourses. Thus, for example, in ch. xix. the execution of the divine command is not given, as it always is in the other parts of the book (xiii. 1–7 ; xviii. 1–3 ; xxv. 15–17 ; xxxii. 7–15 ; xxxv. 3–5); to the name of Jeremiah the honorific official title הַנָּבִיא ("the prophet") is regularly added, which in the case of the discourse-sections only occurs occasionally in superscriptions, xxv. 2, xxxii. 2 (xlvi. 1, 13 ; xlvii. 1 ; xlix. 34 ; l. 1): in the language also some slight differences are noticeable. Especially significant, however, is the relation of xxvi. 1–6 to vii. The latter chapter is undated, but there can be no doubt that it is concerned with the same discourse and the same situation which in xxvi. 1 are assigned to *the beginning*

of the reign of Jehoiachim: in both, Jeremiah speaks in the House of Jahve to all Judah at a great festival gathering; in both he announces the coming downfall of the Temple, and in each case, too, in the form in which he sets forth the fate of Shiloh. That the same author should first of all give a report of a highly important discourse with full details, and then repeat it, in a totally different connexion, in a dry and meagre form, is inconceivable. In ch. vii. we have a reproduction—which goes back to Jeremiah himself, and which, though not a literally accurate report, yet breathes the full prophetic spirit—of that famous discourse in the Temple, while xxvi. 1-6 contains but a brief mention of it, introducing the account of the consequences which resulted from it to the prophet himself. This case of parallelism is highly instructive in forming an estimate of the narrative passages: the centre of gravity in these is throughout the biographical-circumstantial element, while the discourses are treated more briefly, and form rather a *résumé* than even a free rendering of the latter. As Baruch was the constant companion of the prophet and the writer of the discourses actually published by him, it is natural to regard the former as the author of these passages, and, in any case, the writer of the narratives was well informed; they, however, contain many inaccuracies and obscurities which we cannot venture to credit to an eye-witness. We must thus suppose that Baruch's notes, in which he set down in a simple and unassuming fashion his personal recollections of his great friend and master, at first took rather the form of a chronological register, and only later were expanded into a coherent pragmatic recital; and that they have been preserved to us as little intact as the original "roll," but have undergone a far-reaching revision.

6. But even if we disregard the narrative passages, by no means everything that we read in ch. i.–xlv. can go back directly or indirectly to Jeremiah. As in the case of Isaiah, so also Jeremiah—a highly regarded and much read book—was later expanded and subjected to revision. The most radical positions taken up with regard to this point are those of Duhm, who leaves to Jeremiah himself only about 270 four-lined stanzas, all composed in the simplest metre, and dividing up into about sixty very short "prophetic poems"; of the biographical notes of Baruch only about 200 Massoretic verses have been preserved. According to Duhm, all the rest—*i.e.* nearly two-thirds of the entire book—is the work of supplementers, the result of a relentless process of diorthosis continued right down to the first century; the book was never really complete. Erbt also reaches similar, though not quite such radical, results. He distinguishes in our Book of Jeremiah, besides the memoirs of Baruch, memoirs and confessions of Jeremiah and prophetic sentences—all this forming an aggregate of small and very inconsiderable passages. A detailed analysis of both is given in my larger commentary on Jeremiah, which is now available in printed form, and to this I must refer the reader. In my view, both Duhm and Erbt have not sufficiently taken into account the narrative in ch. xxxvi. The original roll of the year 605, even if older notes were utilised in it, could not have been

a mere book of songs, a mere collection of short fragments, but must already have been invested with the character of a *book*, and must thus have been the result of *Jeremiah's own productive and editorial powers*. Duhm has doubtless shown in detail that the whole book has been subjected to revision on a far larger scale than had hitherto been generally supposed: but I cannot regard affairs as being involved in such uncertainty as he does. Of the discourse-passages, I think only ch. xxx. and xxxiii., the second half of which is wanting in the LXX., must be given up altogether: otherwise in ch. i.–xxv. and xxxi.–xxxii. we have throughout at least a genuine basis, and also quite a considerable amount of genuine material.

7. Of longer passages, which are complete in themselves, *Jeremiah's authorship of ch. x. 1–16 and xvii. 19–27 is generally denied*. The discourse about the nothingness of idols and the folly of idolatry in x. 1–16, in the first place, stands there in quite an isolated position, while at the same time x. 17 forms the immediate continuation of ix. 21. Further, the LXX. exhibits divergences; apart from minor differences, it has nothing to correspond to vss. 6–8 and 10 at all, and places vs. 9 between vss. $5a\alpha$ and $5a\beta$. Above all, the relation to the corresponding passages in Deutero-Isaiah is significant, and from this the question further arises whether the presence of these passages there is not due to later expansion: here dependence can only lie on the side of Jer. x. As, moreover, the people appear all through this section as living among a heathen population, and exposed to the temptation of idolatry, the whole paragraph is

to be regarded as a late interpolation which has come into a rather unsuitable position; it may have been formulated in close connexion with ix. 22–23, to which passage x. 14 might refer back. Vs. 11, which is written in the "Chaldean" language, and which clearly rends asunder vss. 10 and 12, must be rejected as a still later insertion.

The paragraph about the hallowing of the Sabbath, xvii. 19–27, bears the impress of non-genuineness on its face. Its linguistic usage and phraseology, indeed, are on the whole Jeremian, but the contents stand in palpable and sharp opposition to the prophetic theology of Jeremiah, who elsewhere never even so much as mentions the Sabbath, and cannot possibly have attached such glowing promises to so merely external an *opus operatum*—and even have made the continued existence of Judah and Jerusalem dependent upon it. We are involuntarily reminded by it of Neh. xiii. 15–22; in view of the undeniably Jeremian colouring of the language, we can only suppose that one who shared Nehemiah's views may have placed this sermon in the mouth of Jeremiah.

8. Ch. xxx. and xxxi. are *disputed*. It has already been remarked that ch. xxx. must be given up (see par. 6 of this section above); the Jeremian authorship of ch. xxxi. *in toto* has been denied by Stade and Smend, and it has been explained by them as of secondary character and post-exilic. On the other hand, Giesebrecht has made a successful protest, and claimed for xxxi. a substantial kernel as belonging to Jeremiah. In its first half it contains an oracle of the first period of Jeremiah's prophetic activity on the theme of Ephraim's restoration, as Duhm also

opines: by later revision the passage was enlarged into a promise of salvation for all Israel, which was intended to form the conclusion of Jeremiah's discourses. Following after xxxi. 22, the famous oracle about the New Covenant (vss. 31–34) still appears to me to be incontestable.

Oracles against Foreign Nations

9. The group of discourses directed against foreign nations which we now read in ch. xlvi.–li. (from which ch. xxv. cannot be separated) demands special treatment. That in particular xxv. 1–14—the LXX. version of which, moreover, is marked by striking divergences—has been worked over to the extent of rendering the original sense completely unintelligible has been convincingly proved by Schwally. If with him we suppose vss. 1–3, 5, 7–10, 11b according to the LXX., and vs. 13a to form the fundamental nucleus, we thus obtain a threat dating from the fourth year of Jehoiachim—the year of the battle of Carchemish, which decided the fate of Hither Asia—to the effect that Jahve, as a punishment for continued disobedience against the prophetic word, will chastise Judah by means of a people coming from the north, and will lead them into bondage under the heathen, lasting seventy years. As this catastrophe will affect not Judah only but also the whole of Hither Asia, and above all Egypt, the prophet receives the command to present to all these peoples, and their kings and princes, Jahve's chalice of wrath. Against vss. 25–29 Giesebrecht, against vss. 30–38 Schwally, have rightly objected; but in their purer form preserved in the LXX. no cogent ground exists for rejecting

JEREMIAH

vss. 15-24, and their authenticity is actually required by a weighty argument drawn from literary criticism. How does it result that the figure of Jahve's *cup of wrath*, which is altogether unknown in the older literature, and is not even used in Nah. iii. 11, becomes all at once, from the time of Jeremiah onward, quite common (*cf.* Ezek. xxiii. 32 f.; Lam. iv. 21; Is. li. 17 ff.; Hab. ii. 16; Ps. lxxv. 9)? It does so, indeed, in dependence on Jer. xxv. (*cf.* also xiii. 12-14).

10. The execution of this divine command obviously receives its fulfilment in the *group of discourses contained in xlvi. 1-12, xlvii.-xlix.*, wherein Egypt (xlvi. 1-12), Philistia-Phoenicia (xlvii.), Moab (xlviii.), Ammon (xlix. 1-6), Edom (xlix. 7-22), Damascus (xlix. 23-27), Kedar-Hazor (xlix. 28-33), and Elam (xlix. 34-39) are announced as doomed to imminent downfall. This in the case of Philistia-Phoenicia (xlvii. 2) and Kedar-Hazor (xlix. 30) it is said expressly, in the case of (Moab xlviii. 40 and) Edom (xlix. 19) figuratively, in the case of the rest it is tacitly implied, will be effected through Nebuchadnezzar and the Chaldeans. But the Jeremian authorship of this group of discourses is denied by Vatke, Stade; and in the most thorough and decisive way by Schwally and Duhm. Yet on *a priori* grounds we should expect to find discourses against the heathen in the Book of Jeremiah, for no other prophet had the feeling from the outset that his commission included his having been sent to the nations outside Israel as well, to the same degree as Jeremiah (i. 5, 10; xxxvi. 2; xviii. 9 ff.; *cf.* also xxvii. 2 ff.); and if the announcement in xxv. 15-24

is certainly authentic, this inclines us to take a favourable view of its actual execution. At the outset we exclude the oracle about Elam, which in a special superscription is attributed to the time of Zedekiah, and thus cannot in any case have stood in the original roll. We then obtain exactly seven oracles against foreign nations. Of these the two last, against Damascus and Kedar-Hazor, appear to be so strongly marked by secondary features and by signs of literary dependence that I feel bound to give them up also. On the other hand, with the five remaining ones the case is different (in this connexion notice that besides Egypt only the four immediate neighbours of Israel remain, and these are found joined together in the same way in Ezekiel!). Ch. xlviii. and xlix. 7–22 are indeed remarkable owing to their length; but in them alien prophecies, more especially Is. xv.–xvi. and Obadiah, have been so recklessly utilised that no serious author can have composed them as a whole. We are thus driven here also, as in the rest of the Book of Jeremiah, to assume a certain amount of revision: Giesebrecht also regards a nucleus of xlix. 7–22, and xlvii. in its entirety as genuine. When in xlvi. 10 the judgment on Egypt appears as Jahve's vengeance, this is very explicable after the death of Josiah and the deposition and removal of Jehoahaz. Such a passage as xlviii. 12 to my mind is only comprehensible in the period prior to 586. A main argument I adduce, however, from the indefinite and general character of the threats against Israel's hereditary foes, Moab, Ammon, and Edom. In particular they are never reproached with profiting by Jerusalem's day of misfortune—

Ammon's occupation of Gad which is blamed (xlix. 1) goes back to the catastrophe which befell Israel, for Gad never belonged to Judah; but such facts as these firmly and irresistibly tie us down to a date before the destruction of Jerusalem, indeed before the end of the reign of Jehoiachim (2 Kings xxiv. 2): what tone such addresses assume under the impression produced by these events is very instructively illustrated by a comparison of Ezek. xxv. and especially of Obadiah with Jer. xlix. Against the whole series Schwally raises the objection that it is inequitable to make the heathen expiate Israel's sins: that Jahve appears here as a God of vengeance, who annihilates the heathen as being non-Israelites, and that He is represented as absolute Lord of the world in a manner that goes beyond even Ezekiel. But *vengeance* is only mentioned in the case of Egypt, and for a very adequate and cogent reason; and if Jahve is directing Nebuchadnezzar as the instrument of His punishment of Judah, it is logically quite impossible to assign to another moving cause the circumstances which prepare the way for and accompany the practical execution of this particular result which has been willed by Jahve: the conception of God which characterises these addresses is simply that of Is. x. 5 ff., xviii. 4 ff. The unoriginal character marking them, which is alleged as a further objection against the addresses, their dependence on other prophetic passages, disappears altogether or else shrinks to the proportions in which this feature is to be observed in the admittedly genuine parts of Jeremiah, if we assume in them the presence of a nucleus which has been largely worked over: the fundamental nucleus of the addresses against five foreign nations is certainly authentic, and since xlvi. 5 ff. presupposes the battle of Carchemish as already fought, it must have been written while the impression produced by that mighty event was still strong, and therefore already belonged to the original roll. The oracle against Elam forms a passage by itself; the impossibly obtained superscription בְּרֵאשִׁית מַלְכוּת צִדְקִיָּהוּ מֶלֶךְ יְהוּדָה ("in the beginning of the reign of Zedekiah, king of Judah") need not be contested. But also the second oracle against Egypt in xlvi. 13–28 or rather 26 (the closing verses xlvi. 27–28, which are identical with the non-genuine verses xxx. 10–11 [the latter missing in the LXX.], are to be struck out absolutely) did not yet stand in the original roll, but is a production dating from the last Egyptian period of the prophet: its genuineness also need not be doubted, for vs. 20—which is wrongly absent in the LXX.—can only have been written before Nebuchadnezzar's expedition to Egypt in 568.

11. One of the addresses against foreign nations— *the oracle against Babylon in ch. l.–li.*—has not yet been considered. Eichorn, and after him many others, disputed the authenticity of these chapters; but more especially by Budde their non-genuineness has been so convincingly demonstrated that now hardly anyone can be found to defend their authenticity. There is no need to point to the prolixity, the poverty of thought, and jejune character of the section, which even exceed the similar features of ch. xlviii.; the deductions drawn from the application of literary criticism will more than suffice.

Ch. li. 25–26 is mechanically imitated from Ezek.

xxxv. 3–5, and elsewhere there occur expressions and phrases which are largely of a specifically Ezekielian character. Further, there is to be observed a persistent dependence on the non-genuine parts of the Book of Isaiah: ch. l. 16 = Is. xiii. 14; l. 30–40, a combination of Is. xiii. 19–22 with Is. xxxiv. 13–14; li. 40 is imitated from Is. xxxiv. 5–7; *cf.* also l. 27. Moreover, the dependent relationship to Deutero-Isaiah is especially close not only in individual words and expressions, but also in fundamental thought. A conclusion which is unmistakable may also be drawn from the points of contact which this section shows with other parts of the Book of Jeremiah itself: thus l. 13 = xlix. 17; l. 30 is verbally identical with xlix. 26; li. 15–19 = x. 12–16; l. 40–46 = xlix. 16 + vi. 22–24 + xlix. 19–21, with purely external alterations where indispensable—but that an author should in this manner be indebted to himself is inconceivable; and when finally l. 7*a* is imitated from the passage ii. 3, and וּמִקְוֵה ("even . . . the hope") in l. 7*b* is borrowed from xiv. 8, xvii. 13, and נְוֵה צֶדֶק ("habitation of righteousness") in the same place is due to a misunderstanding of xxxi. 23, it is clear that the oracle against Babylon is the fabrication, dependent on Jeremiah himself, of a later hand, and against such cogent results of literary criticism the attempt even of a Tiele ("Babyl.-assyr. Gesch.," pp. 480–482) to establish the year 538 as *terminus ad quem* cannot avail. On the other hand, however, the dependence of the whole passage on Jeremiah is too evident and purposeful to admit of its being regarded as a mere accident. The explanation of this phenomenon is furnished by the narrative passage li. 59–

64, the genuineness of which has been so convincingly demonstrated by Budde. According to this account Jeremiah, in the fourth year of Zedekiah's reign, entrusted Seraiah, a high official who was travelling with the king to Babylon, with a sheet on which the announcement of Babylon's coming overthrow had been written, and commissioned him after his arrival in Babylon to read this sheet, and then, having bound it to a stone, to plunge it into the Euphrates. Clearly ch. l. 2-li. 58 is invented, and purports to be the Jeremian prophecy of doom directed against Babylon which Seraiah then sank in the Euphrates: if we reject the words in vs. 60*b* which assert this claim, and assume that a corresponding revision of the whole section has taken place, there remains a short, highly important, and historically interesting narrative-passage, the authenticity of which is rendered all the more credible when we remember that such a journey by Zedekiah to Babylon in the company of a high Jewish state-official as is here described by no possibility can have been invented, especially in face of the mission to Babylon of Elasah and Gemariah, which is mentioned in xxix. 3.

12. This is also the appropriate place to discuss *the divergent form of the Book of Jeremiah embodied in the Hebrew text and in the LXX.*, which is displayed in a specially conspicuous way in the discourses against foreign nations. The LXX. sets forth these addresses in a different order—viz. Elam, Egypt, Babylon, Philistia-Phoenicia, Edom, Ammon, Kedar-Hazor, Damascus, and Moab—and also in a different place, viz. after xxv. 13. With regard to the order in particular, this is in every respect more original

in the Hebrew text: here the seven which date from the fourth year of Jehoiachim are followed first by one from the beginning of Zedekiah's reign, and then by the late non-genuine address against Babylon which is assigned by its genuine conclusion to the fourth year of Zedekiah; in the LXX., on the other hand, Elam can only have been placed in the fore-front because it was believed that by it Persia—at the time of the LXX. the dominant world-power—was intended; the discourse against Babylon, on account of its importance, and because Egypt-Babylon always appears as the conjunction of the great powers hostile to Jahve, was made to follow the address against Egypt; for the sequence of the rest no internal reasons can be adduced, but the substantial agreement with respect to the passage xxv. 19–26, which is handed down in both recensions of the text alike, is an argument for the originality of the Hebrew order of the sections. On the other hand, the position of the group as a whole must be recognised as more original in the LXX. Ch. xxv. 1–13 in its existing revised form in the Hebrew as well as in the Greek text clearly constitutes the introduction to the oracles against foreign peoples in their complete form, the oracle against Babylon included, or at least was so formed with reference to this collection immediately following: in fact, in the words (vs. 13) אֲשֶׁר נִבָּא יִרְמְיָהוּ עַל־[כָּל־]הַגּוֹיִם ("which Jeremiah prophesied against [all] the nations") the original superscription of this group of addresses has also been preserved in the Hebrew text of this passage, and reappears a second time now in xlvi. 1.

But even in the LXX. the position of these chapters

is no longer the original one, because at the first their position naturally can only have been after xxv. 15–26 (38), of which they form the prophetic-rhetorical consummation.

13. There are still some differences between the Hebrew and Greek texts which remain to be discussed. Above all, the LXX. exhibits *an altogether shorter form of text*; some 2700 words are unrepresented in it, *i.e.* about one-eighth of the entire book, while cases of matter in excess of the Hebrew text are of comparatively rare occurrence. And though in such passages as viii. $10a\beta$–12, xxx. 10–11, xxxiii. 14–26, which are absent in the LXX., their non-originality is evident, the decisive character of the LXX. evidence in these cases cannot *a priori* be assumed, because several of these missing passages have —or at least may have—fallen out by homoioteleuton. Of the longer ones, this seems to me to be true certainly of xi. 7–$8ba$, xvii. 1–4 (or more exactly $5a\alpha$), and li. $44b$–$49a$; in the case also of xxix. 16–20 and xxxix. 4–13, in spite of several material difficulties, I should prefer to hold the same to be true. Still, an unbiassed view will be obliged to recognise the form of text given in the LXX. as on the whole the purer and more original. But it is impossible to speak with accuracy of two "recensions"—the agreement of both forms of text is too considerable, and mutual relationship too close, for that: we have in them only two different editions of the same recension.

14. *The origin and formation of the Book of Jeremiah* was in every respect a complicated one. After Jeremiah had once taken up the pen, in the year 605 (or 604), it is to be presumed that he wrote

down also further prophetic addresses and divine revelations that had been vouchsafed to him: at his death there was certainly in existence a book of the *words of Jeremiah* (i. 1.), which could now no longer get lost. The memoirs of Baruch, according to Duhm, existed for a long time independently as a treasured part not of prophetic but of historical literature, so that in this way the two foundation-elements of our present Book of Jeremiah had undergone a separate history. This is indeed possible. But inasmuch as the Hebrew text and LXX. on the whole, and generally, yield the same recension, which can itself only be the result of a long and developed diorthotic process, a connexion of the words of Jeremiah with the Baruch-narratives must have been effected some considerable time before the LXX. Yet even after the Greek form of the text had been separated from the Hebrew, the diorthotic process was continued in the case of the latter, so that the close of the Book of Jeremiah in its Hebrew form brings us down as far as the second century. As yet no one has been able to give a rational explanation of this form: ch. xxvi.–xxxvi. more especially are an unsolved riddle. On the other hand, the words of Jeremiah according to the LXX. show a definitely fixed plan in their arrangement: ch. i.–xxv. 13, contemporary addresses to his own people; xxv. 15 ff., xlvi. ff., to foreign nations; xxx.–xxxi., promises of salvation for the future of Israel and Jerusalem.

§ 26. EZEKIEL

LITERATURE: *Commentaries:* H. A. C. Haevernick, 1843; F. Hitzig, *K.E.H.*, 1847; R. Smend, 2nd ed., 1880; A. B. Davidson, 1882; A. Bertholet, *K.H.C.A.T.*, 1897; R. Kraetzschmar, *H.K.A.T.*, 1900.

Essays, Monographs, etc.: A. Klostermann, *St. Kr.*, 1. 391 ff., 1877; H. H. Meulenbelt, *De prediking van den profeten Ezechiel,* 1888; L. Gautier, *La mission du prophète Ezéchiel,* 1891; on ch. xxvii., C. Manchot, *J. pr. Th.*, xiv. 423 ff., 1888.

On the criticism of the text: C. H. Cornill, *Das Buch des Propheten Ezechiel,* 1886; D. H. Müller, *Ezechielstudien,* 1895; C. H. Toy, *S.B.O.T.*, 1899 (Hebrew and English). On xl.-xliii. specially: F. Böttcher, *Proben A.T.licher Schrifterklärung,* 1833 (pp. 218–385); E. Kühn, *St. Kr.*, lv. 601 ff., 1882.

1. Ezekiel was the son of a priest of Jerusalem named Buzi, and was carried away into exile with Jehoiachin to Babylon (i. 1). There he resided at Tel Abib (iii. 15), on the river Chebar (i. 3, iii. 16 ff.), was married (xxiv. 16–18), and lived in his own house. In the fourth month of the fifth year after his being led away captive (i. 1–2), *i.e.* in July 592, he received in a vision the call to the prophetic office, which he served twenty-two years; the latest date appearing in his book is that given in xxix. 17, the first month of the twenty-seventh year, *i.e.* April 570. The whole character and style of his active prophetic work give the impression that at the beginning of it he is no longer young, but already a mature man, whose intellectual and spiritual development is essentially complete. The elders of the community of the exiles repeatedly resort to his house to question him (viii. 1, xiv. 1, xx. 1), but it was only the fulfilment

of his predictions by the destruction of Jerusalem that was able to give his words additional weight. Of the rest of his career we know nothing.

2. *Ezekiel's Book* falls into three clearly distinct main groups. After an introduction (i. 1–iii. 15) in which his call and consecration to be a prophet are depicted in the grandiose vision of the cherubim-chariots of Jahve, the first part (iii. 16–xxiv. 27) contains a collection of addresses which all have as their theme the imminent destruction of Jerusalem, and make it their object to represent this event as absolutely necessary and in any case inevitable: it is the punishment that visits an immeasurable guilt contracted by Judah, and for the most part by the present generation. The second part (ch. xxv.–xxxii.) contains oracles against seven foreign peoples: Ammon, Moab, Edom, Philistia, Tyre, Sidon, and Egypt, which presuppose the siege and capture of Jerusalem. The third part (ch. xxxiii.–xlviii.) embraces discourses on the subject of Israel's future after the destruction of Jerusalem, which is announced (xxxiii. 21) by a fugitive to the exiles. In this third part the famous vision of the Temple (ch. xl.–xlviii.) stands out as forming an independent subdivision.

3. Hitherto it had been supposed that problems of Introduction did not exist in the case of the Book of Ezekiel. In ch. vii. 1 ff., it is true, a doublet was detected, and objections were also raised to some shorter or longer sections, such as x. 1, 8–17, xxiv. 22–23, xxvii. 9*b*–25*a*; but still the essential integrity of the book was firmly maintained, and it was held that the book still lies before us in the form in which it left the author's hand; and the unity of spirit, as

well as the literary unity, which mark it, and especially the definitely planned arrangement of the whole, were regarded as unmistakable. Thus it was only possible, if doubts were to be raised at all, to resort to a rejection of the whole; but Zunz ("Gottesdienstliche Vorträge der Juden," 1832, pp. 157–162; "Z.D.M.G.," xxvii. 676 ff., 1873) and Seinecke ("Geschichte des Volkes Israel," ii. 1–20, 1884), who actually did so, were quite rightly not taken seriously. Recently Kraetzschmar has propounded the hypothesis that the Book of Ezekiel is a composite work pieced together by the hand of a redactor out of two writings, neither of which goes back to Ezekiel himself: the shorter one speaks of Ezekiel in the third person (*cf.* i. 2 f., xxiv. 24), and can indeed only be an abstract from a more detailed work in which Ezekiel himself is spokesman. But as xxiv. 24 is a speech of Jahve, the third person appears only in the superscription (i. 1–4), which in any case is involved in difficulty, while the whole book throughout contains the first-personal form; differences such as are revealed by a comparison of x. 8–17 with i. are not conceivable in the case of an "abstract," the doublets on closer inspection dwindle markedly, and parallels, in view of the breadth of Ezekiel's style, are not surprising. The remark in Josephus ("Ant.," x. 5, 1) to the effect that Ezekiel left behind δύο βιβλία can be turned as little to account in support of this hypothesis as that of the Talmud that *the men of the Great Synagogue* wrote the Book of Ezekiel. Kraetzschmar's two-source theory does not seem to me to have a sufficiently wide basis of fact, though I willingly recognise the superfluousness of many of the doublets evidenced by him, and the secondary character of such passages as iii. 1–9, 16*b*–21.

4. Independent of these questions is that *regarding the literary method of Ezekiel.* As the all-important conclusion—the vision of the Temple—bears the date of the twenty-fifth year of the exile of Jehoiachin (xl. i.), we shall have to regard this year, *i.e.* October 572, as the term for the completion of Ezekiel's book. But at that time Ezekiel had already been actively engaged in prophetic work for twenty years, and the earlier sections of his book bear earlier dates: thus the *fifth* (i. 2, *cf.* iii. 16), *sixth* (viii. 1), *seventh* (xx. 1), *ninth* (xxiv. 1), *tenth* (xxix. 1), *eleventh* (xxvi. 1; xxx. 20; xxxi. 1; xxxiii. 21, where the Hebrew text obviously by mistake writes *twelfth*), and the *twelfth* (xxxii. 1, 17, and erroneously xxxiii. 21) years of the captivity of Jehoiachin are mentioned. The question now arises, Are these dates merely literary fiction, the whole book having been written in the twenty-fifth year all at once? Or do the passages with the earlier dates really emanate from the time specified? Here Stade ("G.V.I.," ii. 37, rem. 2) has rightly pointed out that the Temple-vision is in one supremely essential point at variance with the earlier prediction in xvii. 22–24. "The observation of this contradiction in Ezekiel's predictions is interesting for this reason, because we here find a definite case in which Ezekiel has disdained to transform an older prediction in accordance with more recent knowledge. This fact certainly tends to predispose us to find that the other predictions also which fall before 586 have, on the whole, been faithfully reproduced." We are led to the same result also by the remarkable little passage

in xxix. 17–21. It is—for i. 1 is not here counted in —the only passage which bears a date later than xl. i., and it quite gives the impression of being an insertion added to the already completed book. As Ezekiel was able to insert this correction, it was just as possible for him to get rid of the prophecy so corrected altogether, or to modify it accordingly, and this he has not done. Ch. xii. 12–13 in any case can only be a *vaticinium ex eventu*: but the matters narrated in xxiv. 2, xxxiii. 22, and xi. 1 ff. do not exceed the measure of actual human capacity of presentiment, or the so-called "second sight," and would, if mere inventions, present a serious difficulty. Ch. xii. and ch. xvii. (cited by Kuenen), which in any case cannot have been written thus in the sixth or seventh year of Zedekiah, are not dated, Kraetzschmar having shown that each date given is applicable only to the prophecy which is immediately attached to it. I also venture to remark that the pieces marked out as oldest by the dating, as regards literary art have not yet altogether attained the height reached by the later ones.

All these considerations compel the opinion that Ezekiel wrote down and elaborated his book as a whole in the twenty-fifth year, but for this purpose availed himself of earlier—and in some cases of much earlier—memoranda, which he has left essentially unaltered. His book has not remained intact, but has undergone redactional modifications, though only to a limited extent, and in this respect occupies a privileged position in the Prophetic literature. Unfortunately, the text has come down to us in a condition so much the worse.

Remark.—According to Talmudic tradition ("Baba bathra," 14*b*), the order of the three greater prophets was: Jeremiah, Ezekiel, Isaiah, as it occurs in many manuscripts, and in the work "Ochla we-Ochla." In this there has clearly been preserved a reminiscence of the fact that Isaiah as a book is younger than Jeremiah and Ezekiel (*cf.* Lagarde, "Symmicta," i. 142). Still, this arrangement may have been occasioned by the circumstance that according to Talmudic tradition Jeremiah compiled the Book of Kings; and in this way the two books ascribed to Jeremiah were linked together.

Special Introduction

CHAPTER XIII

BOOK II.—PROPHETIC BOOKS—*continued*

§§ 27, 28, 29. *Minor Prophets, 1.—Hosea, Joel, Amos*

§ 27. HOSEA

LITERATURE: *Commentaries* on the twelve minor prophets:
Hitzig-Steiner, *K.E.H.* 1886, 4th ed.; J. Wellhausen, *Skizzen und Vorarbeiten*, Heft 5, 3rd ed., 1898; G. A. Smith, 2 vols., 1896, 1898; W. Nowack, *H.K.A.T.*, 2nd ed., 1904; K. Marti, *K.H.C.A.T.*, 1904.

On Hosea: A. Simson, 1851; A. Wünsche, 1868; W. Nowack, 1880; T. K. Cheyne, *Hosea, with Notes*, etc., 1884; J. J. P. Valeton, jr., *Amos en Hosea*, 1894 (German translation by F. K. Echternacht, 1898).

Essays, Monographs, etc.: H. Oort, *De profet Hosea, Th. T.*, xxiv. 345 ff., 480 ff., 1890; W. Riedel, *A.T.liche Untersuchungen*, i. 1–18, 1902; J. Meinhold, *Studien* (see § 24 above), pp. 64–88.

On the criticism of the text: J. Bachmann, *A.T.lichen Untersuchungen*, 1894, pp. 1–37.

1. Hosea, the son of a certain Beeri, to whom Jewish tradition assigns the two verses Is. viii. 19–20, was a citizen of the kingdom of Israel (vii. 5), and according to the very probable conjecture of Duhm was, like the prophet most nearly akin to him in spirit, Jeremiah, of priestly origin. He appeared in the reign of Jeroboam II. (i. 1), and probably towards

the end of it. Weighed down by heavy domestic misfortune (i.–iii.), in which he saw mirrored a picture of grave misfortune affecting all, amid scorn and contumely as well as fierce hostility and persecution (ix. 7–8), he carried on his work in a troubled anarchical time; of his exact fate nothing is known.

2. *The Book of Hosea* falls into two parts which are sharply distinguished in substance and date: viz. ch. i.–iii. and iv.–xiv., which Volz (*op. cit.*, § 24 above) would even derive from two different prophets.

(*a*) Ch. i.–iii., as to the interpretation of which there should, according to Ewald and Wellhausen, no longer be any controversy, are essentially narrative in character. The prophet recounts his domestic misfortune, and how by this very fact prophecy was born in him. The superscription (i. 1), in which, however, the words עֻזִּיָּה יוֹתָם אָחָז חִזְקִיָּה מַלְכֵי יְהוּדָה וּבִימֵי ("Uzziah, Jotham, Ahaz, Hezekiah, kings of Judah, and in the days of . . .) are a later addition (inserted in order to indicate that the prophet was contemporary with Isaiah), dates this passage *in the days of Jeroboam the son of Joash, king of Israel*.' And this datum is correct. According to i. 4, the dynasty of Jehu is still sitting on the throne; it is, however, threatened with overthrow as punishment for the blood-guiltiness of Jezreel (*cf.* 2 Kings ix. and x.), while the manner and method in which this overthrow is threatened show clearly enough that at the time Hosea had not yet seen the catastrophe fall on the ruling house. The fact, also, that ch. ii. can only enlarge upon Israel's arrogance, sensuality, and wealth, while afflictions and punishment still lie altogether in the future, only suits the time of Jeroboam II.

(b) Ch. iv.–xiv.: a series of addresses in which no very exact arrangement or marked development of thought is discernible. They form a closely connected *résumé* of the prophetic preaching of Hosea, written down towards the end of his active career by himself. Here the situation is essentially different from that in ch. i.–iii. The prophet is conscious of anarchy and murdered kings (vii. 3–7, 16; x. 15): princes and kings have been set up, but not by Jahve (viii. 4), they therefore can give no succour (x. 3; xiii. 10–11), but shall be swept away together with Samaria (x. 7). Instead of looking to them, Israel seeks help at the hands of Assyria and Egypt (v. 13; vii. 11; viii. 9; xii. 2); Ephraim is mingled among the nations, foreigners devour his strength, he gets grey hairs and marks it not (vii. 7–9; viii. 8). From all these indications the time at which this second part was composed can be determined exactly. Hosea had evidently lived through the period of anarchy and repeated changes of rulers which followed the overthrow of the house of Jehu; he had also seen the rendering of tribute to Assyria by Menahem in 738. On the other hand, there is no allusion to the events of the years 735 and 734—the years of the Syro-Ephraimitish war, and, immediately following this, the first invasion of Tiglath-Pileser and the loss of the country east of the Jordan (see, on the other hand, v. 1; vi. 8; xii. 12) and of the northern districts: "The Assyrians had at that time already laid their paws on the land, but had not yet shown their claws" (Wellhausen, "Skizzen," i. 54, 1884). This second part of Hosea's book was consequently written down between the years 738 and 735—the first part *circa* 745; as is well known, the chronology of the kingdom of Israel at this interval is specially obscure.

3. The Book of Hosea is individual and subjective in character to a degree that is hardly paralleled in the case of any other prophetic writing. No question as to its authenticity can here come into consideration at all. But yet it has not been handed down to us without admixture in the form in which it originally left its author's hand. In particular, ch. i. 7, which clearly makes reference to the deliverance of Jerusalem under Hezekiah, is certainly a very awkward Judaean interpolation. In one other important point also Judaean revision has intervened in Hosea. The prophet's picture of the future shows no consciousness of a messianic King sprung from the family of David: he knows only Jahve and Israel, without the intervention of any mediating person, and apparently was the first consciously to have deduced from the theocratic idea its logical consequence, that it is incompatible with any human kingship. The fundamental thought of Isaiah and of the later Judaean writers who depend on him of a hope in the future has been interpolated by a process of revision in Hosea also, as Wellhausen and Stade have rightly perceived. We first encounter this view in ii. 1–3, which passage palpably breaks the connexion between i. 9 and ii. 4, and besides anticipates in the most unfortunate manner ii. 25. The transposition (approved even by Kuenen) of the verses in question to follow ii. 25 would indeed obviate the worst awkwardness, but ii. 25 and ii.

2b–3 conflict with each other even more intolerably; besides, ii. 3 parallel with ii. 25 can never have formed the conclusion of a larger address.

To this Judaistic revision are further to be attributed, in iii. 5 the words דָּוִד מַלְכָּם וְאֵת ("and David their king"), which occur in exactly the same way in Jer. xxx. 9, and in iii. 4 the corresponding words אֵין מֶלֶךְ וְאֵין שָׂר ("without king and without prince") —by the removal of which two correct and parallel verses arise—and also iv. 15a, as well as the change of every occurrence of ישראל ("Israel") in parallelism with אפרים ("Ephraim") in v. 10–vi. 1 into יהודה ("Judah"); also viii. 14 and the mention of Judah in v. 5, vi. 11, and x. 11 may be secondary.

Recently, however, criticism has gone further, and refused to attribute to Hosea any share in the moving principle of God's educating love and the hopes for Israel's future based upon this—a view represented most logically by Marti, who regards ii. 15b–25, the whole of iii., v. 15–vi. 3, xi. 10–11, and xiv. 2–14 as secondary in character, not completely inserted until the Greek period. It is possible that ch. ii. and xiv. may bear traces of revision; but the picture of the future given by ch. xiv. is explicable at no time in the post-exilic or Greek periods, and Jahve's re-marriage to the adulterous and defiled beloved one of youth is a representation that even Jeremiah and Ezekiel have not ventured to express —is not this thought explicitly censured through Deut. xxiv. 1–4 ? Nor can it be read out of Deutero-Isaiah, in spite of Is. liv. 5, 6; for in the eyes of the latter Zion is not divorced (l. 1), she is no harlot and adulteress. Whence also did all Hosea's successors derive the conviction that Jahve's covenant of grace cannot be wholly destroyed even by the worst sins of Israel, whence Isaiah his שאר ישוב ("a remnant shall return"), a thought which is steadfastly held by him from the very first as a dogma that he never feels it necessary to justify? Against the forcible separation of ch. iii. from ch. i. all that Wellhausen has said as to the mutual relationship of both seems to me to apply (*cf.* also Stade, "Z.A.T.W.," xxiii., 161 ff., 1903). The interpretation of ch. iii., also, of apostate Israel, *i.e.* of the heretical kingdom of the Ten Tribes, seems to me impossible to carry through consistently: in that case what does the commission given to the prophet to contract a marriage with the fallen spouse of another—which is yet no marriage—mean? Certainly the Book of Hosea offers problems of great difficulty, but there is no need on that account to resort to the use of such doubtful means to solve them.

§ 28. JOEL

LITERATURE: *Commentaries*: K. A. Credner, 1831; A. Wünsche, 1871; S. R. Driver (Camb. Bible), 1897.

Essays, Monographs, etc.: A. Merx, *Die Prophetie des Joel und ihre Ausleger*, 1879; E. le Savoureux-Baumgartner, *Le prophète Joel*, etc., 1888; H. Holzinger, *Sprachcharakter und Abfassungszeit*, etc., Z.A.T.W., ix. 89 ff., 1889; G. Preuss, *Die Prophetie Joels mit besonderer Berucksichtigung der Zeitfrage*, Dissertation, 1891.

1. The book bearing the name of *Joel ben Pethuel* is assigned in the most diverse way to various dates: opinions range over intervals more than 500 years apart, from Rehoboam to the last years of the

Persian Empire. And yet hardly in the case of any other prophetic book do the circumstances with which it deals lie so clearly on the surface as here. The contents briefly are that a plague of locusts, in the description of which allusion is clearly made to Ex. x. 1–19, seems to the author to be the precursor of the Last Day, which is then pictured, with all its expected consequences: signs in nature, judgment over the heathen, and redemption of Israel.

2. To determine *the time of the composition of Joel*, ch. iv. 2–3 and 17 are primarily of critical importance. If Jahve remonstrates with the heathen because they have scattered His people and inheritance among the nations, have divided His land and cast lots over His people, and if in the expected glorious final period strangers are not to set foot in the holy city Jerusalem *evermore* — all this fixes the year 586 absolutely as the *terminus a quo*: moreover, in the earlier period of the kings it could not possibly have been said that captive or plundered Jews could be sold to Greeks (iv. 6 = iii. 6 in E.V.). The absolute ignoring of Israel, as well as the complaint regarding Jew-hatred in Egypt and Edom (iv. 19 = iii. 19 E.V.), would at least be very exceptional in the pre-exilic period. But we must come down a good deal later than 586. For Judah-Jerusalem, which for Joel is identical with Israel (ii. 27, iv. 2 = ii. 27, iii. 2 E.V.), is inhabited, the Temple built and its service going on; thus the writer obviously addresses himself to the community of the Second Temple. With this agree the features that the whole people can, and is called upon to, assemble in the Temple (i. 14; ii. 16),

that the trumpet blown upon Mount Zion is heard throughout the whole land (ii. 1), because it consists only of Jerusalem and its immediate environs, as well as that the *elders* are mentioned as the only governing class (i. 2, 14; ii. 16). The mention, finally, of Jerusalem's *walls* (ii. 9) brings us down to the time subsequent to Nehemiah.

3. In favour of this conclusion also there exist *weighty internal reasons* of a religious-historical, biblical-theological, and literary-critical kind—above all, the entire absence of prophetic denunciation. It is true Joel summons to repentance (ii. 12–13), but we search in vain for any statement or intimation of the sins from which Israel is to turn: of moral delinquencies in the popular life, of defective or unrighteous worship, Joel knows nothing. The amendment and repentance that are referred to are to be effected by *fasting, weeping,* and *wailing,* a combination which only again occurs in Esth. iv. 3 (*cf.* also Neh. i. 4). The pledge of Israel's communion with Jahve is to him the תָּמִיד ("the continual offering"), which he obviously intends by מִנְחָה וָנֶסֶךְ ("the meal-offering and drink-offering") in i. 9, 13, ii. 14, exactly as it is in Dan. viii. 11, xi. 31, xii. 11. With this accords the unreservedly Jewish-particularistic standpoint of Joel. The heathen are no longer the subjects of teaching and preaching, but merely the objects of anger and judgment, while, on the other hand, all Jews are citizens of the messianic kingdom: the famous verses about the outpouring of the spirit (iii. 1–2) refer its outgoing, according to the clear literal sense of the passage, only to all Jewish flesh, and this is conceived in so external a fashion that

even such heathen as stand in a personal relationship to God's people merely as slaves and maid-servants are likewise to participate in the outpouring. Very striking, moreover, is Joel's dependence on Malachi: Joel iii. 4 is obviously a citation from Mal. iii. 23, and in material respects Joel also belongs to a period subsequent to Malachi, because the latter still finds much to denounce, and is compelled to fight energetically for things which for Joel have long since become matters of wont and usage.

4. The *diction and style* of Joel are strikingly smooth and flowing, a fact which has deceived the majority of the book's interpreters as to its true age and the very considerable internal difficulties and obscurities that distinguish it: "but it is the flowing diction of the scholar who is deeply read in the ancient literature, not the spontaneous beauty which marks the creations of genius" (Merx, *op. cit.*, p. 2). That Joel's language, all the same, plainly exhibits the character of the latest period of Hebrew literature has been convincingly demonstrated by Holzinger. In the Book of Joel we possess a compendium of late Jewish eschatology written about the year 400— if anything rather later than earlier—as developed from later prophecy, with its tendency to flow over into apocalypse: in its whole tone and spirit Joel belongs altogether to apocalyptic, although in outward form it has preserved more of the character of older prophecy than Zechariah and Daniel. The attempt made by Rothstein in his (German) translation of Driver's "Introduction" (*cf.* § 2, 7 above) to separate ch. i.–ii. from iii.–iv., and to maintain for the former address at least the traditional date assigning it to

the period of the minority of Joash, has been satisfactorily refuted by Nowack.

§ 29. AMOS

LITERATURE: *Commentaries:* G. Baur, 1847; J. H. Gunning, *De godspraken van Amos*, etc., 1885; Valeton (see § 27 above); S. R. Driver (Camb. Bible), 1897.

Essays, Monographs, etc.: H. Oort, *De profet Amos, Th. T.*, xiv. 114 ff., 1880; H. J. Elhorst, *De profetie van Amos*, 1900; M. Loehr, *Untersuchungen zum Buch Amos, B.Z.A.T.W.*, 1901; W. R. Harper, *The Utterances of Amos arranged strophically*, 1901; Riedel, (*op. cit.*, § 27 above), pp. 19–36; E. Baumann, *Der Aufbau der Amosreden, B.Z.A.T.W.*, 1903; Meinhold (*op. cit.*, § 27 above), pp. 33–63.

On the criticism of the text: G. Hoffmann, *Versuche zu Amos, Z.A.T.W.*, iii. 81 ff., 1883; A. Hirscht, *Z. w. Th.*, xliv. 11 ff., 1901.

1. Amos deserves special attention because he is the oldest of the writing prophets whose work has been preserved to us. His appearance has something marvellous and inexplicable about it, if one reflects how all the great thoughts of literary prophecy already meet us here in clear definition and original freshness. A simple countryman living in the Judaean town of Tekoa, he was taken away by Jahve from following the flock in order to prophesy against His people Israel, *i.e.* the kingdom of the Ten Tribes—to prophesy and announce as the punishment for all its sins against God and man its overthrow and being led into exile by the Assyrians. Expelled from the Israelitish royal sanctuary at Bethel, with the consciousness that the words of Jahve announced by him were spoken not merely for his immediate hearers, but for all time, he wrote down his prophecies in order to preserve them for the future also.

2. As *the time of his appearance* the superscription (i. 1), which is incontestably genuine, mentions *the days of Uzziah of Judah and Jeroboam of Israel*. And this datum fully corresponds with the contents of the book. The picture of external power and prosperity side by side with internal weakness and corruption, of wealth and arrogance, haughtiness and wanton luxury that meets us here, of the foolish proud self-confidence that recks of no danger—all this brings us into the time of Jeroboam II., when Israel lay bathed in the sunset-glow of the earlier brilliance, and it could be believed that the glorious days of David had returned. And in fact we find ourselves not at the beginning, but in the middle or latter half of the long reign of Jeroboam, for according to vi. 14 his military achievements and conquests are complete and finished. That would mean *circa* 760–750. We are led to the same point by yet another historical consideration. Just as the annihilating judgment over all the surrounding peoples is an echo of the great campaign of Ramannirâri III. in 797, so the uneasy feeling of the threatening proximity of the Assyrians appears also to presuppose the events of 773–767, when three times in swift succession Assyrian armies appeared in the Lebanon: a still more definite conclusion would be deducible from viii. 9 if Amos here really had in view the great eclipse of the sun of the year 763. A further indication is afforded by the acquaintance shown by Hosea with Amos (*cf.* Hos. iv. 15, v. 8, x. 5 with Amos v. 5), so that we must assign the date of the latter nearer to 760 than to 750.

3. *The Book of Amos*, the later writing down of

which clearly appears from i. 1, falls into two parts which exhibit a definitely planned literary arrangement: in ch. i.-vi., where again i. and ii. can be divided off as introductory, we have discourses throughout; ch. vii.-ix. contain visions, interrupted by the historically inestimable narrative-passage vii. 10-17. These visions may in reality have been spoken in much the same form at Bethel, and as a consequence the conflict with the High Priest Amaziah may have arisen; but the whole is clearly a quite free *résumé* or amplification of what was enunciated by the prophet in oral speech.

4. As the Book of Amos is a purely literary production, it was natural to trace it back to the prophet himself. But this view has quite recently been vigorously assailed. More especially Harper, Loehr, and Baumann, on the ground of metrical and strophical considerations, have postulated for the book an original form according to which its traditional text can only be the result of a diorthotic process which must be described as almost unscrupulous. It must be conceded that everything is not so clear and simple in Amos as has hitherto been generally supposed, that, *e.g.*, viii. 1-14 would rather be expected to be found within iii.-vi. But is it after all so inexplicable if between the announcement of the end (viii. 1-2) and its fulfilment (ix. 1 ff.) the chiefest of Israel's sins and delinquencies are once again recapitulated? Ch. iii. and v., too, the fragmentary and disordered condition of which Nowack and Baumann especially deplore, are left almost entirely in their traditional order by Loehr. Besides, this view has as its presupposition that the

discourses of Amos were published by him singly as pamphlets, or else were only handed down orally. But what object could have been served by the publication of the six ten-lined strophes of ch. i. and ii. (which are all that are left to Amos) or of the four visions of vii.–ix. by themselves as a single pamphlet? If Amos wrote at all, then, he must be treated as an author, and I still believe that we have to deal with a book composed by him, which has survived with as little alteration as any prophetic book.

Ch. ii. 4–5, iv. 13, v. 8–9, and ix. 5–6 have long been recognised as later additions. The last three of these passages are very closely related, and were obviously written by the same hand; they palpably disturb the connexion and introduce thoughts which are alien to Amos, in spite of his sympathy with nature and his fondness for images drawn from nature's domain. A similar addition occurs also in the LXX. of Hos. xiii. 4. Ch. ii. 4–5 contrasts so markedly with the plastic and concrete reproaches levelled against the rest of the peoples, and is made up of phrases quite general and so specifically Deuteronomic in character, that it can only have been written by a later interpolator, who in the threat of judgments was unwilling to allow Judah to be passed over in the mouth of a true prophet. The doubts expressed by Wellhausen as to i. 9–10, 11–12, iv. 12*b*, and viii. 11–12 are also at least well worthy of attention. In vi. 1 צִיּוֹן ("Zion") is strange, because Amos elsewhere never makes any reference to Judah: with Wellhausen, therefore, who also strikes out vi. 2, vs. 14 must be so modified as to indicate the southern border of Judah.

On the other hand, after Wellhausen's analysis no one will any longer assert the authenticity of ix. 8–15: here " a later Jew has appended the codicil and suppressed the true conclusion, because it sounded too harsh." Elsewhere also revision may have been at work. Elhorst's attempt to explain the book as a pseudepigraph emanating from the beginning of Josiah's reign is simply a curiosity.

Special Introduction

CHAPTER XIV

BOOK II.—PROPHETIC BOOKS—*continued*

§§ 30–36. *Minor Prophets* (continued) — *Obadiah, Jonah, Micah, Nahum, Habakkuk, Zephaniah, Haggai*

§ 30. OBADIAH

LITERATURE: *Commentaries*: C. P. Caspari, 1842; Graf, *Jeremiah* (*cf.* § 25 above), pp. 559–563.

1. The book bearing the name of Obadiah, though the smallest of the prophetic writings, all the same furnishes complicated problems of Introduction. The contents and situation of the book appear first of all to be perfectly clear. A fearful judgment is announced to Edom for its treachery and baseness towards Judah: in the day of Jacob's misfortune, when the enemy pressed into Jerusalem, and cast the lot over it, Edom was as one of them. Therefore Edom is doomed to perish for ever, while Israel is restored to its ancient glory. It is obvious that vss. 11–14 are a description of the capture of Jerusalem by Nebuchadnezzar, and thus a fixed *terminus a quo* appears to be given for the book, viz. the year 586.

2. But the *relation of Obadiah to Jeremiah xlix,*

7–22 must first be established. In this Jeremian oracle against Edom occurs a series of the most striking points of contact with Obadiah. These are as follows: Ob. 1 = Jer. xlix. 14; vs. 2 = xlix. 15; vs. 3a = xlix. 16a; vs. 4 = xlix. 16b; vs. 5 = xlix. 9; vs. 6 = xlix. 10a; vs. 8 = xlix. 7; vs. 9a = xlix. 22b. If we compare these parallels with each other, it must be admitted that on the whole the scale turns in favour of Obadiah. Above all, the verses in Obadiah exhibit a thoroughly logical and good connexion and original structural arrangement, while in Jeremiah we find *disjecti membra poetae* embedded in what belongs properly to the former. Especially striking is Jer. xlix. 16 compared with Ob. 3–4, where the two verses of Obadiah have been rather harshly compressed, and in particular the expression מִשָּׁם ("thence"), which in Obadiah has a *raison d'être*, in Jeremiah is suspended altogether in the air, being without any proper antecedent. Accordingly we must suppose that Jeremiah has imitated Obadiah and had the latter before him: but the prophecy of Jeremiah emanates from the fourth year of Jehoiachim, that of Obadiah at the earliest from 586, so that nothing remains but to assume a third source common to both, an original Obadiah, which Jeremiah freely, and our Obadiah, on the other hand, faithfully, reproduced. And this conclusion is further reinforced by the consideration that, in view of the flagrant contradiction existing between vss. 7 and 18, Obadiah could not have been a literary unity. So Ewald.

3. Giesebrecht (who assumes the existence of a genuine kernel in Jer. xlix. 7–22; *cf.* § 25 above)

has pointed out that the passages dependent upon Obadiah there occur altogether in the secondary parts of Jer. xlix.; thus the latter, as a factor for determining the original Obadiah, ceases to be available. The final solution we owe to Wellhausen, who in vss. 1–5, 7*, 10–11, 13–14, and 15*b* sees the original Obadiah, combines this with Mal. i. 2–5, and refers both to the displacement of the Edomites by the Arabs, though not perhaps to quite the same phase of the latter process, since Obadiah's date fell somewhat earlier. This result lands us in the first half of the fifth century. The revision, which may be dependent upon Jeremiah—just as Ob. 7*aβ* is doubtless derived from Jer. xxxviii. 22,—has for its object to expand the contemporary catastrophe of Edom eschatologically into a world-judgment over the heathen, and the restoration of Israel: its date cannot be determined, as unfortunately vs. 20, which might possibly yield a historical starting-point, is obscure and palpably corrupt.

§ 31. Jonah

LITERATURE: F. Kaulen, *Jonae prophetae*, 1862; K. Budde, *Z.A.T.W.*, xii. 40–42, 1892. The essay of W. Boehme, *Die Komposition des Buches Jona*, *Z.A.T.W.*, vii. 224 ff., 1887, is simply a curiosity.

1. In contradistinction to all the rest of the prophetic writings, the Book of Jonah contains nothing but history, or, at least, is clothed in the form of a historical narrative, detailing the marvellous fate that befell the prophet Jonah ben Amittai. Such a prophet, from Gath-hepher in Galilee, had

really lived in the period of Jeroboam II., and predicted to the latter his successes. As the preaching referred to in the book is directed to Nineveh, and thus the continued existence of the Assyrian Empire is presupposed, there can be no doubt that the hero of the book must be the historical Jonah. But that the book can be a product of the time of Amos or Hosea is on linguistic grounds quite impossible: such expressions as חִשֵּׁב לְ ("was like to be") = μέλλω, i. 4; סְפִינָה ("ship"), i. 5; הִתְעַשֵּׁת ("think"), i. 6; קְרִיאָה ("preaching"), iii. 2; טַעַם ("taste"), iii. 7; וַיְמַן ("prepared"), ii. 1 [= i. 17 E.V.], iv. 6, 8; בְּשֶׁלְּמִי ("for whose cause"), i. 7; בְּשֶׁלִּי ("for my sake"), i. 12; שֶׁבֶּן, iv. 10—all point to the latest period of the linguistic development of Hebrew, and with this feature the character of the whole representation also accords, dependent as it is on older models: thus Jon. iii. 9 = Joel ii. 14; Jon. iv. 2 = Joel ii. 13, Ex. xxxiv. 6, Ps. lxxxvi. 15, ciii. 8; and the story in Jon. iv. of the marvellous tree is obviously imitated from the narrative in 1 Kings xix. of Elijah under the juniper-tree in the wilderness. The manner, too, in which, iii. 3, Nineveh is spoken of, as of a marvellous city of legendary times which has long since disappeared, is inconceivable in the case of an author of the time of Jeroboam II.; finally, the piling up of marvellous features is quite in the style of Chronicles and Daniel.

2. If the book was composed some centuries later than the time of the person who is the subject of its narrative, in view of the peculiar character of the latter we shall rather think of it as a product of the author's free invention, especially when it appears how this narrative has been formed with a very

definite purpose, and directed to the attainment of a very definite object. Even if the author may have utilised to some extent existent material, "yet he has assimilated this to such an extent" to his own purposes "that it has become his own" (Kuenen). Thus we have before us a *parable*, in which the form of historical narrative only serves to give a doubly forcible and impressive representation to the underlying idea. And this fundamental idea clearly points to a very late period. It is a protest against the pernicious arrogance of the Judaism that followed Ezra, which is jealous because God is so gracious, and which is in danger of losing its faith because Jahve does not extirpate and annihilate the heathen, as later prophecy had hoped and promised that He should. In opposition to this the Book of Jonah in its own inimitable and affecting way indicates that God is not merely a God of the Jews, but of the heathen also, that as Creator and Lord of the whole world He is affected towards the whole world with the feeling of love which belongs to the Creator towards His creation, and that such a loveless and self-seeking disposition as that which is here of set purpose embodied in a prophet, merits Jahve's sharpest censure. In this the greatness of the Book of Jonah lies for all time, and also its unique significance in the O.T., to which a tribute of the highest admiration can only be rendered, when one recalls Mt. x. 5–6, xv. 24–26. Whether the unknown author borrowed any features in his account from a tradition cannot certainly be said; it is, however, hardly probable, when it is considered how the whole narrative has been arranged according to definite plan directly with a view to give an embodiment and representation for every thought. The author wrote, at the earliest towards the end of the Persian, perhaps even in the Greek period; the *terminus ad quem* is given by Jesus ben Sira [Ecclus.] xlix. 10. According to Budde, the book originally formed a section in the Midrash from which the Chronicler made extracts (*cf.* § 20, 9 above), and there occupied a place after 2 Kings xiv. 27.

3. The "*Psalm*" *in ii. 3–10*, which offers considerable difficulties, would then, on Budde's view, when the separation from the Midrash was effected, have been interpolated by a later hand in order to secure the actual words of the prayer mentioned in vs. 2, and generally to furnish an example of connected address by the prophet; for this purpose the interpolator made use of the present psalm, which is not a prayer at all, but purely a song of thanksgiving. If the original author had himself produced it, he would at least have made it fit the situation; if he had borrowed it, he would at any rate have inserted it after vs. 11. To see in it any genuine work of the old historical Jonah from which the present narrative has been developed is, in view of its literary character, which marks it as belonging to the latest lyrical poetry, quite impossible.

§ 32. Micah

LITERATURE: C. P. Caspari, *Ueber Micah den Morasthiten*, etc., 1852; T. Roorda, *Commentarius in vaticinium Michae*, 1869; L. Reinke, 1874; T. K. Cheyne, *Micah*, etc., 1882; V. Ryssel, *Untersuchungen über die Textesgestalt und die Echteit des Buches Micha*, 1887; H. J. Elhorst, *De profetie van Micha*,

1891; B. Stade, *Z.A.T.W.*, i. 161 ff., 1881, iii. 1 ff., 1883, and iv. 291 ff., 1884 (against Nowack, *ibid.*, pp. 277 ff.). On ch. ii. 4: B. Stade, *Z.A.T.W.*, vi. 121 f., 1886. On ch. i. 2-4 and vii. 7-20: *Z.A.T.W.*, xxiii. 163 ff., 1903.

1. Few O.T. books and prophets have more certain attestation than *Micah of Moresheth* and his oracle by the noteworthy passage in Jer. xxvi. 18. According to this, Micah spoke the oracle in question *in the days of Hezekiah the king of Judah.* And even though a datum derived from the narrative part of the Book of Jeremiah does not amount to chronological proof, yet it will be found to be correct as a matter of fact: for Micah i.-ii. is most easily explained of the time of Sennacherib, and would accordingly be contemporaneous with the addresses in Is. xxii. 1-14, xxviii. 7-xxxi. Even the threat made to Samaria (i. 6-7), which (differing in this respect from Is. xxviii. 1-4) has in view a complete destruction of the city only, not the cessation of its independence and the end of the kingdom of Israel, would be quite explicable of 701, as the Assyrians did not destroy Samaria in 722.

In the superscription, Jotham and Ahaz are redactional additions.

2. *Ch. i.-iii.* make up a uniform passage, the contents of which are provided by the corruption of the people, especially of the ruling class in Jerusalem, and the penal judgment of God rendered necessary by this. Only ch. ii. 12-13 is foreign to the context and betrays clear marks of being a later insertion. It dissevers ii. 11 and iii. 1 (the וָאֹמַר, "and I said," of iii. 1 is just as much Micah's retort against the false prophets in ii. 11 as iii. 8 is to iii. 7), and in

linguistic features and historical situation contrasts markedly with its whole context: here the whole of Jacob and Israel is scattered, and must first be gathered together like a flock, in order then, when a breach has been made in their fold, to march under the leadership of Jahve and of his king into the gates of Jerusalem—a representation which obviously belongs to the circle of ideas and artificial manner of exilic or post-exilic prophecy. Ch. i. 2–4 may also be objected to. For the rest, however, ch. ii. and iii. closely cohere, and form, according to Stade, three parallel and constantly ascending speech-divisions, viz. ii. 1–7, ii. 8–iii. 1 (without ii. 12–13), and iii. 2–8, which then find their concentrated expression in the fearful concluding threat of iii. 9–12. According to Marti, only the following passages go back to Micah: i. 5*b*, 6, 8, 9, 16; ii. 1–3, 4 ?, 6–11; iii. 1, 2*a*, 3*a*, 4, 5*a*, 2*b*, 5*b*–8, 9–12.

3. The threatening words of iii. 12 are followed immediately, without any sort of connecting link, by the promise of a glorious future which has already engaged our attention in Isaiah. Without repentance, without conversion—at least nothing concerning either stands in the text—Zion appears (which had only just been doomed, on account of the sins of its inhabitants, to be "ploughed as a field," and to become "the high places of a forest") as the place whither all the heathen make pilgrimage in order to secure instruction for themselves about the God of Israel and to walk in His ways. We have already seen (*cf.* § 24, 6 above) that this thought points to a period subsequent to Deutero-Isaiah. And in fact Micah's authorship of ch. iv. and v. in their entirety

has been denied by Stade on grounds which have hitherto been unrefuted, and they have been explained to be a later interpolation which in itself consists of two connected passages. Even the defenders of their authenticity must concede the presence in these chapters of gaps in the connexion, passages foreign to their context and breaks in the thought, and assume larger or smaller interpolations. Ch. iv. 8, with its obscure reference to Gen. xxxv. 21, presupposes the downfall of the Judaean kingdom, and iv. 10*b* the Babylonian Exile; iv. 13 has a decidedly Deutero-Isaianic colouring. The designation of Bethlehem as *Ephrata* in ch. v. 1 is verifiable only at a much later period (Gen. xxxv. 19, xlviii. 7 Rp; Ruth iv. 11; 1 Chron. ii. 19, 50; and אֶפְרָתִי, 1 Sam. xvii. 12, Ruth i. 2 against Judg. xii. 5, 1 Sam. i. 1, and 1 Kings xi. 26), and its characterisation as צָעִיר ("little") is to be understood in accordance with Neh. vii. 26. Ch. v. 1*b* does not give the impression that at the time the House of David was still reigning, and vss. 2 and 3 clearly presuppose the Exile. Finally, the incidental mention as a matter of course of the cessation of מַצֵּבוֹת ("pillars") and אֲשֵׁרִים ("Asherim") in v. 12 (=13 E.V.) brings us down unquestionably below the period of Deut.; their conjunction with פְּסִילִים ("graven images") is a specifically Deuteronomic touch (Deut. vii. 5, xii. 3).

On all these grounds Micah's authorship of ch. iv.–v. must be denied. Only in the case of ch. v. 9–13 does Wellhausen firmly adhere to the possibility of its composition by Micah.

4. But with the settlement of this point everything is not yet finished off. *Within these chapters*

there are still grave inconsistencies. Wellhausen has already rightly seen that iv. 10 is absolutely irreconcilable with iv. 11; iv. 5 following iv. 1–4 is very strange, and iv. 6–7 chronologically should precede iv. 1–4. Finally, the realisation of the messianic final salvation is represented differently in v. 4–5 from vss. 2–3. On the other hand, iv. 11 forms the natural (and an excellent) continuation of iv. 1, and v. 6 of v. 3. Stade, therefore, takes the passages iv. 1–4, iv. 11–v. 3, v. 6–14—which besides are linked together by the sarcastic use of the expression גוֹיִם ("nations") or עַמִּים רַבִּים ("many peoples"), in iv. 2, 3, 11, 13, v. 6, 7 —together as one complete whole: in the future many peoples will come to thee to serve Jahve and to be instructed by thee in His law; now indeed they scornfully band themselves together for thy downfall, and smite thy judges on the cheeks; but then Jahve will raise out of the family of David the messianic King, who shall gather the remnant of Judah to Israel, and under His rule they will dwell in safety and, freed from all sins, teach the heathen, and have no necessity to be in fear of them any more; those who raise any opposition Jahve will Himself annihilate. Into this passage—which throughout displays the spirit and point of view of Ezekiel and Deutero-Isaiah, and which at first was intended obviously to stand after Micah iii. 12—iv. 5–10 and v. 4–5 were then inserted by way of supplement, according to Stade by the same hand that wrote ii. 12–13. The first of these smaller passages clearly depicts the Babylonian Exile and the return therefrom; in the second, which is very obscure, an allusion to the catastrophe that befell Sennacherib may be seen.

These were inserted, on Stade's showing, under the presumption that the other longer passage proceeded from Micah, the contemporary of Isaiah: more exact details as to the place and time of origin of both passages cannot be obtained. Both would gain if the passages iv. 9, 10a and 14—which by some scholars are interpreted as perhaps genuine—were rejected: v. 2 also gives the impression of being a later insertion containing a reference to Jer. vii. 14. That the necessity was felt here at all to revise and expand is explained by the fact that Micah's threatening prophecy lacked the reverse side—that of promise, which all the prophets elsewhere add.

5. With the two *final chapters, vi.-vii.*, a totally new section begins again. In a legal process, which is conducted in the form of a dialogue between Jahve and Israel, the latter is reproached with the unmerited kindnesses received from Jahve, and its own base ingratitude. Israel knows full well what Jahve demands of it, but yet the people walk after the ordinances of Omri, and do the works of the house of Ahab. Now follows an affecting lament of Zion over the corruption of her children, which makes the judgment perceived by the prophet inevitable; yet after this judgment Jahve will compassionate Zion and cast her sins into the depth of the sea. Micah's authorship of these chapters was first denied by Ewald, who interpreted them as the work of an unknown prophet of the time of Manasseh, and in doing so certainly struck the right note. Micah, indeed, if ch. i.-iii. fall about the year 701, may well have lived through the days of stress in the reign of Manasseh; but the spirit which breathes through

these chapters, more especially as it finds expression in vi. 1–8, is altogether too different from that of ch. i.–iii. to allow of one authorship. Here we find ourselves already set in the direction of Deut., already breathing (so to speak) Deuteronomic air. The dejection and readiness to acknowledge and confess sins such as the passage presupposes, undoubtedly at any rate among the pious of the people, offers a forcible contrast with the assurance shown in Isaiah, and is explicable only of a time when sins against Jahve and apostasy from Him were notorious and in evidence before all eyes. The willingness manifested even to offer children in sacrifice for the sin of the soul shows that this custom was then prevalent, and did not merely come to the front in isolated cases of the direst necessity, as in the case of Ahaz; the expression יוֹם מְצַפֶּיךָ ("day of thy watchmen") also, in vii. 4, presupposes a fairly long development of prophecy and a whole series of announcements of disaster, and besides there are worse things, such as levity, inordinate love of pleasure, injustice and outrage, which are here denounced. In only one point is Ewald's view open to modification. As Wellhausen has shown, with vii. 7 the thread of the discourse breaks off, and an entirely new section begins. The predicted punishment is a present reality: Zion has fallen and sits in darkness, but she waits for her deliverance on God, who must defend His own honour against the heathen, and who also will vindicate her after she has borne His anger. Then will Jahve perform wonders, as at the Exodus from Egypt, the heathen will have to submit and serve Him, while Israel's sin is sunk in the sea, and Jahve makes the gracious promise sworn to Abraham become a present reality.

Throughout all this we find ourselves within the circle of ideas and way of regarding things which belong to the Deutero-Isaiah: this section cannot possibly emanate from the time of Manasseh, but at the earliest is to be regarded as the cry of a voice from the oppressed and sorrowful period of the community of the Second Temple; for the residue of Jacob's heritage is obviously dwelling already in the land, but has still to wait for the final fulfilment of Jahve's promises.

Wellhausen also considers vi. 9–16 and vii. 1–6 to be quite isolated passages, of which the first, he thinks, cannot be dated, and the second suggests the period of Malachi and of some of the psalms. But they contain nothing which makes it impossible to assign them to the reign of Manasseh; in particular, adequate parallels for vii. 1–6 are to hand in Jer. v., vi., and ix.

6. The question still remains to be discussed, how, out of elements so various and disparate, *the Book of Micah as it now lies before us* could have arisen. In this connexion it is necessary to explain, first, how vi. 1–vii. 6 could have come to be appended to the Book of Micah, and then to show what relation vii. 7–20 bears to the earlier interpolations.

As regards the first question, we must suppose that the insertion of this passage preceded the working over of ch. i.–iii.: for ch. i.–v. in their present shape form so coherent a whole, and v. 6–14 such a full conclusion, that it is quite impossible to suppose an addition of vi.–vii. on to this complete whole. On

MICAH

the other hand, it can easily be seen that the anonymous piece vi. 1–vii. 6 was appended to i.–iii. In vi. 1 the expression שִׁמְעוּ נָא ("hear ye now") ranges itself beside the similar one (שמעו נא) in iii. 1 and 9, and vi. 2 is strikingly similar to i. 2; further, the particularly joyless and gloomy pessimism that appears in vi. 10–vii. 6 is reminiscent of the manner of ii. and iii.

Thus the first step in the formation of the Book of Micah will have been that the anonymous passage vi.–vii. was added to i.–iii., and the whole so arising was then later subjected to a double process of working over. For the author of vii. 7–20 cannot be the author of iv. 1–4, 11–14, v. 1–3, 6–14, which passages display a strongly marked individuality, but show no points of contact with vii. 7–20. On the other hand, such do occur between the latter and the passages ii. 12–13, iv. 5–10, and v. 4–5; thus there are the figure adduced of the shepherd and the flock in ii. 12, iv. 6–7, vii. 14; the mention of Assyria in v. 4, 5, vii. 12; the promise of the return of the earlier dominion and glory in iv. 8, vii. 14; Jahve's rule as King on Mount Zion (iv. 7) and the homage of the heathen before King Jahve on Mount Zion (vii. 17)—so that it is certainly not too bold a step to ascribe vii. 7–20 to the same hand that framed ii. 12–13, iv. 5–10, and v. 4–5.

Ch. vii. at first certainly had another and different conclusion—an independent section or a whole book could not possibly leave off at vii. 6: here the hand of the final reviser, who interpolated ii. 12–13 and revised the older interpolation iv.–v., later provided a suitable conclusion for the whole book.

Arguing from the view that Micah iv.–vii. exhibits merely a conglomeration of various predictions, Marti elucidates the formation of the Book of Micah in this way, that to its original form (see par. 2 of this section above) first of all only iv. 1–4 and vi. 6–8, linked together by iv. 5, were added; about these two firmly fixed central points various alien elements, gradually accumulating, then established themselves.

The Book of Micah in its present form, which naturally and obviously divides into the three parts, ch. i.–iii., iv.–v., and vi.–vii., in its arrangement shows a striking relationship with Is. i.–xxxix., xl.–lv., and lvi.–lxvi.

§ 33. Nahum

LITERATURE: O. Strauss, *Nahumi de Nino Vaticinium*, 1853; A. Billerbeck and A. Jeremias, *Der Untergang Ninives und die Weissagungsschrift des Nahum*, in *Beiträge zur Assyriologie*, iii. 87 ff., 1895; O. Happel, *Das Buch des Proph. Nah.*, 1902. On ch. i.: H. Gunkel, *Z.A.T.W.*, xiii., 223 ff., 1893; G. Bickell, 1894 (special reprint from *S.W.A.W.*, vol. cxxxi.); W. R. Arnold, *Z.A.T.W.*, xxi. 225 ff., 1901.

1. The Book of Nahum of Elkesi in Galilee has for its contents the subject of Nineveh's downfall, and is thus quite properly and satisfactorily described by its first superscription (which was obviously only added later) as מַשָּׂא נִינְוֵה ("an oracle concerning Nineveh"). For all the oppressions and outrages which the Assyrian people has inflicted upon the whole world, it is overtaken by the merited penal judgment. The picture of this judgment is marked by a lofty dithyrambic movement and by great poetical power, and, as a consequence of this, the

aesthetic-poetical value of the little book is very considerable.

2. For fixing the *time of the book's composition* we have as *terminus ad quem* the year 606; Nineveh is still standing, mankind still sighs under its iron yoke, but the destroyer is drawing nigh (ii. 2); the *terminus a quo* is given by the passage iii. 8–10, where the theme is concerned with a capture and sack of Egyptian Thebes. Such had been carried out on two occasions by the Assyrians: about 670 in the reign of Esarhaddon, and about 662 under Assurbanipal. If it must be assumed that this was still vividly remembered when Nahum wrote—and only the actual presence of some threatening danger to Nineveh and the Assyrian power could have driven him to write—there remains no other assignable period than *circa* 650, the time of the great uprising of Samassumukin of Babylon against Assurbanipal. But against this grave doubts arise. The whole tone of the oracle can only be explained by a direct threatening of Nineveh, while, in view of the importance which Egypt always possessed for Israel, such an event as the capture of Thebes must have remained firmly fixed in recollection. Of operations directly threatening Nineveh we know for certain (as well-founded doubts suggest themselves against accepting the first-mentioned attack by Cyaxares in 624, which is only attested by Herodotus) merely of that of 608–606, which ended in the city's capture; and in favour of 608 an argument may also be drawn from the acute observation of Bertholet,[1] that Nahum

[1] "Die Stellung der Israeliten und Juden zu den Fremden," 1896, p. 105 f.

puts himself in opposition with the greatest animosity to foreigners: for him Judah's sin has passed out of sight, and the sin of the heathen consists just in this, that they lay violent hands on Israel—a clear result of the ideas of Deut. Nahum can scarcely have lived and written in Assyria itself, and it should be observed carefully that a restoration of the kingdom of the Ten Tribes and the return of its exiles is never spoken of.

2. But even Nahum furnishes *questions as to authenticity*. It had already been observed that in Nah. i. traces of alphabetic arrangement appear, and Wellhausen had pointed to the presence of the language of the Psalms, and to the phenomenon that in one set of verses (i. 12, 14; ii. 2, 4 ff.) Nineveh, in another (i. 13; ii. 1, 3) Judah, is addressed, when Gunkel, and coincidently with (though independently of) him Bickell, reconstructed out of Nah. i. 1–14, ii. 1–3 a complete alphabetic psalm with contents of an eschatological character, and with this result secured a good deal of agreement. But Wellhausen quite rightly objects to this that an independent oracle could not begin with ii. 2, and that no reason appears for severing i. 12 and 14 from ii. 2. From this point of view Arnold and Nowack ("Kl. Proph.," 2nd ed.) followed up the problem further: Arnold has convincingly claimed i. 11, Nowack also vss. 9 and 10, for Nahum, while Marti only recovers vss. 11 and 12 for Nahum, and makes i. 12 to be directed to Zion: i. 1–8, 13, ii. 1, 3 have been given up generally. And indeed in Nahum's case it is easy to understand that the necessity for thorough revision was felt, as the religious-prophetic motive had been reduced in his

writing decidedly too far, seeing that unfortunately it is confined to the twice-repeated *Behold, I am against thee, saith the Lord of hosts* (ii. 14; iii. 3).

Remark.—The attempt made by Happel to explain Nahum as a pseudepigraph of the Maccabean period, contemporaneous with Daniel, has been satisfactorily refuted by Nowack.

§ 34. HABAKKUK

LITERATURE: *Commentaries, etc.*: F. Delitzsch, 1843; L. Reinke, 1870; A. J. Baumgartner, *Le prophète Habakuk*, 1885; O. Happel, *Das Buch des Proph. Hab.*, 1900; F. E. Peiser, *Der Prophet Habakuk*, 1903; B. Duhm, *Das Buch Habakuk*, 1906. *Essays, etc.*: B. Stade, *Z.A.T.W.* iv., 154 ff., 1884; H. Oort, *Th. T.*, xxv. 257 ff., 1891; K. Budde, *St. Kr.*, lx., 383 ff., 1893, and *The Expositor*, 1895, 372 ff.; against W. J. Rothstein, *St. Kr.*, lxvii. 51 ff., 1894; M. Lauterburg, *Theol. Zeitschr. aus d. Schweiz*, 1896, pp. 74 ff.

1. As in Habakkuk ch. i. and ii. it is clear that judgment is announced to a godless, wicked power which has harassed and outraged numerous peoples, and as the Chaldeans are the only people mentioned by name, till a short time ago the Chaldeans were generally regarded as forming the theme of the oracle and the object of its threats, and accordingly it was assigned to about the year 605, when the Chaldeans first became a real factor in the affairs of Judah. Giesebrecht, however ("Beiträge sur Jesaia-kritik," p. 190 f.), showed that the descriptive passage which mentions the Chaldeans (i. 5-11) clearly occupies a wrong position, as it dissevers i. 12 from vs. 4, of which the former is the immediate continuation, and Budde also showed that this whole interpretation is shattered on the wording of i. 6, which announces the appearance of the Chaldeans for the first time, so

that the Chaldeans are not the objects but rather the instruments of the judgment threatened by Jahve. That being so, the object of the oracle's address can only be Assyria, and thus it would have as its theme the threatening of Nineveh by the Chaldeans.

If, with Budde, the notoriously misplaced passage i. 5–11 is made to follow ii. 4, where there is an obvious hiatus and where an announcement as to who is to execute the judgment in Jahve's name is imperatively required, the whole oracle from i. 2 to ii. 8 runs smoothly and in a well-ordered sequence. Its date must be fixed at a time anterior to the actual assault by the Chaldeans on Nineveh, but also, on account of the striking way in which Israel-Judah appears as צַדִּיק ("righteous"), and the heathen world as רָשָׁע ("wicked," "godless"), subsequently to Josiah's reform of the cultus, thus somewhere about 615; it appears "as a witness from this period of the goodwill that existed and of the first disillusionment that followed the introduction of the Deuteronomic Reform." If, on the other hand, with Wellhausen, i. 5–11 is regarded as an intruded older oracle, the traditional interpretation of i. 2–4, 12–17, ii. 1–4 can be retained. In that case, however, two consequences are inevitable. If the year 600 is adhered to as the time of the book's formation, Habakkuk belongs to the number of those false prophets against whom Jeremiah waged war to the death. If this is unacceptable, it must be pushed forward to the time of Deutero-Isaiah, and be made contemporaneous with this and Is. xiii. 2 ff., xxi. 1 ff., as in fact has been done by Lauterburg.

2. Hitzig first took exception to ch. ii. 9–20,

and subsequently Stade assigned the whole section to the secondary and reproductive class of literary prophetic authors. Traces of such a purely literary character are unmistakable. In particular vss. 12–14 have been compiled almost entirely out of reminiscences and citations: vs. 12 is reminiscent of Micah iii. 10; vs. 14 an almost literal citation from Jer. xi. 9; and vs. 13 a citation in the same way almost word for word out of Jer. li. 58. Jer. l. and li., however, belong to the latest parts of the Book of Jeremiah, and in so suspicious a context to assume that Hab. ii. 13 is the original of Jer. li. 56 is not to be thought of. Further, vs. 17b is borrowed verbally from vs. 8b, and vs. 20b is derived from Zeph. i. 7.

Budde, on the other hand, thinks it possible to regard vss. 9–11 and 15–17 as original. As vs. 11 is to be reckoned among the most original words to be found in the entire prophetic literature, we willingly assent as regards vss. 9–11. The decision regarding vss. 15–17—a passage palpably dependent upon Jer. xxv.—will depend upon the verdict given as to i. 2–ii. 8: even for Wellhausen it cannot well be the work of a prophet who prophesied before the Exile.

The hypothesis of Rothstein, who thinks Hab. i. and ii. arose in this way: an original oracle delivered in the form i. 2–4, 12a, 13, ii. 1–3, 4–5a, i. 6–10, 14, 15a, ii. 6b, 7, 9, 10$ab\beta$, 11, 15*, 16*, 19*, 18*, about 605, against the godless among the people, in particular King Jehoiachim, was in the time of the Exile altered by revision into the present oracle against Babylon—is too complicated. And I may also apply the same verdict to the hypothesis of Marti, who derives only i. 5–10, 14–16 from the year 605: to this oracle, according to his view, were added towards the end of the Chaldean supremacy the woes in ii. 5–19†, while i. 2–4, 12a, 13, ii. 1–4 form a still later psalm.

3. Ch. iii. bears the special superscription תְּפִלָּה לַחֲבַקּוּק הַנָּבִיא ("Prayer of Habakkuk the prophet"). This passage is distinguished by a method and character of its own, as only in it are musical annotations and data after the manner of the Psalms to be found: we also encounter סֶלָה here three times. This (for the most part) unduly overrated "psalm" exhibits pure rhetoric: for any clearly developed line of thought, any historical situation that may be grasped, one searches it in vain. It cannot have been composed by the prophet Habakkuk, as nothing analogous to it can be produced throughout the whole of the literature of the time. The circle of thought in which the poem moves is that of eschatology tinged with apocalyptic; its mode of expression is the artificial archaising style of such passages, as Deut. xxxii., 2 Sam. xxiii. 1–7, Pss. lxviii. and xc., in common with which it has a corresponding superscription. It was not originally designed to form the conclusion of the Book of Habakkuk, but is derived —as Kuenen conjectured and E. Nestle ("Z.A.T.W.," xx. 167 f., 1900) has proved—from a "song-book," in which it may already have possessed the same superscription, just as the LXX. in fact ascribes five poems of the canonical Psalter to the prophets Haggai and Zechariah. In any case it does not belong to the latest products of post-exilic literature, as Ps. lxxvii.

17-20 furnishes a clear instance of imitation of Hab. iii.

Remark.—With considerable intellectual acumen, Peiser has interpreted the entire Book of Habakkuk as the work, composed in 609 and only partially revised and defaced, of a Jewish prince, interned as a hostage in Nineveh—perhaps a son or grandson of Manasseh—who was well acquainted with Assyro-Babylonian literature. But in view of the literary character of ch. ii. 9–iii. 17 this thesis cannot be accepted.

§ 35. ZEPHANIAH

LITERATURE: F. A. Strauss, *Vaticinia Zephanjae*, 1843; L. Reinke (Commentary), 1868; W. Schulz (Commentary), 1892; H. Oort, *Godgeleerde Bijdragen*, 1865, pp. 812 ff.; F. Schwally, *Z.A.T.W.*, x. 165 ff., 1890; K. Budde, *St. Kr.*, lxvi. 393 ff., 1893. On the criticism of the text: J. Bachmann, *St. Kr.*, lxvii. 641 ff., 1894.

1. *The prophet* bearing this name was undoubtedly a native of Jerusalem. Contrary to the usual custom, his family descent is carried back four steps, up to a certain Hezekiah—according to the prevalent view, the well-known king of that name—so that in this case Zephaniah was a princely member of the royal house; but in view of the definite data given in 2 Kings xx. 18, xxi. 1 this view seems to me to be impossible chronologically. According to the superscription in i. 1, Zephaniah prophesied *in the days of Josiah, the son of Amon*, a detail the genuine character of which is made all the more certain by the fact that it cannot be deduced from the contents of the book itself. But in that case we must assume that the period referred to is the first half of the reign of Josiah. For Zephaniah, besides the usual

complaints as to oppression and outrage, is obliged to denounce specially idolatrous customs (i. 9), syncretistic Baal-worship (i. 4), adoration of the stars (i. 5), apostasy from Jahve (i. 6), as well as heathen conduct and foreign fashions; consequently his appearance must certainly precede Josiah's reform of the cultus, and this conclusion receives further confirmation from the fact that in i. 8 it is not the king personally who is threatened, but the בְּנֵי הַמֶּלֶךְ ("the sons of the king"), the princes of the blood, the palace-camarilla who during Josiah's boyhood actually carried on the government. We should thus be brought to about the year 630.

2. Ch. i., which is one of the most outstanding passages in the whole range of prophetic literature, pictures the יוֹם יהוה ("Day of Jahve") as a terrible world-catastrophe, which more particularly brings to pass the penal judgment over Judah and Jerusalem. It is represented as a sacrificial banquet to which the guests have already been invited (i. 7). The manner of its execution clearly points to the miseries and stress of war: robbery and plundering, trumpet-blast and war-cry, bloodshed and devastation.

In view of the fact that it is characteristic of Old Testament prophecy to be conditioned by the circumstances of the time, we have to look for some particular occasion for a discourse with so strikingly peculiar a colouring of its own, and this is furnished by the terrible Scythian storm which about this time roared through the whole of Asia, spreading terror and devastation everywhere : according to the express testimony of Herodotus (i. 105), the wild hordes came burning and destroying even up to Palestine. Such events, which, at any rate for the moment, loosed all the bonds of order and dislocated everything, were admirably adapted to make the representation of the יוֹם יהוה (" Day of Jahve ") vivid, and to sustain belief in its coming.

3. In ch. ii. (where Nowack rightly rejects vs. 15) and iii. not only has the text been handed down in a very bad condition, but the contents also present grave stumbling-blocks, which were first perceived by Oort and Stade (" G.V.I.," 644, remark 3). The hope expressed that Jahve's dispersed ones shall be brought to Him as an offering of homage from the rivers of Ethiopia (iii. 10) seems very strange in the mouth of a prophet writing in 630 : iii. 14–20 both in phraseology and thought is completely Deutero-Isaianic in character, and also in ii. 11 we encounter in the expression אִיֵּי הַגּוֹיִם ("isles of the nations") a specifically Deutero-Isaianic feature. Schwally, therefore, denies Zephaniah's authorship of almost the whole of ch. ii. and iii., and in the case of ii. 1–15 Budde, in the case of ch. iii. Wellhausen, have pronounced a similar verdict. But ch. ii., as forming the continuation of ch. i., which promises a wrathful judgment on the whole earth, and not merely on Judah, is indispensable; as the judgment of Nineveh still lies in the future, ii. 13–15 must be older than 606, and Jahve's outstretched hand against the north in vs. 13 presupposes antecedent blows against other quarters of the world. Budde's objection that ii. 14–15 takes up a radically different position towards Israel and the nations falls to the ground if, with Wellhausen, we reject vss. 8–11 and regard vs. 7 as having been revised. The suspicion raised against vs. 3, on the other hand,

appears to me unfounded, for בטרם ("before") in vs. 2 clearly presupposes the possibility of a deliverance from the judgment. Nothing of consequence can then be objected against iii. 1–8 and 11–13; in particular vss. 1–4 are covered by Ezek. xxii. 25–29. Accordingly, ch. i. is to be regarded as having been preserved substantially intact, ch. ii. as worked over only to an insignificant extent, ch. iii., on the other hand, as to some extent mutilated.

§ 36. HAGGAI

LITERATURE: A. Köhler (Commentary), 1860; L. Reinke (Commentary), 1868; E. Sellin, *Studien* (see § 21 above). ii. 43–63: W. Böhme, *Z.A.T.W.*, vii. 215 ff., 1887.

1. Of a prophet Haggai some account is given in Ezra v. 1, vi. 14. In conjunction with a certain Zechariah, he came forward in the second year of Darius (520) to urge the people and its leaders to take up the task of rebuilding the ruined Temple. The sacred work was really begun and was completed in four and a half years.

2. *The little prophetic book* which has been handed down to us under Haggai's name quite corresponds to this account. The building of the Temple and the Temple itself are the centre of interest around which all revolves. A severe famine, the result of drought and failure of crops, from which the people were suffering at that time, gives the prophet occasion to utter a sharp reproof: this, he declares, is the punishment they are bearing because the people themselves are living in ceiled houses, while Jahve's House lies in ruins. Only by building the Temple can the divine

anger be averted and blessing received. On the completion of this Temple Jahve will shake heaven and earth, all the peoples of the earth will bring their valuables to it, and David's descendant Zerubbabel, as Jahve's chosen servant, will set up the messianic kingdom, and become the signet-ring on Jahve's right hand.

3. The little book — in connexion with which groundless objections have been raised against i. 7b, 13, ii. 5a (lacking in the LXX.), ii. 17 (= Am. iv. 9): in ch. ii. 14 also the LXX. introduces an addition from Am. v. 10), 18ba with ii. 20–23—takes only a modest place in the prophetic literature; it hardly rises above the level of pure prose, but in its very simplicity and modesty, because it is the utterance of a profoundly moved heart speaking out of an agitating situation, there is something strangely attractive, not to say moving, about it—one would not willingly be without it. From ch. ii. 3 Ewald concluded that Haggai himself was among the few who had seen the Solomonic Temple while still in its ancient glory; accordingly, he must at this time have been over seventy years old.

In accordance with the custom initiated by Ezekiel, the four addresses into which the book falls are dated: i. 1–11, on the 1st day of the sixth month in the second year of Darius, and to this is attached vss. 12–15, containing a historical notice as to the consequence of this address, viz. that on the 24th of the same month a beginning was made with the work; ii. 1–9, on the 21st day of the seventh month; and ii. 10–19, as well as ii. 20–23, on the 24th day of the ninth month. Haggai's active work as prophet accordingly falls within the period from September to December 520.

According to Klostermann ("G.V.I.," 1896, 213) and Marti, the Book of Haggai was not a writing composed by the prophet himself, but simply a historical statement about his prophetic activity.

Special Introduction

CHAPTER XV

BOOK II.—PROPHETIC BOOKS—*continued*

§§ 37–40. *Minor Prophets* (continued) — *Zechariah, Malachi, The Book of the Twelve Prophets, The Book of Daniel*

§ 37. ZECHARIAH

LITERATURE: *Commentaries:* A. Köhler, 2 vols., 1861, 1863; K. Bredenkamp, 1879; C. H. H. Wright, *Zechariah and his Prophecies*, 1879.

Monographs, Essays, etc.: K. Marti, *Der Prophet Zecharia, der Zeitgenosse Serubbabels*, 1892, and in *St. Kr.*, lxv. 207 ff., 716 ff., 1892; Sellin (as cited above, § 36), pp. 63–104.

On ch. vi. 11–15: J. Ley, *St. Kr.* lxvi. 771 ff., 1893.

On the question of a Deutero-Zechariah: (B. G. Flügge, published anonymously) *Die Weissagungen welche bey den Schriften des Propheten Zacharias beygebogen sind*, etc., 1784; E. W. Hengstenberg, *Beiträge*, i. 361–388 (1831), and *Die Christologie des A.T.*, iii., 2nd ed., 327–581, 1856; E. F. J. von Ortenberg, *Die Bestandteile des Buches Sacharja*, 1859; B. Stade, *Z.A.T.W.*, i. 1 ff., 1881, ii. 151 ff., 275 ff., 1882; W. Staerk, Dissertation, 1891; G. K. Grützmacher, Dissertation, 1892; R. Eckardt, *Der Sprachgebrauch*, etc., *Z.A.T.W.*, xiii. 76 ff., 1893, and *Der religiose Gehalt*, etc., *Z.T.K.*, iii. 311 ff., 1893; A. K. Kuiper, *Zacharja ix.–xiv., Eene exegetisch-critische studie*, 1894; A. von Hoonacker, *Ch. ix.–xiv. du livre de Zacharie*, 1903.

1. Side by side with Haggai a prophet Zechariah ben Iddo was mentioned in Ezra v. 1, vi. 14 as a

contemporary and of one mind with him in working for the rebuilding of the Temple. The prophecies of this prophet, who, according to Neh. xii. 16, was head of a " father's house " among the priests, are preserved to us in *the first eight chapters of the Book of Zechariah*: of their identity there can be no doubt, as the author is called in Zech. i. 1 and 7 *Zechariah ben Berechiah ben Iddo.*

The individual sections of this writing also are dated, ch. i. 1–6 in the eighth month of the second year of Darius (November 520), ch. i. 7–vi. 8 on the 24th day of the eleventh month in the same year (February 519), and ch. vii.–viii. on the 4th day of the ninth month in the fourth year of Darius (December 518)—thus the earliest emanates from a time when, according to Hag. i. 15, the building of the Temple had already been begun: but these prophetic passages also have as their theme, directly or indirectly, the building of the Temple and the hopes and expectations bound up with this, so that their authenticity and derivation from the prophet mentioned in Ezra cannot be doubted.

2. Zech. i.–viii. is one of the most remarkable and important sections to be found in the prophetic literature of Israel. In the form of eight night-visions—which in their details are in some respects very obscure, but in their main significance are perfectly clear—interpreted to him by an angel (i. 7–vi. 9), and of an appendix which breaks off suddenly in the middle of a sentence (vi. 9–15), and which Ewald was the first to detect had been purposely misplaced (besides this section, ch. iv. also appears not to have been preserved intact), the prophet gives

expression to his hopes and expectations for the future. The heathen are to be chastised for the wrong done by them to Israel, the Temple and Jerusalem are to be rebuilt in their ancient glory, and curse and sin removed from Israel; then the High Priest Joshua in cleansed raiment, and the governor Zerubbabel as the *Branch* (or *Shoot*), i.e. Messiah, will be the two *sons of oil*, i.e. the anointed ones, of the Lord of the whole earth, and between the messianic King who is crowned by Jahve Himself, and the High Priest who has been purified from sin by Jahve Himself, peace and concord shall reign. Ch. vii.–viii. give some instruction concerning fasting. The regular fast-days which have come to be observed in exile as national days of mourning are to cease as soon as Jahve, immediately on the completion of the Temple, has inaugurated the time of the messianic dominion and of the final salvation. In the case of these eight chapters no problems of Introduction arise.

Zechariah ix.–xiv.

3. When we pass on from Zech. viii. to ch. ix., we feel ourselves transported at a bound into a totally different world. All the highly significant peculiarities of the first eight chapters are absent here, while fresh peculiarities emerge, not a trace of which is to be discovered there. Consequently the recognition of the fact that these two parts of the Book of Zechariah are not derived from one author is one of the earliest attained results of the scientific criticism of the O.T., and had already been definitely expressed as early as 1784 by Flügge. Gradually the view

began to prevail that Zech. ix.–xiv. must be divided into two independent oracles: ch. ix.–xi. presuppose the continued existence of the kingdom of Israel, and make mention of Assyria and Egypt as oppressors and enemies of Israel and Judah, and consequently are to be assigned, it was thought, to the period before 722, and are the work of a contemporary of Hosea and Isaiah; while ch. xii.–xiv. are concerned only with Judah, without taking any account of Israel, and thus fall within the period subsequent to 722; and as the weeping for the dead in the Valley of Megiddo mentioned in xii. 11 can only refer to Josiah's fatal wound and quickly succeeding death at Megiddo, it was regarded as necessary to assign it to the interval between the battle at Megiddo and the fall of Jerusalem, and thus to make it the work of a contemporary of Jeremiah. Ewald later adduced proof to show that xiii. 7–9 must necessarily be taken together with ch. xi., and be ascribed to the author of ch. ix.–xi.

By apologetical writers it was supposed that they had corroborated the authenticity of these chapters in adducing proofs of their post-exilic composition. Eichorn, who—though not with the required decisiveness—had assigned the origin of this section to the period of Alexander the Great, was unheeded, as also were Gramberg and Vatke, who led the way to a right understanding of the whole question. With a full and complete scientific apparatus and in a brilliantly convincing way Stade has shown that Zech. ix.–xiv. is the work of an author who did not himself claim to be a prophet, but was already moving altogether in the track of the later Jewish apocalyptic, and wrote during the wars of the Diadochi, *circa* 259. He is throughout dependent upon the older prophets whom he reproduces, more especially Jeremiah and Ezekiel, as indeed had already been worked out by Gramberg in broad outline and by Hengstenberg in a comprehensive investigation of details.

4. I begin with ch. xii.–xiv. In this case the post-exilic origin is palpable and obvious. Thus xiii. 2–6—where prophecy, without further qualification, is ranked with the spirit of uncleanness and the names of the idols as things which must cease before the final salvation can come — would be altogether inconceivable in the mouth of a contemporary of Jeremiah. The external work-righteousness of xiv. 16–19, where the conversion of the heathen to Jahve is made to consist in their yearly pilgrimage for the Feast of Tabernacles to Jerusalem, and above all the grossly materialistic and crassly particularistic idea of holiness exhibited in xiv. 20–21, where every pot in Jerusalem and Judaea is to be holy to Jahve Sabaoth, are unheard of in pre-exilic prophecy, and go to lengths even beyond Joel. The way in which the author (xii. 7, 8, 10, 12; xiii. 1) speaks of the House *of David* on a par with other *houses*, the manner in which Uzziah (xiv. 5) is called *king of Judah*, and in which complaint is introduced over the self-exaltation of the House of David, which is to be humbled, makes it impossible to suppose that the House of David was reigning at that time; and when, moreover, according to what is probably the essential significance of the very obscure passage xii. 10–14, the House of David and the House of Levi are destined to mourn over a judicial murder which has

been compassed equally by both, the pre-exilic period —when the entire administration of justice was in the hands of the king and of his officers, and nothing was known of a spiritual court—is thereby altogether precluded. Equally unheard of in pre-exilic prophecy is the idea, which dominates the whole of this section, of a violent attack by all the heathen against Jerusalem and God's people, an idea which was first coined by Ezekiel from quite definite theological presuppositions, under the impression produced by the actual destruction of Jerusalem and the Temple. Ch. xiv. 8 also is obviously an exaggerated imitation of Ezek. xlvii. 1–10, while the specifically Deutero-Isaianic type of language is equally in evidence in xii. 1 and xiv. 16, and xiii. 1 goes back to Numb. xix. The post-exilic composition of Zech. xii.–xiv. is in my opinion indisputable.

5. But also in ch. ix.–xi. the marks of post-exilic composition are unmistakable. Did a contemporary of Hosea or Isaiah see conversion to Jahve realised in the observance of the Levitical dietary laws (ix. 7)? In ix. 8, the tyrant is not to pass through Jahve's House *any more*. On account of the covenant of Sinai, Zion's prisoners are to be freed, and their exile (מְגוּרַיִךְ LXX.) is to be doubly recompensed (ix. 11–12). Over Ephraim, also, Jahve will take compassion and lead them back, declaring that they are as though He had never cast them off (x. 6). And when, moreover, in ix. 13 (a passage which is unassailable on critical grounds) the heathen world-power appears in the guise of בְּנֵי יָוָן ("Greece"), we are thereby undeniably brought into or after the period of Alexander the Great, as referring to whose campaign ix. 1–7 may

also without violence be interpreted. But side by side with these undoubtedly late elements it is thought that the presence of old pre-exilic fragments, for the most part from the eighth century, must still be recognised in ch. ix.–xi., and even Kuenen's powerful voice has been raised in defence of this view. Ch. ix. 13 must presuppose the continued existence of the two kingdoms of Judah and Israel, and so also ix. 10. But the return of the Ten Tribes and restoration of their kingdom form a principal feature of the messianic-hopes of the future in Jeremiah and Ezekiel, and ix. 13 is messianic-eschatological in character. And when Jahve in the last decisive war uses Judah as bow and Ephraim as arrow, and thus makes this war to be fought out by means of Judah and Ephraim, and in such a way, too, that they tread down their foes like mire in the streets and drink their blood like wine, it is clear that they must be armed; and thus it can be perfectly well understood how it is that after the entrance of the messianic King the chariots shall be cut off from Ephraim and the horses from Jerusalem, because then, after the overthrow of the heathen, the kingdom of peace appears.

The bringing back of the captives out of Egypt and Assyria (x. 10) has in Is. xxvii. 13 a certainly post-exilic parallel; for an author who notoriously wrote in the Greek period Egypt and Assyria simply stand for the Ptolemies and Seleucids. The consultation of the תְּרָפִים ("teraphim") and diviners is depicted (x. 2) as an earlier custom and as the cause of the Exile which, too, lies in the past, and in a manner also that proves that the author no longer possesses any clear information about these things, and moreover Mal. iii. 5 complains of magic as an evil still in vogue. Finally, xi. 4–17—obscure as its contents are, and deceptive as the application of xi. 8 to 2 Kings xv. 8 ff. is—can on literary grounds only be explained as an imitation of Ex. xxxiv., as also the two staves which appear there are clearly derived from Ezek. xxxvii. 16 ff. The *brotherhood* mentioned as existing between Judah and Israel in xi. 14 is to be understood in accordance with ch. ix.: in historical times such only existed during the reigns of Ahab and Jehoshaphat and their successors. All the arguments brought forward in favour of the time of Hosea and Isaiah thus receive an entirely satisfactory explanation if the authorship is attributed to a later secondary writer, who was steeped in the ideas of Ezekiel and dependent upon that prophet; and though Kuenen regards a clear separation of older and later elements as an impossibility, and on that account recognises Zech. ix.–xi. as an essentially uniform piece of work, this view only throws the real problem back, and is, at any rate, more artificial and complicated than Stade's thesis.

6. If, now, in accordance with Kuenen's view, the author of ch. xii.–xiv. was a later secondary writer living in a world of Ezekielian ideas, the question would have to be weighed carefully whether *ch. ix.– xi. and xii.–xiv. were not written by one hand.* In this connexion we are struck, first of all, by the fact that ch. xi. has no conclusion. If xiii. 7–9, which in its last part is palpably an imitation of Ezek. v. 2–4, is appended, in this way at any rate a superficial conclusion would be secured; but in its contents the

chapter clearly points beyond itself. The breaking asunder of the two staves *Beauty* and *Bands* remains, that is to say, quite without result; that in reality the covenant with the peoples and the brotherhood between Israel and Judah have been broken is hardly intended. When an account is given in ch. xii. of a combined assault by all the nations against the People of God, at which crisis Jerusalem comes into the direst distress and is obliged to fall back upon her own unaided efforts, as Ephraim has completely disappeared and the enemy are even forcing Judah to join the expedition against Jerusalem—all this shows that ch. xii. is the fulfilment and immediate continuation of xi. On account of the people's sins and the sins of the leading circles among them, the complete prophetic hope for the future is not fulfilled: the final salvation—the picture of which is stamped throughout with the characteristic traits that mark Levitical Judaism—will not be brought about by a glorious restoration of all Israel, but through the agency of a miserable remnant living under terribly distressful conditions and the severest hardships. That the special superscription in xii. 1 is no proof to show that a new and independent passage is beginning will soon appear. Wellhausen, basing his view on the presence of inconsistencies and stylistic differences, dissects the six chapters into four distinct sections, independent of each other, viz.: ix., x. 1–3 ?, 4–12, xi. 1–3; xi. 4–5, 7–17, xiii. 7–9; xii. 1–6, 8–14, xiii. 1–6; and xiv. 1–12, 15–21. In spite of material and circumstantial differences, Wellhausen is still of opinion that the chapters might come from the same author, "even if the style were not sufficiently distinctive." Meanwhile, in the case of so motley and kaleidoscopic a collection of passages as jostle each other in Zech. ix.–xiv., in view of the literary characteristics of such late apocalyptic writing (in which it can never be stated with certainty where the use of derived material ends and its own begins), conclusions of too sweeping a character, based on differences of content and style, are to be avoided; Marti even maintains the unity of ix.–xiv.: "Of the total number of passages, perhaps only the small section x. 1 f. cannot be traced back to Deutero-Zechariah." It may be regarded as certain that ch. ix.–xiv. cannot be older than the Greek period, and that when they were appended to i.–viii. these chapters formed a unity (*cf.* § 38, 4 below). Much in them, and especially what the author has given us of his own, will always remain obscure and incomprehensible to us, because our information respecting the whole post-exilic period, and especially of the earliest part of the Greek period, is so extraordinarily defective. The date assigned by Stade in the confusions produced by the wars of the Diadochi, when in fact *the whole earth, everyone into the hand of his shepherd* (רֹעֵהוּ) *and of his king was delivered up* (xi. 6), and when, also, the wintry storms of Ezekiel's prophecy of Gog were recalled, *circa* 280, has every probability in its favour, both internal and external, and is specially confirmed still further by a definite criterion. When it is said (x. 11) that in the messianic time the pride of Assyria, *i.e.* of the Seleucid empire, and the sceptre of Egypt, *i.e.* of the Ptolemies, shall cease, this feature transports us into the interval falling between 301 and 198, when the Ptolemies were the rulers of the land in Palestine. To carry particular parts of these chapters as far down as the period of the Maccabees Wellhausen regards as inadmissible, although one sometimes feels "reminded" of the events of that time "involuntarily": he prefers to suppose, therefore, that xii. 7 was inserted later, because, in contradistinction with what precedes, it harmonises best with the Maccabean period. Thus, in spite of many difficulties which remain unsolved, we can adhere firmly to Stade's thesis.

7. The question *how this appendix became part of the Book of Zechariah* can only be answered when the Book of Malachi has been considered. But in connexion with this a divergence in the description given as to the author of ch. i.–viii. calls for discussion here. In Ezra v. 1 and vi. 14 he is called Zechariah ben Iddo, while in Zech. i. 1 and 7 his name is given as Zechariah ben Berechiah ben Iddo. Now the Hebrew word *ben* ("son") may in itself also be the equivalent of *grandson* (Gen. xxix. 5, xxxi. 28; 2 Kings ix. 20; Neh. xii. 23; *cf.* also Gen. xxiv. 48; 2 Kings viii. 26); but Neh. xii. 4 and 16 (where, corresponding to father and son Joshua-Jehoiachim [*cf.* vs. 10], stand as father and son Iddo-Zechariah) testify to the correctness of the description in Ezra. How the difference is to be explained is also one of the unsolved riddles of the Book of Zechariah. The conjecture of Bertholdt that the unknown Jewish prophet who wrote Zech. ix.–xi. was identical with the Zechariah ben Jeberechiah mentioned in Is. viii. 2 has secured a good deal of approval; the similarity of the names

is supposed to have been the cause of the two writings having been placed together, and ultimately led to the juxtaposition also of the names of the two fathers. If our conclusions are correct, this acute combination cannot enter into the discussion. Besides, if a prophetic piece by one known from the Book of Isaiah to have been a contemporary of that prophet had been preserved, it would have been placed among the prophets of the Assyrian period, among whom even such small books as those of Obadiah and Jonah have found a place. No explanation of the difference of names can be given.

§ 38. MALACHI

LITERATURE: L. Reinke (Commentary), 1856; A. Köhler, 1865; W. Boehme, *Z.A.T.W.*, vii. 210 ff., 1887; J. Bachmann, *A.T.liche Untersuchungen*, pp. 109-112; H. Winckler, *Altorientalische Forschungen*, ii. 3, pp. 531 ff., 1901.

1. The conclusion of the twelve minor prophets is furnished by a writing of no great size which bears on its front the name Malachi. This writing, both as to form and content, is very noteworthy. In accordance with a manner which was already beginning to show itself in Haggai, the form of the representation throughout is casuistical-dialectical: particular concrete questions are discussed in the garb of dialogue: assertion, objection, refutation— we find ourselves as regards formal discourse already on the way to the Talmud. The content, also, of the little book is quite peculiar. Under the pressure of distressful circumstances, Israel is in doubt as to Jahve's love, and does not render Him due honour,

as even the heathen do, who under the name of their scrupulously honoured idols in reality serve Jahve. It is the priests who give the lead to the people with their evil example in displaying indifference and contempt towards Jahve and His commandment: therefore they are destined to be made contemptible and to be severely punished. A further inveterate vice is the wanton divorce of Israelitish wives and the contracting of mixed marriages with *daughters of a strange god*: this Jahve hates and will terribly requite. But God's judicial power is doubted: He will appear suddenly to effect radical cleansing. If the people would conscientiously serve Him and fulfil their duties towards Him, He would be able to alter the present distressful position of affairs. And serving God is no empty folly: the pious will yet come to honour and the godless be extirpated; on that great and terrible day Jahve will send the prophet Elijah, lest He need to smite the whole land with the ban.

2. The *time of* the little book's *origin* is on the whole quite clear. Judah is under the rule of a governor (i. 8), and the Temple is built (i. 10; iii. 1, 10); thus we find ourselves in the period subsequent to Haggai and Zechariah, in the community of the rebuilt Second Temple. But the exact point of time within this epoch to which the book belongs has been defined with considerable variations. We are first of all struck by evidences of a close relationship with the narratives in Ezra and Nehemiah. The delinquencies denounced by Malachi are almost exactly the same as those against which Ezra and Nehemiah have to wage war, and consequently the

Targum already sees in the very strange name Malachi a veiled suggestion of Ezra. But the question now arises, does it indicate a predecessor, contemporary, or follower? The last appears to me to be quite outside the pale of possibility: nothing suggests that the people were aware of being under any solemn obligation to carry out the demands of the prophet, or how rigorously Ezra and Nehemiah had also carried through their work: after it had once been carried through, circumstances such as those depicted by Malachi are inconceivable. According to Kuenen, Mal. iii. 8–10 compared with Numb. xviii. 21 ff. and Neh. x. 38 necessitate making the author a contemporary dependent upon Ezra. But the existence of tithe is presupposed in Gen. xxviii. 22 and Amos iv. 5, and is already demanded by Deut. xiv. 22–29 and xxvi. 12; תְּרוּמָה ("offering," "heave offering") occurs—though with the addition of יָד ("hand")—as early as Deut. xii. 6, 11, 17, and is quite a common word in Ezekiel—in conjunction with מַעֲשֵׂר ("tithe") it occurs, outside of Mal. iii. 8, only again in the three verses cited from Deut.; עִוֵּר ("blind") and פִּסֵּחַ ("lame") also in ch. i. 8 are derived from Deut. xv. 21: thus Malachi throughout is formally dependent on Deut., and relies on the latter, though essentially and materially he already stands within the territory of P. This literary-critical test-case alone is sufficient to fix Malachi's date before the time of Ezra, as Hitzig (who indeed changed his view later), Bleek, Reuss, Stade, and Wellhausen do (Kautzsch regards it as "more probable"). When Ezra himself narrates (Ezra ix. 1) that the obstacle in the way of his proceeding against the mixed marriages was removed by the complaints of the שָׂרִים ("princes") at Jerusalem, we must conclude from this that he already found sympathisers ready to help in Jerusalem; and to this pious and strenuous circle—which was already in evidence in the Promised Land before the advent of Ezra—consisting of those who were written down in Jahve's book of memorial, the author of the Book of Malachi belonged—how short or how long a time before 458 cannot, of course, be stated. Ch. i. 8 also is useful as providing an incidental point for fixing the time of the composition; this passage absolutely precludes the period of Nehemiah's governorship (*cf*. Neh. v. 14–19).

Winckler's assignment of the date to the time immediately preceding the Maccabean revolt is a pure curiosity.

3. No *questions as to authenticity* fall to be considered in connexion with the Book of Malachi. As in the case of Haggai, so also here Böhme regards the conclusion iii. 22–24 as having been added later; but this view has already been well and satisfactorily refuted by Kuenen: more especially in their thoroughly Deuteronomic colouring do these verses—which are directly attested by Jesus ben Sira [Ecclus.] xlviii. 10,—in spite of many peculiarities in detail, show complete agreement with the rest of the book. On the other hand, we agree with Marti in regarding ii. 11–12 as an interpolation, for elsewhere quite other thoughts respecting the heathen are expressed: these verses are a deplorable blot upon a book in other respects so full of good feeling.

4. *The superscription in i. 1* demands a more

detailed treatment. As it now runs, there can be no doubt that מַלְאָכִי ("Malachi") is intended to be taken as the name of the prophet: But such a proper name, even if it be possible linguistically, is on material grounds inconceivable. Further, this superscription is not free from doubt textually, for the LXX. reads ἐν χειρὶ ἀγγέλου αὐτοῦ θέσθε δὴ ἐπὶ τὰς καρδίας ὑμῶν,[1] from which Bachmann, supposing the LXX. reading to have been וְשִׂמוּ בלב, and explaining this to be a misreading of וּשְׁמוֹ כָלֵב ("and his name was Caleb"), infers that the author of the book bore the name of Caleb. In any case the combination מַשָּׂא דְבַר יהוה ("oracle of the word of J."), which only occurs again in Zech. ix. 1 and xii. 1, is strange. And here is the place to take up this question, which has been left over for discussion. If we consider the three headings more narrowly, their close connexion with each other and mutual dependence becomes at once obvious, and, if the correctness of the traditional text is assumed, the original can only be Zech. ix. 1, of which the two other passages are imitations; for in the former passage (Zech. ix. 1) the words דבר יהוה ("word of J.") belong to the oracle itself, and could only have been regarded as forming part of the superscription because they were misunderstood. It is true that מַשָּׂא occurs alone, without any explanatory genitive, again in the superscription in Hab. i. 1; but Zech. ix. 1 is on other grounds suspicious. However, be that as it may—in Zech. xii. 1 and Mal. i. 1 the superscription is undoubtedly secondary in character. In Zechariah the overloading of the verse is a striking feature—xii. 1b would more than suffice;

[1] "By the hand of his messenger. Lay it, I pray you, to heart."

and in Malachi, finally, the superscription, in the form which it has assumed in the Hebrew text, is to be explained simply as due to a misunderstanding of iii. 1.

Now the addition of Zech. ix.–xiv. on to the Book of Zechariah is explained. Both Zech. ix.–xiv. and Malachi originally were anonymous pieces which were appended as such at the end of the collection of minor prophetical writings which were derived from definitely named authors: Zech. ix.–xiv., as being the more extensive, was placed first, the shorter "Malachi" quite at the end. That the latter formed an independent, closely connected, and uniform book is unmistakably clear. Then it was easy to provide it for the first time with a special superscription, by means of which the further advantage was secured that the collected "minor prophets" now made up the significant and favourite number of twelve exactly.

Zech. ix.–xiv., which did not possess such striking peculiarities and characteristics as Malachi, was now included with Zechariah, just as the anonymous work of Deutero-Isaiah was included with Isaiah. Then Zech. xii.–xiv., which appears to be very different in character from what immediately precedes, although it is its direct continuation, was provided with a similarly framed special superscription, for according to this view of the matter the superscription in ix. 1 only marked a subdivision in the same book. Marti points out the similarity with Is. xl.–lxvi., which by the verse-refrain in xlviii. 22 and lvii. 21 was also divided into three fairly equal parts. Even if Zech. xii.–xiv. had been an independent anonymous piece—a view which at any rate seems to be favoured by the existence of this special superscription analogous to Mal. i. 1—in that case the sequence of the arrangement Zech. ix.–xi., xii.–xiv., Malachi must be attributed purely to chance, unless, indeed, the compiler of the collection of the twelve minor prophets shared the opinion of the majority of the latest critics, and wished to arrange his collection in historical order. If the passage Zech. ix.–xi. really should have survived as an independent oracle, preserved under the name of the Zechariah ben Jeberechiah mentioned in Is. viii. 2, right down to the time of the formation of the prophetic canon, its present local disposition is altogether incomprehensible.

The view that Zech. ix.–xiv. and Malachi were two anonymous minor prophetic writings, and as such were placed at the conclusion of the prophetic writings which proceeded from authors whose names had been traditionally handed down, alone satisfactorily explains all the problems involved.

§ 39. THE BOOK OF THE TWELVE PROPHETS

1. In the Hebrew canon the twelve minor prophets together form *a single book*, and it is obvious that we have here before us a collection, a compilation. Having already acquainted ourselves with the books individually, we have now to deal specially with the collection as a whole.

2. The occasion could only have arisen, and the need could only have been felt, for the formation of a final and authoritative collection of the prophetic

writings when the conviction had grown up that prophecy as a living force was extinguished, and it was thus treated as something definitive and final, a historical phenomenon belonging purely to the past, the still extant documents of which it was desirable to collect. For this view of the matter we possess documentary evidence in 1 Macc. iv. 46, ix. 27, xiv. 41, and indeed already in Zech. xiii. 2-6, and to a certain extent also in Mal. iii. 23. If we pursue the attempt to fix the time of the closing of this canon more exactly, we have in Zech. ix.–xiv., which was the last piece to be admitted into the collection, the *terminus a quo*: the *terminus ad quem* is furnished on one side by the circumstance that the Book of Daniel is no longer reckoned among the prophetic writings, on the other by the positive testimony of Jesus ben Sira, who in [Ecclus.] xlix. 10, after Isaiah, Jeremiah, and Ezekiel, speaks of οἱ δώδεκα προφῆται— the passage in question is absolutely unassailable on critical grounds (*cf.* Nöldeke, "Z.A.T.W.," viii. 156, 1888), and in fact has now also been discovered in the Hebrew text. We are thus brought to the period from *circa* 300 to *circa* 200, and so to the middle or second half of the third century.

3. As regards *the principle which guided the arrangement*, it is clear that this was a historical one. Hosea, Amos, Micah, Nahum certainly belong to the Assyrian, Habakkuk to the Chaldean, Haggai and Zechariah to the Persian period. More especially in the case of the last-named the principle of the chronological arrangement is perceptible with particular clearness: the little Book of Haggai could only have been placed before the more extensive and

important Zechariah because Haggai came forward two months earlier than Zechariah (Hag. i. 1, compared with Zech. i. 1). The sequence Nahum, Habakkuk, Zephaniah is explained thus: Nahum introduces for the first time the threatened punishment of Nineveh, Habakkuk makes the first mention of the Chaldeans, and Zephaniah already depicts the complete destruction and depopulation of Nineveh; thus the contents of the Book of Zephaniah might be regarded as the actual carrying out and consequence of Habakkuk's vision, and the Day of Jahve depicted in Zeph. i. as the fulfilment of the theophany in Hab. iii. The admission of the Books of Joel, Obadiah, and Jonah into the series of the Assyrian prophets is explained in the case of the last by the fact that it was regarded as being a work of the historical Jonah ben Amittai of the time of Jeroboam II., in the case of the two former as the result of erroneous traditional opinions regarding the age in which the authors lived. But side by side with the chronological factor other material factors have contributed to the result. The historical Jonah belonged to an earlier period than Hosea and Amos; Amos was earlier in date than Hosea. If in spite of this Hosea opens the Book of the Twelve Prophets, such a result can only have been brought about because Hosea's book is the most voluminous of the writings here collected, just as in the case of the Pauline letters the Epistle to the Romans has been placed at the beginning of the series. Hos. i. 2 might also have contributed to this result. If Jonah, of the three Israelitish prophets from the period of Jeroboam II., occupies the last place, this can only have happened because his book is rather in the nature of narrative than prophecy. The middle position assigned in each case to Joel and Obadiah seems to have been dictated by a desire to make Israelitish and Judaean prophets alternate: Hosea was an Israelite, Joel a Judaean; Amos a Judaean, but working exclusively in Israel, Obadiah a Judaean; Jonah an Israelite, Micah a Judaean. Still other grounds for the arrangement adopted may be discovered. That the historical principle was the governing factor and was consciously acted upon throughout seems to me to be undeniable.

4. But *the arrangement has not been traditionally handed down in an altogether fixed form.* The Alexandrian canon exhibits in the case of the first six books a different sequence: Hosea, Amos, Micah, Joel, Obadiah, Jonah. When we compare the two arrangements together, we must acknowledge that that of the Palestinian canon has altogether the better claim to be original. In Alexandria the books were arranged in order according to their bulk, and Jonah, on account of its purely narrative character, was consigned to the end: how out of this order, on the assumption that it was original, that of the Hebrew text could have arisen is not evident. But the fact that the sequence of the last six books is in agreement in both texts, and that only within the first six were transpositions allowed, testifies to the existence on the whole of an early reached and clearly held opinion as to the grouping of the twelve minor prophets.

§ 40. THE BOOK OF DANIEL

LITERATURE: *Commentaries:* C. von Lengerke, 1835; F. Hitzig, *K.E.H.*, 1850; J. Meinhold, *S.Z.*, 1889; A. A. Bevan, 1892; G. Behrmann, *H.K.A.T.*, 1894; F. W. Farrar, 1895; J. D. Prince, 1899; S. R. Driver, 1900; K. Marti, *K.H.C.A.T.*, 1901.

Essays, Monographs, etc.: J. Meinhold, *Beiträge zur Erklärung des Buches Daniel*, 1888; A. Kamphausen, *Das Buch Daniel und die neueste Geschichtsforschung*, 1892; A. von Gall, *Die Einheitlichkeit des Buches Daniel*, 1895. On ch. iii., E. Nestle (as cited above, § 17), pp. 35-37; on ch. iv., E. Schrader, *Jp. Th.*, vii. 618 ff., 1881. On the seventy weeks of years: A. Hebbelynck, 1887; J. W. van Lennep, 1888; R. Wolf, 1889; C. H. Cornill, in *Theologische Studien und Skizzen aus Ostpreussen*, ii. 1 ff., 1889.

On the criticism of the text: A. Kamphausen, *S.B.O.T.*, 1896; M. Löhr, *Textkritische Vorarbeiten zu einer Erklärung des Buches Daniel*, *Z.A.T.W.*, xv. 75 ff., 193 ff., 1895, xvi. 17 ff., 1896; A. Bludau, *Die alexandrinische Uebersetzung des Buches D.*, 1897; P. Riessler, *Das Buch Daniel: Textkritische Untersuchung*, 1899.

1. If the Old Testament books are treated in accordance with the principle of arrangement by subject-matter and content, the book which bears the name of Daniel must be assigned to the prophetic literature, as indeed the Greek Bible does assign it in placing it among the prophetic books. It divides into two fairly equal parts. Ch. i.-vi. give an account of the experiences of a certain Daniel and his three friends, Hananiah, Misael, and Azariah, who in the third year of Jehoiachim are led captive by Nebuchadnezzar to Babylon, and there come to high honour, but in spite of many temptations remain true to the God and faith of their fathers. Ch. vii.-xii. recount many visions which this Daniel had, and which were interpreted to him by an angel. The

book, from ii. 4*b* (where the address of the "Chaldeans" is given in Aramaic) up to vii. 28, makes use of the Aramaic language. Attempts have been made to explain this double linguistic character in the most diverse fashion. The most probable is the view of Marti, that the author wrote the whole book in Aramaic, but that later, in order to make its admission into the canon possible, both the beginning and the end were translated into the old, sacred language, Hebrew.

2. The book belongs to the so-called *Apocalyptic Literature*, which designedly veils and disguises the things it discloses. In order to understand the contents and aim of Daniel, we must proceed on the basis of ch. xi., where in veiled but yet perfectly clear language historical events are spoken of. Now it is clear, and the point is generally conceded, that ch. xi. 5–20 contains a concise but thoroughly correct survey of the history of the Ptolemies and Seleucids and their mutual entanglements, and vss. 21–39 a detailed description of the reign of Antiochus Epiphanes and of his persecution directed against the faith of Israel and its confessors. In accordance with this absolutely certain evidence the remaining accounts are to be estimated, more especially viii. 9–14, 23–26, vii. 8, 19–27, and ii. 31–34, 40–43. They are all concerned with the kingdoms of the Diadochi, and above all with Antiochus Epiphanes, who forms the peculiar subject and essential theme of the book. Now it would be supposed that the book was written in the time with which it is concerned; but it expressly claims to be derived from a contemporary of Nebuchadnezzar and Cyrus, as a

book which is to be sealed for ever. This self-attestation of the Book of Daniel was first explicitly contested by the neo-Platonist Porphyry, who devoted an entire book of his λόγοι κατὰ Χριστιανῶν to the question of Daniel. At the present time the view which sees in Daniel a work of the Maccabean period is the all-prevailing one: defenders of the traditional date grow ever fewer and rarer. And indeed it is no mere rationalistic repugnance to the marvellous and denial of a supernatural inspiration, but objective reasons of the utmost weight, which render the view of its non-genuineness necessary.

(a) *The position of the author as regards history.*— For the period subsequent to Alexander the Great his knowledge of events is fairly good, for the time of Antiochus Epiphanes he has access to excellent sources of information: all that lies outside these time-limits is for him enveloped in darkness. Especially regarding the older history he has notions such as are altogether inconceivable in the case of one who was an eye-witness. His fixing the carrying away into captivity in the third year of Jehoiachim (i. 1) contradicts all the contemporary accounts, and can only be explained as due to a combination of 2 Chron. xxxvi. 6–7 with an erroneous interpretation of 2 Kings xxiv. 1. To represent that the king in whose reign Babylon was captured and the Chaldean Empire destroyed was named Belshazzar, and was a son of Nebuchadnezzar (ch. v.), is to contradict all the other assured witnesses of the O.T. The same is true when the conqueror of Babylon is called *Darius the Mede* (vi. 1), a son of Xerxes (ix. 1), and represented to be the predecessor of Cyrus. That the

Medes must have captured Babylon is derived from Is. xiii. 7, xxi. 2, Jer. li. 11, 28, in connexion with which the author possessed a dim consciousness of the fact that the Persian Empire had grown out of a Median kingdom, and that once a Darius really did capture Babylon. Of the fact of Susa also having been a seat of the Babylonian court there may be a reminiscence in viii. 2. The impossible character of the edicts ascribed in ch. iii. and iv. to Nebuchadnezzar, and in ch. vi. to Darius, the absurdity of the wish attributed to Nebuchadnezzar in ch. ii., and the incredibility attaching to the supposed incapacity of this king for government, owing to madness, for a space of seven years, need no proof. It must also be pointed out that a writer who makes a pious Jew, and one true to the Law, to be admitted into a society of the Chaldean magicians can only have possessed very confused notions of the latter: the gross blunders exhibited respecting assured historical events suffice to preclude the possibility of his having been an eye-witness. The author's knowledge of the period between Cyrus and Alexander the Great is, however, equally defective. When we find him attributing to the Persian Empire a total of only four kings (xi. 2; *cf.* also vii. 6), this clearly arises from the fact that by accident the names of only four Persian kings are mentioned in the O.T.; when we find that he makes the fourth of these to be exceedingly rich, provoke a mighty war against Greece, and in a triumphant repulse of this attack by the Greek king Alexander the Great to be defeated and dethroned—it is clear that the author has confused Xerxes and Darius Hystaspes by making them one and the same person, and mistaken the latter for Darius Codomannus. The same obscurity recommences with the year 165: all that lies beyond this date is for him nebulous and in direct disagreement with all historical facts (xi. 40–45; vii. 11–14; viii. 25). As it is impossible to assume a limited and partial inspiration of this kind, the only explanation remaining is that the author was a contemporary of Antiochus Epiphanes, who naturally possessed an accurate knowledge of the events he himself had lived through, and had a fair acquaintance as well with the history of the empire of which he was a subject.

(*b*) *The entire absence of any traces of influence exercised by Daniel on the post-exilic prophetic literature.* — If Daniel had been composed by a contemporary of Cyrus, we should necessarily have expected that so peculiar and highly important a work would have shown some evidence of its being known and used. When one sees how echoes and reminiscences of Deuteronomy, Jeremiah, Ezekiel, Deutero-Isaiah are traceable in all the literary productions that were written after them, the same results would be looked for from Daniel. But nothing of this is to be discovered.

(*c*) *The position of the book in the Hebrew canon, where it is inserted, not among the prophets, but in the third division of the canon, the so-called Hagiographa.*—If it were the work of a prophet of the time of Cyrus, no reason would be evident why there should be withheld from it a designation which was not denied to a Haggai, Zechariah, and Malachi—nay, even to a Jonah.

(d) *The non-mention of Daniel by Jesus ben Sira.*
—This author, writing about the year 200, mentions Isaiah (Ecclus. xlviii. 20–25), Jeremiah (xlix. 6–7), Ezekiel (xlix. 8–9), and the twelve minor prophets (xlix. 10): failure to mention Daniel here would be all the more inexplicable because Jesus ben Sira already regards the essential idea of prophecy as consisting in prediction of the future, and thus would have set an especially high value on Daniel. The first certain reference to Daniel occurs in 1 Macc. ii. 59–60, *circa* 100 B.C.

(e) In the case of a contemporary of Cyrus the whole of ch. ix.–xii. (reflection on the subject of Jeremiah's oracle of the seventy years) would be inconceivable; as in the first (or third) year of Cyrus these seventy years had not yet elapsed, it was consequently impossible to indulge in surmises as to the non-fulfilment of the prophecy in question.

(f) The manner in which the term כַּשְׂדִּים ("Chaldeans"), exactly like the Latin *Chaldaeus*, is used in the sense of *soothsayers* and *astrologers* (ii. 2, 4, 5, 10; iv. 4; v. 7, 11) is inconceivable at a time when the כשדים were the ruling people of the world.

(g) The repeated occurrence of Persian and Greek loan-words, among which the composite word סוּמְפֹּנְיָה = συμ-φωνία is a specially convincing example.

(h) The use of the Aramaic language, which presupposes that Aramaic — and that the Western Aramaic of Palestine, not the Eastern Aramaic dialect of Mesopotamia—was the mother-speech of the original readers.

(i) In the face of such overwhelming proofs of an objective kind, it is hardly necessary to adduce reasons derived from Biblical theology and archaeology. But perhaps the following should be mentioned: prayer offered three times daily in the direction of Jerusalem (vi. 11); the importance attached to fasting (ix. 3; x. 3) and almsgiving (iv. 24); abstinence from flesh and wine in intercourse with the heathen (i. 8 ff.); the developed angelology which characterises the whole book right through; the doctrine of a twofold individual resurrection of the dead to bliss and to damnation (xii. 3); and finally the expression הַסְּפָרִים, "the books" (ix. 2), for *the Bible*, τὰ βιβλία, which already presupposes a collection of writings regarded as sacred. All these are things which would not have been intelligible at the time of the Babylonian Exile.

(*k*) Lastly, the whole manner and character of the book, which, in spite of many points of contact with Ezekiel and Zechariah, is just as distinctly remote from all the rest of the canonical literature of the O.T. as it is in close accord with the later apocalyptic and apocryphal books.

3. All these reasons compel us to recognise in Daniel the work of a pious Jew, loyal to the Law, of the time of Antiochus Epiphanes, who was animated with the desire to encourage and support his persecuted and suffering comrades in the faith by the promise that the Kingdom of Heaven had nearly arrived. These exhortations and predictions he placed in the mouth of a divinely inspired prophet of the time of the Babylonian Exile, so that his book is a *pseudepigraph*: the adoption of this method, however, if he wished to be heard and if his allocution was to do its work, was an absolute necessity, because

his age was fully impressed with the idea that prophecy was extinguished (Ps. lxxiv. 9; 1 Macc. iv. 46, ix. 27, xiv. 41). Our author got the name of his prophet from Ezekiel, who (xiv. 14, 20; xxviii. 3) makes mention of a certain Daniel as having been especially pious and wise. This Ezekiel-passage cannot be employed as proof of the historicity of Daniel, because the Daniel mentioned (Ezek. xiv. 14, 20) by the side of Noah and Job cannot possibly be "a Babylonian student" (Reuss) of the days of Ezekiel, but can only be drawn from popular tradition. Whether the latter had already introduced his name in connexion with similar stories of the kind narrated by our author we have no means of knowing: in any case the name and person of a pious and wise Daniel, who lived in earlier times, were for his purpose sufficiently guaranteed by the authority of Ezekiel.

4. Having regard to the altogether peculiar character of the Book of Daniel, *the time of its composition* can be determined almost to a day, when we have once ascertained what events were known to the author. For this viii. 14, according to which it must be concluded that the author had himself lived to see the rededication of the Temple by Judas Maccabaeus (1 Macc. iv. 42–58), is decisive. Nor is the conclusion contradicted by xi. 34, יֵעָזְרוּ עֵזֶר מְעָט ("they shall be holpen with a little help"): in comparison with the marvellous display of Jahve's omnipotence which had been hoped for, all Judas' achievements amounted merely to *a little help*, and according to 1 Macc. v. the position of the Jews at that time was sufficiently depressing; on the other hand, the fact of the Hellenisers joining themselves

to the pious *in hypocrisy*[1] (xi. 34*b*) already presupposes some not unimportant consequences. The dedication of the Temple took place on the 25th of Kislev (December) 165. As the author did not live to see the death of Antiochus Epiphanes in the winter of 164, but expects the end of this tyrant to synchronise with the end of the seventieth week of years in June 164, the book must have been written between the end of December 165 and June 164, thus probably in January 164. Nor is this date excluded by ix. 24 (*cf.* Kamphausen, "Geschichtsforschung," p. 36): even if it were, however, the book could not have been written very much earlier.

5. The unity of the book was much called into question in the earlier period; most recently in particular by Strack—who, however, in the last edition of the "Einleitung" speaks with much greater reserve —and Meinhold. According to this view, ch. ii.–vi. form an Aramaic book of Daniel-stories emanating from the period of Alexander the Great, to which later, under Antiochus, the visions in vii.–xii. were added. But this view has little probability. Ch. ii. cannot in substance be separated from the visions in vii. and viii., and besides ii. 43 likewise contains a strain of quite definite prediction of historical events out of the later history of the Diadochi. Further, in the Daniel-stories in ii.–vi. the penetrating underlying references to Antiochus Epiphanes and his persecution of the Jewish religion are quite unmistakable. Moreover, ch. i. must have preceded ch. ii. from the very first. In spite of a good many, and some grave, inconsistencies in details, hardly any other

[1] E.V. *with flatteries.*

O.T. book is so uniform and written so much in a single strain as Daniel, and therefore I find myself quite unable to agree with the view of a successive composition and publication of the material of the book in " pamphlet " form (Reuss).

6. As later additions (apart from isolated glosses) Gall rejects the prayer of repentance in ix. 4–20, and Marti also rejects i. 20–21 ; the elimination from the text of viii. 13–14 (Giesebrecht, " G.G.A.," 1895, 599) and xii. 11–12 (Gunkel, " Schöpfung und Chaos," 1895, 269, and Marti) seems to me to depend upon an incorrect view of those passages. It is well known that Daniel has been amplified in the Greek Bible by the addition of a number of long pieces.

Special Introduction

CHAPTER XVI

BOOK III.—C. POETICAL AND DIDACTIC BOOKS

§§ 41, 42. *The Psalter, Lamentations*

LITERATURE: H. Ewald, *Die Dichter des Alten Bundes*, 3 vols., 2nd ed., 1866–1867.

§ 41. THE PSALTER

LITERATURE: *Commentaries*: De Wette, 1811; F. Hitzig, 2 vols., 1835, 1836; H. Hupfeld, 4 vols., 1855–1862; F. Delitzsch, *B.C.A.T.*, 1893, 5th ed.; F. Hitzig, 2 vols., 1863, 1865 (an entirely new work); Hupfeld-Nowack, 3rd ed., 2 vols., 1887, 1888; F. Baethgen, *H.K.A.T.*, 1904; B. Duhm, *K.H.C.A.T.*, 1899; T. K. Cheyne, 1904, 2nd ed.

Monographs, Essays, etc.: F. Delitzsch, *Symbolae ad psalmos illustrandos isagogicae*, 1846; C. Ehrt, *Abfassungszeit und Abschluss des Psalters*, 1869; F. Giesebrecht, *Ueber die Abfassungszeit des Psalters*, *Z.A.T.W.*, i. 276 ff., 1881; E. Sellen, *De origine carminum quae primus Psalterii liber*, etc., Diss., 1892; T. K. Cheyne, *The Origin and Religious Contents of the Psalter*, 1891; B. Stade, *Die messianische Hoffnung im Psalter*, *Z.T.K.*, ii. 369 ff., 1892; P. de Lagarde, *Orientalia*, ii. 13–27, 1880, and *Novae Psalterii Graeci editionis specimen*, 1887; B. Jacob, *Beiträge zu einer Einleitung in die Psalmen*, *Z.A.T.W.*, xvi. 129 ff., 265 ff., 1896, xvii. 48 ff., 263 ff., 1897; A. Büchler, *Zur Geschichte der Tempelmusik und der Tempelpsalmen*, *Z.A.T.W.*, xix. 96 ff., 329 ff., 1899, xx. 97 ff., 1900; W. Staerk, *Zur Kritik der Psalmenüberschriften*, *Z.A.T.W.*, xii., 91 ff., 1892, and *Die Gottlosen in den Psalmen*, *St. Kr.*, lxx., 449 ff., 1897; A. Rahlfs, עני *und* ענו *in den*

THE PSALTER

Psalmen, 1892; R. Smend, *Ueber das Ich der Psalmen,* Z.A.T.W., viii., 49 ff., 1888; G. Beer, *Individual- und Gemeinde-psalmen*, 1894; F. Coblenz, *Ueber das betende Ich in den Psalmen*, 1897; H. Roy, *Die Volksgemeinde und die Gemeinde der Frommen im Psalter,* 1897.
On Ps. lxviii.: E. Reuss, 1851; J. Grill, 1883 f.
On the criticism of the text: J. Olshausen, K.E.H., 1853; C. Bruston, *Du texte primitif des Psaumes*, 1873; J. Dyserinck, *Th. T.*, xii. 279 ff., 1878; H. Graetz, *Kritischer Kommentar zu den Psalmen*, 2 vols., 1882, 1883; G. Bickell, *Dichtungen der Hebräer*, iii. 1883; J. Wellhausen, S.B.O.T., 1895, English transl., 1898, and *Skizzen und Vorarbeiten*, vi. 163 ff., 1899.

1. The Psalter or the Book of Psalms is a collection of 150 poems, of very various kinds and value, which, however, possess the common characteristic that they are all of a religious character — with the single exception of Ps. xlv., which only owes its place in the Psalter to the fact that its contents received a new religious interpretation. In Hebrew it is called סֵפֶר תְּהִלִּים, or in a contracted form תִּלִּים or תִּלִּין, i.e., "Hymn-Book," collection of poems for use in divine worship, and for religious edification, the title thus clearly expressing the liturgical character of the collection. The richness and many-sidedness of the contents of the Psalms are endless: all the situations and occurrences of life are debated in the light of the divine way of regarding them, and sanctified and ennobled by piety, so that they are transfigured into prayer and hymn.

2. In connexion with the isagogic treatment of the Psalter, a sharp distinction must be drawn between the individual poems and the collection now lying before us. We must first of all fix our attention on the *individual poems*—of course not in the sense of

investigating the time of origin and the author of each of the 150 psalms, but merely from general points of view, and by taking into consideration questions of principle.

3. In considering the individual poems, the first question must be the one as to *the superscriptions.* With the exception of thirty-four poems, viz. Pss. i., ii., x., xxxiii., xliii., lxxi., xci., xciii.–xcvii., xcix., civ.–cvii., cxi.–cxix., cxxxvi., cxxxvii., cxlvi.–cl. (which the Jews call in consequence יְתוֹמִים, *orphaned*), every individual psalm in the Hebrew text bears a superscription. Much that these superscriptions contain is of a purely musical kind, and includes directions as to the manner of rendering and accompaniment of the psalms, as to the melody to which they are to be sung, or as to the position they are to occupy and their employment in worship: the interpretation of the expressions so used—which only occur outside the Psalter in Chronicles—belongs to exegesis. Pss. lxvi., lxvii., xcii., xcviii., c., and cii. have superscriptions purely of the musical-liturgical kind; the very closely connected group cxx.–cxxxiv. bear the common title שִׁיר הַמַּעֲלוֹת or, in the case of cxxi., שִׁיר לַמַּעֲלוֹת.

From the point of view of Introduction only two categories of superscriptions are important, viz.:—

(a) *Names,* which, too, are all joined with לְ. לְמשֶׁה (Moses), Ps. xc.; לְדָוִד (David), in the case of seventy-three psalms—thus nearly half of the entire number viz. iii.–ix., xi.–xxxii., xxxiv.–xli., li.–lxv., lxviii.–lxx., lxxxvi., ci., ciii., cviii.–cx., cxxii., cxxiv., cxxxi.–cxxxiii., and cxxxviii.–cxlv.; לִשְׁלֹמֹה (Solomon), lxxii. and cxxvii.; לְאָסָף (Asaph), l. and lxxiii.–lxxxiii.; לִבְנֵי קֹרַח ("sons of Korah "), xlii., xliv.–xlix., lxxxiv., lxxxv., lxxxvii., lxxxviii.; לְאֵיתָן הָאֶזְרָחִי ("Ethan the Ezrahite"), lxxxix; לְהֵימָן הָאֶזְרָחִי ("Heman the Ezrahite") by the side of לִבְנֵי קֹרַח ("sons of Korah"), lxxxviii.; further, לִידִיתוּן (Jedithun), side by side with לְדָוִד (David), xxxix.; and עַל־יְדִיתוּן by the side of לְדָוִד, lxii.; by the side of לְאָסָף, lxxvii.

(b) *Historical superscriptions.* In the case of thirteen, all with the designation לְדָוִד (David), viz. Pss. iii., vii., xviii., xxxiv., li., lii., liv., lvi., lvii., lix., lx., lxiii., cxlii., the time and occasion of the psalm's origin are given, and to this class Ps. xxx. might also belong.

4. Before it is possible to enter into a detailed examination of these two categories of superscriptions, *the true state of affairs as affected by the criticism of the text* must first be determined. It is true that they are all found in the LXX., but only in certain manuscripts, and to some extent under suspicious circumstances: the historical superscriptions to li., lii., liv., lvii., lxiii., and cxlii., on account of their peculiar form, can only be the result of later Hexaplaric insertion: moreover, the incredible divergence of the MSS. from each other is at least remarkable. The LXX., however, still has a considerable majority in opposition to the Hebrew text, partly in the denomination of the names, partly in the insertion of musical-liturgical and historical additions. Here also there is an incredible amount of divergence among the MSS., and before an even relatively definite opinion can be given about them the psalm-superscriptions of the LXX. must first, with the aid of all available subsidiary material, be made the subject of special study in the form of monographs. Only

this much can be said at the present juncture, that this surplus matter in the LXX. is not due to Greek additions, but is throughout similar in character to the Hebrew superscriptions, and is perhaps, also, of equal worth: that Ps. xxiv. was the Sunday-, xlviii. the Monday- (lxxxi. in the Old Latin and Armenian versions the Thursday-), xciii. the Friday-, and xciv. the Wednesday-psalm is confirmed by original and independent Jewish testimony. The Hebrew text thus represents the results of a sifting of richer traditional material, which material cannot be simply put on one side and ignored. The Syriac Bible, on the other hand, wholly diverges both from the Hebrew text and the LXX., and has furnished the Psalms with brand-new superscriptions which for the most part give expression to the views of the Antiochene school of exegesis respecting the contents and occasion of the individual poems. In view of this divergence among the three main witnesses, it may confidently be asserted that the superscriptions have never been regarded as an integral part of the sacred text itself.

5. *With regard to the name-superscriptions,* we must start from those which are of most frequent occurrence: לאסף (Asaph), לבני קרח (sons of Korah), לדוד (David). According to the view most widely held, the composer of the respective psalms is in this way intended to be indicated, and consequently a "ל auctoris" is spoken of. The first distinct witness for this view is 2 Chron. xxix. 30, where the contents of the Psalter are described as the *words of David and of Asaph the seer.* But obviously this is by no means the case. Its application to לבני קרח (sons of Korah)

at once produces difficulties, and double denominations such as occur in Pss. xxxix., lxii., lxxvii., and lxxxviii. are on this view unintelligible, for the same psalm cannot have been composed by David (or Asaph) and Jeduthun. That the ל can denote the theme of the psalm is quite impossible in the case of לאסף (Asaph) and לבני קרח (sons of Korah), while, on the other hand, the analogy with לְמְנַצֵּחַ ("for the precentor") cannot for the present be pointed to, and also the variants עַל־יְדִיתוּן, lxii. and lxxvii., by the side of לִידִיתוּן, xxix., are to be observed. So then it will be safest to attribute to these three superscriptions, לדוד also included, a liturgical significance originally, which we understand little more, indeed, than that of the other musical-liturgical annotations; in the case of Pss. lxxxix., xc., and cxxvii. the ל was already in the original sense of the superscription intended to be the ל auctoris, while, on the other hand, in the case of lxxii. (LXX. only here εἰς) it denotes the theme, and in cii. the destination of the psalm (*cf.* Lagarde, " Mitteil.," iv. 346).

6. If, however, the original object of the name-superscriptions was not to announce the composer of the psalm, *the historical superscriptions*, which presuppose this (erroneous) view of their meaning, can only have been inserted later. This conclusion is confirmed by their form, for they are all, partly in wording, partly in substance, derived from Samuel, and in fact from Samuel in the form in which it now lies before us—as well as by the relation they bear to the psalms indicated by them. Every detailed investigation of this relationship—such as, for example, was carried out in the first two editions of this "Outline"

—yields the same result, viz. that they are simply inferences, arrived at by combination (and not always correct and careful combination) of the contents of the poems with the narratives in Samuel. A procedure somewhat analogous was followed also with respect to the ל auctoris in Pss. xc. and cxxvii. Ps. xc. was ascribed to Moses on the ground of the striking points of contact it shows with the " Song of Moses" in Deut. xxxii.; and in the case of Ps. cxxvii. the proverbial character of the diction and the application of vs. 1 to the building of the Temple suggested Solomon as the author.

7. Under such circumstances it is only possible to estimate *the age and origin of the Psalms* in detail *by internal evidence*. Here, in the first place, it is absolutely certain, from Amos v. 23, that already in very early times Israelitish worship claimed the co-operation of the musical art; Ps. cxxxvii., which cannot be later in date than 500, expressly mentions, in connexion with the period of the Babylonian Exile, the existence of *Songs of Zion* or *of Jahve* (*cf.* also Lam. ii. 7), and the King-psalms xx. and xxi. (I purposely do not mention lxi. and lxiii.), should be regarded in the same way. But the fact—as strange as it is undeniable—must be pointed out that the whole pre-exilic literature of Israel shows nothing in the least corresponding to the poetry of the Psalms, nor the smallest trace of having been under their influence. Would it really be conceivable that all the historians and prophets of the pre-exilic period, as if by design, should have passed over the Psalms in silence, and have deliberately ignored this most precious of the spiritual possessions of Israel? Only

in Chronicles and the latest and most secondary parts of the prophetic writings, such as Is. xii., xxvi., xxxviii. 10-20, Jonah ii. 3-10, Nah. i., Hab. iii., do we meet with the psalm-style.

The truth is that the Psalter in its present form is *the hymn-, prayer-, and religious instruction-book of the community of the Second Temple.* For this way of regarding it we can adduce the (doubtless highly questionable) tradition preserved in 2 Macc. ii. 13, according to which Nehemiah is represented to have compiled the Psalter, and it is the most natural thing to conceive the Psalms as having originated in the time whose needs they were designed to serve. This conclusion is confirmed by their linguistic character (Giesebrecht) as well as by considerations based on Biblical theology, since the Psalms presuppose the final completion of Prophecy and the Law: "The Prophets are older than the Law, and the Psalms are younger than both" (Reuss). Therefore Wellhausen has defined the problem quite correctly when he says: "Thus the question is not whether any post-exilic, but whether any pre-exilic poems are to be found in it [the Psalter]." And in so regarding them we are not guilty of depreciating the Psalms, but, on the contrary, we appreciate them fully in their whole wonderful significance for the first time. They mark the reaction of the pious feeling characteristic of old Israel against Judaism, affording a clear proof that the religious genius of Israel was not to be killed by Ezra and Pharisaism, and they thus form in a quite unique sense and degree the binding-link between the Old and New Testaments: the circles which sang the Psalms, and which practised a piety typical of the Psalms, formed the soil from which the Church sprang.

As regards David under the special aspect of a composer of psalms, it is certain that he practised the musical art, and that he vitally interested himself in the cultus; the very ancient narrative in 2 Sam. vi. expressly gives an account of his musical participation in a religious solemnity. But of him as a religious poet (for 2 Sam. xxii. does not belong to the ancient form of Samuel) the whole of the pre-exilic period shows absolutely no knowledge whatever; the only authentic poem of David's that has been handed down to us, 2 Sam. i. 19-27, shows a marked and surprising absence even of religious motive, and the one pre-exilic mention of David's musical achievements outside Samuel, viz. Amos vi. 5, suggests anything but a specifically religious character or any particular interest in or reference to worship as belonging to the then known poems of David. David the singer of psalms meets us for the first time and alone in Chronicles: he is an exilic or post-exilic figure, and an organic link in the chain that connects the different stages in the process—begun by the Deuteronomic historical writers of the Exile—by which the history of ancient Israel was completely transformed into the history of a Church, after Israel, as a consequence of the turn given to national development by Deut., and through the logic of events, had been changed from a State to a Church, from a people into a community. The David who by messianic prophecy had been forced into becoming the focus and centre of religious interest, of whom it was known that he had been a poet and had spontaneously interested himself also in the cultus, could only (it was thought) have been a religious poet, and in this way the entire religious lyric poetry was traced back to him, as was the entire secular lyrical and proverbial poetry to his son Solomon, in accordance with 1 Kings v. 12 (= iv. 32, E.V.).

8. We have primarily to consider *the Psalter as a whole*, for it has come to us only in the form of a book, a collection. First, as regards the arrangement and grouping of the poems united together in it, distinct groups are clearly to be detected in the collection, such as Pss. xlii.–xlix. (Korah-psalms), lxxiii.–lxxxiii. (Asaph-psalms), cv.–cvii. (Hodu-psalms), cxx.–cxxxiv. (psalms of steps), cxi.–cxiii. and cxlvi.–cl. (Hallelujah-psalms). In the formation of the present arrangement liturgical and literary points of view may have been determining factors: the catchwords pointed out by Delitzsch in his *Symbolae* are hardly the result of accident. Hebrew tradition divides the Psalter into five books: I., Pss. i.–xli.; II., xlii.–lxxii.; III., lxxiv.–lxxxix.; IV., xc.–cvi.; V., cvii.–cl. These *books* are marked off by the so-called "concluding doxology" which stands at the end of the last psalm in each case: xli. 14, lxxii. 18–19, lxxxix. 53, and cvi. 48; the last book stood in no need of such, because the whole of the concluding psalm (cl.) is one long-drawn-out doxology. The concluding doxologies both in compass and form are somewhat dissimilar; but all have as common features the benediction בָּרוּךְ יהוה ("Blessed be J."), the עוֹלָם ("for ever"), and the אָמֵן ("Amen"), in the case of the first three books אמן

אמן, and so in the LXX. also cvi. 48. For the division of the Psalter into five books old tradition already pointed to the analogy of the Pentateuch into five books; thus Epiphanius ("De mens.," 5) says: τὸ ψαλτήριον διεῖλον εἰς πέντε βιβλία οἱ Ἑβραῖοι ὥστε εἶναι καὶ αὐτὸ ἄλλην πεντάτευχον,[1] and also the Midrash to Ps. i. 1—which fact at the same time proves that the latter cannot be older than the fourth century, because before the year 400 no "Pentateuch" existed. If we now consider these five books of the Psalter, we are at once struck by the disproportionate brevity of Book III., and therefore a very high amount of probability attaches to Ewald's conjecture that originally the eight Korah-psalms and the one Asaph-psalm in Book II. belonged to Book III., so that Book II. would have consisted of li.–lxxii., and Book III. of l., lxxiii–lxxxiii., xlii.–xlix., and lxxxiv.–lxxxix. This view is rendered almost certain by the subscription in lxxii. 20, which, after the analogy of Jer. li. 64 and Job xxxi. 40, can only have been designed to mark off one homogeneous whole as against something of a different character and kind, so that the writer of Ps. lxxii. 20 can only have read up to that point David-psalms; in Ps. lxxii. he saw a *prayer* of David *for Solomon.*

9. This *collection of the Psalter* did not originate all at once, but by successive stages. Books II. and III. cannot have been edited by the same hand as Book I., nor again Books IV. and V. by the same hand as Books II. and III. An argument in favour of this conclusion is already furnished by the well-

---

[1] "The Hebrews divided the Psalter into five books, so that it also might be another Pentateuch."

known parallel psalms. Ps. xiv. reappears as Ps. liii., xl. 14–18 as lxx., and cviii. is a compilation made from lvii. 8–12 and lx. 7–14. Of still greater importance, however, is another circumstance. Books I., IV., and V. are altogether or mainly Jahvistic, while Books II. and III., at least up to Ps. lxxxiii., are Elohistic throughout: with Ps. lxxxiv. a tendency to vacillate between both is manifested, only to fall back later in Pss. lxxxv. and lxxxix. with ever-growing decisiveness into the Jahvistic nomenclature. That this is the result of deliberate redactional change is shown especially by the parallel psalms, where the יהוה (Jahve) of xiv. and xl. appears everywhere in liii. and lxx. as אלהים (Elohim), while it is even more clearly demonstrated by the appearance of such totally unheard-of expressions as אלהים צבאות and אלהים אלהיך. If, then, these three individual collections were compiled by different hands, it will be desirable first to come to some clear conclusion about them. According to the consensus of opinion, Book I. is to be regarded as the oldest of these, and it must therefore be gratefully acknowledged as a particularly fortunate circumstance that we possess two certain criteria for determining the time at which Book I. originated. One—though it possesses but a relative value—is the relation Ps. xviii. bears to 2 Sam. xxii. It can hardly be supposed that at a time when a whole collection of Davidic psalms was within everyone's reach in the form of a hymn-book this particular one should have been extracted and admitted into 2 Sam.: the character of the superscription also indicates that its original position was in a historical writing. But

2 Sam. xxii. is "an interpolation in an interpolation," which belongs to the latest redaction of all, as to the date of which, indeed, we can give no certain account. An absolutely fixed *terminus a quo* is furnished, on the other hand, by Ps. xix. 2, where we find the term הָרָקִיעַ already in use as a familiar expression for *heaven*. This fact is proof positive of dependence on P; thus at least Ps. xix.—the possibility of which being a later insertion in Book I. is in no wise probable—cannot be older than 400, and this conclusion is in agreement with the division of the whole collection into five books, if the latter was imitated from the Pentateuch. When we carefully scrutinise the two other separate collections, it does not appear probable that Books II. and III. were completed all at once. The obviously disturbed condition of the original arrangement is opposed to this, and still more so the peculiar features present in Pss. lxxxiv.–lxxxix., which no longer exhibit the Elohistic character of the rest of the collection, and by the side of אסף (Asaph) and בני קרח (sons of Korah) provide still other names: the superscription of lxxxviii. is only explicable as due to the violent combination of two quite distinct headings, each of which is independent of the other. The collection also in IV. and V. does not appear to have been planned *uno tenore*. At the outset the division into two books of notably different proportions, which makes a division in the group of Hodu-psalms (cv.–cvii.), is very surprising, and here quite a number of separate groups stand out with special distinctness. It might be supposed that the third collection was composed originally only of Pss. xci.–c., cv.–cvii.,

cxi.–cxviii., cxxxv., cxxxvi., and cxlvi.–cl., a body of poems, homogeneous, and purely liturgical in character, and that later there were admitted into this collection partly separate psalms like xc., cxix., cxxxvii., partly groups of psalms, such as the "step-psalms," cxx.–cxxxiv., and the David-psalms, ci.–civ., cviii.–cx., cxxxviii.–cxlv., in order to have all extant or known psalms in a collected form together.[1] The Psalter as a whole, in the form in which it now lies before us, cannot be older than the fourth century.

10. Can we possibly fix a *terminus ad quem* for the *completion and conclusion of the collection of the Psalter*? In reliance on 1 Chron. xvi. 36, it has been thought possible to assume the time at which Chronicles arose as fixing this, and in fact the concluding doxology of Book IV. recurs in other places. It has therefore been concluded that if the Chronicler read this verse in Ps. cvi., the division of the Psalter into five books must have been known to him already, and consequently must be older than the Chronicler himself. But the relationship in question cannot be determined quite so simply. In 1 Chron. xvi. 8–36 we read a psalm which David caused to be sung by Asaph at the solemnity of the bringing up of the Ark of the Covenant to Mount Zion. 1 Chron. xvi. 8–22 = Ps. cv. 1–15, and 1 Chron. xvi. 23–33 = Ps. xcvi.—that is certain; and now 1 Chron. xvi. 34, 35, and 36 is said to be = Ps. cvi. 1, 47, and 48. That in spite of its possessing some better readings 1 Chron. xvi. 8–33 is just as much derived from Ps. cv. 1–15 and xcvi. as is 2 Chron. vi. 41–42 out of Ps. cxxxii. 8–10 cannot be doubted. A comparison of 1 Chron.

[1] Somewhat differently Riedel in "Z.A.T.W.," xix. 169 ff., 1899.

xvi. 27 בִּמְקוֹמוֹ and לְפָנָיו in vs. 29 with בְּמִקְדָּשׁוֹ Ps. xcvi. 6 and לְחַצְרוֹתָיו in vs. 8 is sufficient to show this. But in the case of 1 Chron. xvi. 34–36 = Ps. cvi. 1, 47, 48 the matter is not so simple. Ps. cvi. 48 falls altogether outside the analogy of the other concluding doxologies, and even if the verse should be regarded as an original part of the psalm which on account of affinity with the concluding doxologies had only been utilised as such later, even so it is contrary to all analogy of other psalm-expressions, while in Chron. in the form it has there it suits the context quite admirably: for this verse at least every unbiassed consideration of the facts must concede the priority to Chron. Moreover, vs. 34 need not be = Ps. cvi. 1, because the latter is quite a common liturgical formula, which occurs, *e.g.*, already in Jer. xxxiii. 11 (though this, it is true, is a secondary passage). Vs. 35 and Ps. cvi. 47 are substantially, though not in all respects, identical. Apart from the minor differences in the first half of the verse, in addition to the וְקַבְּצֵנוּ of the Psalm there appears in Chron. הַצִּילֵנוּ ("and gather us and deliver us"). The קַבְּצֵנוּ ("gather us") in the Psalm is as logical and fitting as it is meaningless in Chron., while with הצילנו ("deliver us") alone the passage fits the context in Chron. admirably. Thus וקבצנו must have been introduced into Chron. from the Psalm, but after eliminating this I feel bound to regard vs. 35 in Chron. as original, because neither of the two other great historical Psalms, cv. and lxxviii., has a similar conclusion. Any cogent conclusion as to the age of the division of the Psalter, which is based on the accord of 1 Chron. xvi. 36 with Ps. cvi. 48, is made the more impossible because Reuss (§ 474), in a very noteworthy investigation, positively asserts "that the whole passage 1 Chron. xvi. 8–36 is a late interpolation, and vs. 37 closely connects with vs. 7"; Stade also gives judgment to the same effect ("G.V.I.," ii. 215, rem. 2).

11. The truth is, we must seriously consider whether we are not obliged to come down considerably below Chronicles in fixing the time of the conclusion of the collection of the Psalter, whether *poems from the Maccabean period* do not occur in the Psalter. Long ago Theodore of Mopsuestia interpreted the following seventeen psalms with reference to the Maccabean period, viz. Pss. xliv., xlvii., lv.–lx., lxii., lxix., lxxiv., lxxix., lxxx., lxxxiii., cviii., cix., cxliv.; later, Calvin more especially directed attention to this point; and in fact in the case of a whole series of psalms the relevant factors are so cogent that even F. Delitzsch concedes the possibility of Maccabean psalms, at least in principle. And also in support of this view appeal may be made to 2 Macc. ii. 14, where immediately after Nehemiah Judas Maccabeus is honourably mentioned with regard to the collection of the sacred writings; and at any rate the superscription of Ps. xxx. must be later than the year 165, if—and this view is supported by the consensus of the meaning of the poem and the testimony of Jewish tradition—it refers to the festival of Chanukka. Above all, Pss. xliv., lxxiv., lxxix., and lxxxiii. fall to be considered in this connexion. It is characteristic of them as a whole that the sufferings of which the poet complains have the character of a religious persecution

brought about through no fault of the sufferers themselves: when W. R. Smith ("O.T.J.C.," 2nd ed., Appendix D), on account of doubts suggested by the history of the collection of the Psalms and of the canon, pleads for the period of Artaxerxes Ochus, it is to be remarked that of religious persecutions of the Jews by Ochus we have not the least knowledge. All the other material criteria also argue, in the case of these four poems, for a Maccabean date as the time when they originated, so that this may be regarded as a widely accepted view: there are also many other poems in the Psalter which we might easily assign to this epoch. Furthermore, I note that the four certain Maccabean psalms all occur in Books II. and III., which in other respects also, on account of their Elohistic character and their dislocated order due to insertions, occupy an isolated position. Thus all honest exegesis must recognise that there are Maccabean psalms; but to proceed to derive the majority of the Psalms, or even the whole Psalter, from the Maccabean period is a grossly extravagant theory, which—not to speak of 2 Chron. xxix. 30—is shattered by Jesus ben Sira [Ecclus.] xlvii. 8–10: according to this passage Jesus ben Sira must already have been acquainted with a "Psalter of David." The testimony of 1 Macc. vii. 7 also argues against it in the most energetic way. This is the only direct quotation from the Bible in the whole of 1 Macc.; and if Ps. lxxix. 2–3 is here cited as "Holy Scripture," κατὰ τὸν λόγον ὃν ἔγραψε, vs. 16, then for the author of 1 Macc., who lived and wrote shortly after the time of John Hyrcanus, *circa* 100, the Psalter cannot be an entirely new book, the formation and "canonisation" of which he might possibly even still remember, but the long-established canonical authority of the older Psalter is even shared by the later interpolated Maccabean poems—it is not a question, in the case of the Maccabean psalms, of anything more than the interpolation of isolated poems, added to the collection which had long been in existence and enjoying canonical authority, and precisely because of the designation of a psalm which is certainly Maccabean as *Scripture* (γραφή) in 1 Macc. vii., it is clear that even these isolated interpolations were not admitted into the collection at an excessively late date: but 1 Macc. ii. 63 also gives an obvious allusion to Ps. cxlvi. 4, and thus to a poem which indubitably belongs to the latest parts of the whole Psalter. The Prologue of the grandson of Ben Sira, of the year 132, defines the *terminus ad quem* for the final closing of the Psalter. That immediately after the death of Alexander Jannaeus the Pharisees should have eliminated themselves and admitted into Holy Scripture the psalms of their mortal enemies the Sadducees, in which they themselves were characterised as rebels and godless (Duhm), is simply inconceivable, and a drastic revision such as Duhm desiderates for a number of Alexander-Jannaeus psalms—a revision which involved in utter confusion not only the original sense, but also the form and metre, and resulted in the common traditional text as it is handed down in the M.T. and LXX.—is not the work of a couple of years: no, a much longer process of literary development has to be reckoned with here. And finally, how could an Alexander-Jannaeus psalm so worked over

—such as Ps. xviii. "clearly" is, according to Duhm—have come into Samuel as an authentic Psalm of David?

12. If the Psalter is a collection of independent poems adapted for liturgical purposes, the question still remains to be discussed whether these poems originally had a liturgical character and destination, *i.e.* whether they were originally *poems for use by the community*. In the case of a large number, especially of those which stand in Books IV. and V., this may be roundly asserted to be the case; in the case of those where the matter is not at once obvious, decision is rendered more difficult by the consideration that we must always allow for the possibility of a revision of the poems having taken place in order to make them available for the purposes of worship or religious edification. And that this is not merely a possibility can be proved. Thus the liturgical epiphonemal conclusions in Ps. xxv. 22 and xxxiv. 23 certainly did not belong to the original form of the two alphabetic poems: in the same direction points the dislocation of the alphabetic arrangement such as is painfully evident to an unusual degree in the originally alphabetic double-Psalm ix. and x., and further criteria of a formal nature, which indicate similar revision, are such as sudden change in the verse-structure, *e.g.* Ps. lxxvii. 17-20, or the irregular appearance of the refrain, *e.g.* Ps. cvii. 6-9, 13-16, 19-22, 28, 32. A combination of originally unconnected poems, or parts of poems, has demonstrably taken place in the case of Ps. cviii., and is practically certain in Pss. xix., xxiv., xl., and cxliv., perhaps also in lxxxi.; the reverse process has undoubtedly

taken place in the case of Pss. ix. and x., xlii. and xliii. In view of such facts as these, it will be necessary to maintain an attitude of great reserve in answering the question raised at the beginning of this section, and to guard against making categorical assertions on the point.

Remark.—In dividing off the individual psalms the Hebrew and Greek texts are not in complete agreement. The sum-total of 150 is the same in both recensions, but the LXX. combines Pss. ix. and x. and cxiv. and cxv. into one, while reckoning Ps. cxvi. 10-19 and cxlvii. 12-20 as separate poems. That in spite of this the mode of the division has in detail been handed down in a relatively old and fixed form follows from the fact that both recensions agree in severing Pss. xlii. and xliii., and, on the other hand, in combining in Pss. xix., xxiv., and cxliv. originally disparate elements. Further, the LXX. inserts at the end a 151st Psalm, with the superscription: οὗτος ὁ ψαλμὸς ἰδιόγραφος εἰς Δαυιδ καὶ ἔξωθεν τοῦ ἀριθμοῦ ὅτε ἐμονομάχησε τῷ Γολιαδ.[1] This " Psalm " has all the marks both in form and manner that characterise Psalm-poetry, and undoubtedly goes back to a Hebrew original; it is, however, a quite late fabrication, depending on 1 Sam. xvi. 1-12 and xvii., and exhibits the characteristic marks of pseudepigraphic authorship without disguise, claiming in the most barefaced way to have been composed by David himself.

§ 42. LAMENTATIONS

LITERATURE: *Commentaries*: O. Thenius, *K.E.H.*, 1855; M. Löhr, 1891, and *H.K.A.T.*, 1893; K. Budde, *K.H.C.A.T.*, 1898.

Monographs, Essays, etc.: Th. Nöldeke, *Die A.T.liche Literatur*, 1868 (see above, § 2, 6), pp. 142-148; S. A. Fries, *Parallele zwischen Thr. iv. und iv. und der Makkabäerzeit*, *Z.A.T.W.*, xiii. 110 ff., 1893; against this, Löhr, in the same magazine, xiv.

---

[1] "This Psalm is a genuinely Davidic one, though supernumerary, [composed] when he fought Goliad in single combat."

51 ff., 1894; Löhr, *ibid.*, pp. 31 ff., *Der Sprachgebrauch des Buches des Klagelieder* and *Threni iii. und die jeremianische Autorschaft des Buches des Klagelieder*, *Z.A.T.W.*, xxiv. 1 ff., 1904.
On the criticism of the text: J. Dyserinck, *Th. T.*, xxvi. 359 ff., 1892; G. Bickell, *W.Z.K.M.*, viii. 101 ff., 1894, *cf.* also *Dichtungen der Hebräer*, i. 87–108, 1882.
On the artistic form: K. Budde, *Das hebräische Klagelied*, *Z.A.T.W.*, ii. 1 ff., 1882, iii. 299 ff., 1883, xi. 234 ff., 1891, xii. 31 ff., 261 ff., 1892, and *P. Jb.*, lxxiii. 461 ff., 1893.

1. In few O.T. books is the situation which they depict so clear and distinct as it is in the little book that is usually denominated by the word which begins ch. i., ii., and iv., and which is characteristic of the dirge—אֵיכָה; according to the witness of Jerome, however, as well as in the Talmud and in the Massoretic *vox memorialis* which is found at the end of the book, its name should rather be קִינוֹת = θρῆνοι, *Lamentations*. Lamentations over the destruction of Jerusalem, which are always reappearing in new forms and phraseology, form its sole content. After terrible sufferings Judah has been carried into captivity; the city is a desolation, the servant of brutal tyrants, an object of scorn and derision to malicious neighbours. All this, indeed, has been brought upon Zion by Jahve Himself as punishment for her sins, her apostasy and disobedience. Everything points to the destruction of Jerusalem in 586, which therefore furnishes the absolute *terminus a quo*. And though hope is not yet altogether abandoned, nevertheless the poet is crushed beneath the load of misfortune and of the Divine anger, and no evidence is anywhere forthcoming that the possibility of a deliverance was present to his mental

vision. So far is this from being the case that the book ends with a despairing and disconsolate question, which, when it was read aloud in the services of public worship, was not allowed to form the conclusion, so that the penultimate verse had to be repeated once more, as in the case of Isaiah, Malachi, and Koheleth.

2. In *form* also the little book is stamped with some marked peculiarities. The first four chapters are alphabetic poems—a method which in the case of the dirge-song was especially likely to be adopted, because it was customary to begin such with איכה. This alphabetic arrangement is in ch. i., ii., and iv. simple; in ch. iii. it is carried through in a threefold way, so adjusted that each letter of the alphabet is repeated three times in succession. Further, these chapters are obviously composed in the "Kina-verse" (*cf.* § 4*a*, 4 above), which in the restoration of the much-injured text here not merely may but must be regarded. Ch. v. occupies an isolated position; it numbers twenty-two verses, it is true, but is neither arranged alphabetically nor formulated in the Kina-strophe.

3. The prophet Jeremiah is regarded as the *author* of Lamentations both in Jewish and Christian tradition. The oldest trace of this tradition we possess is 2 Chron. xxxv. 25, according to which passage Jeremiah sang a lamentation for the dead King Josiah; this lamentation has been preserved *unto this day*, and remains written *in the lamentations* (על־הקינות). Here the view is not to be scouted that Chronicles may have our canonical Book of Lamentations in mind. In ch. iv. 20 there really

does occur a lamentation over *the anointed of Jahve, the breath of our lips,* who has been taken in the pit of the enemy: this verse might be interpreted of Josiah, the last pious king, and thus the statement of Chronicles would receive a satisfactory explanation, and would then be the oldest witness to show that at least Lam. iv. was ascribed to the prophet Jeremiah. The LXX. already extends this tradition to the whole book; for in this version the Book of Lamentations begins with the words: καὶ ἐγένετο μετὰ τὸ αἰχμαλωτισθῆναι τὸν Ισραηλ καὶ Ιερουσαλημ ἐρημωθῆναι ἐκάθισεν Ἱερεμίας κλαίων καὶ ἐθρήνησε τὸν θρῆνον τοῦτον ἐπὶ Ιερουσαλημ καὶ εἶπεν,[1] which quite produce the impression of being the translation of a Hebrew original: the conjecture may be hazarded that Lamentations may have stood with this introduction in the Midrash already referred to (§ 20, 9 above)—the words would naturally and artlessly attach themselves to 2 Chron. xxxvi. 21. Nor can it be denied that the view regarding Jeremiah's authorship possesses a certain probability. If the contents consist of lamentation over Jerusalem, and the descriptions produce the impression of being the work of an eye-witness, then Jeremiah was the personality to whom thoughts would be bound first to turn. Furthermore, Lamentations has a certain prophetic character: the heavy burden of suffering is subordinated to the point of view of the Divine anger, of an inevitable judgment for unpardonable sins, just as Jeremiah had again and again threatened and predicted that it should

[1] "And it came to pass after Israel was taken captive, and Jerusalem made desolate, that Jeremias sat weeping, and lamented with this lamentation over Jerusalem, and said:"

be. The tender, sympathetic character of the prophet's personality would also recommend him as likely to be the poet of these elegies, and ch. iii. appears to argue directly in favour of this view: for the poet is described as a man who is an object of mockery and derision to all his people (vs. 14: here, it is true, the reading is not certain), whom they persecute, and whose life they seek (vss. 52–63), nay, whose life they wish to make an end of in the dungeon (vs. 53). In the LXX. Lamentations is therefore joined with Jeremiah, as also in the Vulgate and German and English Bibles. But this is clearly due to conscious and deliberate transposition. If Lamentations from the first had been an integral part of Jeremiah, it would be quite impossible to explain how it could have been severed from that book, and relegated to a totally different position in the canon; and that its present position in the LXX. is not the original one has been shown in a particularly striking way by Nöldeke, who has demonstrated that the two books have been translated into Greek by two different hands—Lamentations very literally and slavishly, following the Hebrew, while Jeremiah, on the other hand, has been rendered with tolerable freedom.

4. We must therefore test *this tradition* as to its *credibility*. As to that, we find such words as those of v. 7—which, in view of the explicit passage Jer. xxi. 29–30, would be difficult to understand in the mouth of Jeremiah—disconcerting enough. Similarly, it is improbable that Jeremiah should have spoken of prophecy of the time in such a way as that of ii. 9, and that he should have expressed himself in

the unreserved manner of iv. 17 on the pro-Egyptian politics of the people and its leading circles. Even the unity of authorship of the whole of Lamentations is not at all certain, as is evidenced from the divergent order of the letters of the alphabet, which in ch. i. is the regular one, while in ch. ii., iii., and iv. פ precedes ע. Regarding the isolated position of ch. v. remark has already been made. In this connexion Thenius was the first to give a fruitful impulse to the investigation by pointing out that ch. ii. and iv. are distinguished by many marks of superiority from the other chapters: they are characterised by the greatest wealth of thought and the most finished form, and give evidence of the most profound and original poetical power; Thenius thought it possible to save these two chapters, and these alone, to Jeremiah. But even in the case of these two chapters a literary-critical factor of far-reaching significance conflicts with their composition by Jeremiah: they are, in fact, quite clearly dependent upon Ezekiel. Ch. ii. 14*aa* could only have been written by someone who was acquainted with Ezek. xiii. and xxii. 28; moreover, the word חָזוֹן ("vision") in ii. 9 is specifically Ezekielian; in ii. 1 הֲדֹם רַגְלָיו ("his footstool") is at least reminiscent of Ezek. xliii. 7; the combination מַחֲמַדֵּי עַיִן ("those pleasant to the eye") in ii. 4 only occurs again in Ezek. xxiv. 16, 21, 25; iv. 6 is derived from Ezek. xvi. 46 ff., and also in the case of נִלְכַּד בִּשְׁחִיתוֹתָם ("was taken in their pits") one cannot help thinking of Ezek. xix. 4 and 8; finally, כְּלִילַת יֹפִי ("perfection of beauty") in ii. 15 is directly derived from Ezek. xxvii. 3 (*cf.* also vss. 4 and 11 there, and xxviii. 12); a complete list of all points of contact with Ezekiel is given by Löhr ("Z.A.T.W.," xiv. 41–48, 1894). By such facts as these, however, composition by Jeremiah is positively excluded; moreover, the use of ש (relative), which occurs in these chapters (ii. 15, 16 ; iv. 9), is quite foreign to Jeremiah. While, however, the view of Thenius must thus be rejected on this particular point, his opinion, so far as it affects the aesthetic side of the problem, is thoroughly well justified: ch. ii. and iv. emphatically are the most precious as well as the oldest parts of Lamentations. Here not even the faintest shadow of a doubt can arise to question the character of the work as being that of an eye-witness: the way in which the king is spoken of suggests that the speaker is a personality belonging to Zedekiah's circle, and the close acquaintance displayed with Ezekiel so soon after 586 is easily explained in the case of one who was in exile in Babylon (ii. 9, 14). Next in aesthetic value and age to ch. ii. and iv. ranks ch. v., which in all its details gives a clear picture of the lot of those who remained behind in the land, but belongs to the generation subsequent to the catastrophe of 586, and certainly before 538—thus to be dated *circa* 550. Ch. i. and iii. are doubtless considerably younger, as is proved by the many points of contact shown with Deutero- and Trito-Isaiah and with numerous Psalms. Ch. i., in contrast with ii., iv., and v., shows a specially strongly marked penitential tone, so that here the "design of employing it in public worship" (Budde) may already have been a motive at work. In the case of ch. iii., the author of which, according to Löhr, has made use of two independent Individualpsalms, the thought spontaneously forces itself upon one that the גֶּבֶר or אִישׁ ("man") of the poem is intended to be Jeremiah himself; as ch. iii. was clearly designed from the first to be attached to ch. ii., we should have in the author of it the redactor of the present Book of Lamentations, at whose time the Jeremiah-tradition was thus already in existence; he appears also, in order at least to some extent to assimilate it to the other chapters, to have brought ch. v. to the complete number of twenty-two verses, for some well-founded suspicions raise themselves against the originality of vss. 11, 12, and 18. A more exact determination of the date is not possible.

Remark.—The attempt to explain Lam. iv. and v. as Maccabean is a pure curiosity.

Special Introduction

CHAPTER XVII

BOOK III.—POETICAL AND DIDACTIC BOOKS—*contd.*

§ 43. THE BOOK OF JOB

LITERATURE: *Commentaries:* A. Schultens, 1737; M. H. Stuhlmann, 1804; J. G. Stickel, 1842; E. Renan, 1860; F. Delitzsch, *B.C.A.T.*, 1876, 2nd ed.; A. Dillmann, *K.E.H.*, 1891, 4th ed.; F. Hitzig, 1874; G. H. B. Wright, 1883; A. B. Davidson, 1884; K. Budde, *H.K.A.T.*, 1896; B. Duhm, *K.H.C.A.T.*, 1897.

Translations, with short explanatory notes: G. Studer, 1881; E. Reuss, 1888; G. Hoffmann, 1891; G. Bickell, 1894; F. Baethgen, 1897; F. Herrmann, 1900; Friedr. Delitzsch, 1902; J. Ley, 1903; S. R. Driver, 1906.

Essays, Monographs, etc.: K. Budde, *Beiträge zur Erklärung des Buches Hiob*, 1876; J. Grill, *Zur Kritik der Komposition des Buches Hiob*, 1890; J. Meinhold, *Das Problem des Buches Hiob, N. Jd. Th.*, i. 63 ff., 1892; L. Laue, *Die Komposition des B.H.*, Diss., 1895; J. Ley, *Die Abfassungszeit des B.H.*, *St. Kr.*, lxxi., 34 ff., 1898; E. Kautzsch, *Das sg. Volksbuch von Hiob*, 1900.

Its relation to Prov. i.–ix.: F. Seyring, Diss., 1889, and H. L. Strack, *St. Kr.*, lxix., 608 ff., 1896. On ch. xix. 25–28: Stickel, *In Jobi locum de Goele*, etc., Diss., 1832; O. Droste, *Z.A.T.W.*, iv. 107 ff., 1884. On ch. xxvii.–xxviii.: F. Giesebrecht, *Der Wendepunkt des Buches Hiob*, Diss., 1879; Budde, *Z.A.T.W.*, ii. 191 ff., 1882.

On the Elihu-speeches: Stickel, pp. 224-263; A. Kamphausen in Bunsen's *Bibelwerk*; Budde, *Beiträge*, pp. 63–160; G. Wildeboer (*op. cit.*, § 2, 7), pp. 286–384 of the German translation.

On the criticism of the text: A. Merx, *Das Gedicht von Hiob*, 1871; A. Dillmann, *S.B.A.W.*, 1890, pp. 1345 ff.; C. Siegfried, *S.B.O.T.*, 1893; G. Beer, 1895, 1897.

1. With the Book of Job we enter on that literature which, in accordance with its fundamental idea, is usually designated the *Wisdom-Literature*. Of canonical writings there belong to this literature Job, Proverbs, and Koheleth; of the apocryphal books, Wisdom and Jesus ben Sira (Ecclesiasticus). This literature takes an independent place by the side of the prophetic writings, and to a certain extent is the latter's substitute. After Prophecy had been extinguished and the Law had been set up and Scribism had arisen, the religious instinct, so far as it was still spontaneously active and did not exhaust itself in the subjective poetry of the lyric, sought out another region for the display of its energies, and that the intellectual one. And it is quite natural that wisdom should become the central idea here for theology, because wisdom is just that property of God which is most closely related to a purely intellectual knowledge of God. Hebrew wisdom thus furnishes a parallel phenomenon to Greek philosophy, only with a fundamental difference: for the former, knowledge is not, as it is for philosophy, an end in itself—in the Book of Job the possibility of metaphysical knowledge for man is directly and with the greatest emphasis totally denied,—but is always and everywhere conceived of as thoroughly ethical and definitely religious; it is not philosophic, but theological, or—if the term be preferred—theosophical speculation; its problems are not of a theoretic-metaphysical character, but those of practical religion.

A classical characterisation of this specifically Hebrew wisdom is given in ch. i.–ix. of Proverbs: the fear of God is its beginning (Prov. i. 7; Ps. cxi. 10) and its goal (Prov. ii. 5); it proceeds from God and will lead to God, teaching men not metaphysical knowledge but a godly life. Accordingly Prov. viii. proceeds to hypostatise wisdom as the first-fruits of God's creatures, co-operating with Him in the work of creation.

In literary character also the wisdom-writings form a class by themselves, with a strongly marked common body of fundamental characteristics: the new spirit has created for itself a new body, having formed a diction and terminology of its own; specifically new words and ideas meet us here all at once, and are a proof that we must regard this whole literature in its literary history as a unity, and may not rend it asunder chronologically.

2. Its summit and crown is the *Book of Job*, one of the most marvellous products of the human spirit, belonging, like Dante's "Divina Comedia" and Goethe's "Faust," to the literature of the world, and, like these all-embracing mighty works, striving to fathom the deepest secrets of existence, to solve the ultimate riddles of life. The problem of the book is the theodicy: in view of the many baffling perplexities and obvious injustices that mark the course of the world, how can belief in an almighty and just God be maintained? This question is developed under one of the most aggravated and inexplicable of the forms it assumes, the suffering of the righteous. Job, from the land of Uz, is a pattern of piety and blameless virtue, but in spite of this he meets with

the most terrible misfortune, in which it was thought must be recognised in quite a special way the immediate penal intervention of the Deity; the three friends who arrive to comfort him, demand from him confession of his guilt and submission to God's righteous judgment, but this confession Job is unable to offer without making himself a hypocrite: the general sinfulness of mankind he, of course, concedes, but that he himself by any special sinfulness has deserved this terrible fate he feels bound to deny. The soul-torments of one who apparently has been forsaken by God, of the sufferer misunderstood and misjudged of men, who, strong in the consciousness of his innocence, wages and successfully carries through war against a whole world—the heart-struggles of a pious man, who, in spite of everything, clings to his God, and holds fast to one whom he must regard as his foe—have never been depicted more powerfully or movingly than in Job.

3. The many problems set to the lower criticism by this very difficult book—handed down as it is in a form not by any means to be relied on implicitly—belong to the department of exegesis; also the large amount of transposition and elimination of particular verses or sections that has been proposed need not be investigated more closely here. It is obvious that the metrical question in this connexion must play a decisive rôle, and that those who make the entire Book of Job to be composed of four-lined stanzas, with three accentual rises in each line, must either reject or amend all the parts which do not adjust themselves to this scheme; but criteria of a material and circumstantial kind also must incline us to admit

revision and retouching to a considerable extent. Moreover, *higher criticism* has taken exception to whole sections of the book, and considered that their connexion with the original poet is to be denied.

(*a*) *The prologue, ch. i. and ii., and epilogue, xlii. 7–17.*—These passages are written in pure prose, and furnish the necessary orientation with respect to the personality and fortunes of the hero of the poem, and also give an account of the final outcome of the whole matter, and of the latter part of the life of the rehabilitated sufferer. From this very fact, however, their indispensable character appears. Without the prologue the whole of the following speeches would remain suspended in the air, the reader would be entirely at a loss as to how he ought to take Job's constant asseverations of innocence, and might even at last feel tempted to side with the friends against Job: in order to grasp the whole tragedy of the situation, and in order to be just to the hero, and rightly to understand his obstinacy—almost bordering on blasphemy—and with this his unwavering adherence to God, the reader must know the truth of the matter from the mouth of Jahve Himself. We are therefore compelled to maintain that ch. iii.–xli. could never have existed alone and independently without ch. i.–ii.

(*b*) *Ch. xxvii. and xxviii.*, either wholly or in part, have widely been the subject of doubt. More especially xxvii. 11–23 was bound to provoke objection as a speech of Job, because here he goes over "bag and baggage into the enemy's camp," and how ch. xxviii. could possibly justify this proceeding (notice כִּי, "for," xxviii. 11) was not exactly evident. The attempt made from many quarters to extract from the contested passages a third speech of Zophar, is one that, in view of ch. xxv., cannot be maintained, and to transfer particular parts from it to ch. xxv. in order to enlarge the third speech of Bildad is a device which has been exploded by Budde's demonstration of the fact that xxvii. 1–10 is the reply to xxv. 4–6, just as xxvi. is to xxv. 2–3. Long ago Rashi († 1105) took xxvii. 11–23 as directed to the friends whom Job confounds with their own words, in this way welding a piece of recantation at the same time into a weapon against the friends. The development of the thought and the connexion would be rendered clearer if, with Budde, vs. 7 is made to follow vss. 8–10. Ch. xxviii. establishes the indecisive character of the whole of the controversy so far, and proves the utter helplessness and resourcelessness both of the friends who have been silenced and also of the triumphant Job.

(c) *Ch. xl. 15–xli. 26*: description of two marvels from the animal world—Behemoth and Leviathan. The verbose and diffuse delineation of Leviathan, together with the enigmatic middle-passage xli. 1–3 and the almost comically awkward resumption of it in vs. 5, more especially rouse suspicion. With this passage, however, there also stand particular passages and features so poetical and significant that a complete rejection of the section is not to be lightly decided upon. The question must be taken up again (see par. 5 below): here only this much need be said, that the Jahve-episode would attain inordinate lengths if, while Jahve Himself only spoke the two matchless and majestic chapters xxxviii. and xxxix., thereupon followed as conclusion xl. 2, 8–14, and to this again as Job's answer xl. 3–5 and xlii. 2–5.

4. A thorough and detailed treatment is demanded by *the speeches of Elihu*, ch. xxxii.–xxxvii., which have almost universally been abandoned as having any claim to be an original part of the book, even by F. Delitzsch. Nor can it be denied that cogent reasons appear to argue in favour of this view. Especially noticeable is the entire absence of any reference to Elihu in the prologue and epilogue. In the prologue this might indeed be intelligible, but that in the epilogue also he should not receive a single syllable of mention, but be wholly ignored—this fact does seem eloquently to testify to the later interpolated character of the section, and to evidence its being the work of a hand which did not dare to interfere unduly with the traditional contents of the book, but was sensible at the same time of the necessity of material correction. And these considerations are reinforced by the circumstance that xxxviii. 1 appears to be the direct continuation of xxxi. 40; after the friends have been reduced to silence and Job, in the proud consciousness of victory, has challenged the Almighty Himself to a legal duel, Jahve's reply and interposition would be expected to follow immediately. Instead of this being so, six chapters here intervene, with a new speaker who up to this point has not received the smallest mention or notice, and who never gets the smallest notice later in the book, and whose self-introduction (xxxii. 6–xxxiii. 7) cannot be regarded as particularly happy. And to these must be added other subjective factors

and aesthetic considerations: one finds these speeches insipid, verbose, and diffuse; one is conscious of feeling a sensible absence in them of poetic power and artistic capacity, and the employment, too, of a different linguistic usage and of a method of expression which is in many respects peculiar and differs in character from that in other parts of the book is noticeable. That the genuineness of the Elihu-speeches, however, as opposed to the originality of their linguistic character, remains perfectly possible has been conclusively proved by Stickel and Budde. The decisive word must depend upon internal reasons, and above all upon an unbiassed examination of the plan and contents of the book. The poet who can thus drag to the surface the deepest things of the human heart, who with pitiless precision thus sets forth the problem and relentlessly follows it up to its furthest consequences—he surely must have had a solution of the problem to offer: else he would have been attempting a task that exceeded his strength, and would not deserve to be described as an artist so much as a torturer of humanity, who delights in plunging the knife ever deeper and deeper into the mortal wound. Up to ch. xxxi. no solution had yet been discovered; on the contrary, in ch. xxix., xxx., and xxxi. the whole dilemma had once more been displayed with unexampled sharpness and precision, only at last to find an outlet in the confident challenge of God in xxxi. 35–37. On the assumption of the non-originality of the Elihu-speeches, the question would now have to be asked: Do the speeches of Jahve provide the real solution, or any solution at all?

Every unbiassed consideration of the facts can only result in giving a negative answer to this question. Jahve, the Being who has been impeached and challenged, appears in the storm and speaks "the brief, majestic thunder-language of the Creator. He does not dispute: He displays a series of living pictures, and surrounds, stuns, and overwhelms Job with His animate and inanimate creation" (Herder). Not the slightest attempt is made at any refutation or convincing of Job, no friendly or consoling word for the sufferer finds a place in the speeches of Jahve, but all the former obtains is a brusque repulse, clothed in the form of irony, which, under such circumstances, appears altogether out of place. Nor can the solution of the problem be sought in the prologue on the lines that the pious must content himself with the fact that his steadfast endurance of sufferings is a spectacle for angels and men, and marks a triumph for Jahve over Satan; for of what is narrated in the prologue Job knows nothing, and it is absolutely essential that he himself should obtain an answer to his anxious and despairing questioning. Now let us consider the content of the Elihu-speeches. What is the novel and profound wisdom which Elihu promises to introduce? He points out the danger of being blinded, under the influence of isolated cases of apparent injustice, to the love and provident wisdom of God as expressed in the regulated course of the world. If God does not grant men's petitions, that is not because God will not or cannot hear, but because man does not appeal to Him in the right way. Above all, however, Elihu gives a teleological explanation of the suffering of the righteous, recognising in it an instrument of education in God's hand: suffering leads man to self-knowledge, and temptation leads him to recognise the presence in himself of slumbering sin, which, perchance, may have had no opportunity so far of asserting itself in overt act, and this fundamental thought of the Elihu-speeches is already intimated in the words of Satan in the prologue, ch. i. 9–11, ii. 4–5. If man misinterprets this educative character of suffering, he thereby commits a grave sin, and is justly punished by God: if, however, he recognises its true character and takes it to heart, the suffering becomes to him a source of infinite blessing, the highest practical proof of the divine love towards him. In the entire range of Holy Writ there are few passages which in profundity of thought and loftiness of feeling can compare with the Elihu-speeches: in content they form the summit and crown of the Book of Job, and furnish the only solution of the problem which the poet, from his Old Testament standpoint, is able to give, for the true and final solution was shut out from him. Of a life after death, of any hope of a better Beyond, he knows nothing: death, *the king of terrors*, is for him the end of all things. If the poet was thus compelled to set forth the solution of his problem within this life, no grander explanation, or one richer in consoling power, was possible than to recognise in suffering the highest practical proof of the divine love. After repeated and thorough investigation I am unable to change my view, and sincerely rejoice that Wildeboer has frankly accepted it, and that even Duhm—the most formidable scoffer at the Elihu-speeches and their defenders—can see in the Jahve-speeches "no quite satisfactory result," only an "evasion" of the issue: "the wherefore of the misfortune remains an enigma"—in which admission he recognises the basis of our standpoint as justified.

5. But why has the poet not allowed *the solution of the problem* to be given by Jahve at all, but placed it in the mouth *of a man*, although the whole course of the book from the beginning onwards is directed to the appearing of Jahve? This line of action has been followed with the fullest deliberation and with profound wisdom: "his appearance has been wisely and instructively planned in the composition of the whole," is Herder's verdict regarding Elihu. In ch. ix. 34–35, xiii. 20–21 Job had, to a certain extent, prescribed to God the manner of His appearing: He is to divest Himself of His divine almightiness, is to speak with Job as with an equal, is not to crush but convince him. Of all this Jahve does exactly the reverse. The poet has clearly grasped that he must give up the whole poetical effectiveness of the personal appearing of Jahve if he makes Him speak like an ordinary man, and if he allows Him (to borrow Herder's words), "from a wooden pulpit" and in the dry didactic tone of the moralist, to develop and to vindicate the principles of His government of the world—besides, it would hardly be consonant with Jahve's dignity to bandy words in the form of address and reply with a man. At this point Elihu enters the gap. He fulfils the condition which Jahve, on poetical grounds, is unable to fulfil—the verbal agreement of xxxiii. 7 with ix. 34 and xiii. 21 is highly significant in this connexion, and the

transition from Elihu to Jahve's appearing in ch. xxxvii. is a masterpiece of wonderful genius: "he prepares the way for God's advent, and announces it without himself knowing it" (Herder). And is it not a touch of surprising effectiveness that Job, who had confidently challenged the Almighty Himself, is now compelled to silence before a man, whom the poet with the nicest purposefulness and admirable art represents as the youngest of all, unable to throw in the scale either the garnered wisdom of age or the imposing experience of a long life? Thus ever anew and ever from new points of view are the indispensable character and authenticity of the Elihu-speeches being corroborated.

But the difficulties and suspicious features incident to the non-mention of Elihu in the prologue and epilogue, and the not exactly happy self-introduction, still remain in evidence; the latter has been very ingeniously explained by Wildeboer on the lines that the poet took the three friends as well as Job himself from tradition, while he personally was responsible for the introduction of the figure of Elihu, and therefore was obliged to account for his appearance somewhat more circumstantially. Kamphausen, one of the most zealous and successful champions of the Elihu-speeches, makes them to have been interpolated by the poet himself later into the already completed work. A more acceptable way is one that was first followed up by Merx. This scholar (*op. cit. supra*, pp. lxxxix.–cii.) points to two passages which are quite separate and cut off from the rest, viz. xl. 24*b* and xli. 1–4, as well as to the two lengthy descriptions of animals in xl. 15–xli. 26. In all these—whose connexion with the original poet is not to be denied—Merx sees "Paralipomena," *i.e.* "rejected notes made by the poet while at work and thinking"; and the same scholar further calls attention to three palpable doublets in xl. 21 and 22, xli. 8 and 9, and xli. 20 and 21, that are "double formulations of the same thought . . . which look like attempts of the poet struggling after concise expression," and with these may possibly be reckoned "also the whole strophe xli. 10–13." In the same way Budde's remark that, with the exception of certain chapters, the second half of the book is inferior in formal completeness to the first, rests upon a fine and discriminating aesthetic sense and insight. All this, however, suggests that the poet was prevented from putting the finishing touches to his work, that the latter has not been preserved to us in the form which he would have given to it finally, and in this way is explained the awkward manner in which the Elihu-speeches and the description of Behemoth and Leviathan have been inserted.

6. The *time of* the book's *origin* can only be determined by internal and literary-critical indications, for the book itself makes absolutely not the smallest statement as to its author. The old Jewish tradition makes Moses the author, and to have written it before the Thora—obviously taking the historical form and setting which, with conscious purpose, the poet has consistently carried through in his work, as indicating the time of its formation. There is never any mention in it of Mosaism and the revelation of Jahve; indeed, no part of the action is ever laid on Israelitish ground. But in fact the entire Wisdom-literature

manifests the intention and aim of forcing all that was specifically Israelitish into the background before the human and universal, and this is specially in evidence here, because Job is suffering in a struggle, and is searching for escape from a dilemma from the operation of which no human being is exempt: the Book of Job is concerned not about any revealed religion but with the consciousness of God that is inborn in man. Luther threw out the idea that the book may ultimately have emanated in the time of Solomon from one of the latter's famous wise men— a view singularly well adapted to the factors of the case, in so far that Job falls altogether within the category of "Solomonic writings"; henceforth this continued to be the (so to speak) orthodox Lutheran view (Hävernick, Keil, Delitzsch, Zöckler, Hengstenberg). It cannot, however, be denied that the whole book produces the impression of being later; the speculative reflective atmosphere which pervades the poem is not to be met with in the demonstrably older literature, while the subjective character of religion depicted, which is conceived of as a personal affair between God and the individual alone, points to a later period than even the former. Indications of a positive kind are suggested by the literary-critical method of treatment. According to these Job must be later than (a) Jeremiah, as is shown by a comparison of Jer. xx. 14–18 with Job. iii. That Jeremiah, in such a situation as is there depicted, should have produced merely a gleaning from Job is quite a fantastic notion: no, in Jeremiah we have the spontaneous effusion of an agonised heart, in Job artistic lyrical poetry: an unbiassed comparison of both passages must compel the reader to perceive that it is in Job that the artistic transition from the theme struck by Jeremiah is apparent—and all the more forcibly because Jer. xx. 14–18 belongs to the greatest utterances that the literature of the world has to show, while ch. iii. must be counted among the less successful parts of the Book of Job.

(b) Job must, however, be also later than Ezekiel, as is shown by Ezek. xviii. Here the existence of the problem with which Job struggles is flatly denied, and it is asserted that such a thing as guiltless suffering does not exist: Ezekiel could not have written in this way if he had been acquainted with Job. On the whole, the tentative way in which Ezekiel approaches this problem gives the impression that it had only then just entered within the spiritual horizon of the prophets and pious of Israel.

(c) In xlii. 17 there appears a distinct reminiscence of P (Gen. xxxv. 29 and xxv. 8).

(d) Finally, also, Job must be later than the Book of Proverbs, and later, too, than the latest part of that book, ch. i.–ix. A distinct and marked relationship with Proverbs in the circle of its ideas and phraseology has long been remarked; but Job xv. 7 is directly dependent on Prov. viii. 25: without a knowledge of this passage the words of Eliphaz are absolutely unintelligible; the poet could only have written thus if he could assume that this allusion to Prov. viii. 25 would be immediately obvious to every reader. This last completely convincing instance transports us into the latest period of Hebrew literature, and with this accords also the peculiar

"Aramaeo-Arabic" linguistic character of the book, as well as another very strange circumstance: that is, the fact—which was already felt by Herder to be a serious problem—that there is an entire absence of any trace of the book's influence on Hebrew literature; "for a collection of such matchless images and poems we should have expected to discover many more traces of imitation among the Hebrew poets than are now discernible." In fact, this implied neglect of such a work as Job would be impossible to understand if it had been composed by a contemporary of Isaiah (Nöldeke, Merx, Hitzig, Reuss) or of King Manasseh (Ewald, Schrader, Dillmann formerly: recently, time of Jehoiachim or Zedekiah, at the latest, beginning of the Babylonian Exile). Any more detailed investigation regarding the time and person of the poet is, of course, purposeless.

7. In conclusion, we have still to enter into an investigation of the *contents of Job*. Is the story of the book simply a free invention like that of Jonah? Or does any actual fact, or at any rate any traditional material, lie at the basis of it? Here come into consideration more particularly Ezek. xiv. 14 and 20, where a *righteous* Job is mentioned by the side of Noah and Daniel. As we have seen, Job must be later than Ezekiel; thus the prophet cannot be alluding to our book, and, that being so, it follows inevitably that there was in existence in Israel a story of a specially pious and righteous Job, who—as is to be inferred from the manner in which the name is introduced in Ezekiel—had been marvellously rescued out of great danger and misery. And that the poet in fact utilised already existent material is

proved by the relation of prologue and epilogue to the poem proper, which no amount of artificial harmonising has completely brought into agreement: in particular the epilogue, after all that has gone before, must give every sensitive reader quite an aesthetic shock. It has now, consequently, become the prevailing view to separate prologue and epilogue from the poem proper altogether, and to see therein *a book of a popular character* which in simple, popular fashion gave an account of the pious Job, and the author would have utilised this in much the same way as Goethe made use of the old popular book of Doctor Faust. It would not have been possible, indeed, at any time to assert that this popular book lay already before Ezekiel, because the post-exilic composition of prologue and epilogue in their present form is evident, and has been demonstrated positively by K. Kautzsch. The possibility of ascribing these to the author of the speeches is thereby enhanced, and K. Kautzsch has not failed to draw this logical deduction with all possible emphasis: but to me the material difficulties in the way seem insuperable, and I feel compelled despite all to maintain the view that the prose narrative already lay before the poet, or at any rate had assumed so fixed a form in tradition that he did not dare to modify anything in it, and thus simply adhered closely to his material, just as J and E perhaps did to the stories of the patriarchs. In the interesting subscription that follows xlii. 17, the LXX., proceeding from the perfectly correct view that the poet intended the action to be viewed as laid in Edom, identifies Job with the second Edomite king, mentioned in Gen. xxxvi. 33, Jobab ben Zerah, and this Zerah, further, with the descendant of Esau mentioned in vs. 13, by which means Job becomes "fifth from Abraham" ($\pi\epsilon\mu\pi\tau o\varsigma$ $\dot{a}\pi\dot{o}$ $A\beta\rho a a\mu$)—purely in consequence of the similarity of the names $\iota\omega\beta$ and $\iota\omega\beta a\beta$. Later tradition fixes Job's residence in the Hauran.

Special Introduction

CHAPTER XVIII

BOOK III.—POETICAL AND DIDACTIC BOOKS—*contd.*

§§ 44, 45, 46. *Proverbs, Koheleth, Song of Solomon*

§ 44. THE BOOK OF PROVERBS

LITERATURE: *Commentaries*: C. P. W. Gramberg, 1828; E. Bertheau, *K.E.H.*, 1847; W. Nowack, 2nd ed., 1883; E. Elster, 1858; F. Hitzig, 1858; F. Delitzsch, *B.C.A.T.*, 1873; J. Dyserinck, 1883; H. L. Strack, *S.Z.*, 2nd ed., 1899; G. Wildeboer, *K.H.C.A.T.*, 1897; W. Frankenberg, *H.K.A.T.*, 1898; C. H. Toy, 1899.

Essays, Monographs, etc.: On ch. i.–ix.: H. Oort, *Th. T.*, xix. 179 ff., 1885; W. Frankenberg, *Z.A.T.W.*, xv. 104 ff, 1895. On ch. xxx. and xxxi.: H. F. Mühlau, *De proverbiorum quae dicuntur Aguri et Lemuelis*, etc., Diss., 1869.

On the criticism of the text: P. de Lagarde, *Anmerkungen zur griechischen Uebersetzung der Proverbien*, 1863; J. Dyserinck, *Th. T.*, xvii. 577 ff., 1883; A. J. Baumgartner, *Étude critique sur l'état du texte du livre des Proverbes*, 1890; G. Bickell, *W.Z.K.M.*, v. 77 ff., 191 ff., 271 ff., 1891; A. Muller and E. Kautzsch, *S.B.O.T.*, 1901.

1. The Book of Proverbs consists of a collection of aphoristic literature (*mĕšālîm*) of the most diverse kind and form. From the simple distich to the most developed *māšāl*-poem, all kinds of this department of art are represented. Their object is to teach wisdom, *i.e.* wisdom in the Hebrew sense of the term, which

has as its dominating principle the fear of God. Although it is permeated by a large admixture of maxims of common worldly wisdom and merely human and ordinary experience, yet the book as a whole is marked by a distinctly religious character, which made it appear quite worthy of reception into the canon.

2. On fixing our attention to *the book in itself*, it is clear that it divides into a number of quite distinct portions, which in part are marked off as such by superscriptions: (*a*) ch. i.–ix., which now form the introduction of the whole book, with i. 1–6 as superscription. In the form of a father speaking to a son, they give an urgent exhortation to wisdom and an earnest warning against folly, which more especially manifests itself in sins of the flesh. In the famous ch. viii. wisdom is herself introduced as speaking, and the whole is brought to complete and concentrated expression in ch. ix., in an allegory of Mistress Wisdom and Mistress Folly, who each invite men to come to them.

(*b*) ch. x. 1–xxii. 16, with the special superscription, which is lacking in the LXX, מִשְׁלֵי שְׁלֹמֹה ("Proverbs of Solomon"). This section forms the real kernel of the Book of Proverbs, and possesses one outstanding feature of form, viz. that it contains pure distichs only. The thought is exhausted in a single verse; they each and all form an independent and self-contained whole; even xxi. 25 and 26, which many expositors have been disposed to take together, as forming a single aphorism (of four lines), prove to be no exception. In the employment of this simplest form, however, a great amount of variety is displayed.

The larger number of proverbs are antithetical, moving in statement and antithesis: in this form at the outset are the first nine in ch. x. Or they are parallel, the same or a similar thought being expressed in both halves of the verse: *e.g.* xv. 30, xviii. 15, 20, xix. 29. Or they are "single-thoughted," the second half of the verse simply developing the thought of the first: *e.g.* xv. 12, xvii. 23, xviii. 16. Or they contain a figure or comparison. In accordance with the etymological meaning of מָשָׁל this last form would have been expected to play the principal part; but within these chapters only three cases occur where a figure or comparison is drawn out: viz. x. 26, xi. 22, and (though applied somewhat differently) xvii. 12. Or it is a countervailing comparison of two things with reference to their opposed value: *e.g.* xii. 9, xv. 16, 17, xxi. 9.

(*c*) Ch. xxii. 17–xxiv. 22: *Words of the Wise*. All at once the form hitherto rigorously kept to is abandoned, and a larger freedom of movement ensues; xxii. 17–21 was obviously designed to form the introduction to this section. Here again the literary form of address by a father to a son has been adopted, which in (*b*) only occurred in the certainly corrupt passage xix. 27.

(*d*) Ch. xxiv. 23–34 is by its superscription גַּם אֵלֶּה לַחֲכָמִים ("These also are [sayings] of the wise") stamped as an independent appendix to (*c*).

(*e*) Ch. xxv.–xxix., with the important special superscription xxv. 1, which it will be necessary to discuss later.

(*f*) Ch. xxx.–xxxi.: three appendices of very different kinds. In xxx. 1 and xxxi. 1 occur special superscriptions, which, however, are of quite extraordinary obscurity; according to them ch. xxx. would consist of *Words of Agur the son of Jakeh*, a series of enigmatic utterances in form purposely obscure, with here and there a gentle thrust at the frivolous; ch. xxxi. 1-9 consists of instructions to a *King Lemuel by his mother*, in which he is warned against women and wine, and is exhorted to the practice of righteous judgment. Finally, xxxi. 10-31 is an alphabetic poem in praise of *the virtuous housewife*, which is one of the most charming and graceful passages in the O.T.

3. That in the Book of Proverbs we do not possess a collection of proverbial sayings derived from the mouth of the people, but throughout are conscious of moving in the region of pure *poetic art*, is a position in favour of which Delitzsch admirably adduces an illustrative example from 1 Sam. xxiv. 14 [E.V. 13], where a genuine מְשַׁל הַקַּדְמֹנִי ("proverb of the ancients"), stamped with the true popular character, is handed down, and exhibits the same pregnant brevity and severe conciseness by which all really popular and genuine proverbs are distinguished (*cf.* also 1 Sam. x. 12; 1 K. xx. 11; Luke iv. 23; John iv. 37). Of this kind there is not a single example in the whole Book of Proverbs. If, however, the contents of the latter are to be regarded as products of the poetic art, we must next proceed to inquire as to the author. In the general superscription in i. 1, and in the special superscriptions in x. 1 and xxv. 1, Solomon is claimed as such, at least for the main substance of the book, and in consequence of this summary principal title Jewish tradi-

tion, and, following it, also Jerome, have attempted to interpret the obscure superscriptions in xxx. 1 and xxxi. 1 in the same way of Solomon. This tradition finds its principal support in 1 K. v. 12 [E.V. iv. 32], where it is said that Solomon *spake* 3000 proverbs, in accordance with the view of him as the sum-total of all wisdom. But here the difference in the numbers at once strikes us. The Book of Proverbs only has 935 verses altogether; but if a collection of 3000 aphorisms, ascribed to Solomon, had lain before the writer of 1 K. v. 12 [iv. 32], the disappearance of such a collection would be altogether inexplicable. On the other hand, the passage in 1 K. v. 12 [iv. 32] cannot refer to the canonical Book of Proverbs; for in that case the statement as to the number would be quite unintelligible. Thus 1 K. v. 12 [iv. 32] stands completely by itself, while, at the same time, dependence of the tradition regarding our Book of Proverbs on this passage in Kings is at least highly probable. Then again the form of 1 K. v. 12 [iv. 32] deserves notice; here it is only asserted that Solomon *spake* these 3000 proverbs, which need not of necessity mean that they had been also composed by him, although it cannot be denied that this is what the writer of 1 K. v. 12 [iv. 32] intends to be understood. Nor can it be disputed on *a priori* grounds that one man might have composed so large a number of aphorisms. But considerations of a material kind argue decisively against the Solomonic authorship. The purely objective view of kingship as something which ruins the people by the burdens of taxation it imposes (xxix. 4; *cf.* also xvi. 14, xix. 12, xx. 2, xxv. 3), and especially the repeated warnings against fleshly wantonness, and the enthusiastic praise of pure monogamic marriage which we encounter here, would look strange in the mouth of a Solomon: in general the impression received throughout is that these aphorisms proceed from someone who stands in the midst of life's ordinary activities, and not above them.

4. But can we derive the whole Book of Proverbs in general, or only that part of it which tradition expressly traces back to Solomon, from *a single author*? It might, perhaps, be supposed that x. 1–xxii. 16 and xxv.–xxix. are selections made from two different collections out of the 3000 Solomonic aphorisms mentioned in 1 K. v. 12 [iv. 32]; but why selections at all? Must not such a wealth of material have been a source of joy and delight, and would not the disappearance of the entire collection be absolutely inconceivable? To suppose that some two-thirds of it may have been struck out owing to positive suspicions as to the authorship is quite out of the question when it is borne in mind that even Koheleth and Canticles have come into the canon under Solomon's flag. And in that case what possible explanation could be given of the fact that xxv. 14 and xxi. 9, xxvi. 22 and xviii. 8, agree word for word, while xxvii. 12 and xxii. 3 (with the exception of a ו occurring twice), xxvii. 13 and xx. 16 (with the exception of a small difference, which is adjusted by the קרי in xx. 16), xxvi. 13 and xxii. 13, as well as xxvi. 15 and xix. 24, agree almost word for word; and also for the fact that xxvii. 21*a* recurs in xvii. 3*a*, xxviii. 6*a* in xix. 1*a*, xxix. 22*a* in xv. 18*a*, and that xxvii. 15 is simply the continuation of xix. 13*b*?

Similar suspicions and difficulties are suggested, however, within the group x. 1–xxii. 16 and xxv.–xxix. Thus xiv. 22 verbally = xvi. 25, xvi. 2 and xx. 10 almost verbally = xxi. 2 and xx. 23; xvi. 18 is at any rate very much like xviii. 12, and x. 2b = xi. 4b (the first half of the verse in both cases only slightly altered), x. 15a = xviii. 11a, xi. 21a = xvi. 5b, xv. 33b = xviii. 12b; the following are almost alike, xi. 13a and xx. 19a, xii. 14a and xiii. 2a, xiv. 31a and xvii. 5a, xix. 12a and xx. 2a; xvi. 12b and xx. 28b are very much alike; and xxix. 20 almost verbally = xxvi. 12. Analogous phenomena meet us also in the parts which are not expressly ascribed to Solomon: xxiii. 10 verbally = xxii. 28a; xxiii. 11b is similar to xxii. 23a; xxiv. 6 is made up of xx. 18b (with insignificant alterations) and xi. 14b (word for word); and xxiv. 33–34 verbally = vi. 10–11. And in addition to these doublets there is also noticeable the absence of arrangement and connexion. True, in individual cases here and there arrangement according to subject, and, too, in accordance with catchwords, is observable (see Bertheau, Commentary, pp. xii., xiv., xv.); but on the whole no trace of any plan is discoverable. This becomes especially evident in passing from the Proverbs of Jesus ben Sira to our book; in the case of the former a fixed order of subjects is unmistakable.

5. If, now, the Solomonic authorship—in fact, composition by a single author at all—cannot be shown, we must determine the *age and origin* of the book on internal grounds. When we take into consideration their spirit and content, such aphorisms as xv. 8, xvi. 2, xix. 3, xx. 9, xxi. 3, 27 point at least to the

prophetic period, while such dicta as x. 12, xiv. 21, 31, xvi. 4, 6, xix. 17, xx. 27, xxi. 8, xxii. 2, xxiv. 17, 29, xxv. 21-22, xxviii. 13, 14, xxix. 18 suggest a time considerably later still: I at least can see no possibility of finding a place for such thoughts as those expressed in the passages referred to in the older period of Israel. All the struggles which convulsed and dominated the prophetic period are over; Prophecy and Law (xxviii. 4-9; xxix. 18) lie behind the Book of Proverbs as things completed and closed, and the book itself, taking its stand on the pure and lofty plane of the religious and moral ideas attained by those two potent forces, mints the good metal of Prophecy and Law into current coin. It is true there are *scorners* who in arrogant folly and criminal blindness would know nothing of Jahve and His religion; but these writers are no longer called upon to strive for the recognition of principles. All this brings us in our quest to the post-exilic period, and moreover, into by no means the earliest division of that period: back before the Persian period we can hardly come, if indeed we are not compelled to descend right into the Greek period—of details, *e.g.*, *cf.* the use of צְדָקָה ("righteousness") in x. 2 and xi. 4 with the full-blown meaning already of *almsgiving*. In any case, to use Delitzsch's words, "the deflection of what is Israelitish into what is human, of Jahvism into universal religion, of the Law into common morality," such as Proverbs shows, attests the influence of the Japhetic spirit on Israel—most clearly of all in the prologue, ch. i.-ix. Such a composition as ch. ii., which forms one long sentence, is unexampled in the O.T., and with the hypostatising of Wisdom in ch. viii. "the metaphysic of Judaism- and of the Alexandrian philosophy has spoken, not indeed its last, but certainly its first word" (Reuss). Almost the strongest argument is furnished by the relation of Proverbs to Jesus ben Sira. And not only in respect of externals does Ben Sira's work offer an analogy to our book; the spiritual and intellectual kinship of the two works, in spite of much difference in detailed points, is also so intimate and close a one that in respect to the time at which they arose we cannot possibly separate them by an interval of several centuries. Even the royal aphorisms in Proverbs, which are usually adduced as the surest criterion of pre-exilic origin, have their counterpart in Jesus ben Sira (Ecclus. vii. 4–6, viii. 1–3, x. 1–5). It is true the possibility cannot be denied that some small amount of material in the Book of Proverbs may be a "reminted form of older currency" (Stade); but as a whole it may be said with nearly complete certainty to belong to the later epoch, and not to an earlier one. As the solitary valid reason to the contrary it might be possible to point to xxv. 1, according to which the Solomonic collection of proverbs in ch. xxv.–xxix. was *compiled by the men of Hezekiah, king of Judah.* This statement certainly sounds quite authentic, and produces the impression of being thoroughly trustworthy; but one is irresistibly reminded by it of the "historical" superscriptions of the Psalms, and it is easy to understand how such a legend about a literary commission appointed by Hezekiah could have grown up, which then, perhaps, was entrusted with the task of safeguarding from destruction also the literature of the kingdom of the

Ten Tribes, which at that time had been overthrown. In any case it is a highly remarkable circumstance that the Chronicler has not the smallest thing to narrate either of Solomonic proverbial poetry or of Hezekiah's literary activity (Stade, "G.V.I.," ii. 216, rem. 1). The merit of having been the first to express the complete correct view as to Proverbs belongs by right, so far as I can see, to the work of A. Th. Hartmann cited by Vatke (*op. cit.*, p. 563, rem. 2), to which, of course Vatke himself gives his adhesion; later and in the most recent period it has been always gaining ground more and more.

6. No more definite conclusion as to *place and time of origin* of the Book of Proverbs and of its individual parts can, of course, be given. The circumstances presupposed suggest throughout city life, and in fact point to Jerusalem (*cf.* Ecclus. xxiv. 6-12). Of the individual sections, ch. xxv.-xxix. produce the impression of being most original, ch. i.-ix., xxii. 17 ff., and xxx.-xxxi. of being the youngest. Ch. i.-ix. may have been originally an independent book of instruction emanating from the circle of the "wise." Ch. i. 1-6 is the superscription to the book in its entirety: for unless we have in i. 6 a mere accumulation of synonyms piled up from mere joy in meaningless word-assonance, then the חֲכָמִים ("wise") point certainly to xxiv. 23, and the חִידוֹת ("dark sayings") to xxx. Ecclus. xlvii. 17 shows clearly enough that at the time of Jesus ben Sira Proverbs already consisted of its present dimensions and was regarded as Solomonic. For the rest, the passage vi. 1-19 is productive of many difficulties; it intrudes in a very disturbing fashion

between v. and vi. 20–vii. 27, which form a homogeneous whole throughout, and also both in tone and diction somewhat diverges from ch. i.–ix. It is true that the four distinct passages of which vi. 1–19 is made up can only have belonged to the Book of Proverbs from the very first, and have been designed to occupy a place in it: how exactly they came to secure their present place can never be ascertained.

Remark.—A brief word must be said as to *the mutual relation between the Hebrew and Greek text of Proverbs*. If the whole manner of the book involves as a consequence that not much indication of any planned arrangement is to be looked for in it in detail, it is not a matter for surprise to find in the LXX. a considerable amount of divergence in the sequence of the subject-matter. Of the more important cases, it may be specially mentioned that the LXX. has the aphorisms of Agur and Lemuel in another place: it reads xxx. 1–14 so as to follow xxiv. 22, and between both a further passage to which there is nothing corresponding in the Hebrew text; following xxx. 14 it then has xxiv. 23–34, and after xxiv. 34 finally xxx. 15–xxxi. 9. Hereupon follow xxv.–xxix., and xxxi. 10–31 come in it also at the end of the book. Still more significant are the differences with reference to the contents; several portions of the Hebrew text are wanting in the LXX., as, for example, the special superscription in x. 1; in particular, however, the LXX. indicates a not inconsiderable number of additions, which largely can be traced back to a Hebrew original. Decision in every particular case is difficult to arrive at: on all these questions Lagarde's epoch-making work gives exhaustive information.

§ 45. THE BOOK OF KOHELETH (ECCLESIASTES)

LITERATURE: *Commentaries:* A. Knobel, 1836; F. Hitzig, *K.E.H.*, 1847 (Nowack, 2nd ed., 1883); E. Elster, 1855; P. de Jong, 1861; H. Graetz, 1871; F. Delitzsch, *B.C.A.T.*, 1875; E. H. Plumptre, 1881; E. Renan, 1882; C. H. H. Wright, 1883;

448   POETICAL AND DIDACTIC BOOKS

A. Kuenen, *Th. T.*, xvii. 113 ff., 1883; G. Wildeboer, *K.H.C.A.T.*, 1898; C. Siegfried, *H.K.A.T.*, 1898.
Essays, Monographs, etc.: G. Bickell, *Der Prediger über den Wert des Daseins*, etc., 1884; P. Haupt, *The Book of Ecclesiastes* (in *Oriental Studies*, Boston, 1894, pp. 242 ff.); A. K. Kuiper, *De integriteit van het boek Prediker*, *Th. T.*, xxxiii. 197 ff., 1899.
On its relation to Greek Philosophy: P. Kleinert, *St. Kr.*, lvi. 761 ff., 1883; A. Palm, *Qohelet und die nacharistotelische Philosophie*, 1885; E. Pfleiderer, *Die Philosophie des Heraclitus*, etc., 1886, pp. 255–352; P. Menzel, *Der griechische Einfluss auf Prediger und Weisheit Salomos*, 1889.
On the LXX.: A. Dillman, *S.B.A.W.*, 1892, 3 ff.; E. Klostermann, Diss., 1892.

1. As Thersites among the Homeric heroes, so at first sight the Book of Koheleth appears among Old Testament books. *O vanity of vanities! saith Koheleth, O vanity of vanities! all is vain. What result has man from all his toil wherewith he toils under the sun?* . . . *There is nothing better for man than that he eat and drink, and make himself enjoy good in all his toil.* Such strains as these we are not accustomed to have brought before us in the O.T., and so enigmatic a book must therefore be considered with special thoroughness. The first question naturally is directed to inquire as to the author, or at least as to the time of the book's composition.

2. With respect to this there can be no difference of opinion that the speaker in Koheleth is intended to be Solomon: the veiled designation קֹהֶלֶת (Koheleth) — which the LXX. happily renders ἐκκλησιαστής, and Luther *Prediger*, "Preacher"—is, all the same, transparently clear in meaning. As this "Preacher" speaks of himself as son of David

and king in Jerusalem, he can only intend to represent himself as Solomon; and when he goes on to narrate of his wisdom and knowledge, his riches and buildings, his pomp and luxury—all this fully corresponds to the legendary picture of Solomon. There is no need, however, specially to emphasise and set forth the material difficulties involved, to refer explicitly to words and utterance which in the mouth of the historic Solomon would be impossible, or at any rate hardly credible: the language of the book alone, as Delitzsch has thoroughly demonstrated, is sufficient to decide the question. The Hebrew of Koheleth is already involved in the full process of linguistic decay, and moves entirely in the region of the Mishna and of the "Chaldee" parts of the O.T. Such words as פִּתְגָּם, זְמָן, עָבַד, בְּטֵל, לָוָה, כָּשֵׁר, נָהַג are purely Aramaic, while תַּקִּיף, גּוּפָא, רַעְיוֹן, מִלָּאָה, חוּץ מִן, עִנְיָן, the periphrasis with בַּעַל are purely Mishnaic. But almost more strongly than particular word-stems and expressions the whole linguistic character of the book affords proof in the same direction. The frequent abstract formations in ־וּת, ־וֹן, and ־ָן; the explicit expression of the personal pronoun, and its insertion after the verbal form even when no emphasis is laid on it; the use of the participle to indicate the present, of זֶה without the article, and, above all, of such conjunctions as עֲדֵן, אִילּוּ, כְּבָר, בְּכֵן, and of שֶׁ in all possible combinations, such as כָּל־עֻמַּת שֶׁ, and even joined with אֲשֶׁר in אֲשֶׁר—בְּשֶׁל—all this is so absolutely convincing and irrefutable that Delitzsch exclaims: "If the Book of Koheleth be as old as Solomon, then there can be no history of the Hebrew language." The post-exilic origin of the book is therefore conceded by all capable of forming an opinion on the matter, and the only question which need concern us is to arrive at a more exact definition of date within the limit of time so laid down. With that object in view we must subject the contents of the book more particularly to a closer investigation.

3. In no book of the O.T. are *the contents* of so peculiar a character as in Koheleth. Particular passages, considered independently of their context, might appear to express the crudest Epicureanism and the grossest materialism, the doubts of a trifler or dreary despair of all ideals; but it would inflict a grave injustice on the author to think that his last word and real meaning are to be seen in such elements of his book. No, he has not given up faith in a God, and a moral constitution of the world. The contradictions and mysteries of daily life, the harassing enigmas and apparent injustices of the course of the world, he knows and recognises as fully as anybody else: it is a perverted world, where injustice and wrong reign in the place of righteousness, and where the right must suffer violence, where the righteous perishes in his righteousness, and the godless lives long in his wickedness, where through their tears the oppressed look for a comforter in vain, where the fool dies as the wise, the transgressor as the righteous, the pure as the impure—but let anyone deduce the practical consequences therefrom and think to act accordingly, he will be a criminal and a fool. For God has made everything good, and also created man so; only through man everything has been put wrong and perverted. God's action is inscrutable

and His ways enigmatic: and though He apparently allows all to go on as it will, and the sinner for the hundredth time remains unpunished, this is only the case in order that men may be put to the test: God does not renounce judgment, but holds everyone accountable to Him; to fear God is and always remains the best course, and is what He claims to receive from man. What God does man can neither add to nor detract aught from: all that man undertakes is vain and airy striving, the course of the world is unchangeably the same, man cannot alter it, and never fully understands it—nay, he cannot even enjoy life without God. Therefore it is best in this disconsolate and miserable time to endure the evil patiently as a dispensation and trial sent by God, and to cling to goodness, to enjoy it as a gift of God, and always to be mindful of the judgment: for it always goes well with the God-fearing man at the last. Old Testament piety has nowhere enjoyed a greater triumph than in the Book of Koheleth. Even this writer, who has a perception of the misery of the world such as is paralleled only in the case of the most modern pessimists, who everywhere sees nought but discord and unsolved riddles, who shrinks from nothing in pursuing the consequences of his thought—even such a spirit as his is so dominated and permeated with Old Testament piety that he fails to arrive at what seems to be the obvious and simplest solution of the question that perplexes him: to draw from the facts which have been dragged into the light by him with such pitiless clearness the conclusion that there is not a God at all, but that the whole world is simply the plaything of blind chance—that is a thought which lies entirely outside his mental horizon, which he does not even reconnoitre from a distance. It is true, however, on the other hand, that in no other book is it so clearly shown as in Koheleth that the Old Testament has not spoken the last word: for his firm and unshakable faith in a personal God and the moral government of the world is still only a postulate to Koheleth, which stands without any inner adjustment by the side of the misery of the world; he even abandons the attempt at a solution, and falls back resignedly upon his childlike faith, in spite of the fact that it has proved itself inadequate to meet his perplexity.

4. It is easy to understand how tempting it would be to place in the mouth of Solomon such a book as this, proclaiming as it does the futility of all human things; the man whom tradition considered to be both the wisest and most brilliant of all kings was bound to have been the most emphatic "preacher" of such doctrines. But *in what period* did this Solomon *redivivus* live and write? The general picture given of surrounding circumstances and conditions suggests a period of the most complete anarchy, when there is no question as to any ordered civic and public life, when worthless upstarts are in power and drain the land of its resources, and it is regarded as political wisdom to accommodate oneself with apathetic indifference to despotism and tyranny. If Koheleth is post-exilic, these conditions can be satisfied by choice between two epochs, either the last century of Persian rule, when the vast empire of Cyrus gradually broke up in internal corruption and complete anarchy, or the period of the later Ptolemies

and Seleucids, during which Hellenism manifested itself under its least worthy and most depraved aspect in nameless moral corruption and debauchery. It might be possible to arrive at a definite and fixed point from iv. 13–15 and ix. 13–16, where the author obviously alludes to well-known events, if only these were clear to us. We are thus thrown back upon combination absolutely. Hitzig has attempted to show that the year 204, when the five-year-old Ptolemy Epiphanes ascended the throne of the son of Lagus, was the year of the book's origin; and even though all his proofs be unconvincing and actually erroneous, yet substantially he hit upon the right solution. It is hardly possible to bring it down into the period of the Maccabees, when the two sides which Koheleth unites in himself (even though it be in purely external juxtaposition), viz. Hellenistic philosophy and Jewish piety, had completely broken with each other. But, on the other hand, Hellenism is clearly the leavening element which has here brought the Old Testament piety into a state of fermentation. The question whether Koheleth exhibits any immediate acquaintance with and direct dependence on Greek philosophy is an open one: so much, however, appears to be assured, that only a Jewish personality whose spirit had been enriched or at any rate influenced by Hellenism could have produced such a work, and I, therefore, consider the Persian period to be out of the question, and that it is necessary to adhere to the Greek epoch. Koheleth arose in the course of the third century in Palestine, and shows what a profound intellectual and spiritual impression Hellenism had made even there, so that such an enterprise as that of Antiochus Epiphanes could not have seemed by any means hopeless. But the author of our book is simply intoxicated with Hellenism: he has welcomed it with joy as an element of culture, without in the least realising the disintegrating character of this culture, which in his case personally, indeed, had been reconciled with his inherited faith. He was thus, perhaps, a contemporary of Jesus ben Sira, but, unlike the latter, did not write under his own name, but placed a philosophy in the mouth of Solomon.

5. Koheleth offers but few *problems of Introduction* in detail. Objection has been taken to the epilogue, xii. 13-14, on the alleged ground that it is the work of a strange hand inserted in order to obscure the true contents of the book and to blunt the point of it; and for similar reasons xi. 9b and xii. 1a and 7 have also been explained as due to later revision, but wrongly: for exactly the same thoughts, which have only been formulated in a specially pregnant way in these passages, permeate the whole book; the fear of God, and God as Judge, are all through cardinal ideas which often sound strangely in their context, but for that very reason stand out with all the greater impressiveness, not to say pathos. Thus, if the view referred to above were adopted it would be necessary—as in fact has been done especially by Haupt—to assume a systematic revision of the entire book. Further, the unsystematic arrangement and absence of any clear development of the thought have been largely felt to be intolerable in Koheleth, and our author has either been acquitted of blame in this respect or attempts have been made by all sorts

of means to come to his rescue, most energetically and boldly by Bickell, who presses into the service of his interpretation a misfortune of the archetype: this "unfortunate manuscript," it is alleged, was bound up in several layers and wrongly sewn together, and in this way the whole book fell into disorder. But there is no necessity to resort to violent expedients of this kind. The whole work is pervaded by one spirit and one tone, and with this we can be content: a complete and rounded philosophical system, a formal body of doctrines, the author had no desire, and perhaps it was even out of his power, to give, so that it does not seem to be well advised to force him (in a literary sense) into a strait-waistcoat, a proceeding which he himself assuredly would have deprecated. His was a nature full of contradictory elements; in his body lived two souls, in head a Greek, in heart a Jew, as we may best describe him, adapting a well-known saying: and so it is not in the least a matter for surprise when by the frank honesty (that can only be described as pathetic) with which he lets us look into his own heart, a mass of contradictions is revealed. In forming an estimate of Koheleth we should not forget Kant's teaching that; though pure reason can never prove the existence of God and the reality of a metaphysical world, yet the practical reason must hold on unreservedly to both as postulates, without which it cannot act. To this sympathetic and quite typical personality—a personality that is so impressively true even in its contradictions—I firmly adhere, then, in spite of Siegfried, by whose attempt, carried out with great ingenuity and acuteness, to apportion the little Book of

Koheleth among at least eight distinct hands, the fragment-hypothesis has been reduced to absurdity. The question is decided by the fact that, as Nöldeke ("Z.A.T.W.," xx., 90 ff., 1900) "quite contrary to his expectation" confirms it, Jesus ben Sira was already acquainted with the whole of Koheleth, including xii. 7 and 13.

§ 46. THE SONG OF SONGS (CANTICLES)

LITERATURE: J. G. Herder, *Salomons Lieder der Liebe*, 1778. Of decisive importance are the following: K. Budde, *Was ist das Hohe Lied?* P.Jb., lxxviii. 92 ff., 1894, and K.H.C.A.T., 1898; C. Siegfried, H.K.A.T., 1898; P. Haupt, *The Book of Canticles*, 1902; A. Harper, *Song of Songs* (Camb. Bible).
The most important representatives of the dramatising treatment are the following (results mainly embodied in Commentaries): J. F. Jacobi, pub. anonymously 1771 (epoch-making); Stäudlin, 1792; Umbreit, 1820; Ewald, 1826; F. Böttcher, 1850; F. Delitzsch, 1851, and B.C.A.T., 1875; Hitzig, K.E.H., 1855; Renan, 1860; Graetz, 1871; J. G. Stickel, 1888; Öttli, S.Z., 1889; C. Bruston, 1891; J. W. Rothstein, 1893; E. Klostermann, *Eine alte Rollenverteilung zum H.L.*, in Z.A.T.W., xix. 158 ff., 1899.

1. Like Koheleth, the *Song of Songs* also is curiously distinguished among the books of the O.T. For no unbiassed investigator can for one moment be in doubt that the only theme of Canticles, consistently maintained throughout, is love, the love of man for woman and of woman for man. And, moreover, these things are discussed and described with an unreserved explicitness which to our sensibilities almost borders on impropriety, but which by reason of its *naïveté* cannot be characterised as lascivious. We are at once conscious that in Canticles we possess

the work of a true poet, whom some god permitted to say how blest and happy he feels himself to be; especially captivating and impressive is the wonderful and deeply implanted feeling displayed for nature: the poet lives and moves in nature, which is to him the reflected image and witness of his own happiness; everything makes holiday with him and attunes his heart to joyfulness. But who is the poet?

2. The superscription in i. 1 can only mean *the choicest of Solomon's songs*, and thus indicates Solomon as the "philosopher in rose- and myrtle-crown" who created this wonderful work. That Solomon was a poet, and a prolific one, is sufficiently attested by 1 K. v. 12 [E.V. iv. 32], which speaks of 1005 songs of Solomon. With this also the contents of Canticles seem to accord: five times Solomon is mentioned (i. 3; iii. 7, 9, 11; viii. 11), and in three of these places is referred to explicitly as King Solomon (הַמֶּלֶךְ שְׁלֹמֹה); in i. 4, 12, vii. 6 likewise a king is referred to, in vi. 8 and 9 a queen; in i. 9. we encounter the steed of Pharaoh's chariot, and in iv. 4 a tower of David. The repeated mention of the daughters of Jerusalem is also in thorough accord with the same representation. If we now proceed to inquire whether 1 K. v. 12 [iv. 32] stands in any close connexion with Canticles, it is to be noticed that that passage makes no reference to the latter: it is quite inconceivable that by the *1005 songs of Solomon* this book of 116 verses could have been meant, while Cant. i. 1 can very well have been, and certainly was, framed out of regard to 1 K. v. 12 [iv. 32]—thus exactly the same relation is apparent as between 1 K. v. 12 [iv. 32] and Prov. i. 1. If the saying "Thy

speech betrayeth thee" is applicable in the case of any Biblical book, it is so in the case of Canticles, the linguistic character of which indicates a date far later than that of Proverbs, and ranks it immediately beside Koheleth. The constant use of the particle שׁ, such as is evidenced in Canticles, only occurs again in Koheleth and some of the very latest of the Psalms: שֶׁלָּמָה in i. 7 takes its place immediately by the side of שֶׁלְּמִי in Jon. i. 12; in particular the extended adverbial use of שׁ in such combinations as עַד שׁ (i. 12; ii. 7, 17; iii. 4–5; iv. 6; viii. 4) and כְּמָעַט שׁ (iii. 4) is quite late, and finally such expressions as שֶׁלִּי כַּרְמִי (i. 6; viii. 12) and מִטָּתוֹ שֶׁלִּשְׁלֹמֹה (iii. 7) are quite unheard of throughout the whole of the O.T., and are purely Mishnaic. The word פַּרְדֵּס in iv. 13, as a distinguished student of the Iranian languages has established, is specifically Persian, and its occurrence points with mathematical certainty to the Persian period as the earliest possible date, as indeed it only occurs again in Neh. ii. 8 and Koh. ii. 5; while the ἅπαξ λεγόμενον אַפִּרְיוֹן—which cannot be interpreted by any Semitic etymology is = φορεῖον, and is thus a Greek loan-word. Whether in the time of Solomon נֵרְדְּ, "spikenard" (i. 12; iv. 13, 14), and כַּרְכֹּם, "saffron" (iv. 14)—either the words or the things—were known may well be doubted, and likewise whether there were in existence an organised police and regular night-watch service (iii. 8; v. 7). But the linguistic indications alone are absolutely convincing, and force us to regard the Persian period as the earliest one possible for Canticles. Although appeal is constantly made to vi. 4, where Thirza is parallel with Jerusalem, and thence it is supposed to follow that

Canticles must be older than Omri, it may be replied to this, it could never have occurred to a post-exilic Jew to mention Samaria in parallelism with Jerusalem—and the later he lived, this would be even less likely to occur: that Thirza had for a considerable period been a royal residence was, of course, well known from 1 Kings, and moreover this city would be especially recommended by the obvious appellative significance of its name — *Belleville* (*Beauty-town*). Thus even vi. 1 does not raise any serious obstacle to the post-exilic date.

3. In the case of Canticles, however, the question as to the *artistic literary form* of the work must be specially discussed. As it clearly contains speech in the form of address and reply, and there is a constant interchange of these, the prevailing view is to regard it as of the nature of drama, exhibiting a regularly carried through dramatic treatment, after the manner of our plays, with monologue, dialogue, and chorus interspersed, amid constantly changing scenes. In that case the only persons mentioned by name, Solomon and "Sulamith" (vii. 1), must necessarily be *dramatis personae*, and it becomes a matter for discussion whether the whole poem is intended to serve the purpose of glorifying Solomon, or to be a satire upon him. But we have absolutely no knowledge of any occurrence of the drama among Semites at all, in spite of the case of the Alexandrian Jew Ezekiel, who worked up the story of the Exodus from Egypt in the form of a Greek drama; and then, further, how can we form any conception of a stage-piece of 116 verses with as many as twelve changes of scene? In such a case recourse must already

have been had to the opera or the vaudeville. Moreover, of all this there is not the slightest indication in the text itself. Thus, then, a door was opened for ingenuity in combination, and from the tempting and irresistible enticement of employing such methods the regular recurrence of these attempts is easily explained. But the true decisive factor lies at the basis of this way of regarding the matter, viz. that in Canticles it is impossible to recognise a uniform and complete connected poem. The truth is, it divides up clearly into distinct songs, shorter or longer as the case may be, "which are no longer connected together, like a row of beautiful pearls fastened together on a cord" (Herder).

4. If now Canticles is made up from the combination of distinct songs, the composition of the book by Solomon or in Solomon's time is out of the question; but if in spite of this Solomon is repeatedly mentioned, what is *the original sense and the original meaning of these songs?* The explanation is furnished by the East of the present day. Among the Syrian peasantry the seven-day marriage festival is called "the king's week," because on this occasion the young pair are looked upon as king and queen, and, sitting upon an improvised throne, are treated and served as such by their own people and by the neighbouring communities who have been invited. In this connexion a series of rigidly fixed and regulated ceremonies is customary, which are all gone through to the accompaniment of singing, playing, and dancing. It is Budde's abiding merit to have been the first to take up this observation—which we owe to J. G. Wetzstein, and which had been repeatedly pressed

into service for the explanation of Canticles—and carry it through to its logical results, and apply it to the whole book. Scales, as it were, fall from our eyes as we read Budde's essay where proof is adduced of the agreement of the individual songs with the different ceremonies of "the king's week," and also it is very rightly pointed out that according to Oriental ideas Canticles can never depict the love of the bride, but only conjugal love. The "king" is the young husband, who is given the name of Solomon as the most fortunate and richest of all lords. The "Shulamite" (Sulamith) is the young wife, who is extolled as the *most beautiful damsel in all the borders of Israel*, like Abishag of Shunem (1 K. i. 3). And thus the riddle of the book, which it had been thought would have to be given up in despair, has been definitely solved. For that this view really is applicable to the O.T. is shown by Cant. iii. 11, where reference is made to a *crown wherewith his mother crowned him in the day of his espousals* (*cf.* also Is. lxi. 10), and it is well known that among the prescribed Jewish marriage customs the crowning of the bridegroom with the *bridegroom's crown* (עֲטֶרֶת חָתָן) and of the bride with the *bride's crown* (עֲטֶרֶת כַּלָּה) finds a place, crowns of this kind, cunningly made out of pure gold, or from a mixture of gold and silver, and richly adorned with precious stones, being kept in every synagogue.

5. But such being the case, it is not at all probable that the individual songs—which all possess the genuine folk-song tone—were composed by one and the same poet. A collection of particularly beautiful ones at these festivities may have been more or less

customary, but the question has still to be raised whether we are dealing with a mere *collection* or with a *redactional work*. As the order of the poems throughout does not correspond to the order of the festivities—which certainly for the last two thousand years has been the same as it is to-day—and as small isolated paragraphs stand out which prove to be of inferior poetical value and dependent in their wording on the context—where, in fact, the real meaning and, in particular, the figurative language of the older pieces have been misunderstood and taken literally —it might be the safer course to assume redaction. Ch. ii. 9a, iv. 8, viii. 3-4, 13-14 must be rejected absolutely.

6. *The time* at which the songs *arose* is on the whole firmly fixed and defined by the linguistic criteria; the most probable *place of origin* is Jerusalem. The collection and writing down took place in the third or second century. When the work was once available, however, it is easy to understand how, in view of the repeated mention in it of the name of Solomon, as well as on account of its erotic character, the opinion could be formed that it had been composed by Solomon himself. And then it was bound to be received into the canon, and obstacles and difficulties were overcome by means of allegorical interpretation.[1] Still its reception was not accomplished without strong opposition.

[1] *Cf.* W. Riedel, "Die Auslegung des H. L. in der jüdischen Gemeinde und in der griechischen Kirche," 1898.

Division II.—General Introduction

LITERATURE : F. Buhl, *Kanon und Text des A.T.*, 1891 (E.T. by Macpherson, 1892).

CHAPTER XIX

HISTORY OF THE CANON

LITERATURE : K. A. Credner, *Geschichte des Kanons*, 1847 ; A. Dillmann, *J. d. Th.*, iii. 419 ff., 1858 ; H. Ewald, *G.V.I.*, vii., 2nd ed., pp. 448–495 ; J. Fürst, *Der Kanon des A.T. nach den Ueberlieferungen in Talmud und Midrasch*, 1868 ; J. S. Bloch, *Studien zur Geschichte der Sammlung der althebräischen Literatur*, 1876 ; W. R. Smith, *O.T.J.C.*, Lect. vi. ; H. L. Strack, *R.E.*, 2nd ed., ix. 741 ff. ; G. Wildeboer, *Het ontstaan van den Kanon des Ouden Verbonds*, 1889 (German translation by F. Risch, 1891); H. E. Ryle, *The Canon of the Old Testament*, 1892 ; F. Mullin, *The Canon of the Old Testament*, 1893 ; K. Budde, *Der Kanon des A.T.*, 1900 (in English, art. "Canon," *Encyl. Bibl.*).

§ 47. THE IDEA AND DIVISION OF THE CANON AMONG THE JEWS. THE NUMBER, TITLES, AND ORDER OF THE CANONICAL SCRIPTURES

LITERATURE : G. A. Marx, *Traditio rabbinorum veterrima de librorum V.T. ordine atque origine*, 1884 ; W. Riedel, *Namen und Einteilung des A.T.lichen Kanons* (in *A.T.liche Untersuchungen*, i. 90–103, 1902).

1. Under the term *Canon* we understand a collection of writings which are recognised by a religious fellowship or society as inspired by God, and as providing a rule and standard of faith and life. The

word "canon" comes from the Greek κανών, which again is a Semitic loan-word from קָנֶה ("reed"). It is already used by Homer, *Il.* viii. 193 and xiii. 407, of the two transverse stays over which the shield was stretched, and, xxiii. 761, of the shuttle, the fundamental idea in all of these being that of *mere wood*. In literary Greek κανών properly signifies *the rule of the carpenter* (*cf.* קְנֵה הַמִּדָּה, Ezek. xl. 3), but was early employed by metonymy with the meaning *norm, rule, standard*, to illustrate which Stephanus ("Thes.," *s.v.*) adduces quotations from Euripides, Antiphon, Aristotle, Demosthenes, and Lucian, and one specially characteristic from Cicero, who writes to his freedman Tiro: *Tu qui κανών esse soles scriptorum meorum.*[1] The word also occurs in the N.T. (Gal. vi. 16) and ("c. Apion," ii. 17) in Josephus [somewhat differently in 2 Cor. x. 13, 15, 16]. As a *terminus technicus* in the sense here in question it is first employed, according to Buhl (p. i.), by the patristic writers of the fourth century. When we speak of canonical writings a double meaning is implicit: they are *normal*, *i.e.* they give adequate expression to the Divine Revelation, and, as a consequence of this, they are also *normative*, *i.e.* they set the standard for us as a rule of faith and life. With respect to the thing itself, we meet with the idea of a canonical writing for the first time in 2 K. xxiii. 1–7, in connexion with the solemn publication of Deuteronomy and pledged obligation to observe it, which was followed by the second and still more important bond of obligation contracted with respect to the Tora of Ezra (Neh. viii.–x.). The history of the O.T. Canon thus begins with the year

---

[1] "Thou who art wont to be the κανών of my writings."

IDEA AND DIVISION OF THE CANON 465

621. In the O.T. itself, for the oldest trace of the developed idea we must refer to Dan. ix. 2, where הַסְּפָרִים ("the books") is already used quite in the same way as τὰ βιβλία (for Is. xxxiv. 16 see § 24, 16 above).

2. The Jews divide the Canon *into three sections*: תּוֹרָה ("Law"), נְבִיאִים ("Prophets"), and כְּתוּבִים ("Writings"), in accordance with which the whole of the O.T. Scriptures is denoted by them with the abbreviation תנ״ך. The תּוֹרָה ("Law") consists of the so-called "five books of Moses," the חֲמִשָּׁה חוּמְשֵׁי תוֹרָה ("five-fifths of the Law"; see § 5, 1 above), in the division of which both the Hebrew and Greek Bibles agree. The Alexandrians give the separate books descriptive titles, and this seems also to have been the case among the Jews; at any rate the designation תּוֹרַת כֹּהֲנִים ("Law of Priests") occurs for Leviticus, and for Numbers Origen is acquainted with the name αμμεσφεκωδειμ = חוֹמֶשׁ פְּקוּדִים (" fifth part of Precepts "); but it has become customary to denominate them by the first word (or one of the first words) of the text: thus Genesis = בְּרֵאשִׁית, Exodus וְאֵלֶּה שְׁמוֹת, Leviticus וַיִּקְרָא; for Numbers Jerome in the "Prologus galeatus" has the Hebrew designation *Vaiedabber* (= וַיְדַבֵּר), which really is the first word in the text; but it is more usually designated by the fifth word, בַּמִּדְבָּר ("in the wilderness"), which at the same time may serve as a sort of indication of the book's contents; finally, Deut. = וְאֵלֶּה הַדְּבָרִים. 2. The second section of the Hebrew Canon is made up of the נְבִיאִים ("Prophets"), which again fall into two divisions, נ׳ רִאשׁוֹנִים ("former prophets") and נ׳ אַחֲרוֹנִים ("latter prophets"); for the meaning of this designation see § 48, 4 below. As נ׳ רִאשׁוֹנִים ("former

30

prophets") are reckoned the four historical books, Joshua, Judges, Samuel, Kings, the two last of which are counted in the Hebrew Canon as one book each. According to Jewish tradition, Judges and Samuel were written by the prophet Samuel, and Kings by the prophet Jeremiah; Joshua also was a prophet according to Numb. xxvii. 18 (*cf.* Jesus ben Sira [Ecclus.] xlvi. 1: διάδοχος Μωυσῆ ἐν προφητείαις, "Joshua . . . successor of Moses in prophecies"), so that these books have to be regarded as prophetic writings in the proper sense of the term; it is necessary also to take into consideration the fact that these historical books deal to a large extent with prophets, and narrate their deeds and sayings, as well as the fact that their recital is given quite in the prophetic spirit (see §. 19, 1 above). The נ' אַחֲרוֹנִים ("latter prophets") again consist of four books: the three greater prophets, Jeremiah, Ezekiel, Isaiah (*cf.* § 26, remark, above), and the Book of the Twelve Prophets (XII.), which likewise only counts as one book (§ 39, 1 above). Finally, the third section is composed of the כתובים or *Hagiographa*. To this belong the three great poetical books, Psalms, Proverbs, Job, indicated by the Jews in the form of a *vox memorialis* as ספרי א"מת; also the five smaller books of Canticles, Ruth, Threni (Lamentations), Koheleth, and Esther, which are called חָמֵשׁ מְגִלּוֹת, *i.e. the five festival rolls*, because they are regularly read through at five festivals (viz. *Canticles* at Passover, in accordance with an allegorical application of it to the Exodus from Egypt, which is already found in the Targum; *Ruth*, the lovely harvest-idyll, on Shabuoth [*Weeks*] as the festival of Harvest-thanksgiving; *Threni* on the 9th of Ab, the day of

IDEA AND DIVISION OF THE CANON 467

the fast for the destruction of the Temple; *Koheleth*, which preaches a thankful enjoyment of life, united with God and consecrated by the fear of God, as the ultimate aim of wisdom, at Sukkoth [*Tabernacles*]; and *Esther*, of course, at Purim); and finally the three books Daniel, Ezra-Nehemiah, and Chronicles— thus altogether eleven books. We meet with a clear and distinct division of these three sections for the first time in the Prologue of the grandson of Ben Sira, *circa* 130 B.C.

3. Consequently *the sum-total of the canonical books will be* $5 + 8 + 11 =$ *twenty-four*. This number is first expressly attested in 4 Ezra xiv. 44, according to the correct reading ($94 - 70 = 24$), which is preserved in the Oriental translations; it is regular in the Talmud and Midrash, where the O.T. is termed *the twenty-four holy scriptures* (כ"ד כתבי הקדש), or *the twenty-four books* (כ"ד ספרים), and we meet with it also in Jerome, in his "Praefatio" to Daniel, and in the "Prologus galeatus" referred to as the view of *nonnulli*. But side by side with this stands the express statement of Josephus ("c. Apion," i. 8), of Origen ("ap. Eusebius hist. eccles.," vi. 25), of Epiphanius ("De mens.," x.), and of Jerome (in the "Prol. gal.") to the effect that the Jews possessed twenty-two canonical books, in accordance with the number of the letters of their alphabet. The number twenty-two was secured by combining Ruth with Judges and Threni (Lamentations) with Jeremiah. At the same time Jerome is acquainted also (*op. cit.*) with the numbering of twenty-seven books, the five final forms of letters being reckoned in with the twenty-two ordinary letters of the

alphabet.¹ Corresponding to these five double letters, five books were counted double, viz. Samuel, Kings, Chronicles, Ezra, and Jeremiah (*i.e.* Threni was counted as a book by itself); no separate reckoning of Ruth is thought of here either. There can, however, be no doubt that these reckonings are purely artificial and arbitrary, and do not amount to anything more than mere trifling; for the history of the Canon the numbers twenty-two and twenty-seven are quite without significance.

4. Regarding the *nomenclature and sequence* of the canonical books no fixed tradition has grown up, as, for instance, is the case in the N.T. Thus for Numbers we have the designations בְּמִדְבַּר, וַיְדַבֵּר, and חֹמֶשׁ פְּקוּדִים; for Lamentations, קִינוֹת and אֵיכָה; for Kings, Origen ("ap. Euseb.," vi. 25) expressly attests as the Hebrew title ουαμμελεχ δαβιδ = דוד המלך, as, in fact, the first words of 1 K. i. 1 run. The order of the books also varies, which will appear the less strange when we remember that in the first and second centuries doubts were still entertained whether it was at all permissible to write several books in a single volume, and that it required Rabbi's² authority (about 200 A.D.) to invest this custom with general validity (Buhl, p. 37 f.). In the famous Talmudic passage " Baba Bathra," 14*b*, 15*a*, the arrangement is: Pentateuch, Joshua, Judges, Samuel, Kings, Jeremiah, Ezekiel, Isaiah, XII.(= Minor Prophets), Ruth, Psalms,

---

¹ As is well known, five letters of the Hebrew alphabet have special final forms (*literae finales*) in addition to the ordinary forms which are used when the letter is not final.—Tr.

² Rabbi = Rabbi Judah the Prince, compiler of the Mishna.

Job, Proverbs, Koheleth, Canticles, Threni, Daniel, Esther, Ezra, Chronicles. Jerome, in the "Prol. gal.," gives the Jewish sequence as follows: Pentateuch, Joshua, Judges, Ruth, Samuel, Kings, Isaiah, Jeremiah, Ezekiel, XII., Job, Psalms, Proverbs, Koheleth, Canticles, Daniel, Chronicles, Ezra, Esther; Threni, which is not explicitly mentioned here, is included in the reckoning with Jeremiah. A different order still is given in the Alexandrian Canon, about which it will be necessary to speak more particularly later. In the remarkable Canon of Melito of Sardis ("ap. Euseb.," iv. 26), who, with reference to *the books of the Old Testament* (τὰ τῆς παλαιᾶς διαθήκης βιβλία), proposes to fix exactly and accurately *the entire number of them and what their order was* (πάσα τὸν ἀριθμὸν καὶ ὁποῖα τὴν τάξιν εἶεν), although he appeals expressly to Jewish authorities, it is just as impossible to see an official Jewish order of books as in the arrangement of Origen (*op. cit.*); it should be added that both have one characteristic in common, in that they place the Prophets within the body of the Hagiographa, Origen after the Psalms, Proverbs, Koheleth, and Canticles, Melito after these four writings and Job—an arrangement which, following the chronological principle, must be described as having good grounds, because David and Solomon belong to an older age than the Prophets. In the great majority of Hebrew MSS. and in all the printed editions of the Hebrew text the following is the usual order of sequence: Pentateuch, Joshua, Judges, Samuel, Kings, Isaiah, Jeremiah, Ezekiel, XII., Psalms, Proverbs, Job, Canticles, Ruth, Threni, Koheleth, Esther, Daniel, Ezra-Nehemiah, Chronicles; for the Hagiographa

(כתובים) an order is well attested which places Chronicles at the beginning of the division, and then Psalms, Job, Proverbs, Ruth, Canticles, Koheleth, Threni, Esther, Daniel, and Ezra-Nehemiah.

§ 48. Formation and Close of the Canon

1. In many quarters the view prevails, and indeed has the authority of a dogma, that the Old Testament Canon *was established and fixed* SIMUL ET SEMEL *by one man or by a college*, and then *ever afterwards was accepted as valid and binding without a word of opposition*. And in truth — despite the explicit testimony of 2 Macc. ii. 13, which singles out Nehemiah as the man who *founding a library gathered together the books about the kings and prophets, and the books of David, and letters of kings about sacred gifts*[1]—tradition is unanimous in ascribing this function to Ezra: thanks to the much-read and highly influential work מסרת המסרת (*Massoreth ha-Massoreth*) of the German Jew Elias Levita (born 1472, died 1549), the opinion that Ezra and *the men of the Great Synagogue* (אנשי כנסת הגדולה) had fixed the O.T. Canon, as being the supposed official Jewish view, became a dogma for Protestant theological science in the sixteenth and seventeenth centuries. But against this all-prevailing opinion the disposition and general character of the O.T. Canon at once raises emphatic protest: if the entire body of Scriptures of the O.T. had been admitted to canonical authority all at once, the traditional arrangement and

---

[1] καταβαλλόμενος βιβλιοθήκην ἐπισυνήγαγε τὰ περὶ τῶν βασιλέων καὶ προφητῶν καὶ τὰ τοῦ Δαυιδ καὶ ἐπιστολὰς βασιλέων περὶ ἀναθημάτων.

division into the two sections of נביאים ("Pröphets") and כתובים ("Writings") would be altogether unintelligible. True, the separation of Ruth and Esther from the historical writings, and the sundering of Lamentations from Jeremiah, can be explained on liturgical grounds as having been effected with the object of having the "five rolls" (חמש מגלות; see § 47, 2 above) together; but, on the other hand, the separation of Ezra-Nehemiah and Chronicles from the historical writings is a great difficulty, that of Daniel from the prophetic books none at all. The fact also that the Samaritan Canon consists only of the first section of the Jewish, viz. of the Law (תורה), is a very noteworthy factor for determining the history of the Canon; also the divergence in principle of the Alexandrian Jews from the Palestinian on the question of the Canon (which will be discussed in § 48*a* following) would have been quite impossible if by about the time of the birth of Christ a canon in the technical sense of the term had been already in evidence.

2. Before we proceed to consider those factors which can elucidate for us the actual history of the O.T. Canon, there are *still some preliminary questions* to be settled. Wildeboer is fully justified in remarking that the idea implied in the term "canonical" is specifically a Church conception, and, therefore, when the question is one concerning the O.T. and the discussions of the Jewish schools, is only to be applied cautiously, *cum grano salis*. The "canonical" idea is, in the controversies that took place about the Canon, expressed in the peculiar phrase that the books in question *defile the hands* (מטמאים את־הידים).

When in this way it was taught that all contact with the holy books produces a state of levitical uncleanness and demands a ritual washing of the hands, this is but the strongest possible expression of the idea of holiness: but as to the criteria that determine canonicity, why one particular writing is regarded as canonical, or why its canonical rank is called in question—on such points as these the expression asserts nothing whatever; it is a pure judgment of value. We are also further informed that in the case of certain writings it was sought *to conceal* them (לגנוז). At once the characteristic difference of the expressions leads to the conclusion that quite different things are in question, and that the canonicity of writings which it was wished *to conceal*, or *hide*, must have been quite otherwise regarded than in the case of those where it was a matter of controversy whether they *defiled the hands* or not (but *cf.* Budde, pp. 64 ff.). With equal justification, however, Wildeboer also points out that in investigations as to the history of the O.T. Canon a sharp distinction must be drawn between the closing of the individual sections of the Canon, and the process by which they secured canonical rank (their "canonising"), that the two are not completely identical, and by no means coincide. How necessary and important this distinction is will be apparent as we proceed.

3. We begin our discussion with *the first and most important section of the O.T. Canon, the Law* (תורה). Its canonisation began in the year 621, and was accomplished for all time in 444 (see § 47, 1 above). In the estimation of the Jewish people it has always occupied a position apart: it was the revelation κατ'

FORMATION AND CLOSE OF THE CANON 473

ἐξοχήν, the holiest of all revelations: in comparison with it נביאים ("prophets") and כתובים (" writings ") were described merely as אֲשַׁלְמְתָא or קַבָּלָה, *tradition*, *i.e.* these books and their authors had but one aim, viz. to hand down and explain to their contemporaries and to later generations the revelation of God given in the Law (תורה) once for all and finally. The famous distinction of proto-canonical and deutero-canonical writings, which Sixtus Senensis (*cf.* § 2, 2 above) invented in order to hide from view the contradiction between Catholic Church-teaching and scientific truth, may quite properly be applied to the Jewish Canon and the relation subsisting between the Law (תורה) and קבלה. In this way, then, the whole of the O.T. is designated after its most essential part as Law (תורה), and this usage of language is verifiable also in the N.T.: thus in John x. 34 the Psalm-passage lxxxii. 6 is cited, and in John xv. 25, Ps. xxxv. 19 and lxix. 5, and in 1 Cor. xiv. 21, Is. xxviii. 11–12 are alluded to as written ἐν τῷ νόμῳ (*cf.* also John xii. 34: ἡμεῖς ἠκούσαμεν ἐκ τοῦ νόμου ὅτι ὁ Χριστὸς μένει εἰς τὸν αἰῶνα). The canonical dignity of the Law (תורה) has thus been undisputed and held in the highest regard since 444; it is all the more important and instructive, therefore, to notice that for a long time quite a free and independent attitude was taken up with regard even to this part of Holy Scripture, and after its "canonisation" it was by no means regarded as a paper Pope: we have seen that in the "Law" (תורה) elements essentially later than the time of Ezra are found (*cf.* § 12, 12 above), that the redaction of the complete Pentateuch falls within a time considerably subsequent to Ezra (*cf.* § 14, 4 above), that after its completion such a passage as Gen. xiv. could be inserted (*cf.* § 13, 7 above), that even in the time of the LXX. entire sections such as Ex. xxxv.–xl. had not yet become fixed and permanent elements in it (*cf.* § 12, 2 above), and that subsequent to the time of the LXX. redactional work on the Pentateuch was still continued (*cf.* § 14, 4 above). In this way it could happen that on so important a point as the chronology of Genesis the Hebrew text, Samaritan Pentateuch, and the Greek text are completely divergent from each other, and that even in Palestine—as is proved by the Book of Jubilees—a chronology differing from the traditional text, and in many respects showing points of contact with the Samaritan, was at any rate a possibility in the first century after Christ. Thus in Palestine itself there still existed in the first Christian century no canonical text of the Tora! This fact may be commended to the earnest consideration of those who, on the score of Mt. v. 18, think it necessary to be more Jewish than was Judaism itself in the time of Christ.

4. *The second section of the Canon* always confronts us with the "former prophets" (נביאים ראשונים) and the "latter prophets" (נ׳ אחרונים) in separate divisions. We must consider both apart. As the Pentateuch is not merely a law-book, but at the same time also a book of history, *the historical books which have been joined together to form the collection of the "former prophets"* (נ׳ ראשונים) constitute its immediate continuation. In view of the glorified form—as much the result of the beautifying power of recollection as of the painful

contrast afforded by them to the present—which the
"good old times" took on in the hearts and imagination of the Jewish people (those glorious times, to
dream of which was an absorbing joy, and the hope
of whose brilliant revival an undying passion) it can
easily be understood how highly prized and zealously
read those books must have been which alone afforded
any information regarding that wonderful past.
These historical books obtained their substantially
final form in the Babylonian Exile (*cf.* § 19 above),
so that we could push on their "canonisation" fairly
near to that of the "Law" (תורה), in fact we might
make it coincide with the latter. Ewald and Wildeboer have actually understood the statement in
2 Macc. ii. 13 in such a way as to ascribe to Nehemiah
an official collection of those historical books. But
the passage in question is hardly convincing in this
direction. These books are clearly not canonical
writings in the strictest technical sense in the time
of the Chronicler, *i.e. circa* 250, for otherwise he
would not have dared to rectify their historical
representation in the manner he has done. The
radical divergences shown by the LXX. in the case
of Samuel (*cf.* § 17, 5 above) and Kings (*cf.* § 18, 9
above) also point to the same result. But everything
supports the conclusion that the prophetic books
of history were extant earlier than the completed
collection—just as was the case in the prophetic
writings proper—and to this circumstance, as well as
to the further fact that they alone give information
regarding the prophets who are older than the authors
of the writings which are united together in the
"latter prophets" (אחרונים נ״), their designation as

"former prophets" (נ״ ראשונים) may be due; the title, accordingly, has a temporal connotation, and does not arise merely from their external position in the Canon.

5. *The collection of the Prophetic Writings proper*, the "latter prophets" (נ״ אחרונים), also extends with its beginnings certainly up into the Babylonian Exile.√ How busily the men of that time occupied themselves with the study of the older prophets and their divine utterances is sufficiently attested by the prophets of the Babylonian exile, Deutero-Isaiah and Zechariah, with their repeated and significant appeals to earlier prophets (*cf.* Ezek. xxxviii. 17; Is. xl. 21, xli. 26, xliv. 7, xlv. 20, xlvi. 10, xlviii. 3; and esp. Zech. i. 4, and vii. 4, in both of which passages the expression "the former prophets" [הנביאים הראשנים] occurs). Regarding the close of the collection of prophetic writings everything that is of importance has already been noted in § 39 above, and there it has been established that we must assign it to the second half of the third century, *i.e. circa* 200. But for the fact that the prophetic writings at that time were not regarded as canonical we have an unimpeachable witness in the person of the same man who attests the conclusion of the collection as having been effected at that period—Jesus ben Sira. This writer would never have been able to say (Ecclus. xxiv. 33) that he, having been himself illuminated and enriched by the Tora of Moses *as a canal from a river* (ὡς διῶρυξ ἀπὸ ποταμοῦ), *will yet pour out doctrine as prophecy and leave it unto generations of ages* (ἔτι διδασκαλίαν ὡς προφητείαν ἐκχεῶ καὶ καταλείψω αὐτὴν εἰς γενεὰς αἰώνων), could never have made the

boast in ch. l. 29 of his book—a passage which, it is true, is not given in the Hebrew text, here very corrupt—that whoever acts according to the precepts of his book *shall be strong to all things, for the light of the Lord is his footstep* (πρὸς πάντα ἰσχύσει ὅτι φῶς Κυρίου τὸ ἴχνος αὐτοῦ), if he had been conscious of himself and his book being separated from the writings of the prophets by the impassable gulf of "canonicity." Thus in the time of Jesus ben Sira there was a definitely closed and completed collection of prophetic books, so that Daniel could no longer be admitted to a place among them; but they did not yet rank as "canonical" Scriptures!

6. The first positive witness *for the existence of a third section of the Canon* is the Prologue of the grandson of ben Sira (*cf.* § 47, 2 above). But while in the case of the first two sections the designation as νόμος and προφῆται or προφητεία is constant, this section is variously termed τὰ ἄλλα πάτρια βιβλία, τὰ λοιπὰ τῶν βιβλίων, and τὰ κατ' αὐτοὺς [*i.e.* Law and Prophets] ἠκολουθηκότα, whence it is clear that about 130 B.C. no such technical designation for this section of the Canon as כתובים ("Writings") was yet in existence. Outside Law and Prophets other writings were extant which were regarded as holy, and were read for purposes of edification, but for which clearly no special class-name had at that time yet been coined. This third section of the Canon has naturally taken its point of departure from its most important and valuable constituent part—the Psalter. As being the hymn-book of the Temple, and the prayer-book of the community, it could not be looked upon and

treated like an ordinary profane writing, could not "be read as one reads a letter," and thus we already meet with a quotation of Ps. lxxix. 2–3 in 1 Macc. vii. 17 cited as "word of scripture" (*cf.* § 41, 11 above). But as compared with the prophetic writings the Psalter was too much distinguished by a character of its own to have allowed of its being fitted into a place among the "Prophets" (נביאים). Then were ranged by its side, in a position quite by themselves, Job and Proverbs: the "canonisation" also of Ezra-Nehemiah was almost a necessity. If our view as to the date to which the Book of Esther is to be assigned (*cf.* § 23, 3 above) be correct, in the time of the grandson of ben Sira the whole of our present collection of כתובים ("Writings") had not yet been completed, not to speak of the possibility of its having already been canonised; and that as a matter of fact, in dealing with the close and completion of the כתובים ("Writings") we are brought down to a far later time is clearly proved by the controversies as to the Canon that arose within the ranks of Judaism. With a single exception, all discussions of the kind of which we have information refer to writings out of the third section of the Canon. The tradition has been expressly handed down that Ezekiel *would have been hidden* (נגנז), because his words contradict the words of the Tora, unless Rabbi Hananja ben Hiskia had solved these disagreements. This Hananja ben Hiskia was a contemporary of Gamaliel I., the teacher of the Apostle Paul. That at so late a date it could still have been a subject of controversy whether Ezekiel was to be admitted into the prophetic Canon is quite inconceivable: by the expression *hiding* there can only be intended exclusion from public reading in the synagogue, from employment liturgically and for the purposes of worship. The same remarks apply in the case of Proverbs, which likewise *it was sought to hide* (בקשו לגנזו), because the book contained contradictions and elements causing difficulty and offence; yet in the end these were ignored. In this case also the question cannot have been whether Proverbs could be admitted at all, but only whether it would not be more advisable to withdraw it from use. The case is essentially different with the three books, Canticles, Koheleth, and Esther: with regard to these controversy still went on in the second Christian century on the question whether they *defile the hands* or not, and in one passage Jonah and Ruth are even mentioned as the subject of such discussion. In view of the cultural conditions then prevailing and of the decisive influence exercised by the teachers of the Law, a *hiding* of these books might possibly have been carried out, and might have been fully adequate to guard against misuse or serious consequences; when, however, controversy arises on the point whether they *defile the hands*, the question of canonical dignity is involved, and those teachers of the Law who deny this point thereby deny to the books in question canonical dignity, and cannot consequently have admitted them into the Canon, or (if so) must again have excluded them. If, however, the canonicity of the books in question could still be a subject of dispute by authoritative teachers of the Law in the second century, there can at that time have been no officially recognised canon of the

כתובים ("Writings"); in the face of such only a *hiding* of the offensive writings could have been discussed and eventually decided on. A synod held at Jamnia about the year 100 dealt with the question, and expressed itself in favour of the canonicity of the disputed books, and likewise with the greatest warmth Rabbi Akiba († 135), the real father of Talmudical Judaism, while for the Mishna (*circa* 200) the equal canonicity of all *twenty-four holy writings* (*cf.* § 47, 3 above) is fixed; but here and there objection was still raised in the third century, especially against Esther, and of Koheleth Jerome is aware that *hic liber obliterandus videretur*.[1] In view of these facts it is, perhaps, not altogether accidental that from the three books of disputed canonicity mentioned no citation occurs in the N.T., that Esther is passed over in the Canon of Melito of Sardis, and by Origen and Jerome is relegated to a position quite at the end. Thus only in the course of the second Christian century was the O.T. Canon definitively closed, and then circumstances imperatively compelled it. After Jerusalem and the Temple had been destroyed for the second time, and Israel as a nation had been annihilated, it took refuge in its religion and became the "People of the Book": when, however, "the Book" had become the fundamental factor of its existence and its life, the Book itself was bound to be established on a firm basis and raised to a position beyond the reach of doubt. Thus the establishment and closing of the Canon was a necessary and deliberate act for the self-preservation of Judaism.

[1] "This book would seem to be worthy of being expunged."

FORMATION AND CLOSE OF THE CANON

7. But the teachers of the Law of about the time of the end of the first and beginning of the second century did not make the Canon, but only sanctioned it. A *communis opinio,* a fixed "praxis of the spiritual life of the pious of Israel" had already grown up which simply confirmed and justified it theologically. For this purpose, however, they were bound to have a *standard of canonicity and a criterion for determining it.* In view of the position taken up by Judaism to the Tora, it might have been expected that the Tora would have been the norm by which the canonicity of the individual writings would be measured (*cf.* also the tradition, mentioned in par. 6 of this section, with reference to the Book of Ezekiel); but if this had been the case Jesus ben Sira would have been more deserving of admission into the Canon than a good deal of the canonical Hagiographa, and yet such a thing was never thought of. The real norm we can see rather by means of the very remarkable passage in Josephus, "c. Apion," i. 8. This is the oldest positive statement which can be exactly dated regarding the idea of Canon and canonicity from the Jewish side. Josephus is desirous of giving reasons why the Jews regard only a fixed number of books—according to his reckoning twenty-two (*cf.* § 47, 3 above)—as canonical, or, as he expresses it, *consider them to be decrees of God* (νομίζειν αὐτὰ θεοῦ δόγματα) and *things justly believed* (δικαίως πεπιστευμένα). This is true only of the twenty-two books which have been written from Moses *till the reign of Artaxerxes, king of the Persians after Xerxes* (μέχρι τῆς' Ἀρταξέρξου τοῦ μετὰ Ξέρξην Περσῶν βασιλέως ἀρχῆς), and of these only *on account of . . . the precise and definite succession of the prophets* (διὰ . . .

τὴν τῶν προφητῶν ἀκριβῆ διαδοχήν). With this agrees the definite statement of the book "Seder Olam," that *up to this time* (עד כאן), *i.e.* the time of Alexander the Great, prophetically described in the Book of Daniel—the prophets prophesied by the Holy Spirit, while *from then onwards* (מכאן ואילך) only the wise worked; and with this again agrees a Talmudic statement that not all books that arose *from then onwards* (מכאן ואילך) defile the hands (see Buhl, p. 37 ; E.T., p. 33). *Thus the canonical dignity of the books is a result of the inspiration of their authors:* these possess prophetic inspiration (רוח נבואה) in order to write a canonical book. Accordingly the extinction of prophecy which followed the time of Ezra and Nehemiah marks the moment at which the possibility of canonical books arising ceases to exist, and, in fact, the time of Ezra and Nehemiah marks the boundary-limit of canonicity : no book has been admitted into the Canon which was written by an author after this time in his own name, as comes to view with special clearness in the case of the classical book of Jesus ben Sira ; all instances of books of notoriously later date which, despite this fact, have been admitted into the Canon were either deliberately intended to be regarded as older, or, at least, were considered to be older.

8. The history of the Canon thus yields the following result : *it was not Israel, not the Judaism of Ezra or of the Maccabees, that definitively fixed and established the Old Testament Canon, but only Talmudical Judaism at its early stages for the purposes of self-preservation.* And therefore even Jesus cannot be appealed to as witness for the O.T. Canon. He

indeed lived and moved in the holy literature of Israel, towards which He did not take up any different position from that of His Jewish contemporaries, and, in fact, in His days almost the same books were counted as Holy Scripture as are found in our O.T.: but a canon in the sense of old Protestant dogmatics had not yet at that time come into existence. Talmudic Judaism has, however, drawn out the logical consequences of its own creation, the conception, viz., of the Canon as a collection of inspired holy Scriptures unalterably fixed once for all, and in the result has lapsed into the dreariest letter-worship, killing out all living power: *for the letter killeth* (τὸ γὰρ γράμμα ἀποκτεῖνει).

§ 48*a*. THE ALEXANDRIAN CANON

1. The Alexandrian Canon must be considered separately on its own merits. In the question of the Canon, that is to say, there is in Alexandria a marked divergence both as to form and substance from the Palestinians: in form, since there is no trace among the Alexandrians of the threefold division of the Canon which is so essential and characteristic a feature in the case of the Palestinians; and in substance, since a whole number of writings, which no one in Jerusalem considered to be canonical, were regarded as on an equality with the canonical and were classified with them. The question is concerned with the so-called "Apocrypha" as it appears in our Bibles. If from the circumstance that Philo never quotes proof-passages from the Apocrypha one were inclined to conclude that Philo, too, did not

regard the Apocrypha as canonical, there is the parallel fact to be considered that he also never cites from a whole number of undoubtedly canonical books; just as conversely Josephus, after giving the correct Palestinian doctrine regarding the Canon ("c. Apion," i. 8) proceeds to make use of such notoriously apocryphal writings as the Greek Books of Ezra and Esther. In strict correctness an Alexandrian "Canon" should not be spoken of at all; for neither the number of the books admitted nor their order is in agreement in the Greek Bible MSS. It is clear that the Greeks have allowed themselves to be guided simply by the principle of οἰκοδομή ("edification"): all writings of a religious character which they found edifying they read and held in high esteem. But such a proceeding would have been quite inconceivable if at the time of the birth of Christ there already existed in Palestine an official canon, and if the books had already at that time been separated into such as *defile the hands*, and such as do not. In Alexandria the historical books (among which Ruth also was reckoned) were arranged in order together, then the poetical and didactic, and last the prophetic, everywhere being mixed in motley sequence: then at the conclusion of the whole the Books of Maccabees take their place as an appendix. This arrangement yields the following constituent elements for the Alexandrian Canon: Pentateuch, Joshua, Judges, Ruth, βασιλειῶν α′ β′ γ′ δ′ (*cf.* § 17, 1 above), παραλειπομένων α′ β′ (*cf.* § 20, 1 above), Esdras α′ (one of the apocryphal Books of Ezra) and β′ (*i.e.* Ezra-Nehemiah; *cf.* § 21, 1 above), Tobit, Judith, Esther in the enlarged form produced by the apocryphal additions (cf. § 23, 1, 5), Job, Psalms, Proverbs, ἐκκλησιαστής, Canticles, σοφία Σαλομῶντος, σοφία Σειραχ, XII. (in the divergent order set forth in § 39, 4 above), Isaiah, Jeremiah, Βαρουχ, Threni, ἐπιστολὴ Ἰερεμίου, Ezekiel, Daniel with the apocryphal passages (cf. § 40, 6 above), Μακκαβαίων α' β'; in some MSS. there also appear in addition Μακκαβαίων γ' δ'. and the Προσευχὴ Μανασση.

2. *This Alexandrian Canon* derives quite a special importance from the fact that it was *the Bible of the Christian Church*, and, indeed, *in the oldest period its only Bible*. In this way, then, there occur a whole number of allusions to and citations from the Apocrypha, and even the Pseudepigrapha, in the N.T. On the relation of the oldest Christian Church to the O.T. as their only Holy Scripture, cf. the excellent discussion of A. Jülicher ("Einleitung in das N.T.," 1894, § 34):[1] "The last thing Jesus thought of was to add to the sum total or to double these Holy Scriptures; He never took up the pen or furnished His disciples with such a commission. . . . Even Paul did not intend to create a new holy literature; he only wrote occasional writings, and simply endeavoured in his letters to secure a momentary satisfaction for his personal appearance and intervention with regard to definite situations; the perpetual preservation of these letters to the end of time, their diffusion broadcast over the rest of Christendom, their public reading in the services of other—possibly to him strange and foreign—communities, to place them on an equality with Prophets and Psalms—to ask all this never entered his thoughts." It is true "there does exist

[1] E.T. by J. P. Ward (Smith, Elder & Co.), 1904.

in the oldest Christian communities an authority immediately on a par with—unconsciously even higher than—Law and Prophets": Jesus Christ. The words of Jesus were already placed by Paul entirely on a level with the words of God, but "not because they stood *written* in a holy book, but because in his conviction they are *Words of Jesus.*" Only gradually do the Apostles also take a place by the side of the O.T. and Jesus: a formal Canon of the N.T. side by side with the Canon of the O.T., and equal in rank with the latter, was first known to and recognised by the old Catholic Church.

Remark.—The history of the O.T. Canon in the Christian Church does not belong to an Introduction to the O.T.

General Introduction

CHAPTER XX

HISTORY OF THE TEXT

LITERATURE: A. Geiger, *Urschrift und Uebersetzungen der Bibel*, etc., 1857; A. Dillmann, *R.E.*, 2nd ed., ii. 381 ff.; F. Buhl, *R.E.*, 3rd ed., ii. 713 ff.

§ 49. MATERIALS FOR WRITING, AND THE WRITTEN SIGNS

LITERATURE: L. Löw, *Graphische Requisiten und Erzeugnisse bei den Juden*, 1870, 1871; E. A. Steglich, *Skizzen über Schrift und Bücherwesen der Hebräer*, etc., 1876; B. Stade, *Hebräische Grammatik*, i. 23-58, 1879, and the two tables of writing; H. L. Strack, *R.E.*, 2nd ed., xiii. 689 ff.; C. Schlottmann, *Hb. A.*, i. 1416 ff.; H. Benzinger, *Hebräische Archäologie*, 1894, §§ 39 and 40; W. Nowack, *Hebräische Archäologie*, i. 1894, §§ 52 and 53. Numerous facsimiles of old Hebrew handwriting in D. Chwolson, *Corpus Inscriptionum Hebraicarum*, 1882. Further A. Merx, *Documents de Paléographie hebraique et arabe*, 1894. For Semitic palaeography in general, *Corpus Inscriptionum Semiticarum*, appearing in Paris (since 1881).

1. Having already (*cf.* § 4 above) dealt with the question of the age of the use of writing, we must now consider the question of writing materials and the written signs. Regarding the oldest *writing materials* of the Hebrews clear information is afforded by etymology. Of the two common words for *book*,

סֵפֶר properly signifies *an object scraped off* or *smoothed*, and מְגִלָּה something *wound up* or *rolled together*, whence it results that the original Hebrew writing material was the skin of animals prepared and made smooth by scraping off the hair, and able to be rolled up easily. With this agrees the ordinance that the rolls for synagogue use may only be written on parchment, and also the law in Numb. v. 23, which presupposes a thoroughly durable form of writing material. The first historical and indubitable example of such a ספר—by which word is designated not only a book in the proper sense of the word, but also any piece of writing—is the Uriah-letter (2 Sam. xi. 14). To this prepared animal-skin writing was applied by means of an עֵט (Jer. viii. 8 ; Ps. xlv. 2), *i.e.* a *reed*, which could be pointed with a *penknife* (תַּעַר הַסֹּפֵר, Jer. xxxvi. 23). *Ink* also (דְּיוֹ) is mentioned (Jer. xxxvi. 18) and (Ezek. ix. 2) the *writer's writing apparatus* (קֶסֶת הַסֹּפֵר), *i.e.* inkhorn with pen, which was carried on the side. This ink must, however, have been easy to wash off, as appears from Numb. v. 23 and the metaphorical use of מָחָה with the meaning to *wipe out without leaving a trace.* It appears to have been customary to use only one side of the writing material for writing purposes, so that when it was rolled together the unwritten side came outermost: at any rate Ezekiel expressly notes it as something peculiar that the roll which was proffered to him in the vision of his call to swallow was written on both sides (פָּנִים וְאָחוֹר, Ezek. ii. 10). For the purposes of monumental writing *tablets* were employed, which are usually denominated לוּחַ (Is. xxx. 8 ; Hab. ii. 2, etc.), but also גִּלָּיוֹן (Is. viii. 1), or *stones*, which outside the tables of the Law are expressly mentioned only in Job xix. 24 and Deut. xxvii. 2, where, however, the stones are to be plastered with chalk, by which an application of colour rather than an engraving process may be intended to be understood. Engraving in metal is only found in the case of the inscription on the high-priestly ציץ.

2. With reference to the *written signs* a change occurred. Hebrew tradition has itself firmly held to the fact that the present usual form, the so-called "square character" (כְּתָב מרֻבָּע) or, as it is also named, "Assyrian writing" (אַשּׁוּרִי "כ), differs from the old Hebrew character (עברי "כ),[1] and had been introduced at a particular time. And in fact Ezra is said to have brought this writing with him from Babylonia and to have rewritten the holy books in this form. This view is on palaeographical grounds quite untenable. At the time of Ezra the old Semitic script, which is essentially identical with old Hebrew, was still written in Babylonia as cursive; then again the Samaritan Pentateuch, which was still written in old Hebrew script, testifies against such a view. From the circumstance that the legends on the Maccabean coins likewise bear the old Hebrew script-character too much is not to be inferred; in our own case the inscriptions on coins are wont commonly to be formed in Latin uncials. As *terminus ad quem* for the naturalisation of the square character, and also for the writing of the sacred text in it, we have in Mt. v. 18 the time of Jesus. The history of palaeography teaches us that the square character is connected

[1] Also called כ" דַּעַץ and כ" לִיבוֹנָאָה. On these designations *cf.* G. Hoffmann, "Z.A.T.W.," i. 334 ff., 1881.

in the closest way with the Palmyrene, and, in particular, with the Egyptian-Aramaic cursive writing, which we can trace as far up as the Persian period. A remarkable mixture of old Hebrew and the square character is shown by the short inscription of Arâk el Emir, of the year 176 B.C., while the epitaphs of the בְּנֵי חזיר at the so-called "grave of James" at Jerusalem, of the first century B.C., already have almost entirely the type of square character, even possess a ן final, and, like the Palmyrene, a whole series of ligatures.

3. Of *old Hebrew writing* we have monumental examples in the Siloam-inscription,[1] about twenty gems and seals (delineated in M. A. Levy, "Siegel und Gemmen," etc., 1869), and above all in the stone of Mesha,[2] if that is originally derived from Moabites. All these monuments display in common the old Semitic script corresponding to the Phoenician; only it is noteworthy that, as compared with the Phoenician, old Hebrew writing possesses a decidedly cursive character, as is shown by the consistent rounding of the letters: in the case of Phoenician writing the straight line throughout is as dominant as is the curved line in old Hebrew, from which circumstance we have concluded (*cf.* § 4 above) that a longer usage of writing must be presupposed for the Mesha-stone. This old Semitic script was, however, very imperfectly developed. It had no method of

[1] A photograph of the plaster-cast in "Z.D.M.G.," xxxvi. 725 (1882); reproduced in full with transcription in Gesenius-Kautzsch, 27th ed., 1902, p. 592, and with translation in Benzinger (*op. cit.*, p. 286, fig. 138); best separate edition by A. Socin, 1899.

[2] The best treatment of the inscription, with copy, is given by R. Smend and A. Socin in their edition of 1886.

dividing words, and did not even make the end of the line coincide with a complete word. It is true that the Siloam-inscription and the Mesha-stone use a point as word-divider, and the latter also employs a perpendicular stroke as sentence-divider; but the point does not appear regularly throughout, and whether from this usage of the inscriptions it is possible to argue as to that of the common cursive writing is more than doubtful, especially as Phoenician shows no acquaintance with this word-separating point in the inscriptions, and as we ourselves in inscriptions place a point after the individual words, a usage which is never employed in cursive writing. A further defect consists in the failure to indicate the vowels. It is true the so-called *matres lectionis* were in use, but still only in isolated cases, in the Mesha-inscription with a fair amount of regularity, to mark final sounds, in the Siloam-inscription more frequently to mark medial sounds also, when an original diphthong is in question; but even on this point we must think of the cursive script as rather more sparing and less particular than the monumental writing.

4. That the Biblical authors composed their *autographs* in this imperfectly developed old Hebrew writing, and that the latter obtained for a fairly long period in Biblical MSS., has been strikingly shown by Chwolson.[1] More especially it seems to have been the case that even to mark the final sound the *matres lectionis* were for a long time used only very sparingly: in 1 K. viii. 48, Ezek. xvi. 59, Ps. cxl. 13,

[1] " Die Quiescentes הוי in der althebräischen Orthographie " (see " Verhandlungen des Internationalen Petersburger Orientalistenkongresses," ii. 459–490, 1878).

Job xlii. 2 the Massoretes have recognised this, in other passages have half-recognised it, as when, *e.g.*, on 1 Sam. xvi. 4 וַיֹּאמֶר they make the remark סְבִירִין וַיֹּאמְרוּ; in very many cases, on the other hand, they have failed to note it, as, *e.g.*, Ps. xvi. 2. Especially instructive in this connexion are parallel texts, such as Is. xxxvi. 5 אָמַרְתִּי and 2 K. xviii. 20 אָמַרְתָּ; 1 Chron. xvi. 15 זִכְרוּ and Ps. cv. 8 זָכַר; Ezra ii. 62 נִמְצָאוּ and Neh. vii. 64 נִמְצָא; יִשָּׂאוּ Micah iv. 3 and יִשָּׂא Is. ii. 4. For instances of variants in medial sounds I point to the refrain in Jer. vi. 15 and viii. 12, where בְּעֵת פְּקַדְתִּים stands parallel with בְּעֵת פְּקֻדָּתָם, as well as to Jer. xxiii. 5 and xxxiii. 15 (צֶמַח צַדִּיק compared with צֶמַח צְדָקָה). Word-division also appears to have found no place in these autographs, although the double point in the form of the so-called סוֹף פָּסוּק proves that even in Hebrew cursive writing "at certain times the point was in use as a word-divider" (Stade, *op. cit.*, p. 29). And with this result agrees also the testimony of the Samaritan Pentateuch, which regularly avails itself of the point for the division of words. But this can never have been the common usage, and can never have been carried through consistently, because not only do many divergences in the LXX. from the Hebrew text go back to a difference of word-division, but in the Massora itself unmistakably wrong divisions of words are found. In fact, even verses and larger logical divisions cannot always have been made discernible by external signs. Instances of wrong dividing up of words are, *e.g.*, the following (I purposely select examples only from quite late passages): אָמְרָה קֹהֶלֶת Koh. vii. 27, or אֱלֹהִים צִוָּה Ps. xliv. 5—this example is all the more significant because the letter ם is in question, and consequently at the time when this notoriously Maccabean Psalm was composed the final form of the letter (ם) was not distinguished in writing: it is only possible to explain such a corruption as Ps. lxxv. 2 וְקָרוֹב שְׁמֶךָ, as against καὶ ἐπικαλεσόμεθα τὸ ὄνομά σου, from the *scriptio continua*; and if word- and verse-division had been regular the refrain in Ps. xlii. 7 could never have developed such a textual corruption, such a reading as Gen. xlix. 19-20[1] could never have been formed, or such a variant as Jer. ix. 4-5 in the LXX. and Massora possibly have arisen. Jerome, moreover, translates the expression מִכְתָּם (here again a *litera finalis* is in question), which occurs in the superscriptions of certain Psalms, *humilis et simplicis*.

§ 50. Perfecting of the Writing

1. So *undeveloped a script* might have sufficed so long as the language was a living one. When, however, Hebrew died out, and only prolonged an artificial existence as the language of the cultus and the learned, the necessity must then have made itself felt to devise means for aiding the understanding of the consonantal text with its endless variety of possible meanings. The first means to hand for this purpose was afforded by a larger and more extended employment of the *matres lectionis*, as was done quite logically by the old Arabic script, which leaves all short vowels without indication,

[1] Here again a מ or ם is in question, and thereby (assuming the distinction of final from medial מ to have existed) a clear indication of the verse-division given.

but expresses the long by the consonant most nearly related to the sound of the vowel. In the Massoretic text, as it now lies before us, this has been done, but inconsistently; all vowels organically long have not been indicated by *matres lectionis* throughout; in particular a preference is shown for avoiding the occurrence in the same word of two *matres lectionis* immediately following each other, while, contrariwise, vowels merely long phonetically have had the *mater lectionis* assigned to them, as יִפּוֹל (Ezek. vi. 12); in cases where even short *ḥatef*-vowels are indicated by the *mater lectionis,* as in אֲשְׁקוֹטָה (Is. xviii. 4), a pronunciation diverging from the traditional Massoretic one lies behind. The division of words by spacing appears also to have naturalised itself about the time of the birth of Christ, and the separation of the individual verses by means of סוֹף פּסוּק, *sôf pāsûq,* is already attested in the Talmud, which forbids the use of these signs of punctuation in the case of the rolls of the Law destined to serve for purposes of worship, thereby at the same time confessing that these are no part of ancient tradition.

2. The Hebrew text was still without a complete *system of indicating the vowels* in the time of Jerome and of the Babylonian Talmud. Jerome complains of the ambiguity of Hebrew writing in a way which shows clearly that he was still not acquainted with any system of indicating the vowels by writing, and the same is true of the Talmud. That it merely forbids the use of סוֹף פָּסוּק for the rolls of the Law is noteworthy, and there is the additional fact that repeatedly in the Talmudical discussions various possible punctuations are pointed out, and warning is

given as to many readings, which could not possibly have happened if the vocal pronunciation had been indicated in an unambiguous manner by the writing. As *terminus a quo* for détermining the age of the system of vowel-indication we thus have the close of the Gemara of the Babylonian Talmud in the sixth century, and as *terminus ad quem* the oldest (Hebrew) Bible MS. preserved to us, viz. the St Petersburg Codex of the Prophets, dating from the year 916. We shall thus assign the development of the system of vowel-indication within the interval from the seventh to the ninth centuries, and in that case it is an organic link in a long chain of similar phenomena, when the Syrians also felt the necessity for introducing the system of vowel-indication into their writing. In this respect priority belongs to the Syrians, who in so many points became the Greek-inspired instructors of the Semitic Orient. Two systems of punctuation were developed, the so-called system of "Tiberias," which is the one usually found in our printed editions and Bible MSS., and the so-called "Babylonian" (described in detail by Stade [*op. cit.*, pp. 41 ff.]), which we find employed in a number of older MSS.: as however, the system of Tiberias is by far the more consistent and complete—is in fact a magnificent and wonderful production—it has ever more and more tended to reach a position of sole and unchallenged supremacy.

In the closest and most intimate connexion with the vocalisation stands the accentuation. The accents, which at the same time supply the place of punctuation, and tendencies to which also manifest themselves among the Syrians, have likewise been developed among the Jews into a system, complex in the highest degree, and expressive of the most delicate *nuances*, which in the case of the books אמ״ת (*cf.* § 47, 2 above) have developed still more far-reaching refinements. "We may . . . regard the vocalisation and the main part of the accentuation as complete by about 650. What then remained undecided has never been decided at all by universal consent. Hence the differences in the MSS." (A. Merx, "Abhandlungen des funften internationalen Orientalistenkongresses, II. i. 223, 1882).

3. The history of the writing thus furnishes us with the following *result*: the autographs of the Biblical authors were written on leather in the very incompletely developed old Hebrew writing in *scriptio continua*, without any division of words and sentences, and almost entirely without *matres lectionis*. This text underwent a complete change in the kind of writing employed in it, and an almost complete change of orthography; has thus experienced various vicissitudes, which fact leads us to suspect that it has not come off without suffering a good deal of misfortune.

§ 51. THE MASSORETIC TEXT

LITERATURE: J. Buxtorf, *Tiberias sive Commentarius Masorethicus triplex*, etc., 1620; H. L. Strack, *Prolegomena critica in Vetus Testamentum Hebraicum*, 1873, and *R.E.*, 3rd ed., xii. 393 ff.
Collections of the vast mass of material in S. Frensdorff, *Die Massora Magna*, i. *Massorethisches Wörterbuch oder die Massora in alphabetischer Ordnung*, 1876; and D. Ginsburg, *The Massorah*, 3 vols., 1880–1885.

THE MASSORETIC TEXT

Model editions of the Massoretic text of individual Biblical books have been produced since 1869 by S. Baer and F. Delitzsch; the best most recent printed text of the whole: that of D. Ginsburg, 1894, 2 vols.

1. The canonical text of the O.T., as it now lies before us, is usually termed the *Massoretic Text* (M.T.), from מסורה or מסורת, the written form of which word is not quite fixed, but the derivation of which from the Mishnaic מָסַר, *to hand down traditionally*, is undoubted. The MSS. in which this text is extant are none of them old—the oldest that can be certainly dated is the St Petersburg Codex of the Prophets,[1] of the year 916, which is written with the Babylonian punctuation (*cf.* § 50, 2 above), and the oldest that exists in Germany is the famous Reuchlianus at Karlsruhe, of the year 1105–1106. Two factors have contributed to this result: first of all, the rule that every MS. in use for purposes of worship, if damaged in any way, must (in order to guard against any possible subsequent profanation) be consigned to a special room in the synagogue, the so-called גְּנִיזָה (*Genizā*), there to be left to moulder away; and last (but not least) the numerous persecutions of the Jews, which were always first directed against their sacred writings. An edition of the text (which, however, is limited to the consonants only), with variants from over six hundred of the best and oldest available MSS., and some forty of the earliest and most correct printed editions, was published in two strong folio volumes at great expense by B. Kennicott, in 1776 and 1780 ("Vetus Testamentum

[1] Published in photo-lithographic facsimile by H. L. Strack, "Prophetarum posteriorum Codex Babylonicus Petropolitanus," 1876.

Hebraicum cum variis lectionibus," Oxford, 1776 and 1780); this vast mass of material was doubled by J. B. de Rossi ("Variae lectiones Veteris Testamenti," Parma, 1784–1788, in four quarto volumes), but with only the more important passages collated, and (a feature that deserves special praise) the punctuation also being brought within the compass of his work. These immense collections yielded hardly any variants—at least scarcely any worthy of note—and there were not wanting those who in this fact were willing to see a mark of superiority on the part of the O.T. tradition over that of the N.T.

2. But not only are no variants furnished by the MSS. of the M.T.; they also positively agree, both collectively and individually, in many strange and peculiar features of the traditional text. Thus there are letters which are written larger than the usual form, as in Ex. xxxiv. 7, Deut. vi. 4, Ps. lxxx. 16; and also such as are smaller, as in Gen. xxiii. 2, Deut. xxxii. 18, Prov. xxviii. 17: several times a point appears over particular letters, as in Gen. xix. 33, Numb. ix. 10, xxi. 30; or over entire words, as in Gen. xxxiii. 4, Ezek. xlvi. 22, Ps. xxvii. 13: or particular letters are suspended above the line of the rest, as in Judg. xviii. 30, Ps. lxxx. 14, Job xxxviii. 13: in Numb. xxv. 12 the stem of the ו is broken through; in Ex. xxxii. 25 and Numb. vii. 12 the ק is completely closed up by the stem; in Numb. x. 35 and 36 and seven times in Ps. cvii. there occurs an inverted נ; in twenty-eight passages an empty space in the middle of the verse, as in Gen. xxxv. 22, 1 Sam. xiv. 19, Ezek. iii. 16. Long ago Spinoza rightly perceived that these startling features simply mark

errors or external damage in the exemplar of the M.T., and from the regular occurrence of these features in all MSS. and editions concluded that only very few—perhaps two or three—MSS. could have been available for fixing our M.T. Though a few already suspected the true state of the case, it was Lagarde ("Anmerkungen zur griechischen Uebersetzung der Proverbien," 1863, 1–2), who from these very peculiarities of the M.T. strikingly and irrefutably proved to everyone who is willing to see " that our Hebrew MSS. of the O.T. go back to a single exemplar, the correction of whose writing mistakes even they have faithfully copied as correction, and whose accidental defects they have taken over." By the recognition of this fact a firm basis was first given for the scientific treatment of the O.T. and a methodical investigation made possible.

3. Such being the state of the case, the next task must be to arrive at some clear conclusion as to the *age of this single archetype.* And on this point the history of the text, the history of the Jewish people, and a positive piece of evidence are in agreement, so as to make it possible to answer this question with greater definiteness. The LXX. diverges from the M.T. radically, the Targum also to a considerable extent, while the later Greek translators Aquila, Theodotion, and Symmachus reproduce our text almost exactly, and Jerome, with merely unimportant variations, quite exactly. These phenomena would suggest the end of the first and the beginning of the second Christian century as the time when the M.T. was constituted. And with this conclusion the historical development of

Judaism corresponds. We have seen that about this time the last of the controversies about the Canon were settled, and the Canon became definitely fixed. After Jerusalem had been destroyed, and the people had been deprived of their national existence, they sought and found in religion the basis for a continued existence among the nationalities of the Roman Empire. The establishment of the Canon must, however, have involved as a consequence the fixing of the text, and this all the more because the most influential man of the Judaism of that day, Rabbi Akiba, introduced and made all-powerful that treatment of Scripture which bases arguments on the letters, and therefore in its eyes every small point of the traditional text was of high and eventful significance. In this connexion Lagarde ("Materialen zur Kritik und Geschichte des Pentateuchs," i. 230 f., 1868) adduces a late Arabic narrative which recounts that all the codices of the O.T. are copies of a single exemplar which was rescued from Bethar: Bethar, however, where also Rabbi Akiba suffered the martyr's death, is the place which played so important a rôle in the revolt of Bar-Kokba. We shall thus be compelled to concede that Lagarde is entirely right in attributing this archetype to the time of Hadrian. Be the Arabic testimony adduced, when objectively considered, as worthless as it may, Lagarde's thesis does not depend for its validity upon it, and has not, therefore, been overthrown by Kuenen's brilliant and famous essay, "Der Stammbaum des masoretischen Textes des Alten Testaments."[1] By this it is not intended to be

[1] *Gesammelte Abhandlungen*, pp. 82–124.

asserted, of course, that this single archetype had been written at the time of Hadrian exactly; but the recognition of this one text as the only authoritative one cannot be placed before that time so fateful for the Jewish people. And with this conclusion the state of this text itself agrees. That is to say, it is, in the various O.T. books, of very unequal value, and in some cases is in such a condition that only urgent necessity can have compelled the canonisation of the books; Jewish tradition itself gives an account of a fixing of the text on the basis of three MSS. only in the case of the Tora, which, indeed, has been handed down relatively in the best condition. This archetype was, of course, a purely consonantal text, marked by a fairly copious employment of the *matres lectionis*, but on no consistent plan; it already possessed *literae finales* and a system of word-division, because our M.T. has preserved both, even in cases where it recognised that its exemplar was wrong: thus Is. ix. 6 ם in a medial syllable, Job xxxviii. 1 נ and Neh. ii. 13 מ as a final sound are found; or wrong division of words is retained (Ezek. xlii. 9; Job xxxviii. 12), two words are erroneously written as one (Jer. vi. 29; Ps. lv. 16), one as two (Lam. iv. 3).

4. If our consonantal text thus emanates from the time of Hadrian, we have to ask further whether the *age of the vocalisation* can be determined. The Talmud traces this also back to Ezra, and understands the obscure passage Neh. viii. 8 of the insertion of the vowel-signs. We have seen (*cf.* § 50, 2 above) that the vowel-signs arose from the seventh to the ninth Christian century; but the question

as to the age of the vowel-signs is sharply to be distinguished from the question as to the age of the vowel pronounciation. The Talmud is already acquainted with a fixed traditional vocalic pronunciation, as appears from its distinction of אם למקרא and אם למסורת, as well as from the constantly recurring אל תקרא כך אלא כך ("do not read thus, but thus"). The same is true of Jerome, as, *e.g.*, when he explains that the LXX. translation of וַיַּשֵּׁב אֹתָם (Gen. xv. 11) by καὶ συνεκάθισεν αὐτοῖς (which according to the consonants merely is quite possible) is wrong, and says: "In hebraeo habet . . . *et abigebat eas*"[1] ("Quaestiones Hebraicae in Libro Geneseos," ed. Lagarde, 1868, 25), and also of Origen, who has even corrected the vocalisation of Hebrew proper names in accordance with the M.T. Moreover, the divergences of the later Greek translators from the LXX. are due to a large extent merely to the fact that they follow the vocalisation of the M.T., while the LXX., on the other hand, follows a different reading of the consonants. Such being the state of the case, we can suppose that the establishment of the vocalic pronunciation took place contemporaneously with that of the consonantal text, and we may say that the M.T., as it now lies before us, originated at some time in the interval between the end of the first and the beginning of the second Christian century.

5. That this text has been preserved to us up to the present day in a condition essentially unchanged, we owe to the so-called *Massoretes*, the בַּעֲלֵי הַמָּסוֹרָת, who watched over the preservation of the traditional material with the minutest care. Their work was

[1] "In the Hebrew it is . . . 'and he drove them away.'"

essentially that of recorders. They counted the verses and letters of the individual books, noted the middle-point in them, counted the cases of *scriptio plena* and *defectiva* of certain words, giving the reference to the passages where both occur, and made lists of passages which were similar, but not quite alike, and which might easily be confused. These they either noted on the margin of the Bible MSS.—the so-called *Massora marginalis*, in which, again, are to be distinguished a larger, more detailed Massora, which at least cites the quotations, and a smaller one which only gives statistics—or else they compiled independent collections of the Massoretic material, the best known of which, named after its opening words אָכְלָה וְאָכְלָה, was issued in 1864 by S. Frensdorff. Still, even this painstaking work did not succeed in fully fixing the text: variants—very unimportant, indeed, and having no effect upon the sense—occur between the text of the מָדִינְחָאֵי, *the Orientals*, i.e. the Babylonian Jews, and that of the מַעֲרְבָּאֵי, *the Occidentals*, i.e. the Jews of Tiberias. Our printed editions throughout have the text of Tiberias. When later the vocalisation was added to the consonantal text, this again gave rise to differences, apart from the divergence between the Babylonian punctuation and that of Tiberias. The Jews recognise two principal authorities in particular for the punctuation, who lived for some time contemporaneously at the beginning of the tenth century: Rabbi Mose ben David ben Naphtali, usually styled briefly *Ben Naphtali*, in Babylonia, and his somewhat younger opponent, Rabbi Aharon ben Mose ben Ascher, usually styled briefly *Ben Ascher*, in Tiberias, to whom the famous Massoretic work "Dikduke Hat'amim" (edited by S. Baer and H. L. Strack, 1879) is attributed. Ben Ascher[1] became the standard authority for the whole subsequent period. Certain model MSS., which were regarded as being especially accurate and trustworthy, were also used: the more important of them are enumerated by Strack (*Prolegomena*, pp. 15–29).

6. The work of the Massoretes thus consisted essentially in the faithful preservation of the traditional material. But there were cases where it was quite impossible to rest content with what was traditionally handed down, but where its *untenable character* was obvious. In such cases they did not venture to correct the traditional text, but the *amendment* was noted *on the margin* as קרי, *that which is to be read*, opposite to the כְּתִיב, *that which was written*. These Qerê-readings consist either of corrections of recognised scribal errors in the traditional text, as, *e.g.*, 1 Sam. xiv. 27, Qerê וַתָּאֹרְנָה instead of the Ketib וַתִּרְאֶנָה, or 1 Sam. xiv. 32, וַיַּעַט for the traditional וַיַּעַשׂ; or the Massoretes change incorrectly written forms into the usual orthography, as מַלְנָה for מלוכה and מלכי for מלוכי (Judg. ix. 8 and 12), or אֲנַחְנוּ for אָנוּ Jer. xlii. 6. These alterations are not always necessary, may even indeed be quite wrong; but in general it may be testified in their favour that they have correctly diagnosed and amended errors. Their criticism, however, extends even to whole words, they either regarding such as

---

[1] A. Merx, "Die Tschufutkaleschen Fragmente: Eine Studie zur Geschichte der Massora" (*op. cit.*, § 50, 2, pp. 188–225), gives some important material on the subject of Ascher.

superfluous (the so-called כתיב ולא קרי), as, *e.g.*, Jer. xxxix. 12 אם, Ezek. xlviii. 16 חמש, and Jer. li. 3, as being pure cases of dittography; or else thinking it necessary to replace missing words (this = the so-called קרי ולא כתיב), *e.g.* 2 Sam. viii. 3 פְּרָת, 2 K. xix. 37 בָּנָיו, Jer. xxxi. 38 בָּאִים. But yet another kind of Qerê-readings remains to be noticed, viz. those cases where divergence from the traditional text is dictated by religious grounds. To this class belongs the so-called *Qerê perpetuum*, which substitutes אֲדֹנָי for יהוה, and which is already attested by the LXX. in its regular employment of Κύριος. Further divergences are dictated by considerations of propriety, as when the verb שָׁכַב is everywhere substituted for שָׁגַל, and טְחֹר in 1 Sam. v. and vi. is substituted for עֹפֶל, or מַחֲרָאָה (2 K. x. 27) and שַׁיִן (2 K. xviii. 27) and similar expressions are paraphrased euphemistically. In all these cases the consonants of the כתיב were provided with the vowels of the קרי, a fact which Cappellus acutely turned to account as proof of the more recent age of the punctuation. A כתיב ולא קרי is not provided with vowels.

§ 52. The Relation of the Massoretic to the Original Text

1. That the M.T. is *not identical with the original text* of the Biblical authors is already apparent from the interval of time which divides it from the latter. During the centuries that lay between the two any traditional text that depended merely on writing must have undergone vicissitudes, and this applies

peculiarly to our Hebrew text because, as we have seen, within this time there falls a complete change of the written character, as well as a gradual development of the orthography. And besides, in the most ancient period the text was by no means multiplied with the slavish faithfulness with which later the M.T. was copied among the Jews: we possess documentary proof of this fact in the so-called "parallel texts" of the O.T. itself, which often diverge radically from one another, and always show enough to prove that any scrupulosity regarding the tradition cannot be looked for in ancient times. Then, further, there is the possibility also to be reckoned with of involuntary oversight, and consequently of scribal errors, in which connexion it must always be borne in mind that in a script like old Hebrew a single letter is sufficient to transform the entire sense. Such scribal errors which we are able to rectify by means of parallel texts in the O.T. itself are, *e.g.*, לְאַרְצֶךָ 2 Sam. vii. 23 miswritten for לְגָרֵשׁ 1 Chron. xvii. 21, or יָצְרוּ 2 K. xii. 11 for יְעָרוּ 2 Chron. xxiv. 11, or וַיֵּרָא 2 Sam. xxii. 11 for וַיֵּדֶא Ps. xviii. 11. Or to take another common source of mistakes—the falling out of words by homoioteleuton, *e.g.* 1 Sam. x. 1, after מְשָׁחֲךָ יהוה follow, according to the LXX., the words: לְנָגִיד עַל עַמּוֹ עַל יִשְׂרָאֵל וְאַתָּה תִמְשֹׁל בְּעַם יהוה וְאַתָּה תוֹשִׁיעֶנּוּ ; or Ezek. xl. 48, מִיַּד אֹיְבָיו וְזֶה לְּךָ הָאוֹת כִּי מְשָׁחֲךָ יהוה where after וְרֹחַב הַשַּׁעַר in the same way, according to the LXX., should follow אַרְבַּע עֶשְׂרֵה אַמָּה וּכְתֵפוֹת הַשַּׁעַר. A converse case of erroneous repetition, which can be controlled by a parallel text, is 2 Sam. vi. 3 and 4 compared with 1 Chron. xiii. 7, where a copyists' mistake in reverting from the second הָעֲגָלָה to the first has involved the whole text in 2 Sam. in hopeless confusion. But there are also cases where the M.T. itself, independently of any objective controlling criterion, shows clear indications of being wrong. Such a case is Jer. xxvii. 1, where the whole connexion proves that the following mention of יְהוֹיָקִים is a scribal error for צִדְקִיָּהוּ. Of this kind of error *lists* more especially yield a rich harvest. In the list of David's heroes (2 Sam. xxiii. 8–39) the sum total given is thirty-seven, while there are actually only thirty-five individual entries; or again in the survey of the tribal district of Judah set forth in Josh. xv., in vs. 32 the sum total given is twenty-nine, while the items only amount to thirty-seven, and in vs. 36 the sum total is fourteen, the items amounting to fifteen; or again in Josh. xxi., in the list of the Levitical cities the tribe of Reuben has fallen out after vs. 36. The cases, indeed, where for internal and external reasons we must suppose the existence of errors in the M.T. are legion.

2. But in dealing with the O.T. another quite special factor comes into question. We have to allow for the presence not merely of ordinary textual mistakes, but also of *deliberate alterations*. Sacred texts are particularly liable to such deliberate alterations if the traditional material appears to contain things to which exception can be taken, and which are felt to be incompatible with other cherished notions and beliefs. Jewish tradition has itself preserved a clear reminiscence of the fact that the M.T. has been reviewed and revised on these lines. Of comparatively small importance are the cases (five in

number) of the עִטּוּר סוֹפְרִים, *iṭṭûr sôferîm*, where the scribes are said to have deleted an originally existing ו; on the other hand, the eighteen cases expressly handed down by tradition of תִּקּוּן סוֹפְרִים, *tiqqûn sôferîm, i.e.* of a *correction by the scribes*, can only be regarded as "tendency"-alterations of the text, designed to remove exceptionable features, such as Job vii. 20, where, according to the tradition, עָלַי is a correction of this kind for an original עָלֶיךָ, or again Hab. i. 12, נָמוּת for תָּמוּת. But we can also point out cases of such "tendency"-alterations of the text elsewhere also: as when in Samuel בַּעַל in Israelitish proper names has everywhere been changed into בֹּשֶׁת. Saul's son אֶשְׁבַּעַל (as he is correctly called in 1 Chron. ix. 39) appears in Samuel throughout as אִישְׁבֹּשֶׁת, Jonathan's son מְרִיבַעַל (1 Chron. ix. 40) as מְפִיבֹשֶׁת, and even Gideon as יְרֻבֹּשֶׁת in 2 Sam. xi. 21 ; in the case of David the name of his son בְּעֶלְיָדָע (1 Chron. xix. 7) has at any rate been changed in 2 Sam. v. 16 into אֶלְיָדָע, just as יְשׁוִי also, *i.e.* originally אִישְׁוִי, is found in 1 Sam. xiv. 49 for אִישְׁבַּעַל. A similar "tendency"-insertion into the text is the addition of אֹיְבֵי in 1 Sam. xxv. 22 and 2 Sam. xii. 14,[1] as also of אֶל־גּוֹיִם in Ezek. ii. 3.

In view of these facts we, therefore, dare not blindly trust the M.T., but have always to reckon with the possibility of accidental error, and even of conscious and deliberate alterations of the text. To show that the plain and obvious sense has in many cases designedly not been expressed by the punctuation and accentuation, it is only necessary to refer to such an instance as תִּפֹּלוּ, Ezek. xlvii. 22, or to the

---

[1] *Cf.* Fürst, "Z.W.Th.," xxiv. 176, 1881 ; and Geiger, "Urschrift," 267.

APPROXIMATION TO ORIGINAL TEXT

position given to the athnaḥ underneath שֵׁכָב in 1 Sam. iii. 3; the accentuation also of the famous passage Is. ix. 5 has been dictated by "tendency"-considerations of a dogmatic kind.

§ 53. Aids towards Reaching an Approximation to the Original Text

LITERATURE: C. H. Cornill, *Das Buch des Propheten Ezechiel*, 1886, 13–150; V. Ryssel, *Untersuchungen über die Textesgestalt und die Echtheit des Buches Micha*, 1887, 144–198.

1. As the first aid towards arriving at an approximation to the original text, the employment of emendation or conjecture, applied in accordance with philological method, is available. The absolute necessity that exists for the employment of conjectural criticism in the criticism of the O.T. text—which method long ago had a champion in Cappellus—is to-day almost universally recognised; those who would not allow the presence of any error in the M.T. grow ever fewer in numbers, and less positive in their attitude. In one respect, indeed, the O.T. itself very substantially lightens the task of emendation, viz. by its use of *parallelism*, which is the dominant factor in the whole of the poetry, and also is to a large extent perceptible in the prose. Thus to anyone who has the slightest feeling for such matters the parallelism makes it clear at once that וְיִטְרֹף in Am. i. 11 by the side of שְׁמָרָה is a scribal error for וַיִּטֹּר; that אָמְרוּ in Is. iii. 10 must be emended into אַשְׁרֵי, and וְיָבֹא in Is. xli. 25 into וַיָּבָם. The general sense and connexion also of a particular sentence often prove a sure and easy guide, and show

us how to effect the emendation, e.g. to amend בלחמו in Jer. xi. 19 into בלחו, or ומאת in Neh. v. 11 into וּמְשָׁאת. Collections of conjectures and emendations are to be found in the following: C. F. Houbigant, "Biblia Hebraica cum notis criticis," 4 vols., 1753; H. Graetz, "Emendationes in plerosque V.T. libros," 3 fasc., 1892–1894; E. Kautzsch, "Die heilige Schrift des A.T.," Appendices; H. Oort, "Textus Hebraici emendationes," etc., 1900. Still, a certain subjective character attaches particularly to conjectures, and it would not be desirable to have emendations and conjectures as our only aids; for emendation and conjecture, after all, are the *ultima ratio* which only comes into play when tradition, after being maturely weighed and carefully tested, refuses to lend any assistance. In the case of other texts the first task to undertake would be considered to be the collection of all available MSS. in order to reconstruct from them, in accordance with philological method, the purest possible form of the tradition. In accordance with the facts ascertained in § 51, 2, it might seem to be necessary in dealing with the O.T. to renounce altogether the hope of making use of aid of this kind: but this is so only apparently; for in the Samaritan Pentateuch and the translations of the O.T. which were made immediately from the original text itself we still possess some MSS. partly entire, partly in fragments, which are more or less independent of the Massoretic recension. This is indeed a field of operations the cultivation of which demands a large amount of special knowledge and unusual circumspection: for many preliminary questions must first be settled and much preliminary work done before we can utilise these translations in substitution for the Hebrew MSS. underlying them; but these tasks are as rich in reward as they are difficult of execution, and form the indispensable preliminary to a rational criticism of the text of the O.T.

The Samaritan Pentateuch

LITERATURE: E. Kautzsch, *R.E.*, 2nd ed., xiii. 340 ff., and *H.B.A.*, 1st ed., 1347 ff.; W. Gesenius, *De Pentateuchi Samaritani origine indole et autoritate*, 1815; S. Kohn, *Zur Sprache, Literatur, und Dogmatik der Samaritaner*, 1876.

2. The Samaritans having secured spiritual guidance among some priestly elements from Jerusalem which were discontented with the reforming work of Ezra and Nehemiah—Manasseh, the grandson of the well-known Eliashib of Nehemiah's memoirs, is mentioned as their first High Priest and the real organiser of their cultus—looked upon the Pentateuch, as it was finally and fully completed, as their only Holy Scripture. The *Samaritan Pentateuch* thus provides us with a recension of the text, independent of the M.T., belonging to the time shortly after its definitive completion and close; for we must suppose its reception on the part of the Samaritans to have taken place already in the fourth century. This Samaritan Pentateuch[1] coincides substantially with the M.T., though showing some 6000 variants as compared with it, a considerable proportion of which derive special importance from the fact that the LXX. is in agreement with them against the M.T. Of "tendency"-alterations the only demonstrable instance is the

[1] First published by J. Morinus in the Paris Polyglot; printed in Hebrew characters by B. Kennicott and B. Blayney in 1790.

comparatively quite innocent one in Deut. xxvii. 4, where the Samaritans have changed עֵיבָל (Ebal) into גְּרִזִים (Gerizim), in order that the stones with the Law might be made to stand upon their own holy mountain of Gerizim. The written characters of the Samaritan Pentateuch are the old Hebrew ones with some embellishments; the point serves as word-divider, and to distinguish words specially liable to be confused they use a diacritical dash above, of the form of the Hebrew raphe. Besides the old Hebrew Pentateuch they possess a Targum in their own Samaritan dialect, which was also issued by J. Morinus in the Paris Polyglot, and has recently been printed in Hebrew square character by A. Brull (1873–1875); a scientific edition was published by Petermann-Vollers (1872–1891).

The Alexandrian Translation

LITERATURE: The literature dealing with the LXX. is enormous. Copious references are given in Reuss, 2nd ed., § 438; Buhl, §§ 37–42; and Strack, 5th ed., 194–197.

Epoch-making and of fundamental importance for the development of this branch of scientific method is the work of Paul de Lagarde: *Anmerkungen zur griechischen Uebersetzung der Proverbien*, 1863; *Genesis Graece*, 1868; *Vorbemerkungen zu meiner Ausgabe der Septuaginta (Symmicta*, ii. 137–148, 1880); *Ankündigung einer neuen Ausgabe der griechischen Uebersetzung des alten Testaments*, 1882; *Librorum Veteris Testamenti canonicorum pars prior Graece*, 1883; *Novae Psalterii Graeci Editionis specimen*, 1887; *Septuaginta Studien*, i. 1891; *Psalterii Graeci quinquagena prima*, 1892; E. Nestle, *Septuagintastudien*, 4 Hefte, 1886–1903, and *R.E.*, 3rd ed., iii. 2 ff. The best manual ed. of the LXX. is the Cambridge one edited by H. B. Swete, in 3 vols., 1887–1894, and with this *An Introduction to the Old Testament in Greek*, 1900. A new large (Cambridge) ed. of the LXX. is being prepared by A. E. Brooke and N. Maclean, (first part just issued).

3. The oldest and in every respect the most important translation of the entire O.T. is the Greek one which was made in Alexandria, and which is usually termed the LXX. The fables about its *origin* go back to the so-called Letter of Aristeas.[1] Of the apocryphal character of this fabrication there can, of course, be no doubt, but still the question arises whether we can simply ignore its entire contents, whether after all it is not essentially right in representing that it was the "literary zeal of Hellenism and not the needs of the Jewish communities in the matter of divine worship which afforded the immediate occasion for the writing down of the Greek Pentateuch" (Wellhausen). In the first instance, indeed, only the Pentateuch was translated, and it is the Pentateuch alone with which the Letter of Aristeas is concerned; but the rest of the sacred books of the Jews were certainly annexed to this very soon. The Prologue of the grandson of ben Sira already, *circa* 130, shows evidence of acquaintance with ὁ νόμος καὶ αἱ προφητεῖαι καὶ τὰ λοιπὰ τῶν βιβλίων in Greek translation, the imperfections of which he pleads in extenuation of some deficiencies in his own translation of the work of his grandfather. It is characteristic that, wherever any more detailed and intimate information is specified of the translators, it is Palestinians who appear in this rôle. The seventy-two translators of the Pentateuch come from Palestine, six from each of the twelve tribes of Israel; the grandson of ben Sira has recently immigrated into

[1] Printed as an appendix to Swete's "Introduction," by H. St John Thackeray, and also conveniently accessible in E. Kautzsch's "Pseudepigraphen des A.T.," pp. 1–31.

Egypt; and Esther, also, according to its superscription,[1] purports to have been translated by a native of Jerusalem: and this is hardly an accident. "In most cases Palestinians will really have understood Greek better than Jews born in Egypt understood Hebrew" (Buhl, p. 124; E.T., p. 123). The translations of the individual books were, of course, made by various translators, and are, therefore, of very different value and character; from the strictest literalness to the greatest freedom, from admirable competence to the crassest bungling, we thus have practically all varieties represented; but on the whole the work is a marvellous achievement if one considers that the translators, without any aids, made their translation from a language which was already in the grip of decay and death into a totally foreign idiom: in the history of the activities of the human spirit it is the first example of a whole literature being translated into a totally foreign language. To us its value is quite inestimable—not only because it was the means of imparting the O.T. to the entire Christian Church: its text is some centuries older than the period when our M.T. was fixed, and more than a thousand years older than the oldest Hebrew MS.; thus it is for us, apart from the Samaritan Pentateuch, the oldest witness of the O.T. text.

4. That a certain *official character* belonged to this translation from the first has nothing to attest it and is also not probable; but all the same the work met with a grateful and warm reception. Moreover, the possession of Holy Scripture in the Greek world-language constituted an unequalled means for

[1] But *cf.* Jacob, "Z.A.T.W.," x. 280–287, 1890.

APPROXIMATION TO ORIGINAL TEXT

forwarding the Jewish propaganda and winning proselytes. In this way the Alexandrian Bible at the time of Jesus had come to be in universal use; Philo makes use of it exclusively, Josephus and the N.T. writers predominantly; the words of Gen. ix. 27 were applied to it, and it was even permitted to utter the prayer of the שמע (*Shema*) in Greek (*cf.* Buxtorf, "Lex. talm.," 104). But this was very soon changed when after the destruction of Jerusalem Judaism tended to become ever more exclusive in its feeling of nationality, and ever more dogged in its maintenance of the letter-principle, and when, on the other hand, the powerful and growing Church derived arguments from the LXX. against the Synagogue. By this time among the Jews the Greek translation was put on a par with the manufacture of the golden calf, and it was said that at the completion of the LXX. a three-days' darkness descended over the whole earth. As the LXX. did, as a matter of fact, diverge considerably from the M.T., which at that time was beginning to assume a fixed and rigid form, accusations of falsification of the text were raised on both sides; the quarrel grew ever more embittered, the prospect of mutual understanding ever more remote. Thus arose

The Later Greek Translations

LITERATURE: F. Field, *Origenis Hexaplorum quae supersunt*, tom. i., 1875, pp. xvi.–xlii.

5. The oldest of these, and the one which enjoyed by far the highest reputation among the Jews, was prepared by Aquila, about whose person a whole garland of myths has been woven. He is said to

have been a proselyte from Pontus, brother-in-law of the Emperor Hadrian, and first prefect of the town of Aelia Capitolina, which was erected on the ruins of Jerusalem, as well as a pupil of Rabbi Akiba. This last statement is essentially correct in so far that the value he places upon the (mere) letters betrays the influence of Akiba: the time also suits on the whole, for possibly Justin Martyr, and certainly Irenaeus, are already acquainted with his work and make mention of him, so that we must assign his active career to a date well in the second quarter of the second century. His principal effort in the translation is directed towards securing the strictest literalness of rendering: in Gen. v. 2 he writes ἐννακόσια ἔτος καὶ τριάκοντα ἔτος, קרב is always translated by ἔγκατον, לֵאמֹר by τῷ λέγειν, the הֵ by δε as οἴκονδε νότονδε, לָמוֹ by εἰς ἀπό as εἰς ἀπό ἡμερῶν for לְמֵימֵי, the mark of the accusative את, when joined with the article, always by σύν; it is specially characteristic of him to strive to render Hebrew words into Greek by their etymological equivalents: thus ראשית is rendered by κεφαλαῖον, יִצְהָר by στιλπνότης, כְּתַרוּנִי (Ps. xxii. 13) by διεδηματίσαντί με. And in this effort, not content with its first result, he, according to Jerome's express testimony (on Ezek. iii. 15), executed a second (*secunda*) edition *quam Hebraei* κατὰ ἀκρίβειαν *nominant*. It need not therefore surprise us to find that in Jewish circles Aquila's translation attained canonical value in the eyes of all who did not understand Hebrew; Ps. xlv. 3 was applied to it, and how considerable its prestige still was in the sixth century, is shown by a remarkable *novella* (No. 146) of Justinian. Recently a fragment of Aquila's translation of Kings has been discovered in the גניזה (*Genîzah*;

cf. § 51, 1 above) of the synagogue at Cairo (ed. by F. C. Burkitt, 1897). It should be added that Aquila's love of literalness is in no wise due to defective knowledge of the Greek tongue; Field has shown that, on the contrary, he must have possessed a considerable amount of specifically Hellenic culture; —he often, for instance, purposely avails himself of the linguistic usage of Homer and Herodotus—while, at the same time, such a grasp of, and penetration into, the genius of Hebrew speech as Aquila's translation throughout testifies to, is only to be looked for in a born Jew.

6. In time the next following of the Greek translators, and, in fact, not much later than Aquila, is Theodotion, whom Irenaeus expressly quotes by name and describes as a proselyte from Ephesus. According to Epiphanius, he also sprang from Pontus, and was originally an adherent of Marcion. Finally, Jerome calls him an Ebionite. Theodotion marks a quite natural reaction against Aquila, whose Hebrew-Greek remained absolutely unintelligible apart from a knowledge of the original text, and indeed was always more in the nature of a work for experts and scholars than for the great public. Theodotion now adopted the course of revising the LXX. He retained what could be retained of it, always, so far as it was feasible, depending on it and seeking to conform it as much as possible to the M.T., and in this way to effect a compromise between both. His work, consequently, enjoyed a large amount of favour: it is chiefly from this source that gaps in the LXX. have been filled in—in our present Greek Job nearly a sixth is derived from Theodotion, and in the case of

Daniel his translation has almost entirely ousted the old LXX. from Church use. It is characteristic of him often to transcribe Hebrew words into Greek letters, instead of translating them, as φθιγιλ Is. iii. 24, βεδεκ Ezek. xxvii. 27, νωκεδειμ Am. i. 1. The latest investigations have shown that Theodotion did not employ as the basis of his work the Greek text of the Bible which is current among us, and which depends substantially upon the Vatican MS. B— the text in which, on account of its close relationship to Origen, we must recognise the Egyptian Bible,—but one which runs through the oldest Christian literature and Josephus, and which may be a Palestinian recension; on account of its intimate relationship to Lucian (see par. 9 of this section below), A. Mez ("Die Bibel des Josephus," 1895) uses the designation "Ur-Lucian" to describe it.

7. The youngest but by far the most important of the Greek translators is Symmachus, who according to the Fathers was an Ebionite, according to Epiphanius a Samaritan who had come over to Judaism, and who at the time of Origen must have been still comparatively new and unknown. His aim was to translate really into Greek: of every sort of syntactical freedom of language, such as participial constructions, genitive absolute, adjectives and adverbs, he makes prodigal use: *e.g.* 2 K. i. 2 in LXX. runs δεῦτε καὶ ἐκζητήσατε, in Symm. ἀπελθόντες πύθεσθε; Job xxxiv. 29 in Theod. καὶ αὐτὸς ἡσυχίαν καὶ τίς καταδικάσεται, in Symm. αὐτοῦ δὲ ἡμερίαν διδόντος τίς κατακρινεῖ; 2 K. ii. 10 in LXX. ἐσκλήρυνας τοῦ αἰτήσασθαι, in Symm. δύσκολον ᾐτήσω; Ps. lv. 24 in LXX. ἄνδρες αἱμάτων καὶ δοχιότητος, in Symm. ἄνδρες μιαίφονοι καὶ

δόλιοι; Ps. xxxiii. 3 in LXX. ἀγαθύνατε ψάλατε, in Symm. ἐπιμελῶς ψάλατε. Jerome in his translation is dependent to a large extent on Symmachus; the statements of the same Father about an *altera editio* in the case of Symmachus also, are, according to Field, *pro mera ignorantiae excusatione habenda*.

The Activity of Origen and its Consequences

LITERATURE : F. Field, *Origenis Hexaplorum quae supersunt*, 2 vols., 1875, 1876.

8. By about the beginning of the third century the LXX. had passed through a history lasting nearly 500 years—an experience which could not, of course, have been gained without leaving traces of its influence on the text of the version. In addition, Judaism in its M.T. possessed an almost canonical form of its Holy Scriptures, so that we can understand how the numerous and notorious divergences of the LXX. from the *Hebraica veritas* must have been the cause of severe searching of heart to the more earnest and learned Christians. In order to elucidate the matter and make it possible for everyone to put it to actual proof and secure the necessary orientation, Origen during the last years of his life in Caesarea, within the years 232–254, took in hand an immense work, the so-called *Hexapla*. Here in six columns he placed in juxtaposition for the O.T. (1) the M.T. in square Hebrew character, (2) the M.T. transcribed into Greek letters (according to J. Halévy, "Journ. Asiat.," ix. 17, pp. 337 ff., 1901, this was in a certain sense an official work of Hellenistic Judaism at Alexandria), (3) the translation of Aquila, (4) the

translation of Symmachus, (5) a text of the LXX. revised by Origen, (6) the translation of Theodotion. As the first two columns were of little general interest, the last four columns were extracted by themselves and then named the Tetrapla. In some Biblical books Origen also gives fragments of three further translations, a Quinta, Sexta, and Septima. The text of the LXX. revised by him he set forth in such a way that the relation of the LXX. to the M.T. was immediately made apparent: all that the M.T. had no equivalent for Origen indicated by the *obelus* ÷, gaps in the LXX. itself he filled in mostly from Theodotion, and marked such by the *asteriscus* *; the period marking the extent of the application of these signs in each case was indicated by the *metobelus* ⌐. Origen's autograph was still in existence at the beginning of the seventh century in Caesarea: with the capture of Palestine by the Arabs it perished. By good fortune, shortly before this event, in the year 617-618, the monophysite Bishop Paul of Tela made a translation of the LXX. column, accompanied with all the critical signs and a selection of Hexaplaric marginal readings, into Syriac, and with such fidelity was this executed that it is possible to reconstruct accurately from it the Greek original, even to the particles. Of this work the Hagiographa and Prophets are preserved in a MS. which is only about a century younger than the work itself, the famous Ambrosianus at Milan, which was published in photo-lithographic facsimile in 1874 by A. M. Ceriani, as being one of the most precious of treasures available for the whole body of O.T. science; all that is extant besides in fragments of the Syrian Hexapla

APPROXIMATION TO ORIGINAL TEXT

has been collected by Lagarde (" Bibliotheca Syriaca," 1892, pp. 33–254).

9. It is obvious that copies of Origen's gigantic work could not be multiplied. A noteworthy fragment, with the entire Hexaplaric text of two, and parts of nine psalms, was discovered in 1896 in a Milan palimpsest, the main facts and characteristics as to which are given by E. Klostermann in "Z.A.T.W." (xvi. 334 ff., 1896). Such were, however, most certainly the rarest exceptions. As a rule people restricted themselves to utilising the MS. at Caesarea and making excerpts from it: but owing to this very fact the confusion became only more intensified. Then the Church took the matter up, and towards the end of the third and beginning of the fourth centuries we meet with three recensions of the O.T. Biblical text, about which some passages in Jerome, that Lagarde was the first to estimate at their true significance, afford us information. According to this, Eusebius and Pamphilus issued the LXX. column of the Hexapla separately with all the diacritical signs, which text was held in high esteem in the Church in Palestine; for Antioch the presbyter Lucian, for Egypt Hesychius, produced a text which was accepted by the Church in each case; of these, the former certainly, the latter possibly, died a martyr's death in 311. Consequently, as Lagarde has recognised and emphatically demanded, it is the first task and pre-requisite of a truly rational criticism of the LXX. to ascertain the text of these three Church recensions. It is natural to expect to find the text of Eusebius and Pamphilus in the Hexaplaric MSS., and above all in the Syriac Hexapla, to which the famous

Vatican Codex B, as was noted by J. Morinus, stands in the closest relation; but Lagarde ("Mitt.," ii. 56) asserts that only one "Codex of the Oktateuch, which almost certainly reproduces the recension of Palestine," is known. As little success so far has been attained in verifying the recension of Hesychius. With Lucian we are more fortunate, his recension having received official sanction throughout the whole of the East from Antioch to Constantinople : thanks to the fact that in the citations of the Antiochene and Constantinopolitan Fathers, such as Theodoret and Chrysostom, a specially rich mass of material lies ready to hand for controlling the text here, the Lucianic recension can be detected and restored with complete certainty. This has been achieved by Lagarde, who in the "Pars Prior," issued in 1883, published the first part of Lucian; the completion of the work was frustrated by Lagarde's death (22nd December 1891). Regarding the manner in which Lucian produced his recension we are able to form a sufficiently accurate judgment. For him also the *Hebraica veritas* is the determinative factor, but all the same he will not allow the old LXX. text to be eliminated entirely, and thus a characteristic of his work is the working of doublets into the text, correction being written side by side with what is corrected, the latter, however, being woven organically into the text: *e.g.* 1 Sam. xii. 2, LXX. κἀγὼ γεγήρακα καὶ καθήσομαι, Luc. καὶ ἐγὼ γεγήρακα καὶ πεπολίωμαι καὶ καθήσομαι ἐκ τοῦ νῦν. Or again, 2 Chron. xiv. 10 לְאֵין כֹּחַ, LXX. freely καὶ ἐν ὀλίγοις, Luc. ἡ ἐν ὀλίγοις οἷς οὐκ ἔστιν ἰσχύς. The text of the LXX. which Lucian used as the basis of his recension is not the Egyptian text of

APPROXIMATION TO ORIGINAL TEXT 523

Origen, but one with peculiar divergent features of its own, which Josephus, the N.T. writers, Theodotion, and the Old Latin version all equally read, and by which the old Syriac version was influenced—viz. that which has been denominated by Mez "Ur-Lucian" (*cf.* par. 6 of this section above).

10. The text of the LXX. has been handed down to us in numerous *manuscripts*, which are all, however, of later date than Origen; many of the more important ones have already been published in full, and of the three most outstanding of these we are in possession of photo-lithographic facsimiles which fully reproduce the actual codices themselves. The largest collection of material is still the work of Holmes-Parsons ("Vetus Test. Graecum cum variis lectionibus," 1798–1827), in which all MSS. known and accessible to the English editors have been collated, but only a selection of the data printed. In spite of all deficiencies, this remains to-day a work of fundamental importance and quite indispensable, making possible, as it does at the very least, a survey of the entire body of facts. The position of affairs thus revealed is one of truly terrible and desperate confusion—so much so, indeed, that we are forced to look about for aid from other quarters for determining the original LXX. text. And here two sources offer us help: viz. the citations in the Fathers, and the secondary versions of the LXX.

The Citations in the Fathers

11. Here one must always be prepared to move on very uncertain ground. When the Fathers are not writing about a Biblical book *ex professo*, whether in

the case of homilies or commentaries, it may always be assumed that they make their quotations purely from memory: in the matter of occasional quotations this may be regarded as the standing rule. At the best they can only serve to define the character of MSS. or families of MSS.: for in spite of any amount of freedom in the individual citation it is possible, having regard to the whole body of the material, as a rule to determine with tolerable accuracy what form of text on the whole a particular Father had before him. Thus, *e.g.*, it has been made possible purely by the citations in Theodoret and Chrysostom to verify the recension of Lucian in definite families of MSS. Of greater importance and promising results of more immediate value are

The Secondary Versions of the LXX.

12. The O.T. also having become Holy Scripture for the Christian Church, the necessity arose in the case of the non-Greek-speaking provinces of the Church to provide translations, which, of course, were based upon the LXX. Undoubtedly the most ancient of these is

(a) The *Vetus Latina*, which, following an obviously corrupt passage in Augustine ("Doctr. Chr.," ii. 14), is usually called the *Itala*.[1] Numerous fragments of this, mostly in palimpsests, are extant. The question as to the time at which the Vetus Latina was formed, and the place of its origin, has not yet been finally

---

[1] On this question *cf.* L. Ziegler, "Die lateinischen Bibelübersetzungen vor Hieronymus und die Itala des Augustins," 1879, and O. F. Fritzsche, "R.E.," 2nd ed., vii. 433 ff.; also E. Nestle, 3rd ed., iii. 26 ff.

settled; regarding the question also as to whether we are to assume a single old Latin version, or several independent ones, there is still division of opinion, as weighty reasons make themselves felt in favour of both alternatives. The time at which it arose will certainly be during the second century. A characteristic of all the fragments that have survived is a laboured adherence to the Greek wording, which is put into Latin with the most painful fidelity, or rather awkwardness. In view of the scarcity of MSS. of this version, the citations in the oldest Latin Fathers possess here a quite outstanding importance; these have been collected in the elaborate work of P. Sabatier ("Bibliorum Sacrorum latinae versiones antiquae," etc., 3 tom., 1739-1749). What has been accomplished in this department, and what must be accomplished, has been shown by Lagarde in his "Probe einer neuen Ausgabe der lateinischen Uebersetzungen des A.T." (1885).

(b) In the second place come the *Coptic Versions*, for the LXX. was translated into all three Coptic dialects, the Upper, Middle, and Lower Egyptian. Of the first two, which are the older, and for us the more important, only fragments are known (for a survey *cf.* G. Steindorff, "Koptische Grammatik," 1894, pp. 213-217): the Lower Egyptian is extant entirely in MSS., but has only been edited partially—the Pentateuch, Psalter, and fragments of the historical books by Lagarde, Job and the prophets by H. Tattam. These translations should possess a special interest from the fact that they were prepared in the native land of the LXX.

(c) In chronological order the next to be mentioned

would be the *Ethiopic Version* (see A. Dillmann, "R.E.," 2nd ed., i. 203 ff., and F. Praetorius, 3rd ed. of same work, iii. 87 ff.). Christianity was brought to the Ethiopians in the reign of Constantine the Great, and very soon after this event the Bible was translated into Ethiopic. Chrysostom († 407) is already acquainted with this fact. The Ethiopic version is fully available in numerous MSS.: of the O.T., the Oktateuch, βασιλειῶν α'–δ', Joel, and a number of apocryphal books have been edited by Dillmann; the Psalter, hymns, and Canticles long ago by H. Ludolf (1701); Isaiah, Obadiah, Malachi, and Lamentations by J. Bachmann. We must distinguish an older version which was made directly from the LXX., and a later recension which has been revised and corrected in accordance with the M.T. The doubt expressed by Lagarde that even the older Ethiopic version "was made after the fourteenth century, not from the Greek, but from an Arabic or Egyptian translation of the original" ("Ankündigung," p. 28; *cf.* also "Material.," i. pp. iv. and v.), needs further proof.[1]

(*d*) To the fourth century also certainly belongs the *Gothic Version* of Ulfilas (editions by H. Massmann and F. L. Stamm). Of the O.T. some fragments from Nehemiah have been preserved, viz. v. 13–18, vi. 14–vii. 3, vii. 13–15: these fragments, however, already suffice to prove that Ulfilas has translated the recension of Lucian (see Lagarde, "Pars Prior," p. xiv.).

(*e*) The translation of the LXX. into *Armenian* by

[1] *Cf.* also T. O. Kramer, "Die aethiop. Uebers. des Zacharias," i. Heft, Diss., 1898; and A. Heider, "Die aethiop. Bibelübersetzung," i. Heft, Diss., 1902.

Miesrob must have been accomplished in the first quarter of the fifth century; this translation was *integra edita, sed mala fide, et jam ante quam ederetur, identidem corrupta*[1] (Lagarde, "Gen. Gr.," p. 18).

Still later secondary versions of the LXX. need not be taken into account for the purposes of textual criticism; at the best the old Slavonic is useful as serving to control the disposition of the Lucianic text in the second half of the ninth century.

13. How this vast mass of material is to be sifted and treated so as to make it possible with its help to reach the original text of the LXX. has been shown in truly magnificent fashion by Lagarde (see esp. "Ankündigung," pp. 29 and 30). But even so we are not yet at the end of our labours, because, as a matter of fact, we are in search not of the LXX. itself but of the Hebrew text underlying it. Consequently in the case of each individual book of the Bible the method and manner of its translation must be determined in order to make it possible to come to some certain conclusion as to the original lying before the translator: having done this, we shall be in possession of a Hebrew MS. independent of the M.T., and from this we must naturally proceed, because it will set forth the oldest tradition that is available for us.

The Targums

LITERATURE: L. Zunz, *Die gottesdienstlichen Vorträge der Juden*, 1832, pp. 61–81; Th. Noldeke, *Die A.T.liche Literatur* (*cf.* § 2, 6 above), 255–261; W. Volck, *R.E.*, 2nd ed., xv. 365

---

[1] "Put forth as a complete whole, but not conscientiously executed, and even before it had been issued had in many places been corrupted."

ff., and E. Nestle, 3rd ed. of same work, iii. 109 ff.; E. Schürer, *Geschichte des jüdischen Volkes*, etc., i. 147 ff., 1901 ; Z. Frankel, *Zu dem Targum der Propheten*, 1872 ; W. Bacher, *Kritische Untersuchungen zum Prophetentargum und über das gegenseitige Verhältnis der pentateuchischen Targumim*, Z.D.M.G., xxviii. 1 ff., 1874 ; A. Merx, *Bemerkungen über die Vokalisation der Targume*, etc. (*cf.* § 50, 2 above), pp. 142-188, and *Chrestomathia Targumica*, 1888.

14. The more the old Hebrew speech fell into disuse (*cf.* Neh. xiii. 24), to give place eventually to *West Aramaic*, so much the more it became urgently necessary for the purposes of public reading in the Synagogue to offer the text to the people in their own idiom. This was effected in such a way that immediately following the public reading a מְתוּרְגְּמָן (*interpreter*) interpreted the text in Aramaic : in the case of the Tora (Law) after each individual verse, in the case of the Prophets three verses might be taken together. As these Aramaic translations, called Targum, formed part of the cultus of the Synagogue, they must have borne an official character, and consequently at quite an early date must have assumed a substantially fixed form, and it is certain that writing was soon utilised for their reproduction : a written Targum to Job is mentioned as in existence at the time of Gamaliel the elder, the contemporary of Jesus, and according to the tradition, rightly understood, what was disallowed was not the writing out of the Targum, but only the use of a written copy in the Synagogue-exposition. The extant written Targums were, it is true, only revised late, but go back far into the pre-Christian period, as is proved by the entire absence in them of an anti-Christian polemic. Except in the cases of Daniel and Ezra-Nehemiah, we possess

APPROXIMATION TO ORIGINAL TEXT

Targums to all the canonical books of the O.T., and that too in more than one form: to the Pentateuch and Prophets a Babylonian and a Jerusalem one, to Esther three distinct Targums.

15. For our purpose the most important is the *Babylonian Targum*. That on the Pentateuch is said to have been composed by Onkelos, a pupil of Rabbis Eliezer and Joshua (most convenient edition the one by A. Berliner, 1884), that on the Prophets by Jonathan ben Uzziel, the principal pupil of Hillel the elder (most convenient edition the one by Lagarde, 1872). In this tradition it is noticeable that the Targum to the Prophets is regarded as being more ancient than that on the Tora (Law), and this view is certainly correct: for the Targum on the Prophets is freer and more spontaneous than that on the Tora, and, further, the necessity for such a paraphrase must have made itself felt in the case of the Prophets sooner than in the case of the Tora. Neither of the two Targums was composed in the first place in Babylonia, as is proved by the markedly Palestinian character of the language, but they underwent final revision in Babylonia, and enjoyed there special prestige. In Palestine, for reasons that can easily be understood, they appear in course of time to have fallen out of use; hence the fact is explained that Origen and Jerome never make mention of them. Later they were once more held in equally high esteem by all Jews; for the Targum Onkelos there is even a special Massora.[1] On the other hand, the

---

[1] See A. Berliner, "Die Massorah zum Targum Onkelos," 1877; and S. Landauer, "Die Mâsôrâh zum Onkelos auf Grund neuer Quellen," 1896

text of the Targum on the Prophets shows many variants (see Cornill, "Z.A.T.W.," vii. 177 ff., 1887).

16. Of the *Jerusalem Targum* we have a complete text on the Tora, which, in consequence of an incorrect explanation of the abbreviation ת"י, has usually been ascribed to Jonathan too, and also another on the Tora, the so-called fragmentary Targum,[1] while the Jerusalem Targum on the Prophets is known only in fragmentary form through occasional citations by Rabbis or on the margin of several MSS., particularly of the Reuchlianus (put together by Lagarde in the apparatus to his edition, and by Bacher, *op. cit.*). It displays the spontaneous character of a natural production, on which account its contents are of the highest interest: its basis also reaches back into the pre-Christian period. The opinion maintained by some scholars that the Jerusalem Targum is the basis of the Babylonian, and that the latter is merely the result of a systematic revision and abbreviation of the former, can hardly be correct.

17. Of the *Hagiographa* also there are Targums (most convenient edition that of Lagarde, 1873); but these never enjoyed such prestige as the Targums on the Tora and Prophets. They are in detail of very different value; that on Proverbs, as J. A. Dathe rightly perceived in 1764, was made not on the original text, but according to the Syriac version, that on Canticles and two on Esther are diffuse and paraphrastic in the Haggadic manner.

---

[1] See J. W. Etheridge, "The Targums of Onkelos and Jonathan ben Uzziel on the Pentateuch, with the fragments of Jerusalem Targum, from the Chaldee," 2 vols., 1862, 1865; and J. Bassfreund, "Das Fragmententarg. z. Pent.," 1896.

18. In order to utilise the *Targum as evidence in matters of textual criticism*, much circumspection and a considerable amount of tact are needed, such as can only be acquired by complete familiarity with the method and manner characteristic of this branch of literature. That is to say, the peculiar double character of the Targum must be kept steadily in view, the fact, viz., that it is intended to be not simply a translation but also at the same time an explanation for the people, and that on this account the utmost pains was taken to remove and by paraphrase to render innocuous anything which might have given rise to misunderstanding or have given occasion to direct scandal. But yet this freedom is accompanied by such faithfulness with regard to the *litera scripta* that in quite a considerable number of cases it is even possible in paraphrastic renderings of the utmost freedom to detect with certainty the Hebrew text underlying the Targum: under such circumstances the latter must rank as the oldest witness to the O.T. text on its native ground of Palestine.

The Old Syriac Version

LITERATURE: J. Perles, *Meletemata Peschitthoniana*, 1859; E. Nestle, *R.E.*, 3rd ed., iii. 167 ff.; A. Rahlfs, *Beiträge zur Textkritik der Peschita*, *Z.A.T.W.*, ix. 161 ff., 1889. The most convenient manual edition is that of S. Lee, 1823, prepared for the English Bible Society; most correct text, that printed in 1852 by the American missionaries at Urmia. For supplementing these: *Libri VI. apocryphi Syriace e recognitione*, P. de Lagarde, 1861.

19. This version is usually designated by a name which has not yet received any certain explanation—

the Peschittô.[1] According to Syrian tradition, the translation is said to have been made in the time of the pious King Abgar of Edessa and of the Apostle Addai; in any case it is of Christian origin, and the O.T. was translated in conjunction with the New, and it may very likely have been effected in the second century. The O.T. is directly translated from the Hebrew, and therefore originally did not include the Apocrypha, nor, strange to say, Chronicles, the Syriac translation of which was only made much later in accordance with a Jewish Targum.[2] We possess very ancient MSS. of the Syriac version, going back as far as the fifth century (the famous Ambrosianus was published in photo-lithographic facsimile by A. Ceriani, 1879–1883), and, moreover, in the citations of Aphraates and Ephrem a rich store of material from the fourth century is available for controlling the text. For the determination of the old Syriac text of the Bible Rahlfs has pointed out the way in showing how to distinguish an East- and West-Syrian recension, the former being that of the Nestorians; the latter would be divisible into a Jacobite, Melchite, and Maronite text. The Psalter according to the West-Syrian recension, with text-critical apparatus, has been edited by W. E. Barnes (1904).

20. The Peshittô cannot at once be utilised for the purposes of the textual criticism of the O.T., even in

---

[1] The most recent conjecture, and one that is highly attractive, is that suggested by Mez (*op. cit.*, par. 6 of this section above), p. 4.

[2] See S. Fränkel, "J. p. Th.," v. 508 ff., 720 ff., 1879; and W. E. Barnes, "An Apparatus Criticus to Chronicles in the Peshitta Version," 1897.

the event of its original text being determined. For one thing, the Syrian translators have carried out the work of translation with a certain freedom, and then again Targumistic features can be traced, and, above all, LXX. influence is already apparent in the work of the original translators: at a later time the Peshiṭthô was systematically revised or corrected in accordance with the LXX. It is of salient importance more especially for the history of exegesis: that it is distinguished by displaying an essentially correct and good understanding of its original cannot be gainsaid.

Hieronymus (Jerome)

LITERATURE: O. Zöckler, *Hieronymus, Sein Leben und Wirken,* 1865; W. Nowack, *Die Bedeutung des Hieronymus für die Textkritik des A.T.*, 1875; C. Siegfried, *Die Aussprache des Hebräischen bei Hieronymus*, Z.A.T.W., iv. 34 ff., 1884; H. Rönsch, *Itala und Vulgata*, 1869; F. Kaulen, *Geschichte der Vulgata*, 1868, and *Handbuch zur Vulgata*, 1870; E. Nestle, *Ein Jubiläum der lateinischen Bibel, Marginalien* (cf. § 17 above), No. 4 (with special paging).

21. The condition of the text of the Vetus Latina in course of time grew to be such that some means of remedying it became imperatively necessary, and increasingly so as the number of new districts won for the Church in which no Greek, but only Latin, was understood grew ever more numerous. With this task Jerome, as being the most learned of the theologians of the time, was entrusted by Pope Damasus. His object primarily was to correct the Vetus Latina and to eliminate its worst faults. In the case of the Psalter he accomplished this twice over, once in accordance with the LXX. (Psalterium Romanum), and a second time according to the

Hexaplaric text (Psalterium Gallicanum), and interested himself in the plan of revising the whole of the O.T. after the Hexapla, of which his edition of Job is still extant.[1] But he was soon convinced that this was not the right course to take, but that he must rather translate the O.T. entirely afresh from the *Hebraica veritas*, which he had learnt to know and understand at the hands of Jewish teachers. This work he began about the year 392 with the Books of Kings, which are consequently prefaced with the famous " Prologus galeatus," and he brought the undertaking to a close in the year 405 with the Psalter, which, however, did not pass into the usage of Church worship because the congregations had, through the liturgy, become too much habituated to the ancient text. At first his work in general excited the liveliest opposition: two hundred years later it was still not fully accepted, for according to the testimony of Gregory the Great (in the Preface to the " Moralia " on Job) the *sedes apostolica* itself still utilised the old translation by the side of that of Jerome, and it is easy to see that under such circumstances only very small security existed for the preservation of Jerome's work in complete purity. But after it had once secured general recognition its importance became immense, much greater, indeed, than that of the LXX. itself. And though Jerome, following the bent of his somewhat irresolute nature, did not proceed in his task with sufficient vigour and energy, and often left the traditional material untouched even in cases

[1] Edited by Lagarde, "Mitteilungen," ii. 189-237, with which should be compared G. Beer, "Z.A.T.W.," xvi. 297 ff., 1896; xvii. 97 ff., 1897; and xviii. 257 ff., 1898.

APPROXIMATION TO ORIGINAL TEXT

where he perceived its incorrectness, yet his work on the whole and as a whole is a wonderful achievement, one worthy of the highest praise. On the question of his method of translation, *cf.* the painstaking monograph of Nowack.

22. Such are the *positive aids* that are at hand to enable us to approximate to the original text, after all preliminary questions and preliminary work have been so far disposed of that the independent evidence of the texts themselves can be utilised in substitution for the Hebrew MSS. underlying them. This material has then to be worked up, with the unrestricted co-operation of emendation and conjecture, in accordance with the approved principles of philological-critical method. In this way text-critical work has been done by A. Merx on Job (§ 43 above) and Joel (§ 28 above), by C. H. Cornill on Ezekiel (§ 26 above), and by V. Ryssel on Micah (§ 32 above); a critical text of the entire O.T. is the professed aim of the large collective work inaugurated in 1893 by C. Siegfried's "Job" (§ 43 above), which is appearing under the general title, "A Critical Edition of the Hebrew Text: under the editorial direction of Paul Haupt," and of which only the Books of Exodus, Deuteronomy, the Minor Prophets (XII.), and Megilloth have not yet appeared.

Remark.—As being the most accessible mines for reaching this material, THE POLYGLOTS deserve a brief further remark. The first of these is the so-called *Complutensian*, printed (1514–1517) at Alcala, the Complutum of the Romans, in six folio volumes, at the expense of Ximenez, Archbishop of Toledo, who took in hand the entire work, and secured the co-operation of the most important Spanish scholars. The O.T. contains the M.T., with the Pentateuch, the Targum Onkelos, the LXX.

(both with a careful Latin translation), and the Vulgate. The LXX. text is noteworthy because Ximenez accidentally based his printed text upon MSS. which reproduce the recension of Lucian (*cf.* Lagarde, "Mitt.," i. 122 f.). The second is the so-called *Antwerp* (or *Regia*), printed at Antwerp (1569-1572) at the expense of Philip II., in eight folio volumes, by the famous firm of Plantin. For it the learned Dominican Benedictus Arias Montanus has secured the largest amount of credit. In respect of the O.T. it is essentially a reprint of the Complutensian, except that the Targum for the whole of the O.T. is given with Latin translation, not, however, as an independent piece of work, but in accordance with the MSS. of Cardinal Ximenez, which had been left ready for the press (see Merx, *op. cit.*, par. 14 of this section above, pp. 153-157). A substantial advance was effected by the third, the *Paris Polyglot*, printed at the expense of the parliamentary advocate Le Jay in ten folio volumes (1629-1645). The Antwerp Polyglot is reprinted, but to it there are added for the O.T. the Samaritan Pentateuch with Targum, and further the entire Peshiṭtho and a complete Arabic translation—all these accompanied with Latin versions. The richest in content and most valuable is the fourth, the *London Polyglot*, edited by Brian Walton, Bishop of Chester, in six folio volumes (1653-1657), with the co-operation of the famous English scholars Edmund Castle and Edward Pococke. Walton has reprinted the Paris Polyglot, and has added in the O.T. the Ethiopic translation of Psalms and Canticles, and for the Pentateuch the Targum of Pseudo-Jonathan and the so-called "Fragmentary Targum," as well as a Persian translation. All these texts, in comparison with the Paris Polyglot, have been essentially improved, and placed together synoptically; in particular, however, the collection of variants which fills the whole of the sixth volume invests the work with a high scientific value. As a brilliant *finale* there was added in 1669 Edmund Castle's wonderful "Lexicon Heptaglotton" (Hebrew, Chaldee, Syriac, Samaritan, Ethiopic, Arabic, and Persian).

Other so-called Polyglots are destitute of scientific value.

APPENDIX

SURVEY OF THE PROCESS OF DEVELOPMENT THROUGH WHICH THE OLD TESTAMENT LITERATURE PASSED, IN ACCORDANCE WITH THE RESULTS REACHED IN THE SPECIAL INTRODUCTION

Pre-Monarchical Period

The Song of Debora.
Utterances concerning individual tribes.

Period of the Earliest Monarchy

David's authentic poem of the "Song of the Bow," 2 Sam. i. 19-27.
Solomon's authentic utterance on the Dedication of the Temple, 1 Kings viii. 12-13, LXX.
The so-called *Blessing of Jacob*, Gen. xlix. 1-27, in its traditional form.

The Period of the Divided Kingdom.

Israel.	Judah.
The Book of the Wars of Jahve.	The Book of the Upright (Jashar).

The Original Balaam-Oracles.
Beginnings of Written History: the Book of the Covenant, Ex. xxi.-xxiii.

ISRAEL.	JUDAH.

850–750. Ephraimite accounts about Elijah and Elisha worked up in 1 Kings xvii.–2 Kings xiii.

Jahvist (J¹) writing in the reign of Jehoshaphat, *circa* 850.

The so-called *Blessing of Moses*, Deut. xxxiii. (*circa* 800, reign of Jeroboam II.).

Circa 760. Amos, a Judaean, but working exclusively in Israel.

Circa 750. The large historical work of the Elohist.

J² in Genesis (date cannot be exactly stated).

Circa 745. Hosea i.–iii.

Anarchy following the extirpation of the dynasty of Jehu.

Between 738 and 735, Hosea iv.–xiv.

Death-year of Uzziah at the latest 736.

Isaiah's consecration to prophetic work.

Before 722—
  Is. vi.
    ii.–iv., ix. 1–x. 4, v., i. 2–3, 21–31.
    xvii. 1–11, vii., viii.
    xxviii. 1–4.

After the Destruction of Samaria (722)

During Sargon's reign, 722–705 :—
Is. xx. (of the year 711); xiv. 28–32 after Sargon's death.

During Sennacherib's reign :—
From 705–701. i. 18–19, xvii. 12–xviii. 6.
              x. 5–32†, xiv. 24–27.
              xxii. 1–14, xxviii. 7–xxxi.
Before 701.   xxii. 15 ff.

APPENDIX 539

About 701. Micah i.–iii.

After 701. Is. i. 4–17 ; date indefinable, ix. 1–6, xi. 1–8.

Still in Hezekiah's reign (?): Judaean history of the Temple, 2 Kings xi.–xii., xvi., xviii. 4, 14–16, perhaps also 1 Kings vi. and vii. (?).

During the reign of Manasseh :—
Micah vi. 1–vii. 6.

Circa 650. E^2, revision of E by an Ephraimite (who had remained behind in the land) on the basis of the more advanced development of prophetic ideas.

The latest Jahvistic (but still pre-Deuteronomic) passages.

Rj, the union and adjustment of J and E ; second half of the seventh century (still pre-Deuteronomic).

During the reign of Josiah :—
Circa 630. Zephaniah.
    627. Jeremiah's consecration to prophetic work.
    621. Promulgation of the original Deuteronomy (which had been written shortly before), and reform of the cultus on the basis of it.
    615. Habakkuk i. 1–ii. 11.
    608. Nahum.

During the reign of Jehoiachim :—
    605. First writing down of original roll of Jeremiah.
    604. Enlarged second edition of same.

Circa 600. Substantial completion of the Book of Kings by Rd^1.

Before 597. Jer. xiii. 15–17, 20–27, xiv.–xv.†, xvi.–xvii.†, xx. 7–18 ?, xii. 7–18, xxxv.

During the reign of Jehoiachin :—
Jer. xiii. 18–19.

597. Ezekiel deported with Jehoiachin.

During the reign of Zedekiah :—
592. Ezekiel's consecration to prophetic work in Babylonia at the Chebar.

Before 586. Jer. xxiv., xxix., xlix. 34–39, xxii., xxiii., xxi., xxxii. 1–15.

After the destruction of Jerusalem :—Jer. xxxi. 31–34, xlvi. 13–36.

APPENDIX

The Babylonian Exile

First Half

Baruch's biographical memoranda *re* Jeremiah.
October 572. The writing down and final close of Ezekiel's book.
April 570. Supplementary interpolation of Ezek. xxix. 17-21.
Deuteronomistic diorthosis of Deuteronomy. (already begun in the pre-exilic period).
Lam. ii. and iv. later than Ezekiel.

Second Half

Redaction of the large exilic Book of the History of the People of Israel (written in the spirit of Deuteronomy); in the case of the Pentateuch, Joshua, Judges, and Samuel by Rd, in the case of Kings by Rd^2.
Beginnings of the collection and redaction of the pre-exilic prophetic writings.
P^1, first systematic noting down of Toroth of a priestly character.
Lam. v.
Is. xxi. 1-10 (and 11-17), on the first emergence of the Persians on the political horizon.
Is. xl.-xlviii., between 546 and 538.
Is. xiii. 2-xiv. 21, shortly before 538.

The Persian Period

Immediately after 538. Is. xlix.-lv.
September to December 520. Haggai.
November 520 to December 518. Zechariah i.-viii.
Between 538 and 500. Ps. cxxxvii.
Circa 500. P^2 formed in Babylonia.
Before 458. Malachi.
    Union of P^2 with P^1.
Circa 450. The history of the Temple and of the building of the wall, written in Aramaic.
Before 444. Is. lvi.-lxvi.
444. Solemn promulgation of the priestly legislation ($P^1 + P^2$).
    The Book of Ruth.
    The Song of the Exodus, Ex. xv. 1-18 (older than Ezra's memoirs).

APPENDIX 541

After 444. Ezra's memoirs.
After 432. Nehemiah's memoirs.
Between 450 and 400. The original Obadiah and Is. xv.–xvi.?
Circa 400. Hexateuch substantially brought to a close by Rp.
Compilation of and selection from the memoirs of Ezra and Nehemiah by the author of Ezra x. and Neh. viii. 1–ix. 5.

In the Fourth Century

Final form of the historical books. Gen. xiv.
(P^x) in the Hexateuch. Rp in Judges and Samuel.
Joel (at the end of the Persian period, after 400).
Bulk of the Psalter of the period of the Second Temple, and older than Chronicles (thus between 450 and 250).
Proverbs in its older parts.
Canticles (at the earliest).
Final form of Lamentations.
Midrash on the Book of Kings.

348. Is. xxiii., elegy on destruction of Sidon ⎱ by Artaxerxes III
343. Is. xix. 1–15, elegy on the punishment ⎰ Ochus.
of Egypt

Greek Period.

Circa 330. Is. xxiv.–xxvii.
   280. Zechariah ix.–xiv.
   275. Translation of the Pentateuch into Greek: beginning of the LXX.
   250. The Chronicler, who was at the same time author of the book Ezra-Nehemiah in its present form.
Proverbs i.–ix., xxx.–xxxi.
Jonah.
Before the close of the collection of the prophetic writings: its more or less thorough and systematic revision on the basis of the dogmatic system of later Judaism and of the eschatological-apocalyptic hopes of the latter.
250–200. Close of the collection of the prophetic writings.
   Job, in any case later than Proverbs i.–ix.

204. Koheleth (according to Hitzig).
Circa 200. Latest diorthosis (after the LXX.) in the historical and prophetic books.

Maccabean Period

Pss. xliv., lxxiv., lxxix., lxxxiii. (for certain).
January 164 (in any case not much earlier). Daniel.
Circa 130. The Book of Esther (which certainly originated in Persia).

INDEX

I. SUBJECTS

ABEN EZRA doubts the authenticity of the Pentateuch, 35; and of Deutero-Isaiah, 265, 287.

Accentuation at the same time supplies the place of punctuation, 495.

Akiba, Rabbi, maintains the equal canonicity of the entire Scriptures, 480; establishes the treatment of Scripture which depends on the letters, 500; Aquila said to have been a pupil of R. Akiba, 516.

Alexander Jannaeus, the question of Psalms by or concerning, 409 f.

Alterations, deliberate and designed, of the traditional text, 507 f.

Apocalyptic literature, character of, 383; Is. xxiv.–xxvii. (p. 278 f.), xxxiv.–xxxv. (p. 281 f.), Joel (p. 328), and Daniel (p. 383) are apocalyptic in character.

Aquila, translator of the Bible, 515 f.

Archaisms, supposed, of the Pentateuch absent in Joshua, 155.

Archetype of Massoretic text, 499 f.; unequal value of the text of various books in, 501; employed the *literae finales*, and had a system of word-division, 501.

Artistic form of Lamentations, 413; Proverbs, 437 f., 440; Canticles, 459 f.

BALAAM oracles, 121 f.

Baruch, the pupil and friend of Jeremiah, writes the prophet's discourses at the latter's dictation, 297; his biographical chronicle of Jeremiah, 300 f., 313.

Beeri, father of the prophet Hosea, said to have written Is. viii. 19–20, 320.

Ben Ascher, 503 f.

Ben Naphtali, 503 f.

Bethar, the Bible-codex from, 500 f.

Bomberg Bible, the, divides Samuel (p. 181) and Kings (p. 206) into two books.

Book of the Covenant, the (Ex. xxi.–xxiii.), 128–132; was already known to Deuteronomy, and used by the latter, 63 f., 69–73; originally belonged to E, and stood in the latter in the place now occupied by Deuteronomy, 131 f.; is a deposit of old Israelitish customary law, of the early regal period, 131 f.; Rd its author, 141; Book of Deuteronomy also so called, 50 f.

Book of the Upright (or Valiant), *see* Jashar.

Book of the Wars of Jahve, the, 35, 120.
Bow, Song of the (2 Sam. i. 19–27), 203, 400.

CALEB, was the author of the Book of Malachi so called? 376.
Calvin recognises Maccabean Psalms, 407.
Canonicity, criterion of, 481 f.
Canticles, *see* Song of Songs.
Catchwords influence arrangement in Isaiah, 293; in Psalms, 401; in Proverbs, 443.
Chronicles, Biblical Book of, already presupposes P^x as Mosaic Tora, 148; read Samuel in its present form, 196, 202; is counted as one book in the Hebrew Canon, 226; originally formed one book with Ezra-Nehemiah, and is by the same author, 249–252; exhibits the musical-liturgical expressions which occur in the Psalm-superscriptions, 394; only knows David as a singer of psalms, 400; its relation to particular Psalm - passages, 405 f.; it has no knowledge of Solomonic proverbial poetry and of a literary commission by Hezekiah, 446; the book originally lacking in the Peschittô, and then translated later in accordance with a Jewish Targum, 532.
Chronicles of the Kings of Israel and Judah, cited in Kings, *passim*; relation of the same to the old official court-annals and to the author of Kings, 210–213; to the Chronicler, 236 f.
Chronology, of Genesis, relation of the, to the Chaldean, 111 f.; divergent tradition of, 474;

of the Book of Judges, 168–170, 179; in Samuel, 184, 196, 201; in Kings, 208 f., 211.
Circumcision, its place in P, 110.
Conjecture, the necessity and justification for using, 509 f., 535.
Coptic translations of the Bible, 525.
Covenant, Book of the, *see under* Book (of the Covenant).

DANIEL, position of, in the Canon, 386, 471, 477; name and person of, derived from Ezekiel, 389; Greek translation of, by Theodotion, ousts LXX. of, 517 f.
David, elegy of, on the death of Saul and Jonathan, *see s.v.* Bow, Song of the; "last words of" (2 Sam. xxiii. 1–7), 204 f.; David as a Psalmist, and the Psalms ascribed to him, 394–401.
Deborah, Song of, 160 f.
Decalogue, the First, belongs to E^2, 81 f.; E^1 also possessed a Decalogue, 82, 130 f., 138.
"Defile the hands" = canonical, 471 f.; doubted in the case of certain books, 478 f.
Designation of particular books, differences in, 465, 468.
Deutero-Isaiah, how united with the Book of Isaiah, 293, 294.
Deuteronomy essentially distinguished from the rest of the Pentateuchal books, 46; the prophetic character of its legislation regarded as a compromise between prophecy and priesthood, 62; presupposes J E throughout, but shows no trace of P, 69–75; united with J E by Rd, 140 f.; Deuteronomy normative for

the real author of Kings, 209 ; the exilic view of the history determined by it, 222 f.; with its publication the idea of a canonical book appears for the first time, 464 f.

Divergences from the traditional text dictated by religious scruples or on grounds of propriety, 505.

Drama, the, unknown among the Semites and Hebrews, 459 f.

E = ELOHISTIC stratum in Hexateuch. E has knowledge of an Ark, 74 ; is not older than the period of the monarchy, and is younger than J, 76-78; its author an Ephraïmite who wrote in the reign of Jeroboam II., 79 f; revised about 100 years later by E^2, 80-84; possessed no primaeval history, 87; cites and makes use of the Book of the Wars of Jahve, 120 f.; embodied the Blessing of Moses, 125 f.; was worked up with and assimilated to J by Rj, 136-140, but still lay before the Deuteronomic authors in the form of an independent writing, 140 ; the presence of E in Joshua, 153 f. ; in Judges, 171-177 ; prepares the way for the theological pragmatism of Judges, 173, 178; the presence of E in Samuel, 187, 193-201. Traces of E^2 in 1 Sam. vii.-xii., xv. 24-31, 188; in 2 Sam. vii. ? 197; is its presence to be detected in 1 K. xi. 29-39, xii. 1-20, xiv. 1-18? 213.

Elias Levita on the close of the O.T. Canon, 470.

Elihu speeches, the, 425-431.

Elijah and Elisha, history of, contains four distinct Ephraimitic sources, 214 f.

Epilogue, the, to Job, 423, 434 f. ; to Koheleth, 454.

Epiphanius, makes mention of the fivefold division of the Psalter, 402 ; of twenty-two canonical books, 467 ; on Theodotion and Symmachus, 517 f.

Esther, canonicity of, disputed, 257, 479 f.; threefold Targum to, 261, 530; read at Feast of Purim, 466 f.

Ethiopic versions of the Bible, 525 f.

Eusebius and Pamphilus issue the LXX. column of the Hexapla of Origen separately, 521.

Exile, the Babylonian, how far specially favourable in external conditions for the production of P, 114; literary activity in the production of historical work during, 222 f.; the beginning of the collection and redaction of the Prophetic Writings in, 476.

Exodus, Song of the, Ex. xv. 1-19, 118 f.

Ezekiel, the prophet, his relation to P, 108 f. ; his relation to the Law of Holiness, 135 f.; the dating of his prophecies, is it a literary fiction? 317 f.; has knowledge of a Daniel who was pious and wise, 389 ; Lam. ii. and iv. dependent on Ezekiel, 416 f. ; Ezekiel shows no knowledge of the Book of Job, 433; but is acquainted with the name and person of Job, 434 ; Book of Ezekiel in danger of being "hidden," 478 f.

Ezekiel, name of a Jewish-Greek dramatist, 459.
Ezra effects the public recognition of P as binding law on the community, 105 f.; P at this time included P^1 and P^2 (united, but not by Ezra himself); but not P^x, which is younger than Ezra, 112 f.; Ezra's memoirs, 113, 244 f., 247; Ezra said to have fixed the Canon, 470; to have introduced the "square character" in writing, 489; and the vocalisation of the sacred text, 501.
Ezra and Nehemiah, one book in the Hebrew Canon, 241.

FATHERS (the Church), citations from the LXX. in, 523 f.; from the *Vetus Latina* in, 525; of the Peschiṭthô in (Aphraates and Ephrem), 532.
Festival Rolls, the five, 466 f.

GOETHE, on the Pentateuch, 36.
Gothic version, the, of the Scriptures, 526.

H, *see* Holiness, Law of.
Haggai, dating of his discourses, 359 f.
Hammurabi, Code of, parallels to, in the Book of the Covenant, 131 f.
Hananja ben Hiskia, Rabbi, prevents the Book of Ezekiel being "hidden," 478.
Hannah, Song of (1 Sam. ii. 1–10), 202 f.
Hesychius establishes in Egypt a text of the LXX. officially recognised by the Church there, 521 f.
Hexapla of Origen, the, 519 f.; the Psalterium Gallicanum translated from the Hexaplaric text, 534; also Jerome's edition of Job, 534.

Hezekiah, Psalm of, 283 f.; literary commission appointed by, 445 f.
"Hiding" a book, significance of the expression, 472, 478 f.
Hieronymus, *see* Jerome.
Hilkiah, a priest, makes public Deuteronomy, 52 f., 106; this Hilkiah not the father of Jeremiah, 296.
Holiness, Law of (H) = Lev. xvii.–xxvi.; stands midway between Deuteronomy and P, 132 f.; compiled by the author of Lev. xxvi. 3–45, on the basis of an older written collection, but later revised so as to accord with P, 133; its relation to Ezekiel, 135; had already by the time of Ezra been united with P^2, 135 f. (*cf.* also 112 f.); other elements possibly belonged to it (outside Lev. xvii.–xxvi.), 136.
Homoioteleuton, significance of, in the textual criticism of the M.T., 506.

IDDO, the anonymous prophet of (1 K. xiii.), 238.
Inspiration, prophetic, required of a writing admitted into the Canon, 482.
Irenaeus has knowledge of Aquila, 516, and Theodotion, 517.
Isaiah, position of, in the Hebrew Canon, 294, 318, 466, 468.
Itala, *see* Vetus Latina.
Iṭṭûr Sôferîm, 507 f.

J = JAHVISTIC stratum in the Hexateuch. J not older than the period of the monarchy, but is older than E, 76–78; most probably of Judaean origin, and not a literary

INDEX 547

unity, 85 f.; primaeval history in, 87-90; secondary elements in J outside the primaeval history, 90; time of origin and formation, 90 f.; already contained the Blessing of Jacob, 117 f.; included also a full Balaam-history, 121 f.; was worked up into and assimilated with E by Rj, 136-140; J in Joshua, 153 f.; in Judges, 171-177; in Samuel, 189-191, 193-201; J^2 in 1 Sam. x. 8, xiii. 7-15, 189; in 2 Sam. vii.? 197; in Kings, 207; many reminiscences of, in Book of Ruth, 255.

Jacob, Blessing of, 117 f.

Jamnia, Synod of, 480.

Jashar, Book of, 153, 203, 207 f.

"Jehovist," see Rj.

Jeremiah, still read in 1 Sam. vii. a description of the catastrophe at Shiloh, by E^1, and is already acquainted with E^2 in 1 Sam. vii.-xii., 187 f.; said to have written Kings, 319; relation of Jer. xlix. 7-22 to Obadiah, 334 f.; of xx. 14-18 to Job iii., 432 f. Was Jeremiah the author of Lamentations? 413-418.

Jerome, designates Chronicles by its usual name, 226; designates the Book of Nehemiah *Esdrae secundus*, 241; Lamentations, *Cinoth*, 412; interprets Prov. xxx. 1 and xxxi. 1 as referring to Solomon, 441; designates Book of Numbers *Vaiedabber*, 465; counts twenty-two, twenty-four, and twenty-seven canonical books: the order of these, 467 f.; is aware that the canonicity of Koheleth is disputed, and places Esther at the end of canonical books, 480; still in isolated cases diverges from the word-division of the M.T., 493; is unaware of any system of indicating the vowels in writing, 494, but is acquainted with an essentially fixed vowel pronunciation, 502; attests the existence of two editions of Aquila, 516; is largely dependent on Symmachus, 519; attests the existence of three recensions of the text of the LXX. officially recognised by the Church, 521; never mentions a Targum, 529; his activity as a translator of the Bible, 533 f.

Jesus, attitude of, towards the O.T. and O.T. Canon, 482 f.

Jesus Sirach, silence of, respecting Esther, 258; the oldest witness for the Book of Isaiah, 265, 284 f.; *terminus ad quem* for the Book of Jonah, 339, and the collection of the Twelve (minor) Prophets into a single book, 379; makes no mention of Daniel, 387; knows of a Psalter of David, 409; the relation of, to Proverbs (contains royal aphorisms also), 445; attests the existence of the complete Book of Proverbs, 446, also the whole of Koheleth, 456; describes Joshua as a prophet, 466; attitude of, regarding prophetic inspiration, 466 f.; why not admitted into the Canon, 482.

Job, belongs to the Wisdom-literature, 420 f.; a poetical book, 466, with a special system of accentuation, 495 f.; Hexaplaric text of, translated into Latin by Jerome, 534.

Jonah ben Amittai, the prophet, not the author of Is. xv.-xvi.

12, 273, nor the author of the Book of Jonah, 336 f.
Jonathan ben Uzziel regarded as the author of the first Targum on the Prophets, 529, also of a second Targum on the Pentateuch, 530.
Josephus, on Hebrew metre, 15 f.; divergent account by, of Nehemiah's building of the walls, 246; makes use of the term κανών, 464; counts twenty-two canonical books, 467; his conception of canonicity, 481 f.; makes use predominantly of the LXX., 515; his Greek text of the Bible, 522 f.
Joshua regarded as a prophet, 466.
Josiah, reform of the cultus by, based on Deuteronomy, 50 f.
Judaean histories, detailed, on the subject of Temple and cultus in 2 Kings, 216 f.

"KINA"-VERSE, 21 f., 413.
Kings, Book of, in the Hebrew Canon reckoned as one book, 206, 466; author of, dominated by an exclusively theocratic interest, 209 f.; in spite of traces of a diorthosis influenced by P^2 and even P^x, its general character Deuteronomic, 220; is not cited as a source by the Chronicler, 237.
Koheleth, belongs to the Wisdom-literature, 420; read at the Feast of Tabernacles (Sukkoth), 466 f.; canonicity of, disputed, 479 f.

LAMENTATIONS, Book of, read on the 9th of Ab, 466 f.; often counted not as a single independent book, but taken with Jeremiah, 467 f.

Lucian of Antioch, establishes a text of the LXX. officially recognised by the Church, 521 f.
Luther, conjecture of, regarding the author of the poem of Job, 432.

MALACHI, literary dependence of, throughout on Deuteronomy, 103 f., 374 f.
Manuscripts, Hebrew, relatively not of any great age: reasons for this, 497 f.; all depend on a single archetype, 500 f.; how far the text of the versions can be used in substitution for the older MSS. underlying them, 510 f.
Manuscripts of the LXX., 523.
Manuscripts of the Peschitthô, 532.
Massora marginalis, magna, parva. Works dealing with the Massora, 503; a special Massora to the Targum Onkelos, 529.
Massoretes, the, work of, 502 f.
Melito of Sardis, Canon of, 469; does not mention Esther, 480.
Mesha, Stone of (="Moabite Stone"), character of the writing on, 14, 490 f.; employs point as word-divider and a perpendicular stroke as sentence-divider, and makes sparing use of *matres lectionis*, 591.
Metobelus, the, 520.
Midrash, existence of, in several forms to Esther, 261; fivefold division of the Psalter in, 402; recognises twenty-four canonical books, 467.
Midrash of the Book of Kings, a principal source of the Chronicler, 237.
Minor Prophets, *see* Prophets, Book of the Twelve.

INDEX 549

Mishna, the, counts twenty-four sacred Scriptures, 467, regarding them as of equal canonical dignity, 480.
Model manuscripts, Massoretic, 504.
Moses, acquainted with the art of writing, 13 f.; was he the author of the Pentateuch? 34 f.; farewell discourses of, 59 f.; in particular the original Deuteronomy purports to have been written by him, 60–64; composer of Ps. xc., 398; said to be the author of Job, 431.
Moses, Blessing of (= Deut. xxxiii.), 49 f., 125 f.
Moses, Song of (= Deut. xxxii.), 49, 122 f.; its connexion with Ps. xc., 398.

NEHEMIAH, the memoirs of, 245 f.; said to have compiled the Psalter, 399, and to have closed the Canon, 470, 475.
Nehemiah, Book of, see Ezra; designated by Jerome *Esdrae secundus*, 241.
Numeration, varying, of the canonical books, 467 f.

OBADIAH, the original (Ur-Obadia), contents of, 336.
Obelus, the, 520.
Occidentals (the Jewish), 503 f.
Old Slavonic translation of the Bible, 527.
Onkelos said to be the author of the first Targum on the Pentateuch, 529.
Orientals (the Jewish), 503 f.
Origen attests for Numbers the traditional designation αμμεσφεκωδειμ, 465, and for Kings ουαμμελεχ δαβιδ, 468; counts twenty-two canonical books, 467; the sequence of these, 469; places Esther at the end, 480); is already acquainted with an essentially fixed vocalic pronunciation of the Hebrew text, 502; his work on the textual criticism of the O.T., 519 f.; never mentions a Targum, 529.
Original text of the Biblical authors, how to be restored, 535.

P = the Priestly element in the Hexateuch: wholly unknown to Deuteronomy, 69–75; forms a *tout ensemble* sharply distinguished from the other Pentateuchal sources, but is itself the result of compilation; oldest written priestly categories = P^1; the larger writing, forming the kernel of the whole = P^2; younger interpolated elements of various character = P^x, 93 f.; the contents of P^x in detail, 95–101; extent and character of P^2, 101 f.; Ezra brought with him $P^1 + P^2$ (in a combined form), while P^x is younger than Ezra, 112 f. Chronicles marks the inferior limit for the formation of P^x, 148; was worked up and combined with J E D by Rp, 142–147; relation of Rp to P^x, 143 f. In Josh. i.–xii. P only very sparingly represented, 152; in ch. xiii.–xxiv. more considerably (also P^x and still younger elements), 154 f. Judg. ii. 10, viii. 30 and 32 reminiscent of P, 178; 1 Sam. ii. 22b dependent on P^x, 187, as also 1 K. vii. 48, 220; 1 K. viii. 1–11 revised in accordance with P, 208 f., 220; 1 K. vi. 16, xii. 32 and 33 dependent on P, 220; 1 K. xviii. 31*b* a verbal quotation from P, 215, 220. P responsible for the transformation of the traditional history effected by the Chronicler, 231 f.; Ruth. iv. 18 f. dependent on P, 255; Ps. xix. younger than P, 404; Job xlii. 17 dependent on P, 433.

Papyrus Anastasi III., 13.

Parallel texts in Chronicles to Samuel and Kings, 228 f.; convincingly show that the old imperfectly developed orthography persisted for a long time in Hebrew MSS., 492; and that no great care was taken in the ancient period to preserve the purity of the textual tradition, 506.

Paul of Tela translates the Greek Hexapla of Origen into Syriac (retaining the critical signs), 520.

Peschitthô exhibits superscriptions to the Psalms which diverge from the M.T. and the LXX., 396.

Philo, oldest witness for the fivefold division of the Pentateuch, 28; cites from no apocryphal books, but also ignores many of the canonical Scriptures, 483 f.; uses the LXX. exclusively, 515.

Poetical books, the = Psalms, Proverbs, Job, 466; they possess a special system of accentuation, 495 f.

Porphyry, the neo-Platonist, disputes the authenticity of Daniel, 284.

Preacher, the, see Koheleth.

Primaeval history, the, in J, 87–90.

Prologue, the, to Proverbs presupposes the completed book, 446, and is older than Job, 433 f.

Prologue, the, to Job, 423, 434 f.

Prologue, the, of the grandson of Ben Sira, 409, 467, 477, 513.

Prophetic Writings, collection of the, begins in the Babylonian Exile, 476 f.; when closed, 378 f., 476.

Prophecy regarded as extinct, 378 f., 388 f., 482.

Proverbs, Book of, belongs to the Wisdom-literature, 420 f.; a poetical book, 466, with a special system of accentuation, 495 f.; said to have been in danger of being "hidden," 479 f.

Psalms, Book of, a poetical book, 466, with a special system of accentuation, 495 f.; forms the starting-point for the collection of the Hagiographa, 477 f.; three translations of, made by Jerome, 533 f.

Punctuation, the, age of, 405; the two systems of ("Babylonian" and "of Tiberias"), 405.

RASHI on Job xxvii. 11–23, 424.

Rd (= Deuteronomic Redactor), effects the union of J E with D, 140 f.; did he (or they) bring Deuteronomy to its present form? 142; is substantially the author of Ex. xx.–xxxiv., 141, and of Joshua i.–xii., 152 f.; Rd in Judges, 158 f., 163, 165, 177 f.; the Deuteronomic Book of Judges, 167–171; in 1 Sam. ii. 27–36; iv. 15, 18*a*, 187; xiii. 1, 18*b*; xiv. 47–51, 190 f.; 2 Sam. ii. 10, 196; 2 Sam. viii., 197 f.; The Deuteronomic Book of

INDEX

Samuel, 201 f.; the Deuteronomic Book of Kings, 210-216. Here a distinction to be made between Rd^1 and Rd^2, 218 f.; final complete Deuteronomic redaction of the historical books, 222-225.

Rhythm of Hebrew speech anapaestic, 19, 24.

Rj (= Jahvistic Redactor) = "Jehovist": a Judaean: worked up into combined form and harmonistically adjusted J and E, 136-140; Rj in Judges, 177; in Samuel, 189 f., 201.

Roll of Jeremiah, the original, of the 4th or 5th year of Jehoiachim, 297 f.

Royal annals, official, kept from the earliest period of the monarchy, 210 f.; relation of the Chronicles of the Kings of Israel or Judah, cited in Book of Kings, to these, 210-213.

Royal aphorisms in Proverbs and Jesus ben Sira, 445.

Rp (= Priestly Redactor), united J E D with P, 142-147, and in the process preserved and improved upon P as much as possible, 142 f.; relation of, to P^x, 145 f.; withdrawal of, in Josh. i.-xii., 152 f., but is substantially the author of Josh. xiii.-xxiv., 154 f.; freer attitude of, towards P here, 155. A Rp restores to the Book of Judges the passages struck out by Rd, and also inserts the "minor" judges, 178 f.; similarly the passages struck out by Rd in Samuel, 201 f.

Ruth, Book of, read at Shabuoth (Feast of Weeks), 466; largely treated not as an independent book, but combined with Judges, 467; canonicity of, disputed, 479.

SAMUEL, Books of, in the Jewish Canon one book, 180, 466; Book of Chronicles fixes the time-limit for the final redaction of, 196, 202, 205.

Seder Olam, the book so called, on prophetic inspiration, 482.

Septuagint, the (= LXX.), of Gen. xlvii. 4-6, 148; Ex. xxxv.- xl., 96, 148; Deut. i. 39, 72, 148; of Joshua, 155 f.; Josh. viii. 30-35 in, 68 f.; xix. 47-48, 154; ch. xx., 67, 155. Divides Samuel into two books, 180 f.; 1 Sam. ii. 1-10 in, 202; 1 Sam. ii. 22, 107, 187; 1 Sam. iii. 21-iv. 1 (not in M.T.), 185; 1 Sam. x. 27, 183; 1 Sam. xiii. 1, 184; 1 Sam. xvii.-xviii., 191 f. Divides Kings into two books, 206; 1 K. viii. 12-13 in, 207. Variant order and presence of doublets pointing to a different recension of the text of Kings, 220 f. Divides Chronicles into two books, 226. Position of Ruth in, 254. LXX. of Jeremiah, 302, 304 f., 310-313; Jer. ix. 4-5 in, 493; Hos. xiii. 4 in, 332; Mal. i. 1 in, 375 f. Order of the minor prophets in, 381. Psalm-superscriptions in, 395. Divergent numbering of the Psalms in, and a supernumerary Psalm in, 411; Ps. lxxv. 2 in, 493. Has an introduction to Lamentations, 414. The latter book in, not translated by the same hand as Jeremiah, 415. Subscription to the Book of Job in, 435 f. Book of Proverbs in, 438, 447. Its Hebrew original without a system of word-division, 492 f. The name, 513; no official character attaching to it at first, 514;

has influenced the Peschiṭṭhô, 533.
Sequence of the three greater prophets in the Hebrew Canon, 294, 318, 466, 468; of the twelve minor prophets, and the principle guiding their arrangement, 378-381; of the individual books of the Canon, 468 f.
Servant of Jahve, Songs of the, 290 f.
Siloam Inscription, character of the script of; employs a point as word-divider and the *matres lectionis* in isolated cases, 490 f.
Sôf pāsûq as a verse-divider; use of, in Tora-scrolls forbidden in Talmud, 494.
Solomon, his utterance at the consecration of the Temple (preserved in the "Book of Jashar"), 207; his prayer at the consecration of the Temple (1 K. viii. 15-53), 218; as composer of Pss. lxxii. and cxxvii., 394, 398; author of Proverbs, 440 f.; of Koheleth, 448 f.; of Canticles, 457 f., or the theme of the latter, 459 f.
Song of Songs, widely regarded as not canonical, 462, 479 f.; read at Passover, because the Targum applies it to the Exodus from Egypt, 466; the Targum to, strongly haggadic and paraphrastic in character, 530.
Spinoza on the Pentateuch, 36; on the prophetic-historical books, 222; on the peculiarities and origin of the M.T., 498 f.
Stichometrical structure of Hebrew poetry, 16 f.
Strophe, the, in Hebrew poetry, 17, 26.
Superscriptions of the Psalms, 394-398.

Symmachus, translator of the Bible, 518 f.
Synagogue, Great, men of the, said to have fixed the Canon, 470.
Synchronisms in Book of Kings, 219.
Syriac translation of the Bible, see Peschiṭṭhô.

TABERNACLE, the, a projection of the Solomonic Temple, 107 f.
Talmud, the, counts twenty-four canonical books, 467; the sequence of these in, 468 f.; is still unacquainted with vowel signs, 494; but displays knowledge of a firmly fixed traditional vocalic pronunciation, 501 f.
Targum, the threefold, to Esther, 261; applies Canticles to the Exodus from Egypt, 466; the Samaritan, 512; influence of, on the Peschiṭṭhô, 532 f.
Tell-el-Amarna, tablets from, 14.
Tetrapla, the, 520.
Theodicy, vindication of the problem of the Deuteronomic historical literature, 222 f.; and of the Book of Job, 421 f.
Theodore of Mopsuestia interprets seventeen psalms as Maccabean, 407.
Theodotion, translator of the Bible, 517 f.; his text of the Bible, 517 f., 522 f.; completely displaces the LXX. to Daniel, 517 f.
Tiqqûn Sôferîm, 508.
Tradition of the text not handed down with scrupulous care in MSS. of the older period, 505 f.
Trito-Isaiah, the, 289 f.
Twelve Prophets, Book of the, regarded in the Jewish Canon as one book, 378, 466.

INDEX 553

"Ur-Lucian," type of LXX. text so called, 518, 523.

Vaticanus Codex B represents the Egyptian Bible, 518; relation of, to the Hexaplaric text, 521 f.

Vetus Latina, the, 524 f.; corrected and revised by Jerome, but still in official use *circa* 600 A.D., 533 f.

Vocalisation, age of the, not identical with the age of the vowel signs, 501 f.

Wisdom, idea of, among the Hebrews, 420 f., 437 f.; already hypostasised, 421, 444 f.

Wisdom-literature, what belongs to the, 420; its literary character, 421; its essential features, 421 f., 444 f.

Word-division, originally non-existent in old Hebrew writing, only partially indicated by a point, 490 f.; indicated in the archetype of the M.T. already by spacing, 494, 501.

Writing mistakes (scribal errors), in the M.T., 506 f.

Zechariah, name of the father of, 361 f., 371; individual sections in, dated, 362; how ch. ix.–xiv. may have been combined with i.–viii., 377 f.

Zephaniah, not a descendant of King Hezekiah, 355.

II. PASSAGES OF THE OLD TESTAMENT REFERRED TO IN THE SPECIAL INTRODUCTION

(The Biblical books which are subjects of specified sections are not, as such, included here; for passages from the LXX. specially referred to, see Index I. *s.v.* Septuagint.)

Gen.			Gen.—*continued.*	
	i. 1	143	xvi. 9–10	137
	ii. 4	143	xviii. 17–19, 22–33	90
	iv.	86 f.		
	vi. 7	143	xx. 18	137
	vii. 3, 7–9, 22, 23	143	xxii. 2, 14–18	137 f.
	ix. 18–19, 20–27	86	xxii. 20–24	90
	ix. 25	90 f.	xxv. 1–6	90
	x. 21, 24	143	xxvi. 3–5	90
	xi. 1–9	86 f.	xxvi. 5	140
	xii. 10–20	90	xxvi. 15, 18	138
	xiii. 14–17	90	xxvii. 40	91
	xiv.	126–128	xxvii. 46	144
	xv. 13–15, 19–21	144	xxviii. 14	138
			xxx. 31–xxxi. 3	138

INDEX

GEN.—*continued.*
- xxxi. 47–54　138
- xxxii. 10–13　90, 138
- xxxii. 33　138
- xxxiv.　83 f., 144
- xxxv. 1–4　84
- xxxv 9–15, 19 } 144
- xxxv. 21　138
- xxxvi. 1–5　144
- xxxvi. 31–39　90
- xxxvii 14　79, 144
- xxxix. 1 and 20　138
- xl. 15　138
- xliii. 14　144
- xlv. 19–21　138
- xlvi. 1　144
- xlvi. 8–27　95, 144
- xlvii. 4–6　148
- xlvii. 30　144
- xlviii. 7　144
- xlix. 1–27　117 f.
- xlix. 28, 31　144

EXOD. iv. 9, 14–16　144
- iv. 21–23　140
- iv. 27–30　144
- v.–x.　144
- vi. 6–9　144 f.
- vi. 13–30　95, 144
- viii. 18　141
- ix. 14–16, 29 } 141
- x. 2　141
- xii. 14–20　95
- xii. 21–27　141
- xii. 40–42　145
- xii. 43–50　95
- xiii. 3–16　141
- xv. 1–18, 20–21 } 118 f.
- xv. 26　141
- xvi.–xvii.　145
- xviii.　83
- xviii. 2　138
- xix.–xxxiv.　81, 141
- xix. 3–8　141
- xix. 13　82
- xix. 23　138

EXOD.—*continued.*
- xx. 2–17　138, 141
- xx. 11　145
- xx. 18–21　141
- xx. 22–26　130
- xxi.–xxiii.　128 f., 141
- xxii. 27–28　82
- xxiii. 10–12, 14–16 } 82
- xxiii. 14–19　82
- xxiii. 17–19　131, 138
- xxiii. 20–23　130
- xxiv. 1–2, 9–11 } 83
- xxiv. 3–8　131
- xxvii. 20–21　95
- xxviii. 41–43　95
- xxix. 21–42　95
- xxix. 38–42　113
- xxx.–xxxi.　95 f.
- xxx. 13　113
- xxxi. 18　145
- xxxii.–xxxiv.　138
- xxxiii. 7–11　82
- xxxiv. 29–35　96
- xxxiv. 29　145
- xxxv.–xl.　96

LEV. i.–vii.　96, 136
- viii.　97
- x. 6–7, 8–11, 16–20 } 97
- xi.–xv.　97, 136
- xi. 43–45　136
- xvi.　100
- xvii.–xxvi.　132–136
- xxvii.　97
- xxvii. 32–33　113

NUMB. i.–ii.　98
- iii. 1–4, 40–51 } 98
- iv.–vii.　98
- v.–vi.　136
- viii.　98
- ix　136
- ix. 1–14　98
- x. 33　141
- xi.　138 f.

INDEX 555

NUMB.—*continued.*
    xi. 7–9, 10 145 f.
    xi. 14–30 82
    xii. 83
    xii. 16 146
    xiv. 11–21 139
    xiv. 27–38 146
    xiv. 44 141
    xv. 98, 136
    xv. 37–41 136
    xvi. 100 f., 146
    xvii. 1–5 101
    xvii. 27–38 146
    xix. 98, 136
    xx. 1–13 146
    xxi. 4 146
    xxi. 13–15, 17–18, 27–30 120 f.
    xxi. 32–35 83, 141
    xxii.–xxiv. 121 f., 139
    xxii. 4, 7 146
    xxiv. 20–24 148
    xxv. 6–9 99
    xxv. 16–18 146
    xxvi. 99
    xxvi. 9–10 146
    xxvi. 11 146
    xxvii. 1–11 99
    xxviii.–xxx. 99
    xxxi. 99, 146
    xxxii. 141 f., 146
    xxxiii. 100, 146
    xxxiv. 1–15 100
    xxxv. 1–8 100
    xxxvi. 1–12 99
    xxxvi. 13 147
DEUT. i.–xi. 59 f.
    i. 1–5 147
    i. 39 72, 148
    iv. 41–43 67, 147
    vii. 12–24 63
    x. 6–7 67 f., 147
    xii. 53
    xiv. 1–21 53
    xv. 4–6 54
    xvi. 1–8 54
    xvi. 21–xvii. 7 54 f.

DEUT.—*continued.*
    xvii. 8–13 55
    xvii. 14–20 55
    xviii. 14–22 55 f.
    xix. 16–20 56
    xx. 1–9, 15–18 56
    xxi.–xxv. 56 f.
    xxii. 5–9 57
    xxiv. 6–9 57
    xxvi. 1–15 57
    xxvii. 4–8 68
    xxvii. 11–26 68, 147
    xxviii. 58 f.
    xxxi. 1–8 69, 142
    xxxi. 14–15, 23 46, 69, 142
    xxxi. 16–30 69, 124, 142
    xxxi. 19 147
    xxxii. 1–43 122 f.
    xxxii. 44 142, 147
    xxxii. 48–52 46
    xxxii. 49 147
    xxxiii. 125 f.
    xxxiv. 1–8 46
    xxxiv. 10–12 142
JOSH. viii. 30–35 69
    xx. 67
    xxiv. 63
JUDG. i. 1–ii. 5 172, 177
    ii. 6–iii. 6 158
    ii. 10 178
    ii. 22 173
    ii. 23–iii. 3 172
    iii. 7–11 158 f.
    iii. 12–30 160
    iii. 31 171, 179
    iv.–v. 160 f.
    vi.–viii. 163 f.
    viii. 30–32 178
    ix. 166
    x. 1–5 167 f., 179
    x. 6–16 173, 178, 189
    x. 17–xii. 7 166 f.
    xii. 8–15 167 f., 179
    xiii.–xvi. 167
    xv. 20 178
    xvii.–xxi. 174 f., 179

1 SAM. i.–vii. 1	185
ii. 1–10	187, 202 f.
ii. 22	107, 187
ii. 27–36	187
iv.–vi.	189 f.
iv. 15, 18	187
vii. 2–viii. 22	187 f.
ix. 1–x. 16	183, 189 f.
ix. 2, 9	190
x. 8	189
x. 17–27	186 f.
x. 24–25	189
x. 27	183
xi.	183, 189
xi. 8	185, 190
xi. 12–14	190
xii.	186 f.
xiii.–xiv.	183 f., 189
xiii. 1	184
xiii. 7–15	184, 189
xiii. 19–22	184
xiv. 47–51	190
xiv. 52	191
xv.	186, 201 f.
xvi. 1–13	194
xvi. 14–23	193
xvii.–xviii.	191 f.
xviii. 6–8	194
xix. 1–10, 11–17	193
xix. 18–xx. 1	194
xx.	194
xxi. 2–10, 11–16	194 f.
xxii.	195
xxiii.–xxxi.	195 f.
xxviii. 3–25	201
2 SAM. i.–vi.	196
i. 19–27	196, 203, 400
iii. 2–5	196, 198
iii. 33–34	202

2 SAM.—continued.	
v. 13–16	198
vii.	197
viii.	197 f.
ix.–xx.	198 f., 201
xxi.–xxiv.	199 f.
xxii.	203 f., 403 f.
xxiii. 1–7	204 f.
1 KINGS i.–ii.	206 f.
iii.–xi.	207 f.
iii. 2, 3	217
vi., vii.	216 f.
vi. 1, 16	220
vii. 48–50	220
viii. 1–11	208 f., 220
viii. 4	107
viii. 12–13	207
viii. 15–53	218
xii.–xvi.	213 f.
xii. 32, 33	214, 220
xiii.	214, 220
xviii. 31	215, 220
xvii.–2 K.x., 2 K. xiii. 14–21	214 f.
2 KINGS i. 2–16	214, 220
xi.–xii., xvi. 10–18, xviii.–xx., xxii.–xxiii.	216 f.
xvii. 7–41	217 f.
xviii. 13–xx. 19	282 f.
xxv. 22–30	217
1 CHRON. xvi. 8–36	405 f.
JER. xlix. 7–22	334 f.
MICAH iv. 1–4	269 f.
ZECH. ix.–xiv.	375–378 (cf. 363 f.)
PSALM xviii.	203 f.

www.ingramcontent.com/pod-product-compliance
Lightning Source LLC
Chambersburg PA
CBHW052110010526
44111CB00036B/1603